DISCOVERING CANADA

Shaping an identity

EDITOR AND SENIOR AUTHOR
Ronald C. Kirbyson, B.A., B.ED., M.A.
Winnipeg School Division No. 1

CO-AUTHORS
Colin M. Bain, B.A., M.A., PH.D.
Gordon E. Perdue High School

Peter Dreyer, B.A., B.ED.

Karl McCutcheon, B.A., B.ED., M.A., M.ED.
Etobicoke Board of Education

Alan Skeoch, B.A., M.A.
Toronto Board of Education

Prentice-Hall Canada Inc.,
Scarborough, Ontario

For

Dawn, Geoff and Jill

Vi

Susan, David and Sheilagh

Dianne, Pam, Krista and Sean

Marjorie, Kevin and Andrew

Cover photograph of the Snowbirds: Canadian Forces photo by Warrant Officer Vic Johnson.

Canadian Cataloguing in Publication Data

Kirbyson, Ronald C.
  Discovering Canada

Vols. 2 & 3 co-authored by R.C. Kirbyson et al.
For use in elementary and secondary schools.
Contents: (v. 1) Settling a land—(v. 2) Developing a nation—(v. 3) Shaping an identity.
ISBN 0-13-215657-1 (v. 1).—ISBN 0-13-215533-8 (v. 2). —ISBN 0-13-215541-9 (v. 3).

1. Canada—History. I. McCreath, Peter L. II. Skeoch, Alan. III. Title.

FC170.K47   971   C82-094164-6
F1034.2.K47

Accompanying materials

Discovering Canada: Settling a land

Discovering Canada: Developing a nation

Discovering Canada: Teacher's Guide

Prentice-Hall, Inc., Englewood Cliffs, New Jersey
Prentice-Hall International, Inc., London
Prentice-Hall of Australia, Pty., Ltd., Sydney
Prentice-Hall of India Pvt., Ltd., New Delhi
Prentice-Hall of Japan, Inc., Tokyo
Prentice-Hall of Southeast Asia (Pte.) Ltd., Singapore
Editora Prentice-Hall do Brasil Ltda., Rio de Janeiro

ISBN 0-13-215541-9

        4   5   6   BP   88   87

Printed and bound in Canada by Bryant Press

Project Editor: MaryLynne Meschino
Production Editors: Catherine Leatherdale, Eva Judge, Elynor Kagan, Deborah Burrett
Photo Researcher: Barb Pratt
Design: John Zehethofer
Maps, charts and diagrams: James Loates
Illustrations: Ruth Bagshaw
Composition: CompuScreen Typesetting Ltd.

Policy Statement

Prentice-Hall Canada Inc., Educational Book Division, and the authors of *Discovering Canada* are committed to the publication of instructional materials that are as bias-free as possible. The student text was evaluated for bias prior to publication.

The authors and publisher also recognize the importance of appropriate reading levels and have therefore made every effort to ensure the highest degree of readability in the student text. The content has been selected, organized, and written at a level suitable to the intended audience. Standard readability tests have been applied at several stages in the text's preparation to ensure an appropriate reading level.

Research indicates, however, that readability is affected by much more than word or sentence length; factors such as presentation, format and design, none of which is considered in the usual readability tests, also greatly influence the ease with which students read a book. These and many additional features, such as marginal notes and glossary, have been carefully prepared to ensure maximum student comprehension.

Contents

Preface

To you, the student, we wish a successful journey in *Discovering Canada*. In the pages that follow, you are going to meet all kinds of people who have been part of Canada's history. You are going to experience a wide variety of situations and events and places. You will travel by way of stories, explanations, illustrations and photos, dramatizations, letters and diaries, maps and diagrams.

To speed you on your way, we present some of these parts in adapted form. In other words, we sometimes changed language—of a letter, say, or a speech—so that it would be more understandable to a modern student. For other parts, we used conversations or anecdotes or word-pictures to help you "picture" what was going on. We took pains, at all times, to ensure that made-up parts were based on historical fact.

A journey awaits you. May it be a good one. May you find out much about Canada and the world—and about yourself.

Acknowledgements

It would be difficult to exaggerate the amount of support the authors received from the people at Prentice-Hall Canada Inc. Rob Greenaway, Executive Editor, was instrumental in originating the project and keeping it on course through its years of development. Rob's belief in the value of the project encouraged us. His many contributions, especially at times of unexpected difficulty, made its completion possible. MaryLynne Meschino, Project Editor, through her advice and hard work, improved every part of the book. Mary-Lynne was involved with organization, choice of content, the wording and overall pattern of questions, the general readability and style—and even with writing the final draft of some chapters. As editor and friend, she was tough-minded in her criticism but generous with her praise. As a team leader, MaryLynne rallied us with her energy and ideas and cheered us with her sense of humour.

The Production Editors—Catherine Leatherdale, Eva Judge, Elynor Kagan and Deborah Burrett devoted their talents selflessly to the improvement of every page of *Shaping an identity*. Elynor also supervised the photo research, ably assisted by Barb Pratt. Authors could hardly expect more generous, professional support. Their skillful editorial work is greatly appreciated.

The authors would also like to thank all the others who helped to make this book possible: librarians, typists, archivists, colleagues. Certain individuals and organizations helped us at particularly critical times: the staffs of St. Paul's College and the Winnipeg Public Libraries, especially the St. James branch; Dr. Jean Friesen, provost, University College, Winnipeg; Ken Boichuk; Geoff, Jill and Sandy, youthful reviewers; Dawn, who made meeting deadlines a possibility. We extend our thanks to Peter L. McCreath and John Berestiansky.

Students of Argyle Alternative School in Winnipeg, Parkdale Collegiate in Toronto, Nelson High School in Burlington and Gordon E. Perdue High School in Oakville deserve special thanks. Various materials in this book began as ideas tried out with them.

To our families, whom we can never thank enough for their patience and comfort, we dedicate *Discovering Canada*.

1 Entering the twentieth century: What will be the shape of Canadian identity?

Yesterday was Arnold Leatherdale's ninetieth birthday. The celebrations are over and Arnold is relaxing in his favourite armchair by the fireplace. He is looking through his family photograph album. The birthday celebrations have brought back a flood of memories. He looks at pictures of his schooldays in the early years of the century. He remembers how bare his classroom was, how stern the teacher had been, how he had to walk 10 kilometres to get to the one-room school house and how he had to take his turn putting wood in the big pot-bellied stove in the winter.

Arnold turns to pictures of World War I. He sees himself in his uniform and in the trenches in Europe. He thinks about that experience—how afraid he was, how brave he had to be, how much death and destruction he had seen.

Arnold turns a few more pages in the photo album. He finds pictures of himself and his family during the Great Depression of the 1930s. He recalls how he felt during those years—the helplessness of unemployment, the frustration of not being able to do all he wanted for his family, the desperation of himself and his friends and the joy he felt when he finally got a job in 1939.

The memories of his life's experiences continue to flood his heart and his mind as he thumbs through the pages. As he closes his album and turns on the television to watch the launch of a space shuttle, he thinks about how much things have changed over his lifetime and how all his experiences have affected him.

- Put yourself in the place of Arnold Leatherdale. Look at the pictures of the different stages of your life. How many different sorts of surroundings do they show? What have been some of your most important experiences?

- How would these experiences have affected the way you think about the world in which you live?

Now, instead of Arnold Leatherdale, think about yourself.

- Do you think that any features of your own identity are being shaped at this stage of your life? Just as experiences can help shape the way *people* are and the way they think about themselves, so different forces both inside and outside the borders of *countries* can help shape the identity of a nation.

3

Chapter overview

Canada entered the twentieth century with an enormous sense of optimism about the future. People felt that the economy was bound to grow wealthier and stronger, the population would increase and spread across the country, and Canada would become an important country in world affairs. Prime Minister Wilfrid Laurier said that the twentieth century would belong to Canada, and Canadians accepted this statement as a description of fact, not an exaggerated prediction. Such great expectations were the result of many forces at work between 1896 and the start of World War I in 1914.

In this chapter we will take a brief look at some of these forces. We will see that there was hardship and conflict, as well as optimism. We will examine how the issues and events of this period have affected the shaping of Canadian identity.

Signposts

> Setting the scene

> Settling the Prairies

> Farming and mining

> The growth of industries and cities

> The social picture

> FEATURE: Storm clouds in the sunny skies of prosperity and optimism

> Canada and the world

Key words

optimism	distinctive	international
identity	resources	

Setting the scene

This book is called *Shaping an identity*. This title was chosen because it describes one of the major issues in the history of twentieth century Canada. What does "shaping an identity" mean? If we were to look up the words "shaping" and "identity" in a dictionary, we might find definitions like these:

shaping—the act of creating a form that is definite and organized

identity—the individuality or character of a person or object

What do these definitions help us to understand about Canada? At the start of the twentieth century, Canada faced the challenge of trying to establish a set of characteristics—that is, features special to this country. After a time, these characteristics would give an appearance or "shape" that everyone would recognize as distinctively Canadian, and in which Canadians could take pride. In shaping this identity, many parts of Canadian life would play a role and many basic questions would require answers. These questions include:

Will Canadian economic and social life be rural? urban? agricultural? industrial?

Will all Canadians be expected to speak the same language and follow similar customs?

What will be the relationship between Canadians in different regions—the Prairies, the Maritimes, central Canada, the North?

What will be Canada's political future? How will the central government in Ottawa and the provincial governments share power?

What will be the relationship between such groups as employers and workers? farmers and city-dwellers? rich and poor? recent immigrants and long-time Canadians?

What will be Canada's relationship with Britain? the United States? with other countries?

Will Canadians develop their own distinctive arts?

The map in Figure 1 shows some of the dominant developments and questions in Canada at the beginning of the twentieth century. You should be able to see that many of the questions about shaping a Canadian identity were present at that time. Which ones seem to be suggested by the map? What conclusions can you make about this period for the shaping of Canadian identity? Keep these questions and this map in mind as you read this chapter.

5

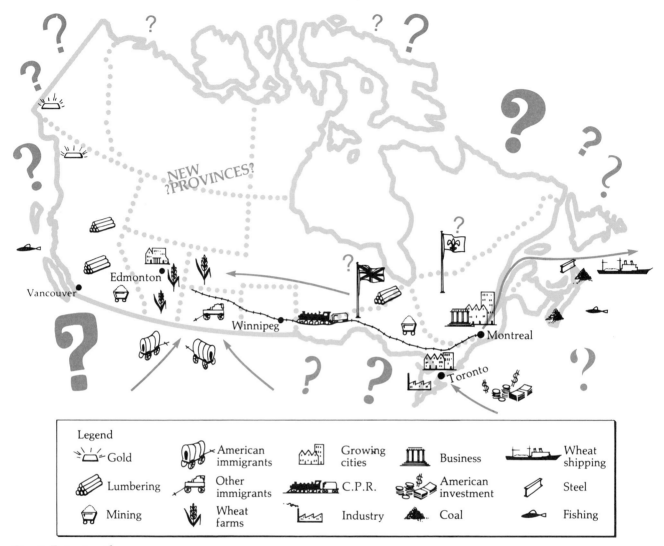

NEW ?PROVINCES?

Vancouver

Edmonton

Winnipeg

Montreal

Toronto

Legend

☀ Gold

🪵 Lumbering

⛏ Mining

🛻 American immigrants

🛻 Other immigrants

🌾 Wheat farms

🏙 Growing cities

🚂 C.P.R.

🏭 Industry

🏛 Business

💰 American investment

⛰ Coal

🚢 Wheat shipping

⊿ Steel

🐟 Fishing

Fig. 1 Entering the twentieth century: what sort of issues and events would shape Canadian identity?

GETTING THE FACTS

1. In your own words, explain what "shaping an identity" means.

2. Examine the map in Figure 1 carefully. In your notebook list two important developments that took place in Canada between 1896 and 1914. List two important questions for Canada at that time.

USING YOUR KNOWLEDGE

3.a) What are some of the characteristics that make up *your own*

identity as a person? List at least four (for example, your likes, dislikes; where you live; your height; etc.)

b) Now list at least four characteristics that make up the identity of a country. Do you think it is harder to describe the identity of a country than of a single person? Give reasons for your answer.

Settling the Prairies

In the early twentieth century, thousands of Europeans and Americans settled on the western Prairies. The arrival of these immigrants was a key reason for the tremendous changes that were soon to take place. Ever since 1869 Canada's leaders had hoped to attract large numbers of settlers to the Prairies. Although it was easy to travel after the C.P.R. was built, the hope had not been fulfilled.

However, around the turn of the century, world trade expanded, and it seemed there would always be a market for all the wheat the Prairies could produce. The Canadian government launched an advertising campaign, offering free land to settlers. These factors combined to bring thousands of immigrants to Canada. In 1900 there were less than 500 000 people living on the Prairies and most of these were in Manitoba. By 1911 there were 1 500 000 on the Prairies, many of them farming millions of hectares of land that had been unsettled.

Not all immigrants settled the Prairies. Many thousands of newcomers went to cities and towns across Canada. In all, over 3 000 000 newcomers arrived between 1896 and 1914. They contributed to the growth of Canada's population to almost 8 000 000 by World War I.

The effect of this influx of people was enormous, especially on the Prairies. Many of the settlers had come from areas of eastern Europe that had not previously sent many people to Canada. They laid the foundation of a multicultural Canadian society. In 1905, two new provinces, Saskatchewan and Alberta, were created on the Prairies. The new Prairie farms permanently altered the Canadian economy. Agricultural produce, especially wheat, boosted trade in both the West and the East at home, and in overseas trade as well. We will note some of these effects as we examine other features of the early twentieth century.

In 1869, after complex negotiations with Britain, the Canadian government bought the vast area between Ontario and the Rocky Mountains from The Hudson's Bay Company. The fur-trading company had controlled this territory for over 200 years.

The building of the C.P.R. and the settlement of the West were two parts of John A. Macdonald's "National Policy." Another aspect was a high tariff on foreign manufactured goods. Designed to build a stronger and more prosperous Canada, Macdonald's National Policy did not meet with success until the early twentieth century and the arrival of Laurier.

GETTING THE FACTS

4. What were two reasons why settlers came to Canada? What were two important results of their settling in Canada?

7

5. Look at the pictures in Figure 2 carefully and answer the questions asked in the captions as a class or in your notebook.

Fig. 2 Settling the Prairies

Advertisements such as this one were spread all over Europe and the United States. Does this poster present an accurate picture of what a settler could expect to find on a Canadian Prairie?

These settlers have just arrived at their new "farm" in the West. How does this picture compare with the poster above? Often, settlers were simply dropped off from trains with a few supplies, and had to work extremely hard to have a home built for the winter.

The Prairie settlers' first homes often looked like this one. They were built from blocks of sod cut from the ground. Why would they not build log cabins or stone houses?

It was only after the family was well-established and producing products for sale, that a home like this one could be built. In what ways would this home be superior to the one above?

Farming and mining

There were tremendous developments in Canadian farming and mining in the early twentieth century. In fact, farming set off the economic boom of this period. Nothing was more remarkable than the growth in the production of wheat. Wheat was especially profitable for the following reasons:

—cities in America and England were growing, and provided ready markets;

—new types of hardy wheat had been developed;

—there were advances in farm machinery;

—ocean freight rates had fallen.

Large scale wheat production and the export of huge quantities of wheat became a basic factor in Canadian life.

In 1891 Canada exported 54 430 tonnes of wheat. In 1916 the export of wheat had reached 4 000 000 tonnes. Wheat had become, as it remains today, a cornerstone of the Canadian economy. Its export was the key to Canadian foreign trade. Indeed, Canadian identity in many parts of the world is often shaped by a vision of a

Fig. 3 One of the first major advances in farm machinery that helped in the cultivation of the Prairies was the development of the steel plough. This family is using a horse-drawn steel plough to break up the ground for the first planting.

country covered with millions of hectares of golden wheat fields.

It was also in the years around the turn of the century that Canada began to take advantage of its natural resources. The wealth in minerals and forests was, for the first time, exploited on a large scale. The Klondike Gold Rush was the first of a series of mining booms that spread across Canada. In southern British Columbia, copper, silver, lead, zinc and gold were mined with great success. Giant smelters and special railway lines were quickly built to take advantage of the mineral wealth. The city of Trail became a refinery centre when the giant Cominco company built its plant there.

Even more spectacular were the developments on the mining frontier of northern Ontario. The discovery of silver near Cobalt set off an incredible rush of prospectors and investors. Soon gold and other metals were found in the rugged rocklands of northern Ontario. Mines and new towns sprang up almost instantly and fortunes were rapidly made. Cobalt, for example, grew from a tent and shanty settlement in 1904 to a town of 10 000 by 1910. It had over 40 silver mines which, by the 1920s, had produced $300 000 000 in silver. In Nova Scotia and Alberta, the mining of coal was a growing

Fig. 4 Early in the century, steam tractors that could pull wide ploughs, threshing machines and other implements began to appear. What advantages would such new machinery bring?

Fig. 5 One of the many
silver mines in Cobalt,
Ontario

factor in economic life. In these years the plentiful Canadian forests,
too, were being harvested to meet an enormous international
demand for lumber, pulp and paper.

All these activities indicate that harvesting or mining of Canada's natural resources had begun on a large scale. Another area of
our identity was becoming clear. Canada was a country blessed with
an abundance of natural resources. The development of resources
was to be a major part of life.

GETTING THE FACTS

6. Why did the great wheat boom happen in the early years of the
twentieth century?

12

7. What do you think is meant by the statement that wheat became "a cornerstone of the Canadian economy"?

8. Assume you were a young person, 22 years old, with a full-time job in a factory in a Canadian city. You were recently married. You have just heard about the discovery of silver in northern Ontario. Would you head for Cobalt to try your luck? Why or why not?

The growth of industries and cities

It is not surprising in this period of great optimism and expansion that business and industry would be growing and changing as well. Most of the industrial growth took place in the cities of southern Ontario and Quebec. Factories were working at capacity—that is, they were producing as much as they could—and many new industries were being established. In 1900 the goods that were manufactured in Canadian factories were worth $215 000 000. By 1910, Canada's factories produced goods worth $564 000 000. Many of these manufactured goods were sold to other countries. In fact, trade was growing faster in Canada than anywhere else in the world.

This growth had important consequences for the people who worked for the manufacturers, and for those who bought the goods that were produced. Ever since factories first developed, most people worked for small companies owned by one family. The workers knew the owner and their fellow employees. Now the small family business was steadily being replaced by large companies called corporations. These were owned by a number of investors. Investor-owners were seldom seen or known by those who worked for them.

There were many giant corporations created in these years. Among them were The Steel Company of Canada (Stelco), The Canada Cement Company, Dominion Textiles and Maple Leaf Milling. These corporations were usually created by combining several smaller companies.

This was also the era in which large department stores, such as those of the T. Eaton Company, began to challenge the traditional corner store as the place where many people did their shopping.

Closely connected with the growth in industry was the explosion in railway construction. The building of the C.P.R. has received much attention, but it was during the first decade of the twentieth century that railroad construction was at its peak. In those years not one, but two more transcontinental railways were begun. It was generally agreed that there was a need to take pressure off the C.P.R. It had neither the track nor the box cars to handle ever-growing

Fig. 6 One of the most successful people in the building of giant corporations was Max Aitken, who later became Lord Beaverbrook. He helped to create the Steel Company of Canada and the Canada Cement Company. Aitken later moved to Britain where he became a key figure in the newspaper business and a Cabinet Minister in the British government.

quantities of wheat that had to be transported to markets, or to terminals for shipment overseas.

There was also a demand for another railway from Prairie farmers. They complained that the C.P.R. charged high rates because it faced no competition. Also, people believed that the Canadian economy would continue to expand rapidly. All these factors helped to bring about the strong support of Laurier's government for the building of the new railways. Millions of dollars in government subsidies were offered to help in their construction. In the optimistic atmosphere of the time, few worried about the cost. Ambitious railroad builders had visions of enormous profits. They began building as many kilometres of track as they could, as quickly as possible. The result was the construction of over 36 000 kilometres of track.

The boom in business and industry increased Canada's wealth. At the same time, however, some people were concerned about the ways it was affecting Canadian life. For example, they were worried about the concentration of business and industry in Ontario and Quebec; the growing amount of American investment and number of American branch plants in Canada; and the size of some of the corporations and their power to control wages and prices. As a result, government increased regulation of business and industry. There was also a growth in the number and membership of unions for industrial workers.

The industrial boom caused the growth of cities. Almost three-quarters of the growth in manufacturing was concentrated in central Canada, and cities such as Toronto and Montreal expanded

It soon became obvious that too much railroad construction had been undertaken in the enthusiasm of these years. After World War I, both new railway companies were in deep financial difficulty. To protect its enormous investment, the federal government took them over and formed Canadian National Railways. The C.N.R. is today still owned by the government.

Fig. 7 Main Street, Winnipeg, c. 1880

rapidly. In the ten years after 1901, Toronto almost doubled its population while Montreal, with 490 000 people in 1911, was Canada's largest city. Montreal was also the chief commercial centre of the country and the focus of international trade. The wheat boom made trans-Atlantic trade more important than ever before, and Montreal had become Canada's main Atlantic port. Traditional Atlantic ports in the Maritimes, such as Halifax, were overshadowed as Montreal's business grew.

Cities in western Canada expanded rapidly as they profited from the wheat boom and immigration to the Prairies. The population of Winnipeg went from 26 000 in 1891 to 136 000 in 1911, while Calgary grew from 3800 to 44 000 in the same period. The growth of these cities showed that, despite the growth of farms on the Prairies, Canada was becoming an urban society. In these years the percentage of Canadians living in cities grew from 36 percent to 45 percent. It would not be many years before over half of Canada's people lived in cities.

GETTING THE FACTS

9. In dollars, how many goods were produced in Canada in 1900? In 1910? How much of an increase in dollars is this?

10. Give three reasons for Laurier's decision to build new railways.

11. What were some of the results of the great growth in Canadian business and industry that caused some Canadians to be concerned about the future?

Fig. 8 Main Street, Winnipeg, c. 1891

12. Examine the photographs of Main Street, Winnipeg. List as many differences as you can. Based on these pictures, what conclusions can you make about the growth of cities in these years?

The social picture

One of the rich was Sir Henry Pellatt of Toronto. He was a multimillionaire, who made some of his millions from investments in the Cobalt silver mines. He built his home, Casa Loma, with 50 rooms, 30 bathrooms, bowling alleys and a rifle range. The horse stable had mahogany stalls and Persian rugs.

One of the characteristics of life in the growing cities was the widening gap between the rich and the poor. To the very rich, city life could mean a luxurious lifestyle. The rich were often the first to travel in that splendid new means of transportation—the automobile. For entertainment the wealthy could attend concerts given by world famous entertainers. They could go to the horse races or attend a lavish party at the home or summer cottage of one of their fellow rich.

Those who had jobs in city shops and factories struggled to build a home and make ends meet. One working-class Toronto man whose family owned a corner store described his neighbourhood:

Not having enough money to order and pay for a full-sized house, most people . . . built their homes by instalments. They would save enough to buy a lot. Then they would save enough

Fig. 9 Casa Loma, the home of Sir Henry Pellatt

to buy the material for three or four rooms; and they would build what was intended to be the rear of the house. . . . This part of the house would contain the kitchen, and perhaps two or three bedrooms. The more prosperous might run into a bathroom. . . . The front was added later and it became the shop, with a hall and a couple of bedrooms above it.

I can recall seeing street after street of these unfinished houses, greyish white blocks, with an entrance on the side, many of which were never finished but stood like clumsy tombstones, as monuments to the unfulfilled ambitions and broken desires of their owners. . . .

There was no government help for those in need. Neighbours tended to look after each other.

In our own store it would be unheard of to stop a man's credit just because he was out of work. That was the very time when he needed what help a little store could give him; and, if he could make arrangements for his milk and his meat, he could get everything else he required. So far as rent was concerned, it did not greatly distress him. He would not be evicted for falling a month or two behind.

From *Cabbagetown Diary* by J.V. McAree.

The poorest were the new immigrant families. Many had no jobs at all. Others had jobs that paid so little they could scarcely afford to rent a place to sleep. The north end of Winnipeg was packed with desperately poor immigrants.

Jacob Lalucki, a Ruthenian who worked in the C.P.R. shops lived there with his Polish wife and two children in one room. Michael Yakoff and his wife had three rooms, but they paid $8 a month rent from Michael's $12 earnings as a caretaker. The Yakoffs took in roomers, and little Pieter Yakoff, age eight, brought in a few pennies scavenging for wood in North End alleys. He never went to school.

From *Into the Twentieth Century* by Alan Phillips.

Working conditions, too, were often difficult and unsafe. As a result, membership of trade unions increased six times during the first decade of the new century. Confrontations between employer and employees were becoming more frequent. The federal government showed its growing interest in the problems of working people by setting up a Ministry of Labour. A future prime minister, William Lyon Mackenzie King, became the first Labour minister. It was becoming clear to many Canadians that city life and urban issues were going to play an important role in shaping economic, social and political life.

Fig. 10 Immigrant families
lived in homes like these. If
you lived in one of these
houses, how would you react
to a home like Casa Loma?
Why? What conclusions
can you draw about life in
the cities? Could you find
similar pictures today?

Those who lived in the rural areas faced their own difficulties. We have already seen some of the problems the Prairie family had to deal with in trying to start a farm and build a first home before the harsh winter began. Once established, however, families helped each other to put up or add to farm buildings.

It was mostly good houses we'd put up. There wasn't a man in the district that wasn't pretty handy with a hammer, a saw. Putting up those houses was duck soup and if everything was ready a gang of men could put up a barn quick too. I've even seen a slap of paint on a barn before the boys went home that night.

There would be a notice in the stores and at the livery barn. Wherever people would be to read it. Tacked on to the fence posts by the schoolhouse, and the preacher would announce it from the pulpit. You know: "There will be a building bee at the John Brown place on the Centre Road this Wednesday starting at eight o'clock." That sort of thing.

At the same time, these people developed their own entertainment to relieve the pressure of hard farm labour.

> I used to love the picnics. They were big events in those times. There would be about two a summer. . . .
>
> Everybody went to those picnics for miles around, and everybody wore their very best. Everybody had pride of appearance and it didn't matter how poor you were, whether you only had a dirt floor in your house, you went to the picnics in your finery.
>
> There were games, baseball, and a lot of tennis. . . .
>
> There always was a big feed. Maybe they'd just spread everything out, the sandwiches and the pies and the cookies, the lemonade and the iced tea, and everybody helped themselves. You all brought your own plates and cutlery.
>
> Then when the picnic was over, everybody would pack up and go home. To the chores. Over those trails, over hills and dale, back to our farms. We were slaves to our horses and cows. A farmer always is.

From *The Pioneer Years* by Barry Broadfoot.

USING YOUR KNOWLEDGE

13. Why did the working-class Toronto man refer to the unfinished homes as "tombstones"?

14. "In the cities and on the farms, neighbours played an important role in people's lives." Find three examples in this section to support this statement.

THINKING IT THROUGH

15. "It is the job of the federal government to help out the poor in the country." Do you agree or disagree with this statement? Give reasons for your answer. If you can, use examples from the section of the chapter you just read.

Storm clouds in the sunny skies of prosperity and optimism

Beneath the prosperity and enthusiasm of the first decade of the new century were signs of difficulty and discontent. Not everyone was happy about what was, on the surface, a great Canadian success story. The chart below indicates some of the groups that were unhappy with their lot while Canada seemed to prosper. The chart summarizes the reasons for discontent, and outlines what was being done to try to improve conditions. Because it received much attention in these years, the issue of French-English relations is dealt with first.

GROUP	ISSUES	EFFECTS
French-Canadians	Continuing resentment over acts of the past, like the execution of Louis Riel	Determination in Quebec to preserve French language, cultural rights and identity
	Resentment over British influence in Canada	Henri Bourassa emerged as leader. He left Laurier's Liberal party to lead the nationalist movement in Quebec (so anxious was he to defeat Laurier that he cooperated with the Conservative leader, Borden, to defeat Laurier in the 1911 election)
	Issues that aroused their hostility:	
	—Canadian assistance to Britain in the Boer War in South Africa	
	—proposed Canadian contribution to build up of British navy	
		Divisions between English-Canadians and French-Canadians appeared to be widening
Factory, mine and construction workers	Dangerous working conditions	Growth of unions
	Low wages and long hours of work	Some signs of open conflict between the workers and owners
		Provincial governments passed laws to control poor working conditions
		Federal government established a Ministry of Labour and passed laws to govern disputes between owners and workers
Farmers (especially on the Prairies)	High C.P.R. freight rates to transport grain	Beginnings of farmer political organizations e.g. the Grain Grower's Grain Company, the United Farmers of Alberta and the national Canadian Council of Agriculture, formed in 1909
	High prices for goods manufactured in central Canada (e.g. farm machinery). Prices high because foreign competition (e.g. American) was limited by Canadian government tariffs	Pressure on federal government to change tariff policy
	The growing Canadian prosperity was based on their production of	Laurier arranged reciprocity agreement with U.S.A., 1910, (lower

GROUP	ISSUES	EFFECTS
	grain but they believed they were not sharing equally in the wealth that resulted	tariffs on American manufactured goods coming to Canada; lower or no tariffs on Canadian agricultural products going to U.S.A.) but it was never put into effect; Laurier lost 1911 election partly as a result of opposition to the reciprocity bill
Native peoples	Most were now residing on reserves, many in poverty They could see land that had been theirs being developed as farms, lumber camps or mines	They expressed unhappiness and resentment, but were not yet well enough organized to have a political impact Their plight was largely overlooked
Maritime provinces	Resentment of growing prosperity in central Canada Ports such as Halifax being by-passed for trans-Atlantic trade by ports such as Montreal	Signs of increasing regional resentments Protests over federal policies which overlooked the Maritimes or helped central Canada at the expense of the Maritime provinces
Women	No political rights Could not vote or stand for political office Could hold only certain jobs—in factories, such as textile mills and in offices. Their pay was usually lower than men's	Gained political experience through such organizations as the Women's Christian Temperance Union (anti-alcohol crusade) Agitation for change by leaders such as Nellie McClung in Winnipeg and Emily Murphy in Edmonton
Immigrants	Although most became very successful in Canada, many ended up in very poor and dangerous jobs in cities, living in slums often with poor sanitation facilities Experienced some prejudice and dicrimination. Suffered anti-immigrant marches and newspaper articles, some destruction of immigrant property, for example, Japanese stores in Vancouver in 1907	Some concerned citizens, especially in the churches, began to take up the cause of the urban immigrants and attempted to assist them Laurier's government followed a policy of welcoming cultural differences Immigrant groups encouraged to establish own language schools, churches and maintain their homeland traditions

THINKING IT THROUGH

16. The ways in which Canadians dealt with these issues or problems would have a great deal to do with the national character or identity that Canada would have in the twentieth century. Look back at the questions concerning Canadian identity in "Setting the scene." Which ones are raised by the problems or issues surveyed in this chart?

Canada and the world

The first decade of the twentieth century was a decisive period for Canada's relationship with the rest of the world. Developments in the world economy were drawing Canada into closer ties with other countries. As we have seen, for example, Canada was exporting more and more grain and minerals to Europe and the United States. Canada, more than ever before, had to be concerned with events in other parts of the world. A war involving European countries could have a serious impact on Canadian trade and, hence, on the prosperity of all Canadians.

Despite this new concern for international relations, Canadian foreign policy was still tied to that of Britain. All of our negotiations were done through Britain and British ambassadors around the world. Prime Minister Laurier did establish an external affairs department but its function was mainly one of passing messages back and forth between Canada and Britain. Canada also depended

Fig. 11 British Colonial Secretary, Joseph Chamberlain, and the Colonial Premiers, 1897. Wilfrid Laurier is standing to Chamberlain's right.

to a large extent on Britain for defense. The small Canadian military force was commanded by British officers and used British weapons. One of the major issues was the fact that there was no Canadian navy.

The role of Britain in Canadian international affairs became a topic of great controversy at the turn of the century. Most Canadians wanted to continue the connection with Britain. However, many wanted to reduce the amount of control Britain exercised over distinctly Canadian affairs. Laurier became trapped in a bitter conflict between those who wanted to maintain and even increase the British connection, and those who wanted it reduced.

Laurier tried to find a uniquely "Canadian" position between these extremes. When the British government proposed to strengthen the ties between the colonies and Britain, Laurier refused. When Britain asked for help in its war in South Africa, Laurier did provide assistance, but it was sent in the form of a volunteer force. The understanding was that this action did not commit Canada automatically to future British wars. When Britain wanted assistance to build up its navy to counter the growing German naval threat, Laurier attempted, rather, to create a separate Canadian navy. This new navy would take over part of the responsibility for the defense of Canada. This proposal failed because of strong opposition from the powerful pro-British element in Canada.

The growth of a sense of Canadian identity was evident, too, in relations with the United States. Many Canadians were angered when the dispute over their border with Alaska was settled in favour of the Americans. Also, Canadian manufacturers rallied opposition to Laurier's proposed reciprocity or trade agreement with the United States.

All these issues show that Canada was entering a crucial period in its relations with Britain and other nations. The direction that Canadian foreign policy was taking would begin to shape the national identity this country was to have, not only for Canadians, but also for the rest of the world.

There were a number of writers in these years who contributed to the reputation of distinctive Canadian literature. Among them were Ralph Connor and Lucy Maud Montgomery. Connor wrote 29 novels including *The Man From Glengarry*. Montgomery wrote over 20 novels, the best known being the "Anne" series which included the famous *Anne of Green Gables*.

There were several internationally famous Canadian athletes at this time. Tommy Burns became the only Canadian to become the heavyweight boxing champion of the world while Tom Longboat, an Onondaga Indian from the Six Nations Reserve in Ontario, became the world champion long distance runner.

GETTING THE FACTS

17. What impact did the growth of trade have on Canada's attitude toward the rest of the world?

USING YOUR KNOWLEDGE

18. Why was Canada's relationship with Britain a particular problem at this time?

Fig. 12 Quebec City, c. 1900. How many signs of the activities of the new century can you identify?

Conclusion

The new century brought great optimism for Canada and its future. Was this confidence justified? Or had Canadians been carried away with their enthusiasm? We have read about tremendous achievements in building Canada in the first part of the twentieth century. Canada now really did stretch from "sea to sea." Agriculture, industry and trade were booming. The population was growing in size and variety. However, did all these developments lead to a clearer sense of Canadian identity?

It seemed that each development in Canadian life also raised problems or questions about Canada's future. Some changes seemed to drive Canadians further apart. Did Canadians have a common purpose at the end of the first decade of the twentieth century? Was there a "shape" to Canada's "identity"? These are the questions that you will try to answer as you work through *Shaping an identity*.

19. Go back to the section called "Setting the scene." Examine again the definitions of "shape" and "identity." Now reread the questions in that section and attempt to answer them, based on what you have studied in this chapter. What answers do you have? How many times did you say, "I'll have to wait to answer that question. I cannot answer it yet"?

20. Select one of the questions or one of the topics in this chapter. Look through this book's table of contents and the "Signposts" in the chapters for sections that deal with this question or topic. Glance through the pictures in the book for those that might relate to the same question or topic. Speculate about the shape that you think Canadian identity is going to take regarding your question or topic. As you read the rest of this book, you may find that you can answer this question and some of the others with more assurance or certainty. Try to keep these questions in mind as we study the story of Canada's efforts to "shape" an "identity" in the twentieth century.

2 Skills: How can we improve our methods of study?

Verilène and Meva have at least one thing in common—they are both teenagers. Though they and their lives are similar in some ways, there are important differences. They live in quite different parts of the world. Verilène is from Quantro, a rich country that belongs to the *developed*, industrialized group of nations. Meva comes from Edgeland. It is poor, *developing* and not equipped with much industry.

On a certain morning, we find them both facing some hard choices. If we could share their thoughts, we might learn the following:

Verilène: This clock-radio needs fixing again. Maybe Dad can do something about it today. It's a miracle I woke up. I could stay in this warm bed all morning!

Meva: *This is going to be a good day. I slept through the night without being awakened by crying from any of my younger brothers or sisters. That's a miracle when you share a room with four others!*

Verilène: I hope we're not having hot cereal for breakfast. If I can't have eggs or caramel flakes, I'd rather have some toast and jam.

Meva: *I feel rested this morning, so I don't mind going without breakfast that much. My turn to eat in the morning was only yesterday, after all. Still, those little flour biscuits are so good. . . .*

Verilène: How can I decide what school to enroll in for next year? Mom and Dad keep reminding me that applications must be filled out soon. I could go to Point Grant, where they have a well-known computer assisted programme, but I like the sound of the sports and music courses at St. Jeffery's. What a hard choice!

Meva: *I must work extra hard in school this week. There just aren't enough schools in Edgeland. If I don't get high marks, I won't qualify to stay at high school. Without an education, I'll spend the rest of my life like my parents— struggling to keep themselves alive.*

Verilène: If only the teacher wouldn't talk so much! Surely they could make school more interesting. If next year is as boring as this one, maybe I'll get a job for awhile. I can always go back to school when I feel like it. I suppose when I am more mature, I'll appreciate school more. Once I choose a career, I'll take education more seriously.

Meva: *High school graduation is an achievement few of us in Edgeland dare to dream about. It could change my life. Perhaps I could get a college scholarship in another country. With special training, in a field like education or medicine, I could come home with skills that could help my people improve their lives.*

- Pick the most suitable title for the scene and explain your choice
  (a) What teenagers think about school
  (b) The rich and the poor
  (c) Hard choices.

- In what ways are the lives of Verilène and Meva the same? In what ways are they different?

- Do you think that one of the two teenagers is faced with more difficult choices than the other? Why or why not?

- What are some examples of "thinking" skills both girls need to make their decisions? Does Meva need any that are different from those of Verilène?

- Suppose you wanted to find out more about the lives of teenagers in different parts of the world. How would you investigate the topic? What skills would you require?

Chapter overview

It is important that the study of history and social studies be useful in everyday life. You should, of course, learn about the history of your country and how it came to be the place it is now. Furthermore, you should develop **skills** for use in your own life, for problem-solving and decision-making.

The more effectively we combine skills in an organized way, the better we can understand and solve problems. In this chapter, therefore, you will work with an organized plan—a model for **inquiry**—for the solving of problems.

You will proceed through a series of steps in the study of an imaginary pair of countries. They are Quantro, a materially rich and developed country, and Edgeland, a materially poor but developing country.

Why deal with imaginary countries? Because we can combine the basic features of many countries into two *types*. Thus we can avoid the time-consuming task of gathering particular facts about a variety of countries. Instead, we can get on with the study of **ideas**, **issues** and **problems**. Provided that our imaginary examples are realistic, we can devise a method that can be used to study any real life example.

Each step you will follow involves posing a carefully worded question that relates to the basic problem. This process is built into the rest of the chapters in *Discovering Canada, Shaping an identity*.

When describing countries, "rich" and "poor" usually refer to average income and other signs of well-being that we can easily point out. These include food and shelter, schools, health care, personal possessions and facilities for recreation.

Fig. 1 We combine skills in an organized way in order to understand and solve problems.

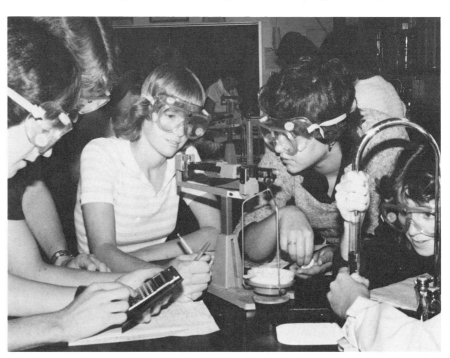

Signposts

Near the beginning of each chapter, you will find "Signposts"—a list of the main section headings which tell you what topic will be studied. In this chapter the signposts are:

> **Examining a problem**

> **Getting the facts**

> **Using your knowledge**

> **Thinking it through**

> **The investigative reporter**

Key words

Following the signposts in each chapter, you will find "key words." These words signal important ideas in the chapter. Understanding them will aid you in working through the topic. Some of the key words are defined in the glossary at the back of the book; others will be defined in the text.

skills	issues	inquiry-model	values
ideas	problems	facts	hypothesis

Examining a problem

In this chapter you begin with the question,

What should be the relations between the two countries, Quantro and Edgeland?

This question sets up a problem for you to study. Through it, you can explore possible ways in which the two countries could deal with each other. Should there be trade between the two countries; should one country promise to support the other in the event of a war; should Quantro give aid to Edgeland; does Edgeland have resources that could be valuable to Quantro?

Then you proceed as follows:
(1) Getting the facts: What are some of the main facts about the two countries, Quantro and Edgeland, that you should know in order to answer the question?
(2) Using your knowledge: What are possible choices in the relations between Quantro and Edgeland?
(3) Thinking it through: What conclusions can you reach, from weighing the evidence, about the most suitable response from Quantro to Edgeland's request for cooperation?
(4) The investigative reporter: How can we use the textbook, *Shaping an identity*, and other sources to study a real problem?

As a result of following this procedure, you should be able to solve the sample problem of Quantro and Edgeland. You will have begun to acquire and develop skills that can be applied to all sorts of problems, from those you encounter in everyday life, to questions asked in the chapters of this book, to problems facing real countries in the world today.

Getting the facts

A necessary step in learning about any topic is "getting the facts" that relate to a carefully worded question. In this section, you want to find out the answer to,

What are some of the main facts about the two countries, Quantro and Edgeland?

So you need to get the facts. Wait a minute. What are "facts"? What are some of the ways we can go about getting them?

A fact is something that actually exists (or has existed), can be observed and can be shown to be real. For example, it is a fact that you are a student who came to school today. It is a fact that you are reading a book called *Discovering Canada*. You can think of many other examples of facts, pieces of information that you can state are true. Only by "getting the facts" can you be sure to know something. Facts, then, are basic to knowledge.

How do you acquire facts? One of the ways is by reading. Reading is a skill; in fact, it is a combination of skills. Whether or not you find reading easy, the chances are that you can improve your reading skills. The key is to know what reading skills are, and to put them to use.

A method, an organized approach to reading, can help you to learn to read better and to enjoy reading more. Take the following passage about Quantro and Edgeland as an example to work with. After you have read it, you will look at a method of sharpening your reading skills.

Quantro and Edgeland had one thing in common, but not much more. They were both once colonies in the empire of Kai, a powerful nation in Europe. Quantro became a rich, developed country in which the people enjoyed one of the world's highest standards of living. The many different resources were plentiful. Most people had jobs. Usually they had to work hard but they made money. Citizens of Quantro came to expect a full refrigerator, good housing, safe working conditions, health care, public transport, well-maintained roads and many other services. People could vote to influence their government. They had freedom of speech and other rights, such as the right to a fair trial.

Edgeland, on the other hand, lagged behind in all respects. The people were mostly poor. They often did not have enough to eat and many were unable to read or write. They lived in fear of a government run mainly by officials from overseas. Why did the two places have such different stories?

Long ago, Quantro became a popular destination for settlers from Kai, the parent country. The climate and landscape were quite

Fig. 2 The development of special skills helps students to improve their own lives and the lives of others in their society.

Resources are a necessary part of developing wealth in a country. *Natural resources*, such as minerals or forests, can be the basis for *resource industries*, that is, when equipment and people are put to work to exploit the resources. Sometimes, one resource is so important, it becomes a *staple*—a product a country depends on for income.

similar to those back home. Immigrants from Kai were grateful to find that Quantro offered a chance to be better off than they could ever hope to be in the homeland. Yet they were determined to be as free in Quantro as were their fellow citizens in Kai. Before too long, therefore, the people of Quantro demanded self-government and gained their independence from the parent country. Yet the parent country and the former colony kept up a commercial partnership. Investors from Kai benefited from putting money into developing Quantro's many resources. The people of Quantro filled jobs in the resource industries—fishing, forestry and farming. Some even went into business for themselves. There were soon more jobs in shops, hospitals and other industries that supplied services to the residents.

Edgeland remained a colony. Governors from Kai ran its affairs. They encouraged business people from the parent country to spend money in Edgeland. These business people developed Edgeland's main natural resources, the rich mineral, atilla. Thus atilla extract became the staple product of Edgeland.

As time went on, some of the people of Edgeland grew resentful of the domination of Kai in their affairs. "We are being used for the advantage of the parent country," was an opinion heard more and more. Those who were dissatisfied were supported by Vastland, a major power unfriendly to Kai. Resistance to the rule of Kai was growing. Talk of independence increased.

Kai became involved in wars with its neighbours and with other

Fig. 3 Do you think this picture was taken in a developed country or in a developing one? Why?

colonies. It strength was reduced. Its popularity in Edgeland was declining, so was its power. Kai was unable to stop the progress of the "Edgeland Liberation Army" in its campaign for independence.

The government of Kai finally realized the hopelessness of trying to keep its colony. Edgeland gained independence and joined the United Nations. The government and people of Edgeland declared their wish to deal with other countries, for trade and other matters, like investment, exchange of skills and tourism.

So Edgeland began life as a new country. Its standard of living was low compared to that of Kai, Quantro and other more developed parts of the world. Edgeland's main problem was that the money made in the atilla mines still belonged to investors from Kai. The Edgeland government decided to nationalize—that is, to take over on behalf of the nation—the atilla industry. The money from the mines would be used to provide services to the people of Edgeland. This action shocked the business people of Kai. They were worried that the government of Edgeland would take over all their investments, so they withdrew their money.

Edgeland was in a difficult situation. The country needed partners among the more developed nations. Increased trade was vital to its economic growth. So were investment money and long-term loans. Expert advice was essential to making its industries more productive and to educating its people. The majority of Edgelanders could not read or write. Poverty was widespread. Health care was scarce.

Edgeland found new partners hard to attract. Vastland offered some aid, but only with "strings attached"—that is, only on certain conditions. Edgeland would have to agree to conditions that would cost it some of its newly gained independence; for example, it would be obliged to accept Vastland troops on its soil and warships in its harbour.

Quantro, as we have seen, was a self-governing former colony of Kai. One day it was contacted by the government of Edgeland. The message was in the form of a question: would Quantro receive a delegation from Edgeland to discuss future relations between the two countries?

1. a) Which of these would be a suitable title for the story? Why?
   i. War and peace
   ii. A tale of new nations
   iii. Rich countries and poor countries
   iv. Protest, violence and social change
   b) What is the main point of the first paragraph?
   i. Quantro and Edgeland were both former colonies of Kai
   ii. Edgeland and Quantro had developed into quite different places

Fig. 4 Do you think this picture was taken in a developing country or in a developed one? Why?

    iii. Life in Edgeland was harsh
    iv. The people of Quantro expected a high standard of living.

c) Another important fact that the story reveals about Quantro and Edgeland is
    i. Edgeland attracted settlers as well as investment money
    ii. The resources of Edgeland were developed mainly for the benefit of the people in the colony
    iii. Quantro attracted both human resources, in the form of settlers, as well as investment that helped improve the standard of living
    iv. Quantro and Edgeland were ready to fight to become countries independent of Kai.

d) Edgeland gained its independence when
    i. Kai decided the time had come to free its colonies
    ii. A war-weakened Kai agreed to the demands of a freedom movement in Edgeland
    iii. Foreign countries came to the aid of Edgeland
    iv. Edgeland chose to follow the same path to independence as Quantro.

e) As a new country, a problem Edgeland did *not* face was
   i. lack of literacy [ability to read and write] among the population as a whole
   ii. the difficulty of obtaining long-term loans
   iii. the need for improved diet and health care
   iv. too many nations competing to be Edgeland's partners

2. In your notebook, write the following items in the correct chronological order:
   a) Edgeland gained its independence
   b) Kai's power as a dominating nation grew weaker
   c) Other countries reacted with mixed feelings to Edgeland's request for trade
   d) Quantro achieved self-government over its own affairs
   e) The Edgeland Liberation Army compaigned against Kai's domination over government in Edgeland

3. a) For what reasons does it seem that Edgeland contacted Quantro in particular to "discuss future relations"?
   b) Suppose you were in a position to help Quantro decide about its answer to Edgeland. Do you have enough facts so far to make up your own mind?

4. With the help of a dictionary where necessary, find the meanings of: colony, resource, independence, investment, developed country, developing country.

What skills did you use in reading and examining the passage? First of all, to answer question 1, you had to "skim"—that is, read quickly—the whole passage. The skill of skimming is helpful in getting an overall view of the content. Remember this as one of the first steps whenever you read.

The next step was to "read for details." To answer questions 2 and 3, you looked at particular points, ideas and descriptions. Reading for details—a more thorough kind of reading—can deepen your understanding of a story or an explanation.

Another step is to "ask questions" about the content. For the above passage, the questions were already given. However, you could have made up your own. Such questions often come from topic sentences, or from other clues, such as headings and pictures. When you read in a questioning way, you are using your brain more actively, digging deeper—and usually understanding better.

Then there is the step of "reviewing," going back over the passage. This enables you to clarify even further the points you have been trying to understand.

You will not always go through all these steps every time you read. If you are reading for enjoyment, you will probably not use such an organized approach. However, if you are reading for information, "getting the facts," you should find this method helpful.

Fig. 5 You can apply the skills you use for reading to pictures. Examine this picture and "ask questions" about its content. What can you tell about the way of life it shows?

How has your reading helped prepare you for dealing with the case of Edgeland and Quantro? Well, you need information in order to answer questions about the two countries. You now have some of that. Perhaps you also have some ideas and impressions that will prove to be valuable later in your study.

Charts and diagrams

Almost every day, television and newspapers use charts and diagrams to help explain events to us. Take weather reports, for

instance. We may not be able to watch, or understand, all the forces of nature that result in a sunny day or a storm. But a well drawn diagram may be able to give an explanation that is easy to follow.

Another thing a chart can do is to organize a large number of facts and statistics. An otherwise lengthy and complicated account can be given in an easy-to-see way. An example of this can be seen in Figure 6, which provides a wide variety of information about Quantro and Edgeland that may startle you:

COLUMN	QUANTRO	EDGELAND
Birth rate, births/1000 people/yr	15	50
Death rate, deaths/1000 people/yr	10	30
Life expectancy	72	47
Average daily food intake, g	1985	1200
GNP, $/person	6000	300
Value of manufacturing output $/person	2800	75
Energy consumption, kg/person	12000	250
Literacy rate, % of total population	97	25

Fig. 6 Could the information in this chart be presented in other ways? If so, how?

This chart is based on figures given by Statistics Canada and by agencies of the United Nations for real countries.

5. a) State three things you can tell, on your own, from the chart
   b) Did any fact on the chart surprise you? If so, which one and why? If not, explain.
   c) Did you find any column headings confusing? If so, which? When using charts and tables, you may have to look for explanations of abbreviations and terms, such as:

   g = grams

   GNP = Gross National Product (total value of goods and services produced in a country)

   kg = kilograms

   literacy = ability to read and write.

   d) Which statistics would be most difficult to change
   (i) in Quantro?   (ii) in Edgeland? Explain.
   e) Compare the two columns of figures in the chart. Does any particular fact influence your own view of what the relations should be between Quantro and Edgeland?
   f) Charts are useful for giving facts, but sometimes there are facts which charts cannot show very well. Give three facts which could help compare the standard of living in Quantro and Edgeland but which do not appear on the chart.

Using your knowledge

Now that you have gathered some of the facts, you can move to the next step in trying to answer the problem posed at the beginning of the chapter. The next step is to deal with the question,

> What are possible choices in the relations between Quantro and Edgeland?

Identifying possible answers

Put yourself in the place of Mario, a student in Quantro. You are following events relating to Edgeland. Your assignment is to report on possible effects of these events on Quantro. In the newspaper, you find a statement by a spokesperson from your country:

> **Quantro should ignore Edgeland's request** *by Reen Grobaway*
>
> Ignoring Edgeland's request seems like the easiest and most sensible decision. Edgeland has few products to trade. It would be risky to sell goods to Edgeland, since the country is poor and would have to buy on credit. We may never be paid. Besides, the government is new and not very stable. It may change soon. Who knows how reliable it would be to deal with?
>
> Since gaining independence, Edgeland has sometimes been hostile. Its government has criticized Quantro. Certain groups there reject Quantro's lifestyle; it reminds them too much of Kai, which they remember as an unfair ruler from the past. Meanwhile, in Quantro, some groups have already held public meetings to object to close ties between the two nations. They fear that immigrants from Edgeland would come to their country.

6. a) State at least four reasons given by Quantro spokesperson, Reen Grobaway, for ignoring Edgeland's request for trade
    b) Prepare a statement that gives a different choice from the one presented by Mr. Grobaway. Use the heading, "Quantro should consider all possible dealings with Edgeland." Refer to the passage on the two countries to get your facts, and give at least four reasons to support your argument.
7. Imagine that you are Mario. Which of the two choices would you expect Quantro to make? Give your reasons.

Distinguishing facts from values

   A. Edgeland requests trade with Quantro
   B. Quantro should ignore Edgeland's request

How are the two above statements different? You may be able to find several differences. However, an important one for your present study is the following: A is a *fact* statement, while B is a *value* statement. The second one, B, as we saw earlier, was made by Mr. Grobaway. It shows his personal viewpoint, his choice of one answer over other possible answers. His statement is not a fact, although he did use facts to back it up.

The ability to distinguish facts from values is an important skill. Why? The way people see facts, gather facts and organize them, depends partly on people's values—their personal beliefs about what is important in life. When giving a description or explanation, people (whether they realize it or not) are often influenced by one value or another. When this happens, some statements given as fact are actually value statements.

Facts, remember, can be shown to be true; for example, it can be accepted as a fact that *Discovering Canada* exists as a book. Figures and

Fig. 7 What is your reaction to this picture? How much is your response based on the facts you learn from the picture, and how much is it based on your values?

graphs from agencies of the United Nations show that some nations have much higher living standards than others have. Values, on the other hand, reflect a preference, a view of what is good and bad, right or wrong. If you say that richer nations *should* cooperate with poorer nations to make the world a better place for all, you are expressing a value.

Facts and values, then, are different, even though they are often mixed together. Keep this point in mind in the following sections.

8. a) What value may underlie Mr. Grobaway's viewpoint: distrust of new governments, dislike for Edgelanders, carefulness in trade? Why do you think so?

b) Does his value position appear to be based mainly on facts or on emotion? Explain, with references to his article.

c) Copy the following statements in your notebook. Beside each factual statement, place an "F"; beside each value statement, place a "V":

   i. Quantro and Edgeland were both once colonies of Kai.

   ii. Kai was wrong in trying to keep control of Edgeland.

   iii. People of Edgeland were right to resent Kai's domination of their lives.

   iv. Edgeland and Quantro were possible partners in trade and other ways.

   v Rich nations should cooperate with poorer nations.

Forming hypotheses

You can often choose one alternative answer over another by forming a *hypothesis*; that is, you *suppose* something to be true, you make a statement of a *possible* explanation. When you first look into a topic, you assume—or take it for granted—that certain statements are true. You put your hypothesis into words. Then you check it in the light of all your evidence, the facts, you can uncover. A hypothesis has much the same use as a carefully worded question—it directs you towards an answer to a problem.

Let us return to the question of Quantro and Edgeland. Suppose you have been gathering facts (through television, radio, magazines, newspapers and books) about several countries in the world today. Some are considered to be "developed" countries, like Quantro. Others belong to the "developing" countries, which remind you of Edgeland. Finally you decide on the following hypothesis:

Cooperation between Quantro and Edgeland is likely to lead to a fairer sharing and use of resources and make the living standards of Quantro and Edgeland more equal.

9. a) Explain how one may go about arriving at a hypothesis.

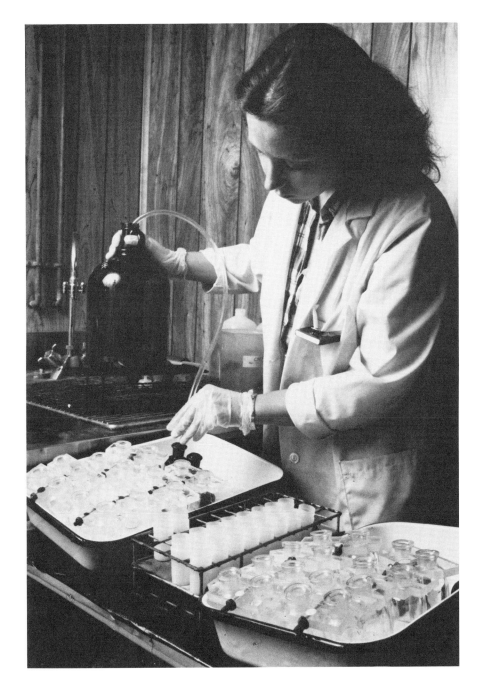

Fig. 8 You have to test a hypothesis to check that it is true. What could be some of the difficulties of testing a hypothesis about an historical problem?

b) Do you think that the hypothesis stated above represents a sound choice? Why or why not?

c) Do you think your values could influence the kind of hypothesis you form? Should they? Why or why not?

d) Devise another hypothesis or two different from the one stated above.

Thinking it through

Now you have a hypothesis. You have to ask the question,

> **On the basis of this hypothesis, do I have an answer to the problem, "What should be the relations between the two countries, Quantro and Edgeland"?**

You arrived at this possible answer by using a variety of skills, including reading, using charts, making summaries, identifying alternative answers, distinguishing facts from values. Now what?

You are about to put the pieces together. You will still be using skills identified in the two earlier sections. That is, you will still be observing, reading for main ideas, making comparisons, and so on. The emphasis, however, will now be on "thinking it through." Your task is to weigh the evidence, in order to reach a conclusion.

In other words, you are testing the suitability of the hypothesis,

> Cooperation between Quantro and Edgeland is likely to lead to a fairer sharing and use of resources and make the living standards of the two countries more equal.

Weighing the evidence

In thinking through a hypothesis, you need to collect evidence. Evidence is made up of facts that relate to, or tie in with, the hypothesis.

Consider the following points. Decide very carefully what is *fact* and what may be based on *opinions* or *values*.

(1) The average person of Quantro consumes nearly twice as much food per day as the average person in Edgeland, and many times more energy, especially in the form of gasoline and other petroleum products.

(2) On the average, more money is spent on petfood in Quantro than is spent in Edgeland for food for humans.

(3) During its long history as a colony of Kai, very little manufacturing was set up in Edgeland. Its natural resources were sold to "developed" countries for processing. The processed goods were then sold in Edgeland. Their cost was high compared with the income received from the colony's natural resources. Edgeland thus lost heavily through much of its trade, and the colony went deeper and deeper into debt. Most of the wealth that did exist in Edgeland was controlled by foreigners and a small class of privileged citizens.

(4) Quantro's heavily industrialized economy continues to expand. The growth of manufacturing, sprawling cities, warehouses

"Privileged" people are those who enjoy the advantages of living in a wealthy, sheltered or comfortable environment.

42

Fig. 9 Distinguish fact from value: On average, more money is spent on petfood in Quantro than is spent in Edgeland on food for humans. Quantro should grant money and supplies to help reduce food shortages in Edgeland.

and parking lots, superhighways and other marks of modern progress are reducing Quantro's agricultural and wilderness land and polluting its air and waterways.

(5) The Third World Relief Agency and various church groups urge the government of Quantro to grant money and supplies to help reduce food shortages in Edgeland.

(6) The first government of an independent Edgeland is overthrown by the army. In an announcement seen on television around the world, General M. . . . states that the revolution was unavoidable. It is the only way, he declares, to end the corruption in Edgeland's government. According to the general, the army will run the nation's affairs until some future time when conditions permit democratic elections.

(7) The Fidget Corporation of Quantro announces a two-stage development plan in which (a) it has contracted with the new government of Edgeland to make the largest purchase of the mineral, atilla, in history and (b) it will start construction, within a year, of a manufacturing plant in Edgeland.

(8) The prime minister of Quantro is welcomed enthusiastically as she begins a good will visit to Edgeland. At a dinner in her honour, General M. . . . praises Quantro as a true friend. "Your

Fig. 10 Distinguish fact from value: 20 percent of the people in Quantro can hardly afford to eat, and some people are homeless. Quantro should not send aid to Edgeland.

country is trusted because it has never had an empire and shows no desire to take advantage of less fortunate countries. Your people have a reputation for being generous."

(9) At Quantro's Parliament Bluff, the Poor People's Committee of Quantro holds a mass rally. Various spokespersons object to aid being sent to Edgeland when 20% of the people in Quantro can only afford a diet of borscht, beans, bologna and tapioca pudding.

(10) a) Do the facts support the hypothesis that "Cooperation between Quantro and Edgeland is likely to lead to a fairer sharing and use of resources and make the living standards of the two countries more equal"?

Why or why not? After "weighing the evidence", have you decided that it actually supports a different hypothesis? Explain.

b) Based on the evidence you have collected, and using the skills you have developed, you can now decide on an answer to the problem, "What should be the relations between the two countries, Quantro and Edgeland?" What is your conclusion? What are the main arguments that support your conclusion?

The investigative reporter

As "the investigative reporter", you will be applying an inquiry (question-based) model—an organized set of skills—to a real world problem.

So far in this chapter, you have been developing the inquiry model by examining an imaginary example. Through the case of Edgeland and Quantro, you have practised the steps of studying a topic systematically: getting the facts, analysing them to identify possible choices, and thinking them through to a conclusion.

Now you should be ready to apply your skills to the investigation of an actual problem. To get started, take the following question:

How can we use the textbook, *Shaping an identity* **and other sources to study a real problem?**

A textbook is often a useful place to start. The next sub-section will give you some guidelines for using a book such as *Discovering Canada: Shaping an identity.*

The textbook: How to use it

As a textbook, *Discovering Canada* is set up to be both a source of information and a programme for using this information. In other words, you will gain knowledge about Canada and also develop a set of skills. These skills will help you to study other social studies topics.

If you know how a book is organized, you will be able to make better use of it. Here are some points about the setup of *Discovering Canada*:

(1) Table of contents: lists chapter titles and the section heading, which are the main topics of each chapter.
(2) Index: lists alphabetically the topics, events, terms, names of people and other specific items found throughout the book. The page numbers where these items are found in the book are also listed.
(3) Chapter organization: every chapter is organized in the same way. Each begins with a two-page spread, consisting of a visual and a brief story or situation. This introduces the main idea of the chapter. Then the chapter overview tells about the content. The signposts and the key words are listed next.
(4) Activities: as you have seen from this chapter, the activities are grouped under four different headings. Each of the headings stands for a group of skills. As you practise these, they will become part of your approach to history and social studies.
(5) Marginal notes: in the margins you will find explanations of

special terms, as well as extra bits of information and items of interest.

(6) Timelines: appear in many chapters. Timelines show where each main event fits in a certain period of time.

(7) Glossary: definitions of glossary words—which appear in bold type and a different colour—are given in a section near the end of the book. Pronunciation guides appear with these where necessary, and with other possibly difficult words throughout the book. The key to the pronunciation guides appears in the back of the book.

When you use other books, begin by looking at how they are organized. You will save yourself a lot of time and effort.

Studying a real problem

With the advice of your teacher, speculate about one problem that Canada shares with other countries. You may be advised to choose a theme such as poverty, the technological revolution, violence, energy, food and water, pollution, unemployment, the

Fig. 11 In what ways might the problems of a developed country differ from those in a developing part of the world? Give several examples of problems that might be typical of a developed country and several that might be typical of a developing country.

power of multinational corporations, the management of sports teams. What questions would you need to ask to try to solve the problem? What sorts of issues and ideas would you have to examine? Now is the time to use the inquiry model you have been learning throughout the chapter.

Your object is to prepare a report. As you work towards this goal, keep the following guidelines in mind:

(1) Remember the old saying about reports and essays: "Say what you are going to say, say it, and then say what you've said!"

(2) In the opening paragraph or two, you should announce to the reader (a) this is what my report is about, (b) here are the main points I am going to talk about. So your *introduction* is a small-scale version of the whole report.

(3) The *conclusion* should sum up the contents of the report and clearly state any ideas, opinions and understanding you have reached about the topic.

(4) In all parts of the report, present your information in your own words. Sometimes you will want to quote words exactly as they appear in a source; that is, a direct quotation. If you do, put a number at the end of the quotation. Then put that number at the bottom of the page, with a *footnote* giving the source. For example, if the following is the fifth quotation in your report:

It would be risky to sell goods to Edgeland, since the country is poor and would have to buy on credit.[5]

5. Grobaway, Reen. "Quantro should ignore Edgeland's request," *The Daily Blab*, Feb. 30, 1983.

(5) The last page of your report gives the *bibliography*, the list of books you used as sources. List them alphabetically according to each author's last name.

(6) A *title page* may be the first page.

Conclusion

You have now had a preview of this volume of *Discovering Canada*. The activities you have worked with are a sample of what is ahead.

Another, and perhaps more important result of this chapter is your experience with an inquiry model. You should have begun to develop an organized set of skills for use in studying a variety of world problems.

3 World War I

"My youth has departed from me"

Nellie McClung was a noted author, politician, and spokesperson for women's rights at the beginning of the twentieth century. She wrote the following words about her 18-year-old son Jack and his friends going off to fight in World War I:

> ... below the surface of my thoughts and forever dulling the pleasure of my many activities lay the blight of war and the dread of Jack's enlistment. When the fateful day arrived, we knew they were leaving their childhood and youth behind them and that even if they did come back they would be changed, so it was more than good-bye we were saying to our boys. It was good-bye—forever!
>
> In my diary I wrote that day, December 4th, 1915:

> This morning we said good-bye to our dear son Jack at the C.N.R. station where new snow lay fresh and white on the roofs and on the streets, white, and soft, and pure as a young heart. When we came home I felt strangely tired and old though I am only forty-two. But I know that my youth has departed from me. It has gone with Jack, our beloved, our first born, the pride of our hearts. Strange fate surely for a boy who never has had a gun in his hands, whose ways are gentle, and full of peace; who loves his fellow men, pities their sorrows, and would gladly help them to solve their problems. What have I done to you, in letting you go into this inferno of war? And how could I hold you back without breaking your heart?

From *The Stream Runs Fast: My Own Story* by Nellie L. McClung.

- What does Nellie McClung mean when she says that her son and his friends were leaving their childhood and youth behind them?

- How do you think Nellie McClung felt as she watched the young men go off to war?

- McClung says that even if the boys came back they would be changed. How do you think war would change the people who fought in it? Would it change people who remained in Canada, far from the battlefields? Explain.

- Why do you think McClung's son and other Canadians would go to fight in a war in Europe?

◀ Mother and son, soon to be separated by war

Chapter overview

World War I was Canada's first major venture into world affairs. Since Britain had great influence over Canada's foreign policy, a British war was automatically a Canadian war. Over 600 000 Canadian men and women joined the armed forces to support Britain and her allies France and Russia in the war against Germany and Austria. Most of these Canadians fought in France. Over 60 000 Canadians died . . . one out of every ten who enlisted. More than 170 000 were wounded.

The changes brought about by World War I were global. The empires of Austria, Germany and Russia were destroyed. Northern France was devastated. The British Empire was weakened. New world powers appeared, the strongest of which was the United States.

Canada was also changed by World War I. It became more industrial, more urban, more independent. Women took on new roles. Relations between French and English, however, were seriously strained by the war.

In this chapter we will survey World War I and focus on Canada's involvement in it.

Signposts

Why the world was headed for war >

What was the war on land like? >

FEATURE: Life in the trenches >

What role did Canadians have on the battlefield? >

The war at sea >

The war in the air >

What was happening at home in Canada? >

How did Canadian women contribute to the war effort? >

1914 Gavrillo Princip assassinates Austrian Archduke Franz Ferdinand / Britain declares war on Germany Canada at war

1915 First Canadians arrive in France Gas attack at Ypres

1916 Battle of Somme – Newfoundland Battalion lost 70 percent of their men at Beaumont Hammel

1917 Canadians take Vimy Ridge Conscription Crisis

1918 Nov. 11, Armistice

1919 Treaty of Versailles signed by Canada separately from Britain

1920 Canada joins League of Nations

Key words

Triple Alliance	income tax
Triple Entente	Military Voters Act
War Measures Act	Wartime Elections Act
stalemate	Victory Bond
attrition	propaganda

Why the world was headed for war

Suppose you were an "average" Canadian in the early 1900s. If someone had asked you "How's it goin'?" you might have replied—

> Canadians have never had it so good. Business is booming. Besides the big railway projects, mining, the lumber industry and manufacturing are on the upswing. Many individuals have opened their own small businesses—grocery stores, hardwares, cafes, barbershops. Jobs are plentiful, and, if you don't like the one you have, you can go west and take up farming on the cheap land available there.

But what about all the trouble overseas? The British must be expecting difficulties in the near future, or they wouldn't be pressuring Canada to help build up the Empire's defenses.

> Well, it's true that we had that war in South Africa, but that's all over now. Europe, where they always seem to be squabbling, is far away. I can't see how a war over there can affect Canadians. Just look at all the immigrants getting out of Europe and coming here to start new lives. For many of them, life in Canada means escape from armies and war-like leaders.

A Canadian in the early 1900s, therefore, was bound to feel safe. Even Europe, where wars had been fought from time to time in

51

Front line
●●●● November 30, 1914

▬▬ Front line
November 11, 1918

Fig. 1 Europe at the outbreak of World War I

Entente is a French word meaning unwritten agreement or understanding. The Triple Entente was an understanding among Britain, France and Russia that they would help each other if attacked by other nations. When the war started, they became allies and fought against Germany, Austria and Turkey.

The Balkan region is a very mountainous region of southeastern Europe extending south from the Danube and Sava Rivers, bounded by the Black Sea on the east, the Aegean Sea on the south, and the Adriatic Seas on the west. Today this region contains Albania, Bulgaria, continental Greece, Rumania, European Turkey and Yugoslavia. Find out what the term "Balkanized" means to increase your understanding of the period.

one region or another, had avoided a widespread conflict for 100 years—since the time of Napoleon.

For several decades, however, Europe had been heading for a different kind of war—a so-called "total war." Two old enemies, Germany and France, were preparing to renew their struggle. In trying to gain an advantage, each had drawn other major powers into opposing sides. By 1914, Germany, Austria-Hungary and Italy—the Triple Alliance—were lined up against the Triple Entente of France, Russia and Great Britain.

How did these European countries find themselves on the brink of war? In many ways, Europe was waiting for an "accident" to happen. The most likely place for the "accident" was eastern Europe. From the Baltic Sea in the north to the Mediterranean in the south, political tempers were rising. Three empires, the Austro-Hungarian, the Russian and the Turkish, had ruled much of the region for many years, even centuries. Each empire included different nationalities, such as Poles, Czechs, Slovaks and Serbs. Among them was a growing desire to be independent, to have separate countries of their own. Nationalists secretly planned ways, including bombings and other violence, to weaken imperial governments. To control such threats to their power, imperial leaders had armies, police and secret police.

Conditions in the Balkan region were particularly unstable. Wars in 1912 and 1913 involved several countries. Turkey was the main loser. It had little territory left west of the Dardanelles. Serbia, on the other hand, had gained territory and population. So far the general peace of Europe had not been endangered. None of the

conflicts had involved any of the major powers, but both Austria-Hungary and Russia were more watchful than ever of shifts in political power in the Balkans. Could some sudden event touch off a chain of events that would draw all the major powers into a war?

On June 28, 1914, a sudden event, an assassination, occurred. The place of the event was Sarajevo [SAR-eh-yay-voh], capital of Bosnia, a province in the Austrian empire. The victims: Archduke Franz Ferdinand, heir to the Austrian throne, and his wife, the Duchess Sophie. The assassin: Gavrilo Princip, an 18-year-old of Serbian background.

Austria felt it had to take strong action against Serbia, or else it would appear weak to the other powers. After nearly a month of confusion, Austria made demands on Serbia that almost equalled a demand to take over that country. Russia, fearful of any spread of Austrian power in eastern Europe, began preparing its armies to back Serbia.

Germany backed Austria in the crisis; France and Britain prepared to support Russia. Once it had declared war on France, Germany launched its surprise invasion through Belgium. Britain had pledged to defend Belgium's freedom from invasion. Thus Britain declared war on Germany on August 4, 1914.

How did Canada become involved in World War I?

Canada was so far from Europe. How did it become part of Europe's "Great War," the struggle that became known as World War I? Canada was still part of the British Empire. Thus when the British declared war on Germany on August 4, 1914, Canada was automatically at war.

The real question in Canada about the war was: In what way will we take part? The answer came quickly. Most Canadians supported a strong war effort. The government wasted little time in passing the War Measures Act. This gave the government the power to take away freedom of speech; the power to arrest, imprison and deport people (send them out of the country); the power to take over the nation's resources and use them for war.

At the beginning of World War I, Canada had an army of 3000. Within weeks, the Canadian government had a war budget of $50 000 000, and by October, 1914, 33 000 volunteers had joined the First Canadian Contingent for training at Valcartier, near Quebec City. They were shipped to England in November for further training. By February, 1915, troops from this force were fighting in France. By the end of 1915, more than 200 000 had volunteered to fight. All together, more than 600 000 Canadians served in the armed forces, and 425 000 went overseas.

Sam Hughes, the first minister of the militia, gave energetic leadership in the recruitment of volunteers.

1. Why would Canadians in the early 1900s feel safe from the unrest in Europe?

2. Name the three main empires ruling eastern Europe. Of the three, which two empires remained powerful after the wars in 1912 and 1913?

3. On June 28, 1914, Archduke Franz Ferdinand of Austria and his wife were assassinated. On August 4 of the same year, Britain declared war on Germany. Starting with the assassination, list all the steps leading to Britain's declaration of war.

USING YOUR KNOWLEDGE

4. When looking at events of the past, it is important for all students of history to have historical perspective. To better understand why a certain event occurred and what its results were, we should keep in mind how people felt at that time.

a) When Britain declared war on Germany in 1914, Canada was automatically at war. Put yourself in the place of a person living in your part of the country when war was declared. In a paragraph, describe how you would feel about becoming involved in a European war. (Keep in mind the strong ties between Canada and Britain at the time.)

b) If Britain declared war *today* and Canada was expected to join in, would you feel the same way about becoming involved in a war in Europe? Explain the reasons for your position.

Allied nations are states which join together to face a common enemy. This term is often used to refer to members of the Triple Entente and nations supporting them. The expressions "Allied cause" or "Allied forces" are also used. Sometimes they were simply called "the Allies." The use of "Allied" can be confusing since "the Allies" fought against the "Triple Alliance." Why do you think that we used "Allied" to refer to the nations and colonies that joined Britain, France and Russia?

What was the war on land like?

World War I was mainly an European war. Eventually other parts of the globe were involved, as conflicts broke out in the colonies and Allied nations of the European rivals. But the bulk of the fighting took place in Europe.

The war on land raged along two fronts, or stretches of territory. One was the eastern front, where the Central Powers (Germany, Austria-Hungary, Turkey and Bulgaria) faced the Russians. The other main battle zone was western Europe. Germany's rapid invasion of Belgium was intended to produce a quick victory over France. The German advance was stalled, however, in Belgium and northern France. Supporting the stand by the French and Belgians were Great Britain and members of its empire, including Canada.

For most Canadians, World War I was mainly the deadly struggle on the western front. Allied resistance to the German invasion

Germany attacks
France 1914

Russia attacks
Germany and
Austria 1914

Turkey attacks
Russia 1914

Austria attacks
Serbia 1914

Allies attack
Gallipoli 1915

(Most Canadians
fought in France)

Turkey attacks
Egypt 1915

Japanese take
Tsingtao 1914

Japanese take
Carolines and
Marshalls 1914

Allies occupy Togoland,
Cameroons 1914-15

British launch
East Africa Campaign
Nov 1914

Anzacs take
New Guinea,
Gamoa 1914

German S.W. Africa
occupied 1915

le of Coronel
Nov 1914

Battle of
Falkland Is.
8th Dec 1914

Fig. 2 The first global war

produced a stalemate that lasted through most of the war. Each side lost thousands of troops daily—to advance, or retreat, a few metres. This was a war of attrition.

Over a stretch of nearly 1000 kilometres, from Switzerland to the North Sea, the land was carved into trenches. From the beginning of the war, troops on both sides had to dig in to avoid mass slaughter by machine guns and cannons. Trenches got deeper and more permanent as the fighting dragged on. Some were even equipped with furniture, stoves and other facilities. But most were damp, cold, slime-filled dugouts infested by lice, fleas and rats. Mud-fields, water-filled shell craters and barbed wire replaced meadows and forests.

From time to time, an army tried to break the stalemate. Thousands of soldiers went "over the top" to charge the other side. Their

Fig. 3 A group of Canadian soldiers goes "over the top," trying to advance on the enemy.

gunners tried to give protection by pounding the enemy trenches with shells. The defenders responded by huddling in their tunnels until the big guns eased their attack. Then they engaged their rivals in an exchange of gunfire and bayonet thrusts. Men fell dead on both sides, but the trench lines remained more or less the same as before.

Poison gas was another desperate device used. Greenish clouds of chlorine were released to be blown by the wind across enemy lines. Heavier than air, the gas flowed into the enemy trenches. It blinded the eyes and destroyed the lungs. But since wind currents were unpredictable, poison gas often proved to be as deadly to the users as to the targets.

Later in the war, tanks were used to assault enemy trenches. Like huge metal dinosaurs, they flattened the rolls of barbed wire set out as protection. Where the ground was firm, tanks were effective. But in the mud of Belgium and northern France where most of the Canadian troops were fighting, tanks often became hopelessly stuck.

Fig. 4 Soldiers test machine guns and other equipment on an armoured car.

Fig. 5 A tank coming out of action. Look closely at the countryside. What can you tell about fighting conditions and the effects of war?

At the end of the war, millions were dead, and the suffering of the survivors was immense. The nervous systems of many people were damaged by the almost constant explosion of big guns. Others would never forget the horror of seeing friends maimed or killed. Nor could they forget the wretched conditions: wet uniforms rotting on their bodies, diseases spread by lice and other vermin, and the hopelessness of sitting for years in the trenches.

GETTING THE FACTS

5. World War I was fought all around the world.
   a) In what two main regions was the war on land fought?
   b) Consult Figure 2 and name at least four other locations where fighting took place.

6. Where did Canadians do most of their fighting?

7. In your own words explain the following terms and use each word in a sentence: front; stalemate; trenches.

USING YOUR KNOWLEDGE

8. Imagine you are a Canadian soldier on the western front. Do one of the following: write a letter home in which you describe battle conditions and your feelings about the war; or draw a picture that will give the people back home a good idea of what life on the front is like.

THINKING IT THROUGH

9. a) In your own words explain what a war of attrition is.
   b) Why did the war on land become a war of attrition? In your answer be sure to discuss how weapons used in World War I were different from those used in earlier wars.
   c) What do you think could be done to end the stalemate? Try to think of a few solutions and then choose the one you think is best. Give reasons for your choice.

What role did Canadians have on the battlefield?

In this section you will learn about the role of Canadian soldiers in key battles on the western front.

Ypres, Belgium, 1915

In mid-April, 1915, the Canadian First Division was sent to the trenches near Ypres [EE-preh], in the Flanders region of Belgium. In

Life in the trenches

Soldiers on both sides spent much of World War I in the trenches dug several feet deep in the muddy ground of western Europe. An underground army was often separated from the enemy by only a few metres of land marked by bomb craters and barbed wire. The following letter sent home by a Canadian soldier gives a vivid picture of life in the trenches:

3 October, 1915

Well, I've been through it and out of it again. That is to say, I have just had five days and five nights in the front line trenches. . . . It really is most extraordinary what one can get accustomed to. Whizz-bangs [shells] and bullets were flying about at the time, and when you found that they missed *you*, you began to feel, at any rate I did, that they would never hit you. But the real 'corkers' are those . . . 'Coal Boxes' [heavy shells]. You hear the brute coming a long way off with the noise of an express train. It's no good hiding anywhere, because you would only be buried by the debris, so you sit tight, hold your breath and pray to God it won't hit you. Then when it lands a most appalling explosion takes place, shakes the earth all round, and then . . . you breathe once more. . . .

My dugout in the trench had other occupants, things with lots of legs, also swarms of rats and mice, so I didn't feel at all lonely. I think I have slept in every conceivable place of filth there is now, and the most extraordinary thing is that you do sleep. I did not have my clothes off my back for the whole time I was in the trenches, and it rained the whole time. We were all wet through. The excitement counteracted the chill. . . .

From *Letters from the Front, 1914-1918* by John Laffin.

THINKING IT THROUGH

10. a) Reread the letter carefully. What does it reveal about the man who wrote it? Discuss at least four characteristics or attitudes that emerge.

b) Would your own attitudes be the same as this soldier's, or different? Explain.

11. Letters were often censored by officials in World War I. Why do you suppose this was done? Do you agree or disagree with this censorship? Give reasons to support your viewpoint.

relief of French soldiers, the Canadians were to defend a section of the front line. A heavy German attack was expected any day.

April 22, 1915 was the day the attack began. It was a warm, calm, blue-skied day until late afternoon when a breeze blew up. This was just what the German army was waiting for. The thunder of its artillery signaled the attack—and a ground-hugging, yellow-green cloud of poisonous chlorine gas rolled toward the opposition trenches.

No gas masks had been issued. Some men were blinded. Others died. When the German attack came, the surviving Canadians were outnumbered two to one, but they kept on fighting and slowed down the German advance. The German attack was stopped, "by the extraordinary heroism of small detachments of Canadian and British troops," wrote a military historian. The stand at Ypres established the military reputation of Canadian troops. It was a reputation that was tested again and again throughout the war.

Fig. 6 The funeral of a Canadian nurse killed in the bombing of a hospital at Etaples in France. The cemetery at Etaples contains over 10 000 military graves from World War I.

Vimy Ridge, France, 1917

Ypres was a defensive action which drew attention to Canadians. It was Vimy Ridge, however, that demonstrated the effectiveness of Canadians as shock troops—that is, as troops used to spearhead an attack. Vimy Ridge was a Canadian victory in a war in which victory was measured by every single square metre of territory taken. In Vimy, all four Canadian divisions were used together for the first time, 100 000 Canadians in total.

Much had been learned by 1917. "Everything had been carefully rehearsed beforehand; each battalion had its own special work, and weeks before, we had studied the ground in front of our trenches . . . from aeroplane photographs," wrote one Canadian before the attack on Vimy. Another soldier described the attack:

A few minutes before the hour I issued rum to the men and then we waited. Right on the dot, pandemonium broke out. Our artillery opened up as one gun. The noise was deafening. The shrieking shells mingled with their explosions and machine-gun fire, trench mortars, etc., was something indescribable. On our flank great drums of burning oil were projected on enemy strong-points. When our time came, we climbed on the parapet [wall or bank] and started over. Looking to either side one could see thousands of men walking slowly but nonetheless certainly into the German lines. Ahead of us our artillery cleared the way. When we reached the German lines we hardly recognized them. What had been trenches were mere sunken lines. . . . The ground between the trenches was so

pitted with shell-holes that it resembled a gigantic honeycomb. The only works left standing were massive concrete machine-gun emplacements. . . . The wood [forest], when I found it, consisted of a piece of ground covered with stumps about one foot high. A machine gun opened up on us and as I was trying to get away from it I stumbled on a bayonet and got a nasty cut in the foot . . . I had to run, sore foot and all, as the ground was being shelled. . . . I was rather surprised to see I had a following; Germans seemed to spring up out of the ground. I counted up and found I had six [prisoners] to guide, so I started them off down the trench and directed them from behind . . . and carried on to the dressing station where I had my foot dressed.

From *Letters from the Front, 1914-1918* by John Laffin.

The attack on Vimy Ridge was successful. 54 heavy pieces of artillery, 104 trench mortars and 124 machine guns were captured, but the cost was high. Over 10 000 Canadians were killed or wounded.

When the war ended, Vimy Ridge was chosen as the site of the Canadian War Memorial. Here the names of each of the Canadians who died are chiselled in stone. The experiences of World War I, particularly Ypres in 1915 and Vimy Ridge in 1917, made many Canadians sad yet full of pride. These experiences contributed to the feeling that Canada had matured and was ready to have more control over its own affairs.

THINKING IT THROUGH

12. a) Why do you think the experiences of World War I would make many Canadians feel that the country had matured and was ready to have more control over its own affairs?

b) Do you think that the World War I experiences prepared Canada to take more control of its affairs? What other factors, if any, would also be necessary for Canada to act more independently?

13. The description of Vimy Ridge, taken from a soldier's letter, is an example of a primary source document.

a) Suggest some other primary sources.

b) Why are letters and other primary sources valuable to students of history?

c) "When using primary source documents, we must be careful to understand the author's point of view or personal bias. If not, then we may accept a biased or distorted picture as fact." Do you agree or disagree with this statement? Give reasons for your answer.

Fig. 7 Wounded soldiers of the Allied forces. What sort of conditions do you think these men could expect in a field hospital?

Fig. 8 H.M.S. Niobe was the flagship of Canada's navy. This ship was supposed to defend Canada's east coast, but made only one journey before retiring from service.

The war at sea

In the summer of 1914 Canada had a navy consisting of two aging cruisers, the *Rainbow* and the *Niobe*. They had been purchased from Britain as training ships. This was to be the first step in creating the Royal Canadian Navy. Plans to build new, modern warships had been interrupted when, in the election of 1911, the Laurier Liberal government was defeated. The Conservative government, led by Robert Borden, preferred a policy of contributing money to expand the British imperial navy. The naval issue was still unsettled when

World War I began. Only by stretching the meaning of the word "navy" could Canada be said to have a navy at all.

But with the world's largest and strongest navy, Great Britain had been "mistress of the seas" for a century. In February, 1906, Britain launched the huge battleship H.M.S. Dreadnought. It was the first of many such battleships. The dreadnoughts were so large and equipped with such powerful guns that they made earlier warships seem like toys by comparison. Britain was declaring to the world, "We British are determined to continue as the Number 1 naval power."

Germany's mighty army made it Europe's most powerful nation on land. But in the years leading up to 1914, it was also challenging Britain's supremacy on the high seas. Germany had its own programme of building giant battleships. Germany and Britain were engaged in an arms race. When World War I broke out in August, 1914, each was trying to gain a military advantage over the other.

The struggle at sea, therefore, was mainly a contest between the British and German navies. As the war dragged on, the British goal was to use its navy to blockade Germany—that is, to block off the country from contact with the outside world. On the other hand, Germany attempted to cut Britain off from Canada and other overseas suppliers of food and weapons.

On the surface of the oceans, Britain and its allies kept control. The Battle of Jutland, off the coast of Denmark, was the only major showdown between the rival navies. Though Britain suffered heavy losses, it convinced Germany that it would not win an all-out confrontation. Germany turned to submarine warfare, surprising both British military and passenger ships with high-explosive torpedoes fired below the water line. The most spectacular example was the sinking on May 7, 1915, of the *Lusitania*, a passenger liner. Of the 1198 lives lost, 128 were citizens of the United States. The U.S. was not yet involved in the war, but was angered by the loss of American lives to German weapons. The U.S. anger worried the Germans, who were anxious to avoid bringing the Americans into World War I.

German submarines were known as U-boats because the German word for submarine starts with a "u".

Two developments reduced the effectiveness of German submarine warfare. One was the desire to stay away from provoking the United States to join the anti-German war effort. The other was British war tactics. The British used mines and torpedoes to protect their ships. They also used convoys, which were ships travelling together for protection.

The submarine war was spreading toward North America. By the final months of 1916, Britain was doubtful that its navy could continue to protect Canada's coastline. Canada was asked to build and operate a fleet of patrol boats. They played an important part in Britain's convoy system, providing larger ships with protection against attack by submarine.

Canada contributed far more to the Allied naval effort than anyone expected when the war began. Several thousand Canadians served in the British navy, and, in addition, the Royal Canadian Navy became a navy in fact as well as in name. Its warships numbered more than 100, including two submarines bought from the United States. The number of officers and sailors rose from fewer than 350 to more than 5500.

GETTING THE FACTS

14. In your own words, explain the naval issue in Canada just before the war started. What policy did the Conservatives favour? the Liberals?

15. The struggle at sea in World War I was a struggle between which two nations?

16. a) What is a blockade?
    b) How did the Germans use U-boats in the blockade plan?
    c) How did Britain reduce the effectiveness of German submarine warfare?

THINKING IT THROUGH

17. In question 14 you explained how Canadians before the war disagreed about which naval policy to follow.
    a) Describe the contribution to the Allied naval effort that Canada had made by the end of the war.
    b) Do you think that this action helped Canada develop as a nation, or did it hurt the country? Give reasons for your opinion.

THE INVESTIGATIVE REPORTER

18. Below is a list of some World War I battles in which Canadians participated, and some Canadians who were prominent in the war. Consult your library for information on the battle or person, then write a brief one-page report for delivery to the class. If you choose a battle be sure to describe its main feature, as well as the Canadian contribution to the war effort. If you choose a person, outline that person's role and major contribution.
—Festubert and Givenchy, May-June 1915
—St. Eloi Craters, March-April 1916
—Mount Sorrel, 2-13 June 1916
—The Somme, July-November 1916
—The Scarpe, April-May 1917
—Capture of Hill 70, 15-25 August 1917
—Passchendaele, October 26-November 10, 1917

The war in the air

In 1914 the Canadian air force consisted of an unpaid commander and his assistant and one plane purchased in the United States for $5000. When the Minister of Militia, Sir Sam Hughes, refused to grant any more money to the air force, the two flyers went their separate ways. One returned to Canada. The other joined the Royal Air Force (British) and was killed on his first solo flight. Meanwhile, the only Canadian plane had been lost somewhere in England.

In 1914 only eleven years had passed since the Wright brothers' famous flight at Kitty Hawk in the United States. Airplanes were flimsy, awkward, undependable machines. Yet by the end of World War I, air forces had become vitally important to the outcome of the war. More than 20 000 Canadians joined the Royal Air Force (R.A.F.). In 1923 the Royal Canadian Air Force was established as part of Canada's military force.

How can we account for such changes in so short a time? The war resulted in a race between the rival sides to improve the quality of the planes, their equipment and their uses. At first, planes were slow but valuable for watching enemy troop movements. Soon, pilots of both sides were arming themselves with chains, bricks, pistols, rifles—anything they could hurl at an enemy aircraft or drop on soldiers below. By the latter part of the war, planes were better built and flying twice as fast. Machine guns were mounted on the planes. An interrupter gear made it possible to fire forward without shooting off the propeller.

Fig. 9 As planes became more efficient, so did the weapons used against them, anti-aircraft guns.

The air aces

By 1917, combat in the air had become common. "Aces" were pilots who managed to shoot down five enemy aircraft. Both German and Allied air forces soon had developed groups of skilled and deadly pilots. The most widely known was the German, Baron von Richthofen ("the Red Baron"). He shot down 80 Allied planes before he himself was shot down by the Canadian ace, Roy Brown, in April, 1918.

Fig. 10 Billy Bishop

Canada's top ace was W.A. "Billy" Bishop. Strangely, he had one serious shortcoming as a pilot; he could hardly land a plane without damaging it. In the air, though, he was a marvel. He shot down 72 German planes, thanks to his sharpshooting skills learned hunting squirrels as a boy in Owen Sound, Ontario.

Was the life of an "ace" as glamourous as it sometimes sounds? In the musical *Billy Bishop Goes to War*, the hero writes a letter about his experiences and feelings:

Dearest Margaret. We are dropping bombs on the enemy from unarmed machines. It is exciting work. It's hard to keep your confidence in a war when you don't have a gun. Somehow we get back in one piece and we start joking around and inspecting the machine for bullet and shrapnel damage. You're so thankful not to be dead. Then I go back to the barracks and lie down. A kind of terrible loneliness comes over me. It's like waiting for the firing squad. It makes you want to cry, you feel so frightened and so alone. I think all of us who aren't dead think these things. Thinking of you constantly, I remain. . . .

From *Billy Bishop Goes to War* by John Gray.

19. a) Compare Canada's air force in 1914 with its air force at the end of the war.

   b) Why did the air force change so much in so short a time?

THINKING IT THROUGH

20. a) What do you think the qualities of a hero or heroine are? Was Billy Bishop a hero according to your definition. Give reasons to support your viewpoint.

   b) The Allies gave the "Red Baron" a full burial with military honours although he fought against them in World War I. How would you explain this?

THE INVESTIGATIVE REPORTER

21. Many Canadian pilots became aces and the stories of their adventures reveal much about the evolution of military airplanes. Consult the index of books in your library dealing with World War I and prepare a report on one of the following fliers:

Roy Brown	George Barker
Ray Collishaw	Alan McLeod
Ellis Reid	Donald MacLaren
J.E. Sharman	G. McElroy
J.E. Nash	W.G. Claxton
Mark Alexander	Frank Wrigly
Wilfred May	F.R. McCall

What was happening at home in Canada?

Total war! That's how World War I came to be described by 1916. Not just a struggle between rival armed forces, it was a war between whole populations. Though far from the battlefields, people across Canada—in Antigonish and Trois-Rivières and Kitchener and Portage la Prairie and Kelowna and in all the other towns and cities and on farms—found their daily lives changed. All Canadians were expected to do their part to help the war effort.

   Canadians produced more goods than ever before. The Prairies became the "breadbasket of the Empire" because of the overseas demand for such food supplies as wheat and flour, beef, bacon and butter. The need for minerals, particularly nickel, copper and lead, stimulated mining. From the forests came increased quantities of lumber, wood pulp and newsprint.

Fig. 11 The government issued posters to encourage all Canadians to play a part in the war effort.

Fig. 12 Progress of Canada in wartime

	1913	1919	PER CENT INCREASE
Field crops			
Total area ....acres	35 375 430	53 049 640	49.96
Total value	$552 771 500	$1 452 437 500	162.75
Fisheries	$ 33 389 464	$ 58 000 000	73.70
Forest products			
Lumber, lath, shingles, pulpwood	$ 77 887 730	$ 131 668 122	69.04
Livestock ....Number	15 098 986	21 213 408	40.49
Horses, cattle, sheep and swine	$659 308 222	$1 296 602 000	96.66
Minerals	$145 634 812	$ 173 075 913	18.84
Trade			
Exports	$377 068 355	$1 216 443 806	222.60
Imports	$670 089 066	$ 916 429 335	36.76

From *CANADA: To the Delegates of the Ninth Congress, Chambers of Commerce of the British Empire,* Toronto, Sept. 18-22, 1920.

Fig. 13 Production of war supplies

YEAR	VALUE OF CANADIAN MUNITIONS
1914	$ 28 164
1915	$ 57 213 688
1916	$296 505 257
1917	$388 213 553
1918	$260 711 751

The rise in manufacturing was most spectacular and the main reason was the munitions industry—the manufacture of guns, shells and other explosives. At the beginning of the war, Canada had no such industry. However, a variety of companies obtained the necessary equipment, changed over their factories, trained workers and received rich contracts from the government. By 1917, according to some estimates, one of every three or four shells fired by armies of the British Empire was made in Canada. Canada, and in particular Ontario and Quebec, had one of the world's leading war industries.

The economy was good. Unemployment had almost disappeared. Businesses were raking in profits. Farmers were enjoying "bumper" crops. Prices were rising along with people's incomes.

Yet the war overseas was never far from people's minds. Too many awoke each morning wondering about loved ones they had not seen for months, even years. Letters to and from the front lines travelled slowly, but telegrams travelled quickly from the government's Casualty Branch. It had the grim job of notifying relatives of people wounded, killed or missing in action.

GETTING THE FACTS

22. Find three facts that support the following statement: "World War I was a major cause of the growth of Canada's economy from 1914 to 1918."

USING YOUR KNOWLEDGE

23. Statistics show how the war increased Canadian production of

food and other goods. Examine the statistics in Figure 12 and Figure 13 closely. Suggest at least three changes that occurred in Canada due to the increased production.

24. Hypothesize: During the war the Canadian economy boomed largely because of the great demand for food and war products. What problems do you think could arise when the war ended? Explain why you think each problem would occur.

How did government become so involved in the lives of Canadians?

Voluntary efforts were important, and individuals and private organizations kept on donating their time and materials—from food to new socks. However as the war dragged on, the Canadian government wanted to monitor (supervise) the country's contribution to the war effort more closely. The War Measures Act, as we have seen, gave the government unusual powers over the lives of Canadians—and it was only the first step.

A big government worry was shortages. A variety of boards were set up to encourage Canadians to conserve. They did not go so far as to establish rationing (to limit what consumers could buy). They did, however, make rules limiting the amount producers could sell and setting prices. Companies selling coal, gas and wood were required to report their business dealings to the government. The same was true of food dealers and restaurants, for which limits were set on the amounts of meat and sugar that could be used.

The general approach to controls in Canada during World War I has been described as follows:

> . . . most food control effort took the form of persuasion towards voluntary restraint from waste and encouragement of change in eating habits. Films condemning waste or emphasizing the merits [benefits] of nourishing but little-used products were shown in theatres and churches. Each province had a 'Keep a Hog' campaign and a 'Soldiers of the Soil' movement, which enrolled boys for farm labour. Slogans such as 'Eat fish as a patriotic duty' or 'Eat fish and reduce the cost of living' were broadcast across the country. . . .

Paying for the war effort was another main concern of Canadians. The familiar methods of raising money—donations, taxes on imports, the borrowing of money from bankers in London and New York—eventually fell short. By 1917, the government was tapping the savings of Canadians by selling them bonds, called Victory Bonds. These bonds were similar to the modern Canada Savings

Fig. 14 How would buying Victory Bonds help keep all Canadians busy?

From *Canada, 1896-1921: A Nation Transformed* by R.C. Brown and R. Cook.

Fig. 15 Scouts encouraging passers-by to support the Victory Loan

Bonds sold by the federal government each year. They were sold to investors who were attracted for two reasons—a desire to help the war effort and a chance to earn interest on the money invested.

It was only a matter of time before the government began to use new methods of raising money for the war effort. Canadians, both wage-earners and employers, were profiting from the war. The government, therefore, decided it was only fair to introduce new forms of taxes. The result was taxes on business profits—and income tax. Begun as "temporary" kinds of taxation, these have become a well-known fact of life in Canada.

THINKING IT THROUGH

25. a) List at least three ways in which government became involved in the lives of Canadians during the war.

b) Which of the government actions you listed in (a) continued on after the war? Which were ended?

c) Do you think that in times of crisis government should take more control of the lives of Canadians? Be sure to explain your viewpoint.

How did Canadian women contribute to the war effort?

The following recollection suggests the attitude of Canadian women toward their part in World War I:

> I wanted to help do my share, and I joined the Red Cross and helped roll bandages and knit socks. My first ones were big enough to fit an elephant, and after that, I became very proficient—*so* proficient that I knit a pair of socks a day without any trouble. We rolled bandages, and we distributed wool for knitting, and we would go and deliver it to older people that could do it. There were a thousand-and-one things. . . .
>
> You see, *everybody* felt they [sic] had to do something. You just couldn't sit there. . . .
>
> The women involved in the Red Cross were mostly wives and mothers of the soldiers, I would say. There were all different classes. . . .

From *The Great War and Canadian Society: An Oral History* edited by Daphne Read.

As men went overseas by the tens of thousands, Canadian women took on many new roles besides their traditional ones. Some women went overseas as nurses or VADs (members of the Voluntary Aid Detachment of the Red Cross). The majority, however, remained in Canada. In the early part of the war, volunteering brought women out of the home and into Canada's public life. The Red Cross, Women's Institute, Patriotic Associations and other organizations showed spirit and a sense of duty. A notable example was the Canadian Patriotic Fund. Headquarters in Ottawa directed the work of volunteer committees across Canada. The fund provided up to $50 a month to soldiers' families. The services of volunteers ranged from family counselling to helping families deal with a government that was growing more complex.

Women were also instrumental in the recruitment leagues, formed to seek out men who had not joined the armed forces. One tactic was to present men in civilian clothes with white feathers—a mark of cowardice. Another was to hold public meetings at which women speakers urged other women to have nothing to do with slackers.

Women also went to work for pay. They harvested grain, drove trucks, ran businesses and worked in factories. By war's end more than 30 000 women had worked in munitions factories and thousands more worked in jobs not held before by women.

The demands of war brought new roles for women—and new attitudes too. In the minds and on the lips of growing numbers of women were the questions: Why should we be limited to housekeeping

Fig. 16 How does this poster portray the role of women in the war?

Fig. 17 Women did much of the work previously done by men who had gone to war.

and raising children? Why can't we participate more fully in the life of our nation?

The suffragette movement was soon to meet with success. People like Nellie McClung, first in Manitoba and later in Alberta, Emily Murphy in Alberta and Mrs. W.F. Hatheway in the Maritimes had been campaigning before the war for female suffrage; that is, the right for women to vote. Manitoba, in 1916, became the first province in which women won female suffrage. Saskatchewan and Alberta were next and other provinces followed suit. In 1917, the Canadian government gave the vote to all women who were either serving in or related to someone in the armed forces. Finally, in 1918 all women obtained the right to vote in federal elections.

GETTING THE FACTS

26. Reread the quotation at the beginning of this section. According to the woman quoted, what was the attitude of Canadian women about their role in World War I?

27. List at least three ways Canadian women contributed to the war effort.

USING YOUR KNOWLEDGE

28. a) What does the term "non-traditional role" mean? Why did women take on many non-traditional roles during the war?

b) Do you think women's new roles because of the war would affect their attitudes and roles *after* the war? For example, do you think women would want to keep any new attitudes and jobs they had during the war or would they want to return to the way things were before the war? Explain your answer.

29. a) When did women across Canada win the right to vote in federal elections?

b) Why do you think the government gave the vote only to those women who were serving in or related to someone in the armed forces in 1917?

THE INVESTIGATIVE REPORTER

30. Nellie McClung and Emily Murphy achieved much for women. Consult your library for reference to these women and then write one-page biographies of their lives.

How did the war divide Canadians?

Many people across Canada entered the war with patriotic enthusiasm. They were willing to postpone normal living and make sacrifices in order to defeat the enemies of the British Empire and France. The future, not only of these "mother countries," but of freedom and a decent way of living, seemed threatened.

However, unity among Canadians began to crack. The war did not end, as expected, in three or four months. It dragged on for many months, then years.

Criticism of the government was rising. There were accusations of shady deals and fat profits by companies getting contracts to make munitions. A particular target was Sam Hughes, the Minister of Militia. He was believed to be handing get-rich-quick deals to friends. In 1916 he was forced to resign.

Yet the most pressing problem facing the government was manpower for the armed forces. As the losses of people wounded and killed on the battlefields continued, the demand for more soldiers rose sharply. By the end of 1916, there were not enough volunteers to meet the demand.

Two years before, passing a law requiring people of a certain age to enlist had been unthinkable to Canadians. Now, however, such a conscription law was gaining support, at least among many English Canadians whose attachment to Britain was strong. Other

Fig. 18 Sometimes men who did not volunteer for the army were considered cowards. Some received white feathers, symbols of cowardice, in the mail.

Fig. 19 Recruiting for the army in Toronto, 1916. What might the man in the car be saying?

Fig. 20 A recruitment poster aimed at French Canadians

Fig. 21 An anti-conscription rally in Quebec

groups did not share this feeling. French Canadians, for example, felt differently. They had been cut off from France for 150 years. They had no feelings of attachment to Britain. Forceful leaders like Henri Bourassa were questioning Canadian involvement in a far away war.

French Canadians had many reasons for thinking their contribution to the war effort was not appreciated. As early as 1913, Ontario had outlawed French as a language for teaching pupils in the province's primary schools. Manitoba, in 1916, took a similar action. French Canadians who enlisted were scattered among English-speaking units. Few French Canadians were appointed as officers.

Canadians were divided. French Canadians who criticized their country's part in the war could ask: Why fight for a future in which they had little control? English Canadians accused them of failing to fulfill their duty—even of being disloyal to their country.

In February, 1917, the House of Commons decided to stop meeting so that Prime Minister Robert Borden could attend the Imperial War Conference in London, England. There he was pressured to agree to conscription. It was the only way, he was told, to replace the heavy losses suffered by Canadian troops.

Back in Canada in May, Borden found increased support for conscription. He invited Sir Wilfrid Laurier and the Liberals to join a coalition government, as a step to introducing conscription. Laurier refused to agree unless Canadian voters were given the chance to give their views. Borden would not go along with this.

Instead, Borden's government moved swiftly in the summer of 1917. With the Military Services Act, it introduced conscription. Passed by Parliament in August, it split the Liberal party. Many of its English-speaking members voted with the Conservatives.

The Conservative government followed on August 31 with the Military Voters Act. This gave the vote to all men and women serving in the armed forces and took it away from groups opposed to the war. The next step was the Wartime Elections Act. Women related to servicemen overseas now had the right to vote. The Conservatives appeared to be the party determined to win the war.

Sir Wilfrid Laurier was faced with a terrible dilemma. If he agreed to conscription, he would lose his French-Canadian supporters. If he did not, English-speaking Liberals were likely to join the Conservatives. He decided that opposing Borden was the lesser of two evils.

The result of the December, 1917 election was a foregone conclusion. English-speaking Liberals joined the Conservatives in a Union government. The election slogan was "Win the War." The Union party won 153 seats compared to 82 for the Laurier Liberals.

Conscription was promptly put into effect. Close to 100 000

Fig. 22 Arrangements were made for all serving Canadians to vote in the 1917 election, although so many were out of the country. Votes were brought from army camps in the United States, and shipped back from Europe. Even those on ships crossing the Atlantic registered their votes.

men were called up, but anti-conscription meetings and riots erupted in Quebec. To the surprise of the government, western Canadians were also angry. Farm workers, convinced they were needed for the war effort at home, were known to shoot off a toe to avoid the draft.

Was conscription worth the price of a divided nation? The split between French and English Canadians lasted for many years. Furthermore, western Canadians felt their wishes had been ignored by those in the East, particularly in Ontario. Ironically, the war ended before most of the soldiers that had been conscripted went overseas.

GETTING THE FACTS

28. a) Which Canadians tended to be in favour of conscription? What were their reasons?

b) Which Canadians tended to be against conscription? List their reasons.

29. List all the steps that Borden and the Canadian government took in order to deal with the conscription issue. Start your list with February, 1917 and end with the December, 1917 election.

THINKING IT THROUGH

30. The conscription issue was a problem for the leaders of both the Conservative and Liberal parties. Laurier in particular was faced with a terrible dilemma.
a) What was Laurier's dilemma?
b) Which solution did he finally choose?
c) If you were in Laurier's position would you have made the same decision or chosen a different solution? Explain.

31. Debate the following question: "Was conscription worth the price of a divided nation?" Before beginning your discussion, review the arguments for and against conscription. In your discussion be sure to support your opinion with facts.

Propaganda—Necessary in wartime?

If you were involved in running a country that was taking part in a war, what would you do to ensure that people in the country would support the war effort? This was a problem facing Britain, Germany, Canada and the other countries involved in World War I. One major solution used by all countries was propaganda. Propaganda is a system of spreading ideas to convince people to support a particular viewpoint or way of thinking. In World War I, newspapers, radio broadcasts and posters were important media used to encourage people to support the war effort and to keep up morale. For example, newspapers reporting on battles would use statistics released by the government; these statistics were often changed by government officials to keep the public's spirit up. For instance, a newspaper in London reported that in one particular German raid on London, 107 German planes were shot down. The real figure was 41.

Posters were another form of propaganda widely used by all countries. They were designed to do a number of things, from creating a fear of the enemy, to persuading men to enlist. All posters used for the purpose of spreading propaganda shared certain characteristics. In general they were designed
—to have mass appeal;
—to attract the eye at a distance;
—to catch the attention of even the casual spectator;
—to inspire a sense of righteousness in the viewer.

Examine the posters in this chapter and answer the following questions:
1. For what audience were they made?
2. What feelings are they supposed to arouse in the viewer?
3. Which of the characteristics listed above do the posters display?
4. Do they succeed as a piece of propaganda?

The Halifax explosion

With its seaboard location and deep, natural harbour, Halifax was an important naval base during World War I. In Bedford Basin, at the upper end of the harbour, convoys assembled for the dangerous trip across the North Atlantic carrying troops and supplies. At 8:45, on December 6, 1917, the French munitions ship, the *Mont Blanc*, was on its way to Bedford Basin. Chugging through the Narrows, it collided with the *Imo*, a steamer heading out to sea with supplies for Belgium. The *Mont Blanc* caught fire. Unable to sink the ship, the crew abandoned it and made for the Dartmouth shore. Tragically, there was no way to warn others that the *Mont Blanc* was a floating bomb—crammed with highly inflammable and explosive materials.

At 9:05, the *Mont Blanc* exploded with such force that the northern part of the city was flattened and the air was filled with flying glass and debris. Windows were broken in Truro and the sound reached Sydney and Charlottetown. The *Mont Blanc* had disintegrated into fragments of hot metal. A column of smoke, fire and steel bits rose to a height of three kilometres, then rained down on the harbour and parts of the city with the force of gunfire. The explosion unleashed a tidal wave that demolished ships, docks and buildings.

Though the physical damage was incredible, the human suffering was beyond measure. Estimates of the number killed varied from 2000 to 3000. Thousands more were injured. Local hospitals were overflowing, so trains took the less seriously hurt for treatment in towns up to 100 kilometres away.

The recovery of Halifax from the disaster is a story of patience, strenuous effort and courage. Work parties were organized almost immediately. A citizens' committee, including members of the Halifax and Nova Scotia governments, the police and the army, was set up to coordinate the relief effort. Doctors and the other medical people worked tirelessly through the day and night. Supplies arrived from all over Nova Scotia, and, in the days ahead, from as far away as Manitoba and Massachusetts. When people were thanked for their contributions, the familiar answer was, "What else could we have done?"

Fig. 23 Peace celebrations in Winnipeg

Conclusion

More than four years passed between the start and the end of World War I. After the many victories of the Allied nations in 1918, an armistice (cease-fire) took effect on November 11, 1918. It was "the eleventh hour of the eleventh day of the eleventh month." Fighting continued in Russia, where the revolution of 1917 overthrew the government of Czar Nicholas II and led to a civil war. The signing of the Treaty of Versailles in June, 1919, however, meant that World War I was officially over.

Of the more than 600 000 Canadians who served in the war, one in ten did not return home. Besides the loss of life, Canada faced enormous financial costs. The country had gone deeply into debt to fight the war, and would spend even more money to return its people to a peacetime existence.

Canadians were determined that their sacrifices during the war would lead to more control of their own affairs. As Canadians, rather than as members of the British Empire, they wished to decide their country's role in war and peace. Consequently, the Canadian prime minister, Sir Robert Borden, insisted on Canada's right to take part in the peace settlement. Then Canada signed the resulting Treaty of Versailles as one of the countries which had helped defeat Germany and its allies. When the League of Nations, a world-wide organization for keeping world peace, was formed, Canada joined as a member in its own right, rather than as part of the British Empire.

On the eve of the 1920s, Canada was a contradiction. To the rest of the world, the message was: We have a new feeling of pride in being Canadian because of our accomplishments over the past five years. Canadians themselves, however, were seriously divided. Neither French Canadians nor English Canadians would soon forget the conscription crisis. The West felt ignored by central Canada. Ethnic minorities, particularly those from countries which had been enemies in the war, were the objects of discrimination. The Winnipeg general strike was a symptom of the deep suspicion between business people and organized labour. In some respects, the 1920s looked like a rough road ahead.

Yet many Canadians were confident about their country's future. They were relieved that the war was over and they looked forward to an era of peace and overall economic growth.

THINKING IT THROUGH

32. Discuss the statement, "If we were alive on November 11, 1918, Remembrance Day would have much more meaning for us."

33. What do you think were the two most important results of the war for the Canadian people? The two main achievements? The two biggest problems? Give reasons and facts to back your statements.

THE INVESTIGATIVE REPORTER

34. Research and write a report on one of the following:
   —The League of Nations: What part did Canada play in it?
   —Daily Life in Canada at the beginning of the 1920s.

4 The two faces of the twenties: Problems and prosperity

Examine these pictures carefully. They represent the ways in which two different artists viewed the twenties.

- Look closely at the first picture and describe the view of life that the artist is presenting.

- Describe the view of life presented in the second picture.

- When you think of the 1920s, which picture comes to your mind? Have the pictures on these pages changed your own idea of the period in any way?

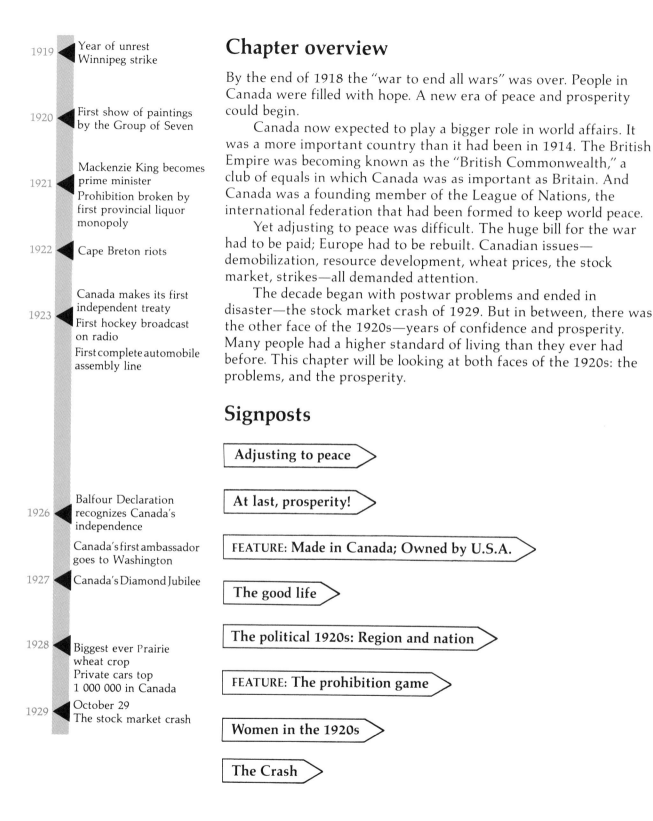

1919	Year of unrest Winnipeg strike
1920	First show of paintings by the Group of Seven
1921	Mackenzie King becomes prime minister Prohibition broken by first provincial liquor monopoly
1922	Cape Breton riots
1923	Canada makes its first independent treaty First hockey broadcast on radio First complete automobile assembly line
1926	Balfour Declaration recognizes Canada's independence Canada's first ambassador goes to Washington
1927	Canada's Diamond Jubilee
1928	Biggest ever Prairie wheat crop Private cars top 1 000 000 in Canada
1929	October 29 The stock market crash

Chapter overview

By the end of 1918 the "war to end all wars" was over. People in Canada were filled with hope. A new era of peace and prosperity could begin.

Canada now expected to play a bigger role in world affairs. It was a more important country than it had been in 1914. The British Empire was becoming known as the "British Commonwealth," a club of equals in which Canada was as important as Britain. And Canada was a founding member of the League of Nations, the international federation that had been formed to keep world peace.

Yet adjusting to peace was difficult. The huge bill for the war had to be paid; Europe had to be rebuilt. Canadian issues—demobilization, resource development, wheat prices, the stock market, strikes—all demanded attention.

The decade began with postwar problems and ended in disaster—the stock market crash of 1929. But in between, there was the other face of the 1920s—years of confidence and prosperity. Many people had a higher standard of living than they ever had before. This chapter will be looking at both faces of the 1920s: the problems, and the prosperity.

Signposts

Adjusting to peace >

At last, prosperity! >

FEATURE: Made in Canada; Owned by U.S.A. >

The good life >

The political 1920s: Region and nation >

FEATURE: The prohibition game >

Women in the 1920s >

The Crash >

Key words

inflation	branch plant
surplus	media
investment	leisure
natural resources	stocks
mass production	credit

Adjusting to peace

In the wake of war Europe remained troubled. Rioting broke out in Berlin, Budapest and Vienna. In giant Russia, the greatest revolution of all was raging on. The leaders of countries that had "won" the war, saw this unrest as a threat to the entire world.

Europe would never be the same again. And when Canada's fighting men came home, they found that their land too had changed in many ways. It had become more urban. For the first time, most of the people in most parts of Canada were living in towns and cities. These towns and cities were dotted with smoke-stacks: the country's war effort had stimulated the growth of industry.

Canada, like Europe, was troubled. Wartime jobs were vanishing. Suddenly there were no more huge government orders for items like guns and boots. Wartime shipping of men and materials had meant soaring revenues for the Atlantic ports; now they were quiet. The only thing that showed no sign of slowing down was inflation. The cost of food and clothing had more than doubled since 1914, and it kept rising.

There had been few changes in society during the war. Now pressure for change was building up. Farmers began to voice their concern over railway freight costs and crop surpluses. Workers were worried that jobs and pay would be cut. Servicemen were furious when they came back from the war to find there was no work for them. During this difficult time, Canadians were discovering that wartime industries had made huge profits. Some sort of conflict was inevitable.

In 1917 Russian workers and soldiers, led by Nikolai Lenin, staged a violent revolution that overthrew the Russian monarchy. They established the first communist state, the Union of Soviet Socialist Republics, or U.S.S.R.

The value of raw materials rose steeply during World War I. As a result, prices increased and more money was needed to buy goods such as wheat, iron, steel and various manufactured goods, including weapons. For each year of the war more money was needed to buy these materials. To do this the government printed more paper currency. Thus, the value of money fell. This process is called inflation.

USING YOUR KNOWLEDGE

1. Suggest an explanation for each of the following points made in the text you have just read:

—After the war, Canada became more urban. Why would this be true?

—There had been few other changes in Canada during the war. Why would this be so?

—Some wartime industries made huge profits. Why would this happen?

2. Choose one hypothesis from question 1. Using books from your school or local library, find facts to support your hypothesis. Write up your findings as a one-page report. If your investigation *disproves* your hypothesis, explain why your first explanation was incorrect. Write a new and accurate explanation.

Winnipeg: Attack

May of 1919 was strike month in Canada. Workers were striking everywhere: 6000 machinists in Toronto, all the builders in Halifax, 4000 from Montreal's big railway-car factory. In Windsor, crowds attacked streetcars when "blacklegs"—workers who take strikers' jobs—replaced striking drivers. In the West, Vancouver's union council voted in favour of a "general strike."

A general strike is a walkout by all workers together, not just a

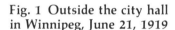

Fig. 1 Outside the city hall in Winnipeg, June 21, 1919

strike by one union. Many Canadians saw such a strike as the only way to get enough pressure for higher wages and better working conditions. To many other Canadians, a general strike sounded like the Russian Revolution.

It was in Winnipeg that the general strike was put to the test. It was a logical place for it to happen. The Manitoba capital was the largest city in the West and had a strong labour movement. Workers were more united in western Canada than they were in the East. In Calgary that spring, separate unions had formed the "One Big Union," or O.B.U., for Westerners only.

On May 1, Winnipeg's machinists went on strike. The issue was "collective bargaining," or the right of a trade association to talk to employers as a group. The machinists wanted the new Metal Trades Council, a member of the O.B.U., accepted as their official voice.

The employers would not agree. They wanted to keep negotiating separately with their own workers. There was deadlock. To increase the pressure, the Trades and Labour Council of Winnipeg voted for a general strike. It was to begin on May 15.

On that day the city firemen stopped working. Postal workers struck, and so did the telephone and telegraph workers. The newspapers were shut down by their printers. There were no streetcars. Bread and milk deliveries were halted.

The list of strikers mounted until some 30 000 people had left their jobs. Most of them were not even in any union. Ex-servicemen were joining in the thousands. Even the police voted to go out on strike, but stayed on duty by permission of the Strike Committee which represented all groups taking part in the action. The Committee also allowed vital food deliveries to start again.

Winnipeg was paralyzed. The anti-strike citizens labelled the strikers as communist revolutionaries. They arranged for "specials"—special citizen constables—to patrol the streets. Winnipeg's mayor appealed to Ottawa for help. The federal government threatened striking employees with loss of jobs and pensions unless they went back to work. Tension grew. The Mounted Police and the army were standing by in case of violence.

On June 21 several strike leaders, who had been arrested a few days earlier, were released. To protest against their arrest a throng of strikers and veterans gathered in the area around the city hall. A streetcar arrived, driven by a "blackleg." The crowd turned on the streetcar, and smashed and burned it. The Mounted Police charged. One striker was shot dead and dozens were injured.

Another man died before the Mounted Police and the army brought about the collapse of the strike on May 26. Seven leaders were jailed for "plotting to overthrow the government," even though the government's own investigation into the cause of the strike put the blame on high prices and low wages.

In 1932 farmers, industrial workers and socialists joined together to form the Co-operative Commonwealth Federation or CCF. This was a political party pledged to establish fair wages, old age security, accident protection and safety standards. (See the chapter on *The Great Depression* for more information.)

The general strike had met with defeat. The O.B.U. would never be an important force again. Yet this did not mean that there had been no changes in Winnipeg and the West. Labour had shown its strength, and its candidates continued to keep winning elections. One strike leader, John Queen, served a long term as mayor of Winnipeg. Another, J.S. Woodsworth, went on to lead the forerunner of the New Democratic party, the C.C.F. or Co-operative Commonwealth Federation. The Winnipeg general strike left its mark on Canadian society.

GETTING THE FACTS

3. In your notebook create a "labour union vocabulary list." Choose six words related to strikes from the account of the Winnipeg strike. Define these words briefly and then write a sentence for each one.

4. What is a general strike? Why did the general strike of 1919 occur in Winnipeg?

USING YOUR KNOWLEDGE

5. "The Winnipeg general strike: Useful labour action or waste of time?" In your notebook divide a page down the middle. In one column give the viewpoint of a Winnipeg machinist on the question above. In the second column give the viewpoint of a company manager.

THINKING IT THROUGH

6. Based on what you know about the Winnipeg strike and about the labour movement in general, which of the viewpoints in question 5 do you most agree with? Give reasons to support your view.

Cape Breton: Defense

By 1920 Canadians were realizing that the economic slump was going to last a while. In some places, like Winnipeg, people fought for better working conditions. In other parts of the country, people had to defend their right to work at all.

On craggy Cape Breton Island, in the East of Canada, the mainstays of the economy were the big steel plant at Sydney and the coal mines of Glace Bay. These belonged to BESCO, the British Empire Steel Corporation. The company was owned and run by investors outside Nova Scotia. There were no other industries, so there were no other jobs. The two communities were dependent on BESCO.

The end of the war in Europe meant that there was less demand for steel. Demand for coal also fell: industries began using oil to power their machines, and the Sydney steel plant was buying less coal for its furnaces.

In 1922, BESCO demanded a 35 percent wage cut. That year the United Mine Workers union was calling strikes all over North America to defend rates of pay. The workers of Cape Breton, who belonged to the international union, vowed that they would fight the wage cuts "to the last ditch."

"Our job is one of the most dangerous in Canada," said one miner citing the death of 153 men in the mines in 1917 and 1918 alone. "For this kind of risk we are asked to take less pay."

The conciliation board supported a pay cut. The workers reacted by rioting and looting in Cape Breton. The machines for pumping water out of the coal mines were sabotaged. When soldiers were sent from Halifax, they were pelted with rocks.

There was a truce for a while, but in June, 1923, 2700 steel-workers walked off the job and 8000 coal miners followed. Again there were riots, and again the army arrived, and arrested the strike leaders.

From *Class Conflict in the Coal Industry of Nova Scotia* by Frank David in *Essays in Canadian Labour History* edited by G.S. Kealey and P. Warrian.

Fig. 2 Lawren Harris painted these miners' houses in Glace Bay in 1925. What does the painting suggest about life on Cape Breton Island?

The Cape Bretoners went back to work a few weeks later. They had gained nothing. They were still at the company's mercy: they had no alternatives. The company itself went out of business two years later. Since there was no local market for what it produced, it depended on outside customers. The Atlantic area got the worst of Canada's bad times, and when the good times did come, they came to the Atlantic last.

GETTING THE FACTS

7. Suggest two reasons why BESCO demanded a 35 percent wage cut.

8. Describe the reaction of the steelworkers and coal miners to the proposed salary cut.

At last, prosperity!

The after-effects of the war were wearing off by 1923. The country repaid loans that had covered the cost of the war. Foreign companies, mainly American, began investing in Canada. Europe recovered, and could buy from Canada again. There was an air of confidence in the land.

The prosperity of the 1920s did not reach everyone in Canada, or even every part of the country. But more Canadians than ever before had a little extra money to put into savings, to spend, or to invest. They could feel part of Canada's growth.

The leading areas in the rapid growth of the mid-1920s were:

—farming
—minerals
—pulp and paper
—manufacturing

The map in Figure 5 shows where in Canada the growth, and the prosperity, were concentrated.

The wheat boom

After the Russian Revolution, western Europe could no longer buy wheat from the Ukraine. It needed to buy more wheat from Canada. Prairie farmers helped by good weather, grew bumper crops. They produced 452 million bushels of wheat in 1923. Because world demand was high, prices were soon three times what they had been after the war. Settlement expanded northward. The Prairie population rose by 20 percent.

Yet farming on the great plains was still a risky business. Crops were attacked by drought, early frost, grasshoppers, and a fungus called stem rust. After harvest, there was the problem of getting the crop to market. The new Panama Canal had made Vancouver a major grain port, but the cost of rail freight over long distances to the port was still high.

To cut their costs western farmers decided to stop using "middlemen"—railway and elevator operators—to transport and store grain. The middlemen were suspected of cheating when they weighed the wheat. Between 1923 and 1925 the farmers set up "wheat pools" in Alberta, Saskatchewan and Manitoba. The wheat pools were cooperatives, owned jointly by the farmers. They took over all the business of storing and shipping.

Fig. 3 The Panama Canal

The cheapest way to transport bulk goods, like grain, is by ship. The Panama Canal cut the length of the sea route to European markets, as the map shows. The alternatives would have been to sail across the Pacific Ocean, or around the tip of South America.

Fig. 4 Wheat elevator, Saskatchewan, 1920. Using books from your library find further information on the wheat pools. What problems were they supposed to solve? How well did they succeed?

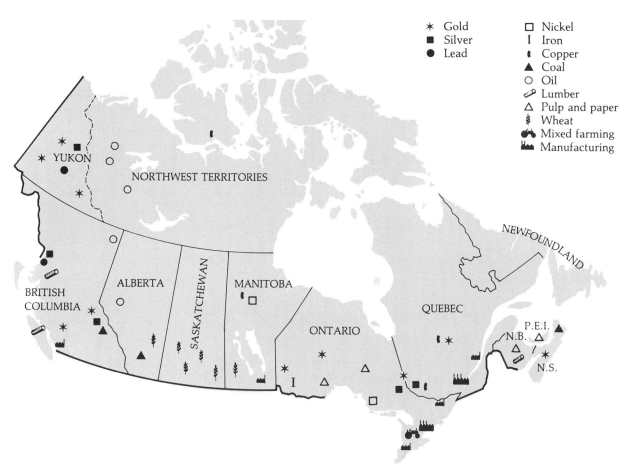

Legend:

- ✳ Gold
- ■ Silver
- ● Lead
- □ Nickel
- I Iron
- ❙ Copper
- ▲ Coal
- ○ Oil
- Lumber
- △ Pulp and paper
- Wheat
- Mixed farming
- Manufacturing

YUKON

NORTHWEST TERRITORIES

BRITISH COLUMBIA

ALBERTA

SASKATCHEWAN

MANITOBA

ONTARIO

QUEBEC

NEWFOUNDLAND

P.E.I.

N.B.

N.S.

Fig. 5 Industry and natural resources in the 1920s

The growth of industry

There was growth in other "primary" industries—industries based on Canada's natural resources. Stock raising, dairying, and lumbering all prospered. There was a mining boom on the Laurentian Shield. Huge copper finds around Rouyn [rOOahn], Quebec and Flin Flon [flan flohn], Manitoba attracted many investors. Such remote areas were now easier to reach, thanks to the new airplanes.

Resource industries developed with the help of Canada's abundant supply of hydroelectric energy—electricity produced by water power. In the 1920s output of hydroelectric power increased 300 percent. Paper mills used this cheap power to meet a soaring world demand. New mills sprang up across the country. Their main customer was the United States, where much of the timber had been used up. Soon Americans were buying more than half their newsprint from Canada. By 1929, Canada was exporting more pulp and paper than all other countries combined.

Cheap energy also stimulated the growth of manufacturing. At that time manufacturing industries differed from primary industries in two important ways. First, primary industries depended on exporting products; manufacturing sold to Canada's own markets. Second, primary industries were owned mainly by Canadians; manufacturing was based on American finance and technology. As U.S. companies moved in to take advantage of cheap power and new markets, Canadians enjoyed such modern wonders as rayon, cellophane, linoleum, radios, vacuum cleaners—and motor cars.

What effect did the new prosperity have on the country? Clearly, regions rich in natural resources profited the most. The historian D.G. Creighton offers one interpretation of the "boom time":

> ... though the economic life of the whole country unquestionably grew richer and more varied, the bounty of the post-war period seemed unequal in its distribution. ... In the pre-war age, wheat had been the one great export staple, ... but now there were half a dozen distinct staple-producing regions, each with its own important export specialty or specialties, ... each with its individual successes and misfortunes. While some provinces ... profited superlatively [soo-PIR-la-tihv-lee] from the new enterprises, others ... benefited only moderately, and still others ... gained little advantage at all. ...

Canada's rich resources could not be developed without vast investment. Since the Canadian investment community was small, American investors were encouraged to buy shares of Canadian companies. As a result, Canadians became more dependent upon foreign money for their prosperity.

From *Canadian Annual Review* 1924-1925.

Fig. 6 By 1925 nearly every Canadian home had a gramophone.

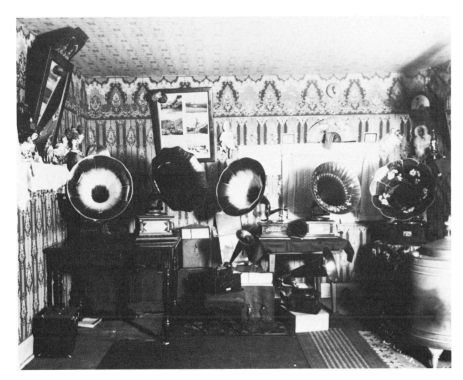

9. List four major areas of growth in the mid-twenties.

10. Why was farming on the Prairies risky, in spite of the boom?

USING YOUR KNOWLEDGE

11. Identify one cause for each of the following events of the mid-twenties: high demand for wheat; boom in primary industries; great pulp and paper exports; increase in manufacturing.

12. Explain how the Panama Canal would benefit Vancouver.

13. Reread the quotation from D.G. Creighton.

a) In your own words summarize what he says about the mid-twenties boom in Canada.

b) Examine the map in Figure 5. Identify six regions that were enjoying economic growth. For each region, state the reasons for the growth. Were many of the key resources exported?

c) Based on your analysis of the map, do you agree or disagree with Creighton? Give reasons to support your viewpoint.

Case study in manufacturing: Automobiles

The mass-produced automobile revolutionized the lives of Canadians in the twenties. Cars were now relatively cheap, and by 1929 one in three Canadian families owned one.

Canadian cars, and the assembly lines on which they were made, were designed in the United States. Gradually the Canadian motor industry was taken over by what became the American "Big Three": General Motors, Chrysler and Ford. These large companies could be more efficient than small ones. American Ford perfected mass-production, and the new cars rolled off assembly lines.

Canadians, like Americans, began their love affair with the automobile in the 1920s when machinists, inventors and investors combined to construct a bewildering number of new cars. The chart on the following page shows just a few of the makes. Canadian-made cars were built in cities across Canada. Few survived very long as the big American car makers steadily took over the Canadian market in the 1920s.

Americans gained control of the gasoline business as well. At first, motorists bought gas by the bucketful from the corner store. By the end of the 1920s there was a country-wide network of service stations, supplied by 25 modern oil refineries. These were run by huge U.S. companies like Imperial Oil.

Fig. 7 A driver for Imperial Oil waits outside a filling station in Moosejaw, c. 1921.

MAKE	YEARS	LOCATION
McLaughlin	1908-22	Oshawa, Ontario
Galt	1914-27	Galt, Ontario
Gray-Dort	1915-25	Chatham, Ontario
Forster	1920	Montreal, Quebec
Winnipeg	1921-23	Winnipeg, Manitoba
Brooks	1924-29	Stratford, Ontario
Derby	1924-27	Saskatoon, Saskatchewan
Frontenac	1931-33	Toronto, Ontario

From *Cars in Canada* by Hugh Durnford and Glenn Baechler.

Fig. 8 Cars of the 1920s

The boom in the car industry created many jobs for Canadians. There was work assembling cars, or making parts and trimmings. There were new jobs in roadside cafés and at gas pumps. Then there was work building better roads for motorists. In 1918 only one kilometre in five of Canadian roads was surfaced. In the 1920s 17 000 km of road were paved, and gravel was laid on 108 333 km. This produced another boom: the improved roads helped attract 4 000 000 American tourists a year.

Within a decade the automobile industry had become a kingpin of Canada's economy.

Fig. 9 Shops like this were becoming commonplace by the early 1920s.

14. Why did the automobile industry in Canada come under U.S. control?

15. List at least four kinds of jobs that the automobile industry created.

16. a) What kind of freedom would a car give someone in the 1920s that could not be matched by a horse or bicycle?

 b) Think of one invention that could revolutionize your own life today as much as the car changed life in the twenties.

Made in Canada; Owned by U.S.A.

It's better because it's Canadian. It uses lumber from Canadian forests and steel made in Canadian mills from Canadian ore, smelted by Canadian foundrymen. It purchases from Canadian sources vast quantities of brass and copper, of wire and glass, of nickel and fabrics, oils, paints and finishes—and all that mass of materials which enter into the making of a modern automobile.

The advertiser was General Motors of Canada. Its president was Sam McLaughlin. His family had begun building cars in Oshawa, Ontario in 1907, under licence from U.S. General Motors. This meant the McLaughlins paid the American company for the right to use their designs and manufacturing methods. U.S. companies often sold rights like these to Canadians. The lack of a strong Canadian patent law—that is, a law to prevent new inventions being copied—made it hard for them to refuse. However, General Motors of Canada belonged to the McLaughlin family. They managed it, and the profits were theirs.

In 1918 General Motors bought the McLaughlin's business. The family knew if they refused to sell, General Motors could take away their licence. Also, the American company would probably build a factory in Canada anyway, which would drive the McLaughlins out of business.

Sam McLaughlin still ran the factory, but he was now an employee. The Canadian-built models still had maple leaves on their hubcaps, but all the profit from sales belonged to General Motors in Detroit. All important decisions had to be approved in Detroit. Oshawa was a "branch plant."

The story of General Motors was typical of the way investment in Canada worked in the 1920s.

In the past, nearly all of the money needed to build Canada's railways and factories had come from Britain. Usually British investment took the form of a debt, like a loan from a bank. When Canadians repaid the debt, with interest, they owned the railways or factories.

By 1925 over half the outside investment in Canada came from the United States. Most of the investors were large manufacturing companies setting up branch plants. They owned the new factories completely and permanently.

Canadian industry suffered in several ways. First, the smaller businesses found it hard to compete with huge American companies. Second, because branch plants were financed from the United States, Canadians did not have much opportunity to invest their money in new industries. Third, branch plants used the designs and technology of the American companies: there was little encouragement for Canadian inventions.

When the 1920s ended, U.S. companies controlled almost all of Canada's car industry and a high proportion of its oil business. Nearly half of the machinery and chemical industries, and over half of the rubber and electrical industries, were American-owned.

USING YOUR KNOWLEDGE

17. Explain how U.S. investment in Canada was different from British investment.

18. a) Suggest two ways in which Canada benefited from U.S. investment in the twenties. Suggest two disadvantages.

   b) Why do you think U.S. investment was generally welcomed at that time?

The good life

In the mornin', in the evenin',
Ain't we got fun!
Not much money, Oh but honey,
Ain't we got fun!

This popular song captures the mood of the "roaring twenties." With better working hours and good wages, more Canadians than ever before had leisure time and money to spend. They used it to have "fun." There were carnivals and crazy stunts and big sports events of all kinds. There was jazz and freedom and a feeling that anyone could strike it rich.

People in the 1920s did other things besides having fun. Religion was as basic in Canadian life as it always had been. One of the most important events of the decade was the formation of the United Church in 1925. But when it came to leisure time in the towns and cities, there was a wealth of new entertainment.

The movies and radio were the wonderful new media. The movies brought the glamour of Hollywood to the main street of town. The crackling radio receivers brought the great entertainers of the world right into Canadian homes.

In the arts, the Group of Seven became Canada's first original school of painters. There were also new writers. One of the most popular was Mazo de la Roche, who published the first volume of her *Jalna* series, on the story of a Canadian family, in 1927.

Examine the pictures in this section. They will give you some idea of Canada's good life in the twenties.

The United Church of Canada was formed by the union of three Protestant churches: Methodist, Congregationalist and a large group of Presbyterians. These churches aimed to demonstrate Christian unity, and hoped that other Christian groups would join them.

Fig. 10 Crazy stunts provided popular entertainment.

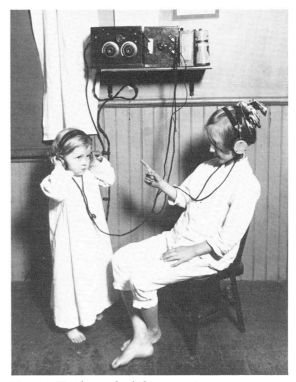

Fig. 12 By the end of the twenties, one Canadian family in five owned a radio.

Fig. 11 Movies and their stars were often from the U.S. Their popularity symbolized the growth of American influence over Canadian culture.

Fig. 13 Lunch counter and newsstand, C.P.R. station

19. In your own words, define "leisure." Why was more leisure time available to many Canadians during the twenties?

20. In this section you looked at some of the things that were "fun" and "popular" in the twenties. Choose three of these amusements; would they be popular today? Explain your answer.

21. Research and write a one-page biography on one of the following: one member in the Group of Seven; Emily Carr; Mazo de la Roche; L.M. Montgomery.

The political 1920s: Region and nation

The map in Figure 5 shows that most of the economic growth was taking place in British Columbia, Ontario and Quebec. The gap between rich and poor provinces was widening.

The poorer regions produced protest movements. In the West, the Progressive party stood for cheaper tariffs and freight costs. The party had sweeping success in the Prairies in the elections of 1921.

On the Atlantic coast the Maritime Rights Movement was formed to protest that eastern provinces did not have enough money to provide modern services. For example, they couldn't afford the kinds of schools and roads people had in British Columbia. As a result the federal government doubled its grants to the region.

The elections of 1921 were won by the Liberals. The new prime

Fig. 14 William Lyon Mackenzie King

Fig. 15 Arthur Meighen

Fig. 16 Thomas Alexander Crerar

The prohibition game

For many years, groups in Canada had been campaigning for "temperance"—abstaining from alcohol. Churches, women's organizations, labour unions, all had supported the idea.

These groups had some good arguments. Public drunkenness was a familiar sight in Canada. It was obvious that alcohol ruined the lives of many individuals and families. Drinking prevented people from doing their jobs properly.

Eventually the campaign succeeded. It succeeded partly as a result of World War I. As a gesture of respect for men in the trenches who were making many sacrifices, King George V gave up drinking. Canadians followed his example. In 1918 the Ottawa government started "prohibition" [pro-ih-BIH-shihn]. It was prohibited—against the law—for anyone to make, transport, or sell alcohol anywhere in Canada.

However, there were also arguments against prohibition. There was the argument of public feeling: many Canadians were not against alcohol, but the abuse—bad use—of it. There was the argument of effectiveness: the law could not be enforced. It was too easy to make "booze," and too many Canadians were willing to buy it.

Gradually, prohibition was given up. Provincial governments could see that prohibition was almost impossible to enforce due to its unpopularity. They also realized that liquor could be a great source of tax revenue. Many groups believed that controlling the liquor traffic was more desirable than prohibiting it, hence the development of government liquor stores and 'control' boards. In 1921, Quebec became the first province to set up a liquor control board. It soon showed a profit of $5 000 000 a year. By the end of the 1920s, most provinces in Canada were selling alcohol through government monopolies.

In fact, prohibition did cut Canada's alcohol consumption by about half. In the United States, the prohibition lasted much longer, and contributed to the growth of organized crime. Organized crime increased in both the United States and Canada: a lot of the illegal liquor drunk in America came from north of the border.

The Canadian government had no objection if distilleries made alcohol for export. In the dead of night, fast cars ferried whisky across the New Brunswick-Maine border. Ships left Halifax loaded with rye for Peru and appeared to make the round trip in two days. Others, it seemed, went to the Bahamas six times a month. What they were really doing was meeting their American customers in offshore waters, and then returning at full speed for more cargo. It was big business, and it happened at every border point in Canada. In Windsor alone, 90 docks were in use for shipping liquor to America.

USING YOUR KNOWLEDGE

22. a) What arguments were given in support of prohibition in the 1920s? Against prohibition?

b) Which arguments would apply today? Give reasons for your answer.

minister was William Lyon Mackenzie King. He was to become a major figure in Canadian politics. When he retired in 1948 he had held office longer than any other prime minister in the Commonwealth.

In the 1920s King was determined to make Canada more independent. He wanted Canada to have the right not to be drawn into the quarrels of other nations. In 1922 King refused to support Britain in a plan to invade Turkey. In 1923 he insisted that Canada alone—without Britain—could sign a west coast halibut fishing treaty with the United States.

In 1926 the British government passed the Balfour Declaration. King had worked for such a declaration. It stated that dominions like Canada had the right to decide their own foreign policy. Canada sent its first ambassador to Washington in 1927.

As a member of the League of Nations, Canada again avoided entanglements. In 1924, the League debated the Locarno Treaty that promised aid to members who were attacked. The Canadian delegate told the League assembly: "We live in a fireproof house, far from inflammable materials." North America, separated by two oceans from the political difficulties of Europe and Asia, was in no danger. Why should Canadians become involved?

Fig. 17 Election results in the 1920s

1921 Election	1925 Election	1926 Election
Liberals 117 (King)	Conservatives 116 (Meighen)	Liberals 116 (King)
Progressives 64 (Crerar)	Liberals 101 (King)	Conservatives 91 (Meighen)
Conservatives 50 (Meighen)	Progressives 24 (Crerar)	Progressives 13 (Crerar)

From *Historical statistics of Canada* by M.C. Urquhart and K.A.H. Buckley.

THE INVESTIGATIVE REPORTER

23. Examine the election results in Figure 17. During the twenties, Canadians turned away from the Liberals briefly and elected a Conservative government. Using references in your school or local library, find out:

    a) Why the Liberals fell out of power
    b) Why the Conservatives held power for only one year
    c) How successful the Progressive party was during the twenties.

24. Using books from your school or local library, find information on the Maritime Rights Movement. Report your findings in one of the following ways: a one-page report; a fictional story based on the facts; a short "picture journal" in which you present important information in a series of drawings.

Women in the twenties

In the 1920s the ordinary women of Canada improved their position in some important ways. In the home they were finding freedom from drudgery. There was a great increase in conveniences like hot and cold running water, flush toilets, telephones, canned foods, electricity, and labour-saving appliances. Orders could be placed by phone. Vacuum cleaners saved time. Refrigerators cut down the need for daily shopping.

Women could go out more freely on their own. Their women's service organizations took them into community work. They were also more liberated in political terms.

One way of checking on women's status—their position in society—is to look at their role in the labour market. By the end of the 1920s, one Canadian woman in five was working outside the home. This was an increase of 50 percent over the figure for 1900. The increase is partly explained by the rapid growth of Canada's cities, where most of the paid jobs for women were found. It is also explained by the greater numbers of independent, "career" women.

Yet there were still very few women in professions such as medicine. Most worked in low-paid jobs with no real chance of promotion—as secretaries, switchboard operators or seamstresses. When they did compete with men they were paid as much as 50 per-

In 1918 women secured the right to vote in federal elections. The right had been won earlier, in 1916, in Manitoba provincial elections. By 1922, they could vote in every province except Quebec where they were denied the vote until 1940.

Fig. 18 Until the twenties it would have been unusual to see women travelling, as they are here, unaccompanied by men. Why?

Fig. 19 Students, University of Toronto, 1928. Do you think many women attended university before this date? Give reasons for your view.

In 1925 the first woman M.P., Agnes Macphail, told the House of Commons: "If the preservation of home means the enslavement of women, economically or morally, then we had better break it. . . . So, when we have a single standard for men and women . . . we shall have a home that is well worth preserving."

cent less, for doing the same job. A man was supposed to be the sole support of a family; women were supposed to be waiting to get married. When they did marry they often lost their jobs. It was accepted that a wife's place was in the home.

Women had made progress, but Canadian society was still run by men. This became clear in the "Persons Case."

In 1916 in Alberta, Emily Murphy became the first woman magistrate in the British Empire. Her appointment was challenged. The grounds for the challenge were that only persons could be judges, and the laws specifically defined persons as men. The challenge was dismissed by the Alberta high court.

Emily Murphy turned out to be an excellent judge. She was much admired for her work with cases involving women and poor people. In 1921 the Montreal Women's Club asked Prime Minister Arthur Meighen to appoint Emily Murphy to the Senate. The old problem came up again. Meighen refused because the British North

America Act, Canada's constitution, stipulated that senators had to be persons.

In 1927 Murphy decided to take her case to the courts for a ruling. The Supreme Court of Canada ruled that, at the time the British North America Act was drawn up, women were not considered persons. In those days women were not expected to run for public office.

Emily Murphy took the case to the British Privy Council. This was a court higher than the Supreme Court of Canada. In 1929 the British Privy Council ruled that women *were* persons. It described the exclusion of women from public office as "barbarous."

By the time the decision was made, Arthur Meighen's government was no longer in power. Emily Murphy, a Conservative, was not called to the Senate. Prime Minister King appointed a woman Liberal instead. Cairine Wilson became Canada's first woman senator in 1930.

Fig. 20 Emily Murphy

GETTING THE FACTS

25. What new inventions supposedly gave women more freedom?

26. In your own words, summarize the "Persons Case."

27. Debate the statement: "The 'Persons Case' was an important step in changing Canadians' attitude about women's place in society."

The Crash

The "good life" in Canada came to an abrupt end in the late twenties. This happened for many complex reasons, some of which were to do with countries outside of Canada. For example:

- U.S. companies realized that they had produced too many goods, so they slowed down production. The U.S. raised its tariffs on imported goods to the highest levels ever. This was done to encourage Americans to buy up their own surplus goods rather than foreign ones. Thus Canada's sales to the U.S. sagged.
- Britain and other European countries also increased tariffs on foreign goods to protect their own products.
- By 1929 competition from Argentina, Australia, and the U.S.S.R. glutted the world wheat market. Canada could no longer sell its wheat in huge quantities.

Fig. 21 One cartoonist's view of the dangers of investing on the stock market.

A Dangerous Animal to Play With

In Canada, the declining price of wheat lowered farmers' incomes dramatically. The farmers' problems caused a chain reaction throughout Canada. Railways, flour mills, farm equipment manufacturers, and many other related industries immediately experienced sales slumps. These industries were forced to slow down production and lay off workers. Unemployment grew rapidly as other export products also suffered slower sales in world markets.

Through the decade consumers had been encouraged to "buy now, pay later" through credit buying campaigns. Many Canadians had gone into debt in order to pay for the goods they purchased. Farmers had borrowed money to buy new equipment. Companies

had taken loans to expand their plants and produce more goods. As companies' stock values continued to rise on the various stock exchanges, more and more people invested in the stock market. They believed share values would always rise. Most investors also bought stocks on credit or "on margin," and gambled they would be able to pay their debts by selling the stocks at a profit. By 1929 credit buying was an accepted practice for many Canadians.

As unemployment began to rise people found they could not pay for goods they had bought on credit during the boom. Companies' inventories—that is, their stores of goods—continued to grow, but sales continued to fall. Because of heavy debt incurred for expansion in earlier years, many companies lost profits. Many others went bankrupt—that is, they were unable to pay their debts and had to go out of business.

A 'stock market' is a place where shares (stocks) in companies are bought and sold. The value of these stocks is determined by several factors. Is the company profitable? Is it likely to be profitable in the future? Are the shares in high demand?

Stock	Value of Stocks		
	1929 High	1932 Low	Percentage Decline
Abitibi Pulp and Paper	$57.75	$1.00	98.3%
Bell Telephone	183.00	78.00	57.3%
Canada Cement	36.00	2.25	93.8%
CPR	67.50	8.50	87.4%
Consolidated Bakeries	43.00	4.00	90.7%
Dominion Textile	118.00	39.00	66.9%
Ford of Canada	70.00	5.75	91.4%
Imperial Oil	41.25	7.40	82.5%
Massey-Harris Farm Implements	99.50	2.50	97.4%
Hollinger Gold Mines	9.55	4.31	54.8%
Steel Company of Canada	69.25	11.00	84.1%
Winnipeg Electric	109.50	2.00	98.1%

Fig. 22 Stock Market Collapse

Stock values plunged. Throughout North America people lost confidence in growth and prosperity. Big and small investors alike sold everything in hope of getting out of the market before they were ruined. The panic peaked on "Black Tuesday"—the stock market crash of October 29, 1929. Because there were many sellers and few buyers, stock prices fell lower and lower. The stock exchange was flooded with sell-orders for stocks that had become worthless, as there were soon no buyers at all.

At the exchanges, traders panicked, wept, fainted. The effects of the crash were immediate. A Toronto investor went home that night to tell his wife that he had resigned from seven clubs, sold their second car, advertised for someone to rent the garage, and cancelled most of their charge accounts. Before going to bed, he fired the maid.

The investor still had assets (things of value)—a car, at least.

The maid probably had none. With the collapse of the stock market, the economic system toppled. The effects would reach into every part of Canadian society in what became known as the "Great Depression": the ruin of the hopes and plans of a whole generation.

USING YOUR KNOWLEDGE

28. Identify at least three causes for the economic slowdown in Canada. Explain why each of them would create problems in Canada.

29. "A large part of Canada's problem in the late twenties was its dependence on its export trade." Using facts from this chapter, either support or disprove this statement.

Fig. 23 The Elks Jazz Band, 1922. Look up a definition of "jazz" in an encyclopedia, and find out when this kind of music became popular.

Conclusion

The historian, Desmond Morton, has renamed the "roaring twenties" the "unroaring twenties." Most working Canadians, Morton maintains, had to struggle through the period while only a few were able to enjoy the automobiles, the dancing, the stock profits—the good times. The period began with economic distress in Winnipeg and Cape Breton and ended with economic collapse when the stock market crashed. Whether you agree with Morton or not, the twenties were complicated years of booming growth in some places, and inactivity in others. They were years of change. When the twenties ended, a new decade began that was distinctly worse.

From *Working People: An Illustrated History of Canadian Labour* by Desmond Morton.

GETTING THE FACTS

30. Review this chapter to find as many facts as you can that contributed to the economic collapse of 1929. List them in your notebook.

USING YOUR KNOWLEDGE

31. Do you think the signs of trouble could have been manipulated to prevent the disaster of 1929? Give reasons to support your ideas.

THINKING IT THROUGH

32. Write a one page essay supporting Dr. Morton's view that the period is best described as the "unroaring twenties."

33. Write a one page essay arguing that the 1920s were years of frantic activity best described as the "roaring twenties."

34. Explain which argument you find most convincing.

5 The Great Depression: Challenge and change

Action: A farmer abandons his farm

After the third bad year the missus said she wasn't going to take any more and somehow we got through that winter and lit out for the Okanagan Valley in the spring.

Sold what stock we could, gave the rest away, scrub stuff, there was nothing but scrub stuff by that time, and put two trunks on top of the car and left everything behind. Houseful of furniture, implements, crusher, harness, windmill, batteries, you couldn't give it away. The missus never looked back, just straight ahead down the road. . . .

From *Ten Lost Years* by Barry Broadfoot.

- Why do you think the Saskatchewan farm family would leave so many possessions behind them when they left their farm?

- If you were forced to leave your home with your family, what would you take?

◀ **A farmer drives his "Bennett buggy" across drought-stricken lands.**

1929	Stock market crash
1930	R. B. Bennett elected Prime Minister
1932	Government relief camps established
1933	Unemployment reaches 32.1% C.C.F. formed at Regina Conference
1935	Social Credit elected in Alberta Union Nationale elected in Quebec Regina riot MacKenzie King re-elected Prime Minister
1936	Communist Party of Canada made illegal
1937	G.M. Canada workers strike
1939	WWII begins

Chapter overview

The date was October 29, 1929. Newspaper headlines shouted "Stock Prices Crash!" The stock market crash of 1929 was the beginning of ten years of hard times called the "Great Depression."

In this chapter you will learn how the Great Depression affected Canadians from coast to coast. You will find out how ordinary Canadians and government leaders responded to the problems of the Depression.

The 1930s were years of challenge for all Canadians and the Great Depression brought about dramatic changes to the Canadian way of life.

Signposts

What happened to people across Canada during the Depression?

FEATURE: **Should relief be repayable?**

The people protest

FEATURE: **Government camps: Good or bad?**

Did anyone have a better way of dealing with the Depression?

Did everyone suffer equally during the Depression?

Key words

relief	world market	free enterprise
tariffs	communist	socialism
domestic market	"New Deal"	

What happened to people across Canada during the Depression?

By 1933 close to one million people were without work—approximately 30 percent of the Canadian labour force. No region, no province and no town was untouched by lay-offs.

Fig. 1 What does this graph reveal about unemployment between 1930 and 1940?

Fig. 2 The decline in average income per person, by province

	1928-29 AVERAGE $ PER PERSON	1933 $ PER PERSON	PERCENTAGE DECREASE
Saskatchewan	478	135	72
Alberta	548	212	61
Manitoba	466	240	49
British Columbia	594	314	47
Prince Edward Island	278	154	45
Ontario	549	310	44
Quebec	391	220	44
New Brunswick	292	180	39
Nova Scotia	322	207	36
Canada	471	247	48

NUMBER 8 DIET

Tea, Coffee or Cocoa............⅛ lb.
Sugar ....1 lb.
Butter ....½ lb.
Rice, Tapioca, Rolled Oats,
    Granules or Flour................2 lbs.
        or 1 lb. each of any two
Vegetables ....3 lbs.
        or 2 lbs. beans
        or 2 lbs. split peas
Prunes or Figs.........................1 lb.
Tomatoes or Corn....................1 tin
        or ½ lb. butter
Laundry Soap...........................1 bar
Matches ....(Small) 1 box
Apples ....2 lbs.
Potatoes ....5 lbs.
Milk ....4 pts.
Meat, Fish, Eggs or Milk........30c
Bread ....4 lvs.
        or 6 lbs. flour and yeast

Per Month

Salt ....1 bag
Pepper ....½ oz.
Baking Powder........................4 oz.
Toilet Soap (pkg. of 3)..........1 pkg.

Fig. 3 The standard of living of most Canadians was drastically changed by the Depression. How is this apparent in the food suggestions listed on this chart of diets for unemployment relief?

In Ontario, relief applicants had to disconnect their telephones and turn in their drivers' licences in order to receive relief vouchers.

Canada had never faced such a massive unemployment problem. There was no unemployment insurance, no family allowance and no organized welfare system to help the thousands of Canadians who were out of work. Many people could not even afford to buy food and clothing. Young Canadians decided to leave their homes in order to ease the burden on the family. With no hope of work in the home area, thousands of Canadians, young and old alike, travelled across Canada in a fruitless search for work.

The government and relief

At first the Canadian government did nothing to help the unemployed. Prime Minister Mackenzie King and the Liberal party were in power as the Depression took hold in 1929. Like many people, King believed that the hard times would be short lived and that good times were just around the corner. King ignored demands for government action to assist the unemployed.

In the 1930 election campaign, the Conservative party, led by Richard Bedford Bennett, launched a vigorous attack on the Liberal party and Mackenzie King. Bennett charged King with ignoring the distress caused by the stock market crash and unemployment. He promised to give $20 000 000 to the provinces to aid the unemployed. He also promised to put the unemployed back to work by using tariffs to "blast a way into world markets." When other countries raised their tariffs on Canadian goods, Canada would raise her tariffs to protect Canadian industry. If another country lowered its tariff policy and bought Canadian goods, then Canada would lower its tariffs in return. R.B. Bennett's policy and promise for action sounded good to Canadian voters. The Conservative party won a majority government with 137 of 245 seats in the House of Commons.

Bennett quickly acted on the two main promises of his campaign by raising tariffs and providing funds for relief. By 1930 provincial and municipal governments were establishing relief programmes for the needy. These relief programmes were considered short term emergency "handouts" to prevent starvation. To qualify, those who requested relief had to prove they were residents of the community and had no relatives to support them. Relief vouchers could be exchanged for food and other essentials. No "luxuries" like newspapers, tobacco, haircuts, lipstick or movies were allowed. The food allowance varied from city to city. A family of five was allowed $3.25 per week in some Quebec cities. A family of the same size could receive as much as $7.80 a week in certain Ontario towns. In most cases relief vouchers were accompanied with suggested diets and economy measures.

Government relief camps

Although provincial and municipal relief programmes helped many people, thousands of Canadians were wandering from town to town in search of jobs. Many of them travelled back and forth across Canada on freight trains and slept in hobo camps beside the railway tracks. They had no home. Because they were no longer living in one particular town or city, they did not qualify for relief.

By 1932, the concern over the number of homeless people "riding the rods" became so great that the government of Canada established a nationwide programme of relief camps. The camps were operated by the Department of National Defense and were usually located in undeveloped areas of northern Canada. They provided single males 18 years or over with food, lodging, clothing, medical care and 20 cents a day. In return, the men were required to build barracks, roads, landing strips, drainage ditches, railway spurs. The camps were also intended to quiet the unrest and frustration of unemployed men by providing them with a place to live and useful work.

Although originally planned to house about 2000 men, eventually as many as 20 000 were stationed in the camps at one time. Before they were closed in 1936, over 170 000 men had spent some time in a government relief camp.

Under some of the freight cars there were a series of parallel iron rods that could hold a person, but "riding the rods" was a very dangerous way of hitching a free ride.

Fig. 5 R.B. Bennett

GETTING THE FACTS

1. Describe three effects that the Depression had on the lives of Canadians.

2. List two promises made by Bennett that helped him win the 1930 election. Explain why each promise would win votes from Canadians in the thirties.

3. In your own words, briefly explain the term relief and summarize how the relief system of the thirties worked.

4. State three facts about government relief camps.

USING YOUR KNOWLEDGE

5. Examine the unemployment graph in Figure 1.
    a) In what decade was unemployment highest? In what year?
    b) What does the graph show about 1939? Why do you think this happened?

6. Look at the incomes in Figure 2.
    a) In which two provinces did incomes decrease the most?
    b) In which two provinces did incomes increase the least? Does this mean that these regions suffered very little during the Depression? Explain. (HINT: Look at the 1928-29 incomes.)

7. a) Examine the diet in Figure 3. How does it compare with yours? List at least five items in your diet that do not appear on the list.
    b) Could you follow the thirties diet and be healthy? Would you want to follow the diet? Explain.

THINKING IT THROUGH

8. a) It is difficult to determine which items are necessities and which are luxuries. How would you define necessities? luxuries?
    b) What were some items considered to be luxuries in the thirties? Would they still be luxuries today? What other luxuries would you add to today's list?

"D—R—O—U—G—H—T . . . it means five, six, seven years of dried-out crops, a great rich land without rain, and heat which would fry the edges off a muleskinner's boots, heat every day, too hot to fight and too hot to sleep in at night. . . ."
From *Ten Lost Years* by Barry Broadfoot.

Depression on the Prairies

The Prairie provinces suffered immensely during the Depression. First, the world wheat market collapsed and wheat prices fell lower and lower. Second, a drought ruined the wheat. Third, plagues of grasshoppers devoured the crops that had survived the drought conditions.

YEAR	ACRES	YIELD	PRODUCTION	VALUE OF WHEAT SOLD OFF FARMS
1928	13 791 000	23.3	321 215 000	$218 000 000
1929	14 445 000	11.1	160 565 000	134 932 000
1930	14 714 000	14.0	206 700 000	72 293 000
1931	15 026 000	8.8	132 466 000	44 407 000
1932	15 543 000	13.6	211 551 000	56 889 000
1933	14 743 000	8.7	128 004 000	52 301 000
1934	13 262 000	8.6	114 200 000	57 950 000
1935	13 206 000	10.8	142 198 000	68 400 000
1936	14 596 000	8.0	110 000 000	81 000 000
1937	13 893 000	2.7	37 000 000	16 000 000

Fig. 6 Wheat production in Saskatchewan

From *Men Against the Desert* by J.H. Gray.

Fig. 7 The Palliser triangle is a farming area near the U.S. border, mainly in southern Saskatchewan, but including smaller parts of Manitoba and Alberta. During the 1930s, drought, wind and insects combined to convert the Palliser triangle into a desert spotted with abandoned farms.

The following excerpt is taken from a letter dated December 16, 1931 and was written by a Saskatchewan woman. In the letter she outlines the problems caused by the drought and talks about the relief received from her fellow Canadians.

You will remember the scores of teams lined up at the elevators this time of year, delivering grain, and the train loads pulling out for the East. We still have lines of teams—but receiving not delivering. Not a loaded car has left this winter, but every day I sign for cars shipped in loaded with relief fodder for distribution at Osage, Fillmore and Creelman. Cars of hay, of oat sheaves, of straw, of oats and of barley. Do you realize that 85% of our farmers are receiving relief in some form? Food for man, fodder

[coarse food] for beast and fuel are the articles provided so far—
later we will have to distribute all grain required for seed next
spring. For all of this repayment is expected . . . but little of it
will ever be repaid.

In addition to all this government provision we had much
direct relief (thanks to the United Church in Ontario) for which
no repayment is asked. . . .

Fig. 8 Winnipeg Grain Exchange, 1937. What sort of activities would be conducted here?

Should relief be repayable?

The Attorney General of Saskatchewan argued that the people who received relief payments of $10 per month or more should repay the money once they began earning a suitable income again. His argument was presented in 1931 when the full impact of the Depression was yet to be felt in Canada.

I may say that we are fully of the opinion that to give free gifts at this time would strike a blow at the independence of the population, which would be very serious, and again there is a body of sentiment, and it is the sentiment of the very best element of those in the stricken area, that it would resent the idea of charity. They want to repay, and should be given the opportunity to do so. The element, and unfortunately it is not small, which would take everything that it could get for nothing, will have a curb placed on its desires when it realizes that there is an obligation to repay.... It would be most unfortunate in our opinion if the belief should be entertained on the part of the population in the south or any part of the Province that they would have the right to free food for the period that will be covered.

From *Bennett Papers*, Volume 778.

THINKING IT THROUGH

9. In your opinion, should the relief given during the thirties be paid back? Do you think any kind of financial aid or welfare given today should be repaid? Explain your views.

Depression in the Maritimes

The Maritimes' economy depended on the export of fish, timber products and coal. Like the Prairie provinces, when the markets for their natural resources disappeared, the Maritime provinces suffered greatly. As the Depression wore on, fishermen did not go out to sea. Workers at fish processing plants were laid off or had their hours of work reduced and wages cut.

The total annual marketed value of all fish landed in the Eastern Division of the Department of Fisheries, comprising the provinces of Nova Scotia, New Brunswick and Prince Edward Island and the Magdalen Islands of Quebec was as follows:

Fig. 9 Values of fish sold in the Maritimes

1926	$19 823 557
1927	17 280 216
1928	18 524 697
1929	19 334 431
1930	17 026 070
1931	13 680 034
1932	10 914 306
1933	10 266 474

From *Royal Commission on Price Spreads and Mass Buying*, 1937.

The coal industry in Cape Breton also suffered a serious setback as did the pulp and paper industry in Nova Scotia and New Brunswick. The incomes of eastern farmers fell, but not as many farmers were forced off the land as in the West. They were more diversified [dih-VER-sih-fid] than the grain farmers of Saskatchewan and could live off their own production even if their cash incomes dropped.

Look at the following letter. How was this family affected by the Depression?

In 1932 the net cash income of the average New Brunswick farm was $20.

Fairview, Nova Scotia,
July 20, 1935,
Premier R.B. Bennett

Dear Mr. Bennett,

I am a young lady in which is having bad luck. My father has never worked since February and with this terrible depression I am scared we are going to lose our home. We have a mortgage of $1,000 and we cannot pay the payments and live. So I thought when I seen your picture in the paper and so much about it would do no harm to ask you. Would you be so kind to lend me $75.00. We owe $70.00 and if we don't get that they will close the mortgage and take the house from us. So if you would kindly lend me that amount I will give you a $100.00 fur for security until I make ends meet to pay you back. But if I can help my father out in any way I must try and do it, as he is all that my sister and I owns and my sister isn't strong. We were very well off in our day but my father invested all his money in a coal mine and lost it all and then this terrible depression came and we had to put a mortgage of $1000 on our home. I do not want this depression to down me as I am a staunch Conservative to the bone.

Yours lovingly
Miss E.L.G.

R.B. Bennett kept many of the thousands of letters he received during the Depression. You can find copies of these letters in *The Wretched of Canada* by Grayson and Bliss.

Although Prime Minister R.B. Bennett did not encourage people to send letters like this to him, they came anyway. As prime minister, Bennett was a natural person for Canadians to look to for help. The fact that he was also a very wealthy man was further encouragement. Bennett did not send any money to Miss E.L.G. although small amounts of money ($5-10) were sent to other people whom he judged more needy. Why do you suppose he decided to do nothing in this case?

Fig. 10 A common form of transport during the Depression was the "Bennett buggy"—a car with its engine removed, and pulled by a horse. Why do you think cars were used in this way, and why were they given this name?

GETTING THE FACTS

10. What was the value of wheat sold in 1928? in 1937? What happened during that time to create such a difference? Give two reasons.

11. Name three major industries in the Maritimes which suffered during the Depression.

USING YOUR KNOWLEDGE

12. a) The economies of the Maritime and Prairie provinces were the same in one important aspect. What was it?

   b) Because of this factor both regions were hit especially hard during the Depression. Explain why.

13. a) Define primary source. What examples of primary sources are found in this section?

   b) Select two sentences in each letter that you find especially interesting. Why are primary sources such as these important in the study of history?

THE INVESTIGATIVE REPORTER

14. Both geographic and historic factors combined to bring about the tragedy of the Palliser Triangle. Write a one page report explaining why the tragedy occurred. Consult both geographic and historical sources. How is the land in the Palliser Triangle used today?

The Depression in central Canada

Domestic market refers to the goods bought and sold within a country. World market refers to the goods bought and sold outside a country.

Ontario and Quebec were both agricultural and industrial provinces. In general, the varied agriculture and industry in central Canada protected many from the total devastation that the Depression brought to the Prairie and Maritime provinces. Farmers in central Canada tended to grow a variety of crops. Thus they could supply many of their own food requirements and the needs of the local community. The industries in central Canada that were protected by tariffs and had a domestic market managed to carry on despite the hard times.

However, some industries depended on world markets. Since the Depression was world-wide, customers in foreign countries bought fewer Canadian-made products. Goods began to pile up in Canadian warehouses. Some workers were fired. Some were laid off. Many who managed to hold onto their jobs experienced work load increases and salary cuts.

Because Canadian workers had less money to spend, the domestic market was soon affected. The downward spiral of wages and prices also affected farmers in central Canada as well as the Maritimes and the Prairies. Those who did not own their land or machinery soon found their income from sales of grain and animals did not cover their debts. Many foreclosures resulted—that is, farmers lost their land because they were not able to keep up the payments on it.

Fig. 11 It was not only farmers who were turned out of their homes. In the cities, families unable to pay rent or mortgages were sometimes evicted.

Government investigation of the clothing industry revealed many non-union shops to have poor working conditions and undesirable pay scales. Dressmakers were often paid according to a system known as piecework. The workers received a salary based on the number of garments completed rather than on the number of hours worked.

In 1934, a government investigating committee interviewed Miss Nolan, a seamstress working for the T. Eaton Company. Miss Nolan told how falling prices and falling wages affected workers in her factory. In 1929 she received $12.50 per week and was expected to make 42 dresses. By 1934 her wages had not changed but the number of dresses she had to make had doubled to 84. In effect, Miss Nolan had to work twice as hard to make the same amount.

Question: Miss Nolan, were you employed by the T. Eaton Company Limited of Toronto?

Answer: Yes, I was . . .

Q. And what was the result, first of all, physically from this drop in rates?

A. Well, you had to work so hard, you were driven so fast that it just became impossible to make $12.50 and you were a nervous wreck. The girls cried. I was hysterical myself. It almost drove me insane.

Q. Was that condition general or did it only happen to you?

A. It was general. All the girls were the same.

Q. And did you break down by reason of it all?

A. Yes. I went into hysterics several times and I had to go to the hospital and a nurse said, "What is the matter? You girls are always coming here."

From *The Dirty Thirties, Canadians in the Great Depression* by Michael Horn.

USING YOUR KNOWLEDGE

15. It is important to examine different views of an historical event. Do you think that the implication that the T. Eaton Company was unfair to its workers is correct or incorrect? Read the following quotation:

"Some people accused Eaton's of running a sweatshop. That wasn't my experience. In 1934, they paid a fair wage and extra money if you were a good worker. I was glad to have the work, the employee's benefits such as medical care and a discount at the store. No one seemed unhappy on our floor. Of course, I was a fast worker."

Elsie Freeman

How would you answer the above question after reading this quotation?

Fig. 12 Elsie Freeman

16. You are a lawyer hired by the T. Eaton Company to prepare a statement for the investigating committee. What evidence would you use to defend Eaton's actions?

The people protest

The Depression caused severe hardship for many Canadians from British Columbia to Nova Scotia. Some endured the Depression quietly. But other Canadians seriously questioned the government's relief programmes and strategy for economic recovery. A number of Canadians actively protested the government's actions.

Bennett was in political trouble. The high tariff policy failed to blast Canada into the world market. Farmers, particularly in the West, resented the Conservative tariff policy because it protected eastern manufacturers but did not help Prairie farmers sell their

Fig. 13 A parade of the Single Men's Unemployed Association. What is the meaning of the statement on the front placard?

What Makes the Wild West Wild

KEEP FREE FROM SPECULATION AND WILD DREAMS OF SUDDEN WEALTH AND YOU WILL BE HAPPY AND CONTENTED!

INDUSTRIAL EAST

TARIFF PROTECTED INDUSTRIES

AGRICULTURAL WEST

With apologies to "The Country Gentleman"

Fig. 14 What point is this cartoon making about Prime Minister Bennett's farm policies?

grain on world markets. By 1935, the cost of government relief in Canada had reached $173 000 000. Bennett would not allow the government of Canada to go into debt to increase relief to the unemployed and needy. Thus, Bennett gained the reputation of being insensitive to the poor.

A dramatic form of protest during the Depression was the "On-to-Ottawa Trek." In 1935, some of the men living in relief camps in British Columbia planned a peaceful protest against the living conditions in the B.C. camps. They left the camps and gathered in Vancouver to organize a march to Ottawa to present their demands to the government. The march was really more like a ride, as the men boarded freight trains in Vancouver to travel across the country to Ottawa. At first, public opinion was against the trekkers. In Kamloops the reception could even be called hostile. Some men talked of quitting the march, but most decided to proceed. As the trek progressed

Fig. 15 The trekkers change trains at Kamloops.

A trekker is a person who has undertaken a long and difficult journey.

From *Recollections of the On To Ottawa Trek* by Ronald Liversedge.

advance parties were sent ahead to persuade townspeople to greet the trekkers. By the time they reached Golden, B.C., things had turned around.

"Boys, you are really going to get a surprise at Golden," promised Arthur "Slim" Evans, the protest leader. One of the marchers describes the surprise:

We were soon marched on to a large expanse of park-like land, richly grassed, with large shade trees scattered here and there. But what was more to the point, under those trees were cooking fires, and suspended under the fires were various kinds of makeshift cooking vessels full to the brims with simmering, bubbling, thick, heaven-smelling beef stew. The cooking pots were makeshift because they had to be big. Over one fire (and this is the gospel truth) was suspended a full-sized bathtub, also full to the brim with beef stew. There were long trestle tables with thousands of slices of golden crusted bread. Around each fire were just two or three quiet, smiling women, salting, peppering and tasting. It was incredible, it was heart-warming, it was beautiful.

As the trekkers moved across the Prairies, more and more men joined the march. Government officials became increasingly alarmed, not only by the number of marchers, but also by their army-like precision and organization. Finally on June 14, 1935, R.B. Bennett ordered the R.C.M.P. to stop the trek in Regina. Bennett claimed the marchers were defying the law and were part of a plot to overthrow the government of Canada. Only the trek leaders

Government camps: Good or bad?

I got a job at Barriefield relief camp in 1932 when I was 15. Dad was only working two days a week and I thought it would be better to get my meals at the relief camp than at home. So off I went ... meals plus 20¢ a day and I could hitch-hike home if it got too rough. I was supposed to be 18 but a lot of 15 and 16 year olds were admitted. We slept in big army bell tents, maybe a dozen to a tent. Stealing was common. Dad used to send me 25¢ every week but for three weeks the mail never came. The government finally traced the theft to my boss who was already earning 40¢ a day. There were a few communist agitators around the camp but no one paid much attention to them as far as I could see. [An agitator tries to stir up support for a cause.] If the truth were known, I didn't mind the camp much at all.

From an interview with J.R. Sutton of Oshawa, Ontario.

Were government camps good or bad? While some men were pleased to have a place to live during the Depression, other men who lived in the government camps made numerous complaints about crowded living conditions, lack of medical facilities, poor food, camp discipline, low pay (20 cents a day) and isolation. Because of the complaints, British Columbia appointed an inquiry into relief camps. The findings of the Macdonald Commission indicated the camps were providing the necessary relief. The commission found the quality of food to be generally good and most of the other complaints to be only minor problems.

In 1935 R.B. Bennett stated that "... the camps have won the warm support and approval of those who have inspected them, including people well able to arrive at the conclusion how single, homeless, unemployed men might be cared for, and some of the most

Fig. 16 Another government relief scheme was the Rolling Hills Project.

distinguished social workers from other countries have expressed warm approval of the action that has been taken."

However, the remoteness of these camps and the lack of wages led to discontent among relief camp workers.

... they griped about the food, the clothing, the bedbugs, the overcrowding in the dormitories, the ... regime, the latrines, and any other grievance they could conjure up. ... All the investigators who roamed the camp—social workers, preachers, Members of Parliament, and Royal Commissioners—were unanimous on this point: the single unemployed regarded themselves as Canada's forgotten men. They had been filed and forgotten and nobody cared if they lived or died.

From *The Winter Years* by J.H. Gray.

THINKING IT THROUGH

17. Based on what you have learned about the Depression, do you think government camps were a good idea? Explain your viewpoint.

were allowed to continue on to Ottawa and present their demands to the prime minister. The remaining trekkers waited in Regina for their leaders to return.

The Six Demands of the Ottawa Trekkers

1. That work with wages be provided at a minimum rate of 50 cents an hour for unskilled labor; union rates for all skilled labor. Such work to be on basis of five-day week, six-hour working day, and minimum of 20 days' work per month.

2. All workers in relief camps and government projects be covered by the Compensation Act. Adequate first aid supplies on all relief jobs.

3. That democratically elected committee of relief workers be recognized by the authorities.

4. Relief camps be taken out of the control of the department of national defence.

5. A genuine system of social and unemployment insurance in accordance with the provisions of the Workers' Social and Unemployment Insurance Bill.

6. That all workers be guaranteed their democratic right to vote.

Talks between Bennett and the strike leaders failed. Bennett did not seem to think that their demands should be answered:

> I endeavoured to explain to the delegation that these camps were in no sense regarded as permanent camps, that they were . . . created to supply shelter, clothing and under discipline, and the only restraint imposed on them was that of good conduct. They were not compelled to work, but work was provided for them, and they were paid a very small sum, not as charity, but to enable them if they so desired to purchase small comforts. They received twenty cents per day.

Communism is a political and economic system where all property and business are owned by the community rather than by private individuals. All people should share equally in the work and the prosperity of the society.

The strike leaders returned to Regina. Nearly 3000 marchers remained in the city. The government's fear of communist influence among the men led the R.C.M.P. and the Regina Police to break up a public meeting and arrest the leaders. A riot broke out. One police officer was killed and many police officers and trekkers were injured before the riot was stopped.

After the riot the government provided two passenger trains to take all the original trekkers back to Vancouver. Other men who had joined the trek were given free transportation to their homes. The government also provided food for their trip.

Conditions in the relief camps changed in the months following the "On-to-Ottawa Trek." Most significantly the Department of National Defense turned over the camps to the provinces. The provinces tended to view the camps as public works camps rather than relief camps and paid the men 40 cents an hour for their labour.

For a fuller understanding of the On-to-Ottawa Trek, read *Recollections of the On to Ottawa Trek* by Ronald Liversedge.

GETTING THE FACTS

18. In one sentence, explain what the On-to-Ottawa Trek was.

19. Give two pieces of evidence to show that the trek was planned.

20. Why did riots break out in Regina?

USING YOUR KNOWLEDGE

21. a) According to Prime Minister Bennett, what was the purpose of relief camps?

b) Now review the six demands of the trekkers. Do they seem to have a different idea about what relief camps should be? Explain.

c) Why do you think Bennett was upset by the trek?

Fig. 17 In a communist society, "all people should share equally in the work and prosperity of the society." Would this sound appealing in hard times? Probably, but after the Russian Revolution many people were afraid that a similar revolution might occur in Canada.

The extent of this fear can be seen in this picture. Here a detective sorts through some of the so-called communistic publications seized in a raid in Montreal in 1938. This kind of attitude toward communism meant that R.B. Bennett rallied support to check the On-to-Ottawa Trek, because it was rumoured that some of the trek leaders were communists.

Did anyone have a better way of dealing with the Depression?

Roosevelt supported the need for the government to intervene in the economy to help end the Depression. He provided more money for unemployment relief, built highways, reforested waste land, offered farmers bonuses for cutting production. Minimum wages were set, maximum hours, unemployment insurance, and old age security.

By late 1934, Bennett was convinced his policies would not end the Depression nor would they gain his party re-election. In a series of radio speeches he announced to Canadians a "New Deal" that was modelled on President Roosevelt's "New Deal" in the United States. Bennett introduced unemployment insurance, a minimum wage, a compulsory day of rest, and a maximum number of hours of work a day. It was a radical change in policy. Bennett was known as a strong supporter of the **free enterprise** system. He believed that "the country that governs best is the one that governs least." Canadians believed the "New Deal" was an attempt to gain votes in the approaching election.

Mackenzie King attacked Bennett's "New Deal" throughout the 1935 election campaign. On October 24, 1935, the Canadian people rejected R.B. Bennett and the "New Deal." The Liberals swept to power with a majority government, winning 171 seats to the Conservatives' 39. Bennett's "New Deal" laws were taken to court and declared illegal. Yet Mackenzie King's new government still faced huge problems and had no clear-cut policies to solve the problems.

King did not promise big changes in government policy, but he did abandon Bennett's balanced budget policy. The Liberal government provided millions of dollars for additional relief and for local improvement projects. It encouraged investment by giving tax exemptions to Canadians who invested in new mines. Taxes were not increased to pay for the increased government spending. The government of Canada was spending more money than it earned from taxation and went deeper into debt than at any time during the previous years of the Depression. Then King waited for the world economy to recover.

A commission was appointed by the King government to study why the provinces were unable to pay for the social programmes they were responsible for under the BNA Act. In 1940 the Rowell-Sirois Commission recommended big changes in the existing system of government, but the world economy had already begun to recover.

GETTING THE FACTS

22. Summarize King's ideas about how government should deal with the Depression.

23. How did King's policies affect Canada's budget?

THINKING IT THROUGH

24. a) The free enterprise system allows private business to operate for the profit of the owners with little government control.

Bennett believed that "the country that governs least governs best." Explain what he meant by this statement. How did his policies reflect this attitude?

b) Do you think that Bennett's policy of "little government" was a good one for the Depression? Would it be a good policy for times of prosperity? Give reasons for your answer.

THE INVESTIGATIVE REPORTER

25. Using books in your school or local library, find answers to the following questions about the Rowell-Sirois Commission: What were its main recommendations? Which ones were taken and when were they put into effect? What overall changes were made to our system of government?

New political parties

Many angry and unhappy Canadians were not prepared to wait patiently for the world economy to recover and stop the Depression. Many were not prepared to accept the Conservative and Liberal methods of dealing with the Depression. The Great Depression gave old and new political ideas new life. It created a number of new and influential political parties in Canada. These new parties proposed unique solutions to Canada's problems and caused changes in Canada's political life.

Extremist parties such as the Fascist and Nazi parties also flourished during the 1930s. Why do you think this happened?

The Cooperative Commonwealth Federation

The C.C.F. party, led by J.S. Woodsworth, was committed to replacing the free enterprise system with socialism. It wanted the government to own all productive businesses, financial institutions, and communication networks. It thought that all the profits should be used to provide social benefits to everyone equally. The C.C.F. party's policy dealt with the problems of the Depression and included:

—unemployment insurance
—sickness and accident insurance
—old age pensions
—family allowances
—national minimum wage
—free medical care
—crop insurance
—public works projects to improve living conditions and to provide jobs for the unemployed

Socialism is a political and economic system where all property and business are owned by the community rather than by private individuals. Thus all people should share equally in the work and prosperity of the society. Socialists attempt to bring about a socialistic society by gradually changing a capitalistic society through the democratic electoral process.

The C.C.F. entered candidates in provincial and federal elections in 1933. The party won considerable support in western Canada, although their socialist policies frightened many voters away

from the party in the early years. In 1935 the C.C.F. won 7 seats in the federal parliament and has continued as a major third party since that time. In 1961 the C.C.F. changed its name to the New Democratic party. The New Democratic party has formed provincial governments in Saskatchewan, Manitoba and British Columbia and has been the official opposition in Ontario. Some of the party's policies have been adopted and implemented by both Liberal and Conservative governments.

The Social Credit party

William Aberhart, a high school principal and radio preacher, created the Social Credit party in Alberta. He blamed the Depression on the banks in general, and, in particular, on the Bank of Canada's policy of not increasing the supply of money. He wanted to provide a social credit of $25 per month to every adult of the province. By placing purchasing power in the hands of every citizen, he believed that the Depression could be stopped and that prosperity would return.

Aberhart's promise that every citizen would share in the natural resources of the province and receive a "Prosperity Certificate" for $25 each month helped to elect a Social Credit government in Alberta in 1935. The party policy was a unique mixture of free enterprise capitalism and government spending to get the economy moving again. Social Credit's policies about banks and "Prosperity Certificates" were declared illegal, but the party remained in power in Alberta for many years. The Social Credit party eventually became a federal party and gained substantial support from Alberta and Quebec in a number of federal elections. The Social Credit party of British Columbia won the provincial election in 1952 under W.A.C. Bennett. W.A.C. Bennett was premier of the province from 1952 to the early 1970s. His son, Bill Bennett, brought the Social Credit party back to power in 1975.

Fig. 18 Prosperity Certificates were often called "funny-money" but merchants accepted them for payment of goods or services. Each time a certificate was used, the merchant would attach a 1¢ tax stamp to the back. When 104 stamps were attached, the holder could claim $1 back from the government. In this way, the tax stamps covered the value of the certificate.

Fig. 19 Maurice Duplessis (right) and Camillien Houde, Mayor of Montreal. Duplessis urged French Canadians to develop a strong sense of their own identity.

Union Nationale

The Union Nationale was a French Canadian nationalist party founded in Quebec in 1935. The party identified the English minority in Quebec as the cause of Quebec's economic problems. Because the English were generally rich and in control of the province's natural resources and industry, the French speaking population was attracted by the Union Nationale's policy.

Maurice Duplessis led the party to victory in the 1936 provincial election by vowing to defend French language, religion and culture against English businessmen, the federal government and communists. Duplessis promised to increase provincial authority so that the party could carry out its economic policy. That policy included improved working conditions, securing new markets for Quebec's farm products and building low income housing.

Duplessis and the Union Nationale were to control the political life of Quebec from 1936-1959 with the exception of the years 1939-1944. The Union Nationale consistently defended the rights of the Québécois and remained a strong voice in Quebec provincial politics until the Parti Québécois became the strongest voice for French-Canadian nationalism in the 1970s.

GETTING THE FACTS

26. In your notebook, draw the following chart and use it to summarize the three new political parties that become important during the thirties.

PARTY	WHERE IT WAS MOST POPULAR	LEADER	MAIN POLICIES

Fig. 20 Grey Owl captured the imagination of many Canadians. He pretended to be an Indian philosopher, but was really an Englishman by the name of Archie Belaney.

Some 1930s prices:
rib roast   9-12¢/lb.
blouses and
skirts   50¢-$2.00
dress shirts $1.00
shoes $4.50

American magazines such as Reader's Digest, Time Magazine and Life were also very popular in Canada.

USING YOUR KNOWLEDGE

27. Choose one of the three parties discussed in this section and review its policies carefully. Why would the party seem to offer better choices to many Canadians than the Liberals or Conservatives could?

THE INVESTIGATIVE REPORTER

28. Many other "solutions" to the Depression were proposed during the thirties. Some were impractical, some were discriminatory, and most had little or no lasting impact on Canada. Find more information on one of these solutions and describe it in a one-page report. At the end of your report give your own evaluation of the solution. Choose one of the following or find your own:

—Grey Owl and the move back to the land
—deporting immigrants
—extremist parties such as Nazis and Fascists
—youth work corps
—firing women workers

Did everyone suffer equally during the Depression?

The good life was still available despite all the poverty and suffering of the Depression. If you had even a little money you could take advantage of the low prices.

> When I went to work for the Free Press for $20 a week. . . . the highest paid reporter on the Free Press staff, in 1935, earned under $40 a week, and the senior news editors were paid little more. Yet a family of three such as ours could get by comfortably on $20 or $25 a week. Rents were depressed and clothing prices were simply unbelievable. Our three-room suite cost us $15 a month and later we were able to pick and choose among five-room bungalows renting for $25 a month. Few of us ever paid more than $21.50 for a two pants suit, or more than $20 for a warm and wearable overcoat. Only one reporter owned a car in 1937. Cars were not something everyone had to have. They were things people hoped to be able to afford some day.

From *The Winter Years* by J.H. Gray.

Radio was an inexpensive form of entertainment available to many Canadians during the Depression. Comedians such as Amos and Andy, Jack Benny, George Burns and Red Skelton flourished in these hard times. American radio programmes became such a part of

Fig. 21 King George VI and Queen Elizabeth visited Canada in 1939. In Toronto they went to the Woodbine Race Track to present a prize of 50 guineas to the winner of the "King's Plate."

Some popular films were Snow White and the Seven Dwarfs, Top Hat, and Gone With the Wind.

Canadians' way of life that Prime Minister Bennett established the Canadian Radio Broadcasting Commission in 1933 to check this influence and improve Canadian broadcasting. This led to the formation of the C.B.C. in 1936.

The American movie industry was experiencing its golden age. Romance, comedy and adventure movies dominated the screen. Few movies gave any hint that North America and the world were in the middle of a major world depression.

Sporting activity grew in popularity during the Depression. Skating, curling, hockey, baseball, football, swimming, were all pastimes for children and adults. Professional spectator sports, like baseball and hockey, began to build national audiences because of the magic of radio. Horse racing was also popular in the 1930s. Raising and racing horses was a hobby for the rich, while the less wealthy hoped to make their money multiply at the betting windows. There were no legal lotteries in the 1930s. The only legal form of gambling available to Canadians was at the racetrack.

Fig. 22 The Civic Auditorium in Winnipeg was built in 1932, as part of a relief project.

The good life was available, even in the 1930s—it was simply a question of who could afford to take advantage of it. For those Canadians with a job, life was pretty good. For the wealthy, there was no limit to the form or variety of fun available. But for the unemployed and poor, the good life of the 1930s was something to dream about.

GETTING THE FACTS

29. Why was a little money the key to good times in the thirties?

30. When was the C.B.C. formed? Why was it created?

USING YOUR KNOWLEDGE

31. In hard times, entertainment, especially comedy, seems to flourish.

a) Find evidence in the section you just read to either support or disprove this statement.

b) Is the statement true for Canada today? Explain your answer.

32. Imagine that you are a teenager from a very poor home during the 30s. Write an account in your diary of what the good life would be for you.

Conclusion

The 1930s were years of challenge and change for Canadians. Canadians responded to the challenges in many different ways, from providing relief, to forming political movements, to suggesting major changes in the capitalist system. The diversity of the responses to the Depression perhaps indicates how serious and confusing the problems and challenges were in the decade.

THE INVESTIGATIVE REPORTER

33. As you have seen, the thirties were tough years for many Canadians and good years for a few. Interview a Canadian who lived through the period. Design a series of five questions using the information in this chapter. Record the results of your interview in the form of a class report. Assess each interview (point of view, reliability, does it shed new light on the period?, etc.).

34. Perhaps someone in your community who lived through the Depression would be willing to visit your class. What questions would you ask such a person?

6 Canada and World War II: Service at home and abroad

This picture shows a group of Canadian soldiers marching off to war. Study it closely. Although we cannot tell for sure, most likely a conversation was taking place when this picture was taken.

- Imagine that you are each of the three main figures in this photograph. What might you be saying as this picture was taken?

- Often what we say and what we think or feel are not the same. Once again, imagine that you are each of the three main figures in this photograph. What might you be thinking or feeling that you are not saying at this time? Is what you are thinking or feeling influenced at all by what you know about World War I? Why or why not?

- The title of this chapter includes the word "service." When we think of "service" in wartime, we usually think of people who "serve" and fight in the armed forces. Is this the only kind of "service" that people give when their country is at war? What other forms of "service" can there be? How might the woman and the young boy in this picture "serve" during the war?

Chapter overview

World War II lasted from 1939 to 1945. During those six years of war, many Canadians—men, women and children—found themselves in situations in which they performed great services for their country. Some of these people became famous while many others remained unknown. Canadian men and women toiled on the warfront while others served on the homefront.

In many parts of the globe, World War II meant bombed out cities and villages, ruined farms, and suffering and death for incredible numbers of people. Canada was spared direct attack but Canadians still felt many of the other effects of war.

Many Canadians died, were wounded, or taken prisoner while fighting on the land or seas or in the skies. Others worked in industries and on farms providing the weapons and other materials with which to fight the war. Still others served as volunteers on the homefront, doing everything from writing letters to homesick soldiers or knitting socks for the troops, to collecting scrap metal for the factories to turn into guns. Seldom has Canada seen such commitment to one cause from so many of its people.

At the same time, there were some Canadians who were not so committed to the war effort. As in World War I, the need for soldiers led to angry divisions over the use of conscription. To organize its people and resources for the enormous war effort, the Canadian government took away some of the usual democratic rights of its citizens. This action caused great discontent among Canadians.

In this chapter, you will learn about many different aspects of World War II. You will see how life changed for Canadians as well as people in other countries affected by the war.

Signposts

Hitler invades Poland!

Major events of World War II

Canadians on the warfront—On land

Canadians on the warfront—On the seas

Canadians on the warfront—In the air

FEATURE: The Holocaust: How should Canada and other nations react?

On the homefront the war meant ...

Timeline (left margin):

- Sept 1939 — Outbreak of World War II
- Dec 1939 — First Canadian troops reach Britain
- June 1940 — Evacuation of Dunkirk / Battle of Britain begins
- Aug 1940 — Battle of Atlantic begins
- Dec 1940 — Wage and price controls in Canada
- June 1941 — Germany invades U.S.S.R.
- Dec 1941 — Japanese attack Pearl Harbour / U.S.A. joins war
- Apr 1942 — Conscription plebiscite
- Aug 1942 — Dieppe raid
- July 1943 — Allied invasion of Sicily and Italy
- Sept 1943 — Italy surrenders
- Dec 1943 — Battle of Ortona
- June 1944 — D-Day / Normandy invasion / Liberation of Europe begins
- Oct/Nov 1944 — Conscription crisis
- May 1945 — Germany surrenders (V-E day)
- Aug 1945 — Atomic bombs dropped on Japan / Japan surrenders

Not all Canadians supported the war >

FEATURE: One community's service in World War II >

FEATURE: A democracy at war—How much freedom should be surrendered? >

Key words

militia	neutrality	internment camps
Blitzkrieg	plebiscite	

In 1914, Canada was still a colony within the British Empire and when Britain declared war on Germany, Canada was automatically at war. By 1939 Canada was an equal member of the British Commonwealth of Nations and had full control over its own international affairs.

The first Canadian soldiers to fight in World War II fought in far-away Hong Kong against the Japanese rather than in Europe against Hitler's armies.

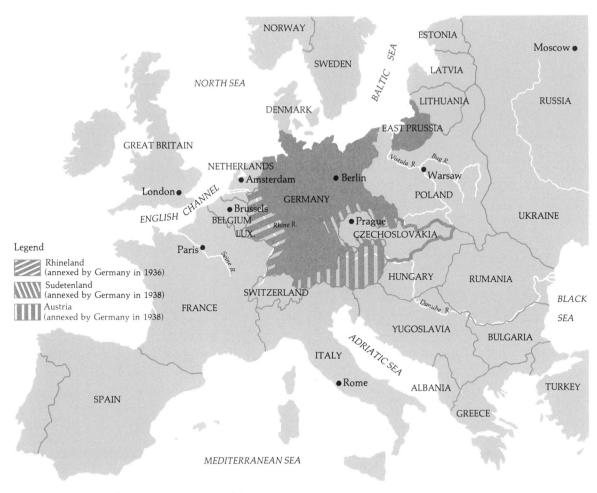

Legend

Rhineland
(annexed by Germany in 1936)

Sudetenland
(annexed by Germany in 1938)

Austria
(annexed by Germany in 1938)

Fig. 1 Europe at the outbreak of World War II

139

The Daily Reporter

SATURDAY, SEPTEMBER 2, 1939   PRICE: 3 CENTS

HITLER INVADES POLAND!

CANADA AND THE WORLD AWAIT THE RESPONSE OF BRITAIN AND FRANCE

Nazi planes bomb Poland: huge German armies sweep towards Warsaw

Special to the Daily Reporter from our London bureau, September 2, 1939.

At daybreak yesterday upwards of a million and a half soldiers of the German armies poured across the border of Poland in a sudden and overwhelming invasion of their eastern neighbour. Attacking from the north, south and west they appear to have as their major target the capital city, Warsaw.

London, September 2, 1939

Both Britain and France sent strongly worded notes to Hitler. In these notes they have stated that, if Germany did not withdraw its troops from Poland, they would declare war.

Silent crowd watches Nazi booth dismantled

Toronto, Ontario, September 2, 1939. While a crowd of several hundred stood watching silently, the German exhibit at the Canadian National Exhibition was quickly pulled down by workmen yesterday. German officials in charge of the exhibit said that the action was taken "In view of the serious international situation."

Based on the Globe and Mail

The final failure of the League of Nations

The League of Nations was created at the end of World War I in the hope that friendship and cooperation among nations would prevent new outbreaks of war. It has never been successful. It failed to stop Japanese expansion in the Far East and Italian aggression in Africa. League members were unwilling to take the actions necessary to stop such attacks. Hitler showed his contempt for the League by taking Germany out of its membership four years ago. Since that time, he ignored all requests and actions of the international organization. Much of the world concluded some time ago that the League has been a failure. Its ineffectiveness in this latest crisis seems to be the final blow in its unfortunate life.

Japan's intentions uncertain

Tokyo, September 2, 1939. The world is not sure what Japan will do in response to the news of Germany's surprise invasion of Poland. Germany and Japan have been drawn closer together by an agreement they have signed for co-operation against possible expansion by Communist Russia.

At this point, it would appear that the best that the rest of the world can hope for will be a Japanese declaration of neutrality.

Canada prepares for war

Ottawa, Saturday, September 2, 1939. Prime Minister William Lyon Mackenzie King and his Cabinet have been meeting all day in response to the news of Hitler's invasion of Poland. Urgent steps are being taken or planned to place Canada on a war footing and to get all possible aid to Britain as soon as possible. Among the actions planned or already taken are:

1. Parliament has been recalled for next Thursday (September 7). All Members of Parliament are making arrangements to hurry back to Ottawa. It is expected that after a short debate a formal declaration of war will be made.

2. The Ministry of Defense has sent telegrams to all military headquarters in the country ordering a partial mobilization of the militia. The permanent army at present numbers only 4000 men. The militia has approximately 50 000 partly-trained men.

3. The R.C.A.F. has been instructed to recruit new members to bring it up to full strength as soon as possible.

4. The Navy is already on patrol. Reserves will be called up as soon as they are needed.

5. A War Supply Board is to take control over all key industries in the country.

6. Censorship of information will begin tomorrow.

7. All companies already having contracts to manufacture munitions have been instructed to deliver the munitions as soon as possible.

8. The War Measures Act, which will give the government special powers to censor news, arrest and deport people and control the economy, will be implemented immediately.

9. The Cabinet is moving to give the government firm control over harbours, ports, all territorial waters, exports, imports and transportation.

10. The Prime Minister will likely address the nation on C.B.C. radio tomorrow.

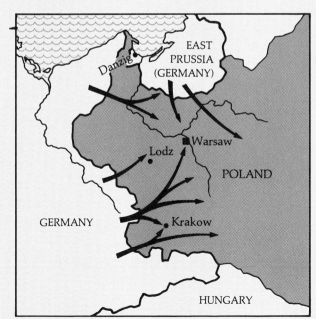

The German blitzkreig on Poland

Peace causes war!

Reacting to yesterday's attack on Poland by Germany and the threat of another world war, many observers are looking back to the peace treaty which ended World War I as one major cause of our present difficulties.

In the treaty, Germany not only lost important territory along its borders, but was compelled to take full blame for the war and pay enormous sums of money to the other countries. The German armed forces were dismantled and Germany could not rearm. Hitler had used this treaty to whip up German anger and desire for revenge. His people applauded when he broke the treaty by taking back conquered territory and rebuilding Germany's military might. When he was not punished by Germany's World War I foes for his violations of the treaty, Hitler was encouraged to move into Austria and Czechoslovakia and now Poland.

Will Mussolini join his ally, Hitler?

Rome, September 2, 1939. The events of recent days have left much of the international community wondering what Mussolini intends to do. It is suspected that although he will offer Hitler what help he can, he may not join his ally at this stage in the actual fighting.

Hitler's rise to power and march to war

A review of the major events that led to this crisis

1921   Hitler founds the Nazi Party in Germany

1929   The Great Depression begins—the economy collapses, money almost worthless, unemployment enormous

1930-1932   The Nazis make big gains in German national elections

1933   Hitler appointed Chancellor of Germany and converts government to a one-man, one-party dictatorship

1934   Concentration camps are started and persecution of Jews begins on a large scale

1935   Germany drops out of the League of Nations

1936   Hitler occupies the Rhineland in defiance of the Treaty of Versailles
Formation of "Axis" between Germany and Italy

1938   Hitler takes over Austria (The Anschluss)

Hitler signs Munich Pact with Britain and France—Hitler promises no more conquests if he is allowed to take the Sudetanland area of western Czechoslovakia

1939   Hitler takes all of Czechoslovakia

Hitler and Stalin sign a pact promising not to attack each other

September 1—Hitler launches Blitzkrieg on Poland

Based on information from newspapers in 1939

1. What did German armies do on September 1, 1939?

2. How did Britain and France respond to the German action?

3. In the article on Canada's preparation for war, find four ways in which the government took greater control over the lives of Canadians. (See the feature, *A democracy at war*, for a discussion of this issue.)

USING YOUR KNOWLEDGE

4. Examine the list of Hitler's actions up to 1939. In it find pieces of evidence that show he was not to be trusted and was prepared to use any means to achieve what he wanted.

5. After reading about Hitler's earlier actions and after studying the map of Europe, explain why Hitler might want to attack Poland.

6. Why would the world be anxious about what Italy and Japan might do?

7. Explain the meaning of the newspaper headline, "PEACE CAUSES WAR" after reading the article.

Fig. 2 German expansion in Europe

August 1939

June 1940

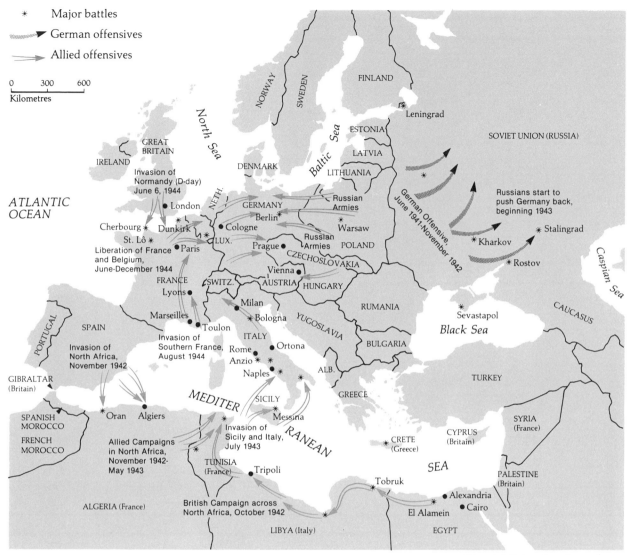

Fig. 3 Major fronts and battles of World War II

Major events of World War II

INVOLVING CANADIANS		INVOLVING OTHERS
	1939	
	Sept.	Germany attacks Poland
	Sept.	Britain and France declare war on Germany
Canada declares war on Germany	Sept.	
First convoy of ships leaves Canada	Sept.	
First Canadian Division reaches Britain	Dec.	
The British Commonwealth Air Training Plan (B.C.A.T.P.) agreement is signed	Dec.	

INVOLVING CANADIANS		INVOLVING OTHERS
1940		
	Apr. & May	Germany overruns Denmark, Norway, Belgium, Luxembourg, and the Netherlands
	May	Churchill becomes prime minister of Britain
	May	Germany invades France
	May-June	Evacuation of Dunkirk
Canada declares war on Italy	June	Italy declares war, joining Germany
National Resources Mobilization Act passed	June	France surrenders to Germany
First Canadians graduate from the B.C.A.T.P.	July-Sept.	Battle of Britain (many Canadians in R.A.F.)
Battle of the Atlantic begins	Aug.	German bomber attacks on England
	Sept.	Germany, Japan and Italy sign pact
First wage and price controls introduced	Dec.	
1941		
German submarine fires on St. John's, Newfoundland	March	
	Apr.	Greece surrenders to Germany
	Apr.	First German offensive in North Africa
Hyde Park Declaration (with U.S.A.)	Apr.	
Canada takes over convoy duty in the Northwest Atlantic	May	The "Bismarck" is sunk
Canadians invade Spitsbergen Islands in Arctic	June	Germany invades Russia
Total freeze on wages and prices begins	Oct.	
	Dec.	Japan attacks Pearl Harbour—the U.S.A. joins the war
	Dec.	Britain and allies declare war on Japan
Canada declares war on Japan	Dec.	
Canadians defeated and captured in Hong Kong	Dec.	Hong Kong surrenders to Japanese
1942		
Japanese Canadians moved from the west coast	Jan.	Japan expands into South Pacific
Conscription vote (plebiscite)	Apr.	
	May	First '1000-bomber' raid on Germany by R.A.F.
Vancouver Island shelled by Japanese submarine	June	
Battle of the St. Lawrence	June to Dec.	
The Dieppe raid	Aug.	
	Aug. Sept.	Battle of Stalingrad
	Oct.	Battle of El Alamein (North Africa)
	Nov.	Record sinkings of Allied shipping by German U-boats
	Nov.	Allied invasion of North Africa

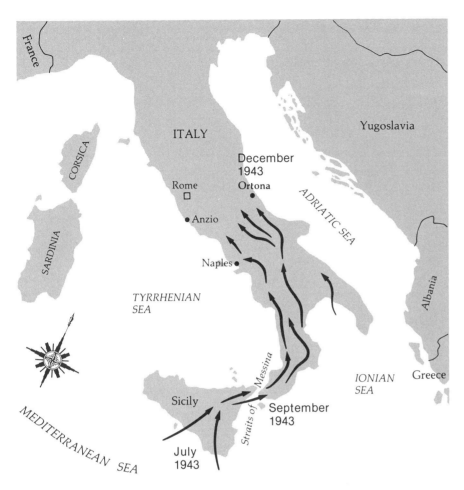

Fig. 4 The Battle of Ortona

The cost of the battle for Ortona was enormous. 650 soldiers of the Canadian 1st Division were killed or wounded before they forced the Germans to retreat. Ortona was an ideal town for the Germans to defend: its streets were dark and narrow and they set their weapons up to point from many of the windows or slatted floors. The Canadians realized it would be too dangerous to fight their way up the streets, so they found a way to move directly from one building to another. They would blast a hole through a connecting wall in a top storey. Before the smoke cleared, troops raced through the hole, throwing grenades and firing machine guns. The technique was called "mouseholing", and soldiers worked their way down entire blocks without ever going into the street.

INVOLVING CANADIANS		INVOLVING OTHERS
	1943	
	Feb.	Germans surrender at Stalingrad
	May	Allies are victors in North Africa
"Dambusters" destroy the Ruhr dams	May	
Battle of Atlantic ends, U-boats withdraw to coastal waters of Europe	May	
Canadians invade Sicily	July	Allied invasion of Sicily
	July	Mussolini dismissed
Canadians invade Italy	Sept.	Allied invasion of Italy
	Sept.	Italy surrenders
	Oct.	Italy declares war on Germany (Germans continue fight in Italy)
Battle of Ortona	Dec.	

INVOLVING CANADIANS		INVOLVING OTHERS
1944		
	June	Allies enter Rome
Canadians land in Normandy (D-Day)	June	Normandy Invasion (Operation Overlord)
	June	First V-1 rockets hit London
	June	First B-29 bombing raids on Japan
Capture city of Caen	July	
	July	Hitler wounded in assassination attempt
Take Falaise	Aug.	
	Aug.	Paris liberated
Break through the Germans' "Gothic Line" in Northern Italy	Aug.	
Liberate Antwerp	Sept.	
Enter Dieppe	Sept.	
Capture Boulogne	Sept.	
Liberate Calais	Oct.	
	Oct.	Athens liberated
	Oct.	Americans invade the Phillipines
Conscription crisis	Oct.-Nov.	
Japanese "Balloon bombs" sent over Canada	Dec.	"Battle of Bulge" begins
1945		
	Jan.	Russians capture Warsaw
	Jan.	"Battle of Bulge" ends
	Jan.	German army in retreat
	Feb.	City of Dresden is fire-bombed
	Mar.	Allies cross the Rhine River
Canadian units in advance towards Berlin	Mar.	
The last Canadian troops leave Italy for northwestern Europe	Apr.	
The Netherlands is liberated	Apr.	Russians reach Berlin
	Apr.	Mussolini executed by Italian partisans
	Apr.	Hitler commits suicide
Canadian forces link up with Russians	May	Germans sign unconditional surrender, V-E Day
	Aug.	Atomic bombs dropped on Japan
POW's released Canadians begin to return to Canada	Aug.	Japan signs unconditional surrender

In the month of September 1939 over 58 000 people enlisted in the Canadian armed forces.

As the summary chart shows, Canadians served in many areas and in many battles in World War II. We cannot examine them all here. In the next section of this chapter, we will read the story of several of Canada's battles—some victories and some defeats. We will also read the stories of some remarkable Canadians who played important roles in these battles.

Fig. 5 Canadian soldiers and equipment on the Dieppe beach after the withdrawal

Canadians on the warfront—On land

Dieppe: Nine terrible hours of war

The German armies had driven the last British forces into the English Channel at the French coastal town of Dunkirk in June of 1940. Since that time, the Allies had been anxious to return to the mainland of western Europe. The Russians were pressing their allies to open a second front in the west to take some of the German pressure off them on the eastern front. Those who were planning future military activities were eager to try a sea-based invasion of the shores of Europe if only to practise for a major invasion later and to discover German defensive strategies. Canadian soldiers, who had been sitting in British training camps month after month, were demanding some action. All these factors combined to bring about the raid on the French coastal resort of Dieppe on August 19, 1942.

The Dieppe invasion turned out to be an incredible disaster for the entire Allied war effort but especially for the Canadians. Sea and air support was insufficient for the Canadian soldiers: they were dumped on the open, stony shore into a continuous German crossfire. The German planes, artillery, machine guns and snipers were all highly organized and in many cases well-hidden and protected. The tanks that were to lead the Canadian foot soldiers bogged down

"Allies" refers to Britain and its Commonwealth partners, France, Russia, the United States (after December 7, 1941) and the many other countries that were fighting alongside them. The term "Axis" was often used to describe Germany and its partners. The term comes from a pre-war agreement between Germany and Italy called the Rome-Berlin Axis.

In contrast to the heavy action experienced by the Allied soldiers during the Blitzkreig and its aftermath, the Canadians referred to their long wait in Britain as the "Sitzkreig."

147

Fig. 6 The location of Dieppe

in the deep, stony beach or were quickly disabled by the Germans. To get to the cover of the buildings of Dieppe, the troops had to run through the heavy German fire across the beach, up a sea wall and across a flat open park. Many Canadians were quickly shot down.

It was miraculous that some Canadians *did* make it into the town to fight it out before being forced to retreat. Other Canadians attacking from the outskirts of Dieppe met similar resistance. Despite the difficulties, a few units managed to get some distance inland.

The Canadians had landed on the beaches at 4:30. At 12:30 the order to withdraw was given. Many more Canadians were killed in desperate efforts to run or swim or crawl to the evacuating landing craft. The fighting had lasted only nine hours but had resulted in enormous casualties. Approximately 5000 Canadians had landed at Dieppe, 900 were killed, 1000 wounded and 1900 were taken prisoner. Only 2200 made their way back to England. Canadians immediately began to debate the value and wisdom of the Dieppe raid. The debate continues to this day.

GETTING THE FACTS

8. What were the two reasons for the Dieppe raid?

9. Why was the raid such a failure?

THE INVESTIGATIVE REPORTER

10. a) Consult some books on World War II. Research and summarize the arguments that have been made both for and against the Dieppe raid.

b) Based on your research, should the raid have been made and was anything gained from it? Write a one-page answer to this question.

Fig. 7 Padre John Foote, was awarded the Victoria Cross for his bravery at Dieppe. During the attack he carried wounded soldiers to arriving landing craft. He saved the lives of at least 30 men, and organized others to help carry more wounded. As the last evacuation vessel pulled away, Foote jumped out, and remained to care for the wounded on the beach. He spent the rest of the war in a prisoner of war camp.

D-day: "The greatest attack in history"

"Operation Overlord" was the Allies' attempt to establish a front in western Europe by landing in France. The grand plan was to squeeze Hitler's armies from the east, where the Russian front was now pushing the Germans back; from the south through the increasingly successful Italian campaign; and now, it was hoped, from the west.

During the night of June 5-6, 1944, the invasion began. Having learned the lessons of Dieppe, thousands of planes and ships, many of them Canadian, began an enormous bombardment of the Normandy shores and inland towns. Thousands of paratroops were dropped and then thousands of infantry with their supporting tanks

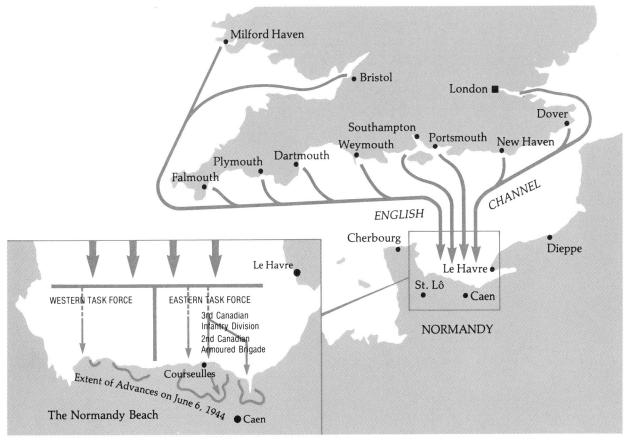

Labels within the image:

Milford Haven

Bristol

London ■

Dover

Southampton
Portsmouth
New Haven
Weymouth

Plymouth
Dartmouth
Falmouth

CHANNEL

ENGLISH

Cherbourg
Le Havre ·
St. Lô
· Caen
Dieppe

NORMANDY

Le Havre

WESTERN TASK FORCE
EASTERN TASK FORCE

3rd Canadian
Infantry Division
2nd Canadian
Armoured Brigade

Courseulles

Extent of Advances on June 6, 1944

The Normandy Beach
· Caen

Fig. 8 The invasion of Normandy

and armour were sent ashore from the landing craft onto the beaches of Normandy.

While American, British and other Commonwealth forces landed on neighbouring beaches, soldiers of the 3rd Canadian Infantry Division and 2nd Canadian Armoured Brigade stormed ashore at Juno beach. Despite the devastating air and naval bombardment, they met tough resistance from the German defenders.

Ross Munro, one of Canada's famous war correspondents, was able to provide an eye-witness account of the experience of the Canadian soldiers involved in the landing at Juno beach. This is his story of the Royal Winnipeg Rifles who, with several other Canadian units, were to go ashore in the first assault at the little fishing village of Courseulles. They aimed to establish a beachhead in preparation for a quick push inland to the main highway to the city of Caen.

> . . . just before eight a.m. leading companies of the western brigade touched down on the Courseulles beaches. The Winnipegs were on the right . . . of the inlet as planned. Tanks of the 1st

One infantry division has in it 3 brigades. Each brigade is made up of 3 battalions. Each battalion has approximately 850 soldiers. Hence a division is made up of between 7500 to 8000 fighting soldiers. There will be additional personnel with support duties attached to each division.

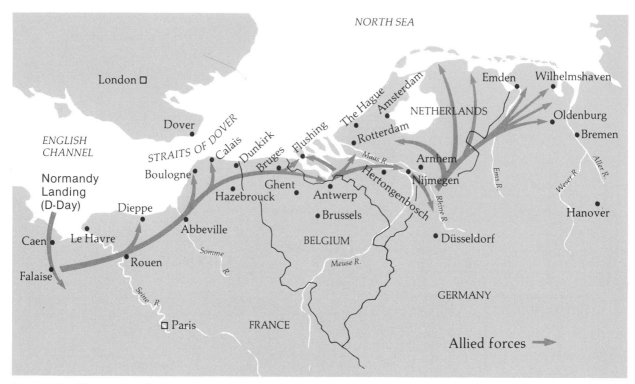

NORTH SEA

Fig. 9 The liberation of North West Europe after D-Day

"Casemates" and "pillboxes" are holes or hollows in the ground, often in the side of a hill, which have been fortified with stone, concrete or steel. From narrow openings, soldiers can fire at their enemy with rifles, machine guns and mortars. Sometimes, larger casements will contain heavy artillery.

From *Gauntlet to Overlord* by Ross Munro.

Hussars were with them. . . . Every unit had to cross from one hundred to two hundred yards [90 to 180 metres] of open beach. . . .

The Germans responded rapidly, shelling the beaches, mortaring them and spraying them with machine-gun bullets. The Canadians ran down the ramps of their assault craft into the face of this fire. Men dropped crossing that open beach but the main force got over it and struggled through the snarled mass of barbed wire at the base of the sand dunes. Gaps were cut and the infantry stormed into the German defence positions. Tanks worked along the beach helping the infantry by shelling casemates and pillboxes and machine-gunning the trenches. Naval craft which had closed in to the shore lent their fire support to the attack on the beach strip defences, while out to sea the big guns of the fleet pounded away at inland positions which were firing on the beaches.

. . . . The Canadians ran into cross-fire. They were shelled and mortared mercilessly even in the German positions but kept slugging away at the enemy. The 1st Hussars' tanks churned through the dunes in close support and after a struggle which was as bitter and savage as any on the British-Canadian sector, the Winnipegs broke through into open country behind the beach.

By the end of the day, all of the Allied forces were in control of the beaches but were having difficulty penetrating as far inland as had been hoped on the first day. The Canadians had managed, however, to fight their way five or six kilometres inland by dark. They were positioned to continue the attack on their initial inland target of Caen. However, this success was achieved at considerable cost: 359 Canadians were killed on D-Day while another 715 were wounded.

Over the next several months, the Allies rolled across Europe liberating towns, cities and countries from Nazi control. The invasion began on D-Day and ended in the spring of 1945 when the forces advancing from the west linked up with the Russians advancing from the east and forced the Germans to surrender.

GETTING THE FACTS

11. What was the grand plan of which Operation Overlord was a part?

12. What difficulties did the soldiers face when they landed on the beach?

13. In point form, list the main events of D-Day which are described in the text you have just read.

USING YOUR KNOWLEDGE

14. Based on what was done at Normandy that was not done at Dieppe, what lesson had been learned from the disaster at Dieppe?

THINKING IT THROUGH

15. Imagine you are a Canadian soldier who has just landed on the beaches of Normandy.

   a) Write a short paragraph describing how you feel.

   b) Now imagine you are a German soldier in a defense position at Courseulles. Write a short paragraph describing how you feel.

   c) Are the feelings expressed in the two paragraphs similar or different? Explain your answer.

THE INVESTIGATIVE REPORTER

16. a) The Normandy invasion is often called "the greatest attack in history" because of the size of all the forces involved. Consult books on World War II and find information on the forces. Present your findings in a written report or poster.

   b) Would you agree or disagree that Normandy was the greatest attack in history? Give reasons for your answer.

Fig. 10 A vivid record of the effects of the war is found in the works of Major Charles Comfort. Comfort had been an art professor at the University of Toronto before he became an official war artist for the Canadian army. In all, he painted 188 battlefield scenes.

Fig. 11 H.M.C.S. Chambly, a corvette.

Life for the crew of a corvette was damp, uncomfortable and crowded. The crew often numbered over ninety men. This was double the crew that had been intended by the designers of the boat. It was wet because water tended to seep in from everywhere. The crew could never get its clothes, bedding, food or even air dried out.

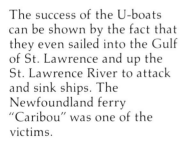

The success of the U-boats can be shown by the fact that they even sailed into the Gulf of St. Lawrence and up the St. Lawrence River to attack and sink ships. The Newfoundland ferry "Caribou" was one of the victims.

All citizens, especially those in port cities were urged not to talk about the arrival or departure of ships in the ports.

Canadians on the warfront—On the seas

If the Allies were to have any chance of winning the war, it was essential that raw materials from Canada reach Britain. These included iron ore, all types of weapons, ammunition, and vehicles, as well as fuel and food. Germany was aware of this, and was determined to cut Britain off from its supplies. Hundreds of German submarines were sent into the Atlantic Ocean to harass and sink the supply ships. These submarines known as U-boats, often moving in groups or "wolf-packs," torpedoed hundreds of slow and almost defenseless merchant ships. The U-boats became so successful that it became necessary to devise a new means of protecting the merchant ships and getting the desperately needed supplies safely to Britain.

Very early in the war, merchant ships were organized into convoys—groups of ships in rows spread over many square kilometres of ocean. Protection of these convoys from U-boat attacks became a particular problem. To solve this problem, a newly designed ship was rushed into production. It was called a *corvette* and it was to become "the ship that won the Atlantic war."

The corvette was somewhat dumpy and squat. It was also rather small, about sixty metres long and ten metres wide, but it

was tough. One of its great assets was that it could turn very quickly in a very small area. This was important during the twisting and turning chase of the U-boats.

The corvette would take up position on one side or at the rear of the rows of merchant ships loaded with their precious cargo. A destroyer led the way. With the rapid expansion of the corvette fleet, many ships left port to tangle with the U-boats with a very inexperienced crew. Often the training took place while at sea on convoy duty.

Women were also very much involved in naval activity during the war. An important development in 1942 was the expansion of the Canadian navy to include women. The Women's Royal Canadian Naval Service was created. By the end of the war, almost 7000 women had served as "Wrens." Their duties involved working as wireless operators, coders, drivers, and operational plotters.

The men and women of the R.C.N. and merchant ships faced many crises and fought many battles through the 2000-day Battle of the Atlantic. Their success in this long battle played a crucial role in turning the tide in the war.

Fig. 12 WRENs boarding a ship

GETTING THE FACTS

17. What was a convoy? Why had the convoy system become necessary?

18. What was the corvette's responsibility with a convoy?

USING YOUR KNOWLEDGE

19. Construct a chart with two columns labelled "advantages" and "disadvantages." List them for the corvette.

THE INVESTIGATIVE REPORTER

20. Find out what other ships sailed in the Canadian navy. Choose one and write an account of its size, equipment, crew and purpose.

21. Consult books that discuss women's roles in World War II and find more information on the Wrens. Present your findings in one of the following ways:
—A newspaper report
—A short story about the life of a woman in the Canadian Naval Service
—A poster showing various activities of women in the naval service

Spray from the North Atlantic would freeze on the corvette and several centimetres of ice would coat the ship. Sailors would have to risk their lives to chop it away to avoid the danger of the top-heavy vessel capsizing.

In July, 1941, the Canadian Women's Army Corps had been established. By war's end over 21 000 women had served including 2900 in posts overseas. In addition to training in the usual army discipline and routine, the women also developed skills in over two dozen different trades. As a result, they served in roles as varied as clerks and tailors, drivers and draftswomen, mechanics and welders.

The Royal Canadian Navy—The wartime record

SIZE OF NAVY 1939	SIZE AND ACHIEVEMENTS OF NAVY 1945

—13 ships
  —6 destroyers
  —5 minesweepers
  —2 training vessels
  —0 corvettes
	—*373 fighting ships

	—over 130 corvettes were built
	—100 000 men served in R.C.N.

—3000 men in Royal Canadian Navy
  —1800 full time permanent sailors and officers
  —1200 in reserves (fully trained but not on full time service)
	—almost 2000 sailors died

—no women in R.C.N.	—7100 women served in R.C.N.
	—R.C.N. ships convoyed over 43 000 ships carrying 235 000 000 tonnes of war supplies across the Atlantic
	—credited with sinking or helping to sink 29 enemy submarines as well as the sinking or capture of 42 surface vessels
	—31 Canadian warships were destroyed or sunk during the war

*The German U-boat fleet alone totalled 463 by March of 1945. This compares with 27 U-boats in 1939.

Canadians on the warfront—In the air

At the outbreak of war in 1939, the Canadian air force consisted of 3000 men and eight squadrons of aircraft. Only a few of the aircraft were combat-ready. By the end of the war Canada had the fourth largest Allied air force consisting of a quarter of a million men and women and 88 squadrons.

Not only did Canada contribute to the air war through its air force, but also through the British Commonwealth Air Training Plan. Canada became a school for pilots and air crews from many countries. By the end of World War II the massive training programme produced 50 000 pilots and 80 000 other air crew.

Beginning in July of 1941, Canadian women began to play a major role in the success of the air war. The Canadian Woman's Auxiliary Air Force, later renamed the R.C.A.F. (Woman's Division) was established. By war's end, 17 000 women had served.

Beginning in the fall of 1944 the Japanese sent bomb-laden balloons across the Pacific Ocean. Carried by the prevailing winds, the Japanese hoped they would land in Canada and the U.S.A., causing forest fires and panic among citizens when they exploded. Of the 9000 launched, only 80 landed in Canada, half of them in British Columbia. One got as far as Manitoba. No Canadians were ever injured by the balloon bombs although 5 American children and a woman were killed in Oregon. The Japanese gave up the "Balloon bomb" war in the spring of 1945.

22. What was the British Commonwealth Air Training Plan?

23. Assume you are a 19-year-old woman during World War II. Why might you want to join the R.C.A.F. and be trained as an airplane engine mechanic?

Some of Canada's air war heroes

Squadron Leader Leonard *Birchall*, while on patrol over the Indian Ocean in March 1942, spotted a huge Japanese fleet on its way to a surprise attack on Ceylon. After sending a warning he was shot down and spent the rest of the war as a P.O.W. in Japan.

Pilot Officer Andy *Mynarski* was on a mission over France when his plane was hit by enemy fire. As the flaming aircraft plunged, Mynarski was about to bail out when he spotted a crewmate trapped in the wreckage. Ignoring his own safety, Mynarski tried to free his crewmate. Unsuccessful, Mynarski bailed out but died of burns received during his rescue effort. Miraculously the crewmate survived to tell the story of Mynarski's sacrifice.

Fig. 13 Buzz Beurling

Fighter "ace" Buzz *Beurling* was known for his skill for sighting and shooting down enemy planes. By the end of the war Beurling had shot down at least thirty-one enemy planes. Beurling survived World War II, but was killed in 1948 in a plane crash while serving in the Israeli Air Force.

Fig. 14 This plane is a bomber, the Lancaster. The best known fighter planes were the Spitfire, the Hurricane and the Mosquito. What do you think the main differences between a bomber and a fighter would be?

Canadians who served in the Armed Forces—The numbers

	MEN	WOMEN	TOTAL	NUMBER WOUNDED OR INJURED	NUMBER KILLED
The Canadian Army	708 535	21 624	730 159	52 679	22 917
*1· The Royal Canadian Air Force	232 632	17 030	249 662	1 416	17 101
The Royal Canadian Navy	98 474	6 781	105 255	319	2 024
Totals	1 039 641	*2· 45 435	1 085 076	54 414	42 042

*1· Among those who served overseas as aircrew, there were actually more Canadians in Britain's R.A.F. than in Canada's R.C.A.F. They are not included in the numbers here.

*2· At least another 4518 women served in the medical services, mostly as nursing sisters.

9045 Canadian servicemen were prisoners of war (POW's) during the war.

Based on Arms, Men and Governments: The War Policies of Canada, 1939-1945 by C.P. Stacey.

Fig. 15 Royal Canadian Navy/Air Force operations room, St. John's, Newfoundland, 1943. What sort of work would be carried out here?

The Holocaust: How should Canada and other nations react?

The Holocaust is a term currently used to describe the most tragic event in a long history of prejudice against Jews (anti-semitism) in Europe. After the National Socialist Party (Nazi) became the government of Germany, an official government policy of persecution of all people who were not Aryan—or pure caucasian of non-Jewish descent—was initiated. This policy affected blacks, gypsies, the mentally retarded, and almost anyone the Nazi Party chose to identify as enemies of the State of Germany. By far the largest group to suffer because of the Nazi policy was the Jewish population. In 1933, the official policy restricted citizens from purchasing goods from Jewish stores. By 1935 the anti-Jewish campaign grew to include exclusion from public office, restrictions on freedom of movement, and removal of voting rights and citizenship. Jews were encouraged to leave Germany, but were not allowed to take any of their material possessions.

Other than a few official protests of the German action against the Jews, the nations of the world, including Canada, took no major action to prevent the persecution or assist the persecuted. Most were even unwilling to accept those Jews who escaped from Germany before the war broke out. In one particular incident in 1939, 930 Jews fled Germany on a ship called the *St. Louis*. Both Canada and the United States refused entry to the Jewish immigrants. Eventually the *St. Louis* was accepted by the Netherlands. However, when the Nazis overran the Netherlands in 1940, the passengers of the *St. Louis* were again under the Nazi regime and most died in the concentration camps.

After the beginning of World War II, the Nazi Party expanded the anti-Jewish campaign and deported Jews from Germany to the conquered territories. Ultimately the Nazi Party began a systematic attempt to execute all the Jews in the conquered countries of Europe. Execution methods included mass shootings, gassing and medical experiments that eventually caused death. Between 1942 and 1945 millions of European Jews were transported to and put to death in camps such as Auschwitz, Belsen and Buchenwald. In all, over six million Jews died as a result of the Nazi persecution.

The Nazi treatment of minorities and other enemies meant many other groups suffered as well. It is estimated that close to nine million Soviet, Polish, and other prisoners of war, civilians, political prisoners and gypsies were systematically murdered by the Nazi regime. Many thousands more who escaped with their lives, were left emotionally and physically scarred for life.

The startling discovery of the death camps towards the end of the war shocked the world. After the war, an international court set up in Nuremberg, Germany, convicted many Nazi leaders with crimes against humanity. Many other Nazis fled to South America, the United States and Canada before being charged.

How should Canada and the other nations of the world have reacted to the knowledge of the persecution of the Jews in Germany? Should Canada have accepted the people of the *St. Louis*? What action should Canada and the other nations of the world have taken to prevent the Holocaust from happening? Today people continue to feel revulsion and horror over the Holocaust and they are still asking questions about where international responsibility lies.

THE INVESTIGATIVE REPORTER

24. One of the most famous stories of courage to come from the Holocaust is *The Diary of Anne Frank*. You may wish to read this fascinating story. Consult your local or school library for other material about the Holocaust.

On the homefront
the war meant . . .

Loyal citizens do not hoard

RATIONED

SUGAR ½ lb. a week PER PERSON

TEA ½ of the usual PURCHASE

COFFEE ¾ of the USUAL PURCHASE

Foodstuffs that were rationed included meat, butter, sugar, coffee and tea. Food rationing began in 1942.

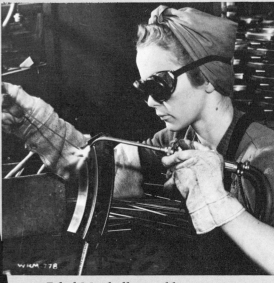

Ethel Mitchell is welding a gun magazine in a munitions factory. Why is a woman doing this job? What do you think Ethel's attitude towards her work would be? Why?

These Scouts collected paper for the war effort.

In 1939, 689 000 women were employed in industry. In 1945 the number was 1 015 000.

Ration books were delivered by postal service.

CARELESS TALK BRINGS TRAGEDY IN WARTIME

1 THE SOLDIER TOLD HIS SWEETHEART (ALL ABOUT THE TROOP TRAIN)

2 THE SWEETHEART TOLD HER FATHER

3 THE FATHER TALKED AT HIS CLUB (WHERE A SPY OVERHEARD)

4 THE SPY INSTRUCTED THE SABOTEUR

5 THE SABOTEUR WRECKED THE TRAIN

Canada's Production Record 1939-1945	
Aircraft	16 000
Rifles	900 000
Military vehicles	815 000
Merchant ships	410
Landing craft	3 302
Navy tugs	254
Tanks	6 500
Escort ships	487
Machine guns	244 000

Value of Canadian Exports	
1939-	$ 936 000 000
1942-	2 385 000 000
1945-	3 267 000 000

The manufacture of some products was either stopped or greatly reduced. These included:
—radios
—aluminum
—refrigerators and other appliances
—record players
—silk stockings
—cars and parts

Approximately 60% of all production in Canada in the six war years was for war uses.

25. Imagine you are a teenager living in Canada during the war. Write a letter to a friend describing how the war has changed the way you and your family live.

26. What results would food rationing have for the planning of family meals?

27. Although some people tried to find ways to "beat" the rationing system, almost all Canadians accepted rationing with little protest. Why?

Not all Canadians supported the war

Now that you have reached this point in the chapter, you might think that there was total support for the war effort from Canadians. This was not the case. Large numbers of Canadians were not willing to serve in the war effort. Different attitudes to involvement in the war can be better understood by looking at the conscription issue.

You will recall that in World War I, the attempt to use conscription to provide soldiers for the armies had caused a serious split between anglophone and francophone Canadians. Prime Minister Mackenzie King was desperately anxious to avoid a similar situation. Thus, even before the war had begun, and repeatedly during its early years, King promised that he would not conscript troops for service overseas.

At the beginning of the war there was no concern about the number of troops because young men volunteered in large numbers. To free these volunteers for overseas service, part of the National Resources Mobilization Act, passed in June of 1940, gave the government the power to conscript men for military service for home defense. Tens of thousands of so-called N.R.M.A. men were subsequently conscripted under this Act.

There were many groups of Canadians—both English and French-speaking—who did not favour conscription. Many French-Canadians still held to their long-time opposition to Canadian involvement in European wars. This attitude did not change much, even after Hitler's conquest of France in June of 1940. An important factor in the French-Canadian attitude was the lack of concern in the armed forces for the French language. Despite the lesson of World War I, the army had only a few French-speaking regiments. The navy had no francophone units and the air force made little

The move to conscription did not result in a repeat of the major riots of 1917. There were, however, isolated riots and numerous desertions among the N.R.M.A. men. Union Jacks were burned in at least two Quebec towns. Protesting marchers in Montreal and Quebec City broke windows in several buildings and the Quebec provincial government passed a motion of censure against the federal government. The general relations between anglophone and francophone Canadians had been further aggravated.

160

One community's service in World War II—A case study of the Six Nations Reserve

The people in many communities across Canada made extraordinary contributions to Canada's role in World War II. The Six Nations and neighbouring New Credit Indian Reserves in southern Ontario demonstrated the kind of commitment, dedication and sacrifice that could have been found in many parts of Canada. At least 233 men and women from the Six Nations Reservation served in either the Canadian or American armed forces. Of those from the Six Nations and New Credit reserves who served in the Canadian forces, 22 were killed.

There were many stories of dedicated service from everyone in this Native peoples community. Among them were:

—3 soldiers were killed and a brother of one taken prisoner during the attack on Dieppe.
—Sergeant Leslie Capton of the R.C.A.F., a plowing champion before the war, was killed while on an operation over Germany in 1942. When word of his death reached home, his sister, Delma, immediately enlisted. She served for four years in the R.C.A.F.
—An Overseas Committee was formed in the spring of 1942. It included representatives from clubs and organizations on the reserve. It co-ordinated fund-raising to help their soldiers overseas. By Christmas, groups such as the Women's Institute and school classes had raised over $300 to send Christmas gift packages overseas.
—In January, 1942, the *Pine Tree Chief*, the newspaper of the Six Nations Young People's Society, published an editorial very strongly supporting compulsory selective service, including military service, to increase Canada's war effort.
—The women of the Six Nations Red Cross spent hundreds of hours sewing and knitting various goods for sale. Proceeds were handed over to the Canadian Red Cross Society.
—Lance Corporal Lee Sloat was awarded the Military Medal for gallantry. In February, 1945, several wounded men in his company were cut off from the rest while under heavy German fire. Ignoring his own safety, he made 3 trips across over 300 metres to rescue those badly wounded men.
—Frequent salvage drives by the children of the schools collected iron, rubber, paper, bottles, and bones for contribution to the war effort.

Canada's Native people could take considerable pride in their contribution to World War II. Including those from the Six Nations and New Credit Reserves, over 3000 served in the Canadian army and many others in the air force and navy. Among them was Canada's most decorated soldier of World War II, Tommy Prince. A total of 213 Native people were killed serving in the army, while 93 others were wounded; 72 Native women also served in Canada's armed forces.

Resources from Woodland Indian Cultural Educational Centre, Brantford, Ont.

Fig. 16 To boost recruitment, the Canadian army reminded the public of both the heroism and the devastation of the Royal Rifles of Canada in Hong Kong. Almost 400 soldiers had died and almost 500 were wounded in savage fighting against the Japanese at the start of the war. How might you have reacted to such a poster during the war?

The men conscripted under the N.R.M.A. came to be nicknamed Zombies by some Canadians. The N.R.M.A. men faced harsh criticism from other Canadians—these Canadians felt N.R.M.A. lacked patriotism.

provision for French-speaking Canadians. Almost all of the training manuals and instruction for the armed forces were in English. It was not an atmosphere to encourage large numbers of French volunteers to sign up for service.

By mid-1941, the Canadian armed forces had been expanded to such a large size that the generals became concerned about keeping up the numbers of persons in uniform and available for duty on the warfront. As well, some Canadians—especially English-speaking Canadians—felt that those soldiers conscripted for home defense should be sent overseas. These issues put pressure on Prime Minister King to change his position on conscription.

Still not anxious to change his policy, King conducted a national plebiscite. King asked the people of Canada whether his government should be released from its commitment not to send conscripted soldiers overseas. The results of the plebiscite were not surprising. Across the country 64 percent voted "Yes" and 36 percent voted "No." However, in Quebec, 72 percent of the population voted "No," while in the rest of Canada, 77 percent voted "Yes."

In the face of francophone suspicions and anger, King tried to indicate that he did not intend to adopt conscription immediately. Trying to keep both anglophones and francophones happy, he only added to the confusion by stating that his policy was "not necessarily conscription, but conscription if necessary."

By the end of 1944, King was forced to act on the conscription issue. After a long Cabinet crisis and the resignation of a key Quebec Cabinet minister, King finally agreed to send 16 000 conscripts to Europe. They were to be taken from the N.R.M.A. men. King preferred to do this rather than impose a total nation-wide conscription. Conscription resulted in more Canadian troops being sent to serve in the war—and the cost of conscription was high. Canada's national unity was dangerously threatened.

Fig. 17 Anti-conscription speech, Montreal, 1939

28. Imagine you are each of the following people. Explain, in no more than three sentences for each, your feelings on conscription for overseas service.

    a) Prime Minister Mackenzie King
    b) a francophone parent of a son eligible for conscription
    c) an anglophone parent of a son serving overseas
    d) a francophone Cabinet minister
    e) a Canadian soldier attempting to cross northern Europe after D-Day

Fig. 18 These pictures show the extent to which some towns in Europe were damaged in the fighting. What do you think life was like for civilians in Europe during and after the war?

A democracy at war—How much freedom should be surrendered?

One of the most difficult questions for a democracy—such as exists in Canada—during a wartime emergency is: To what extent can the government take away the rights of the country's citizens?

At different times during World War II, the Canadian government had the power to:

—ration the production and sale of consumer goods and food, and limit the amount each person could obtain
—prevent a worker from changing jobs
—remove workers from "non-essential" work to work in "essential" industries
—fix the prices of any product
—draft men into the army
—control rents
—censor news and information
—conduct searches of private property without a search warrant

A question of human rights

By far the most serious and shocking case of the violation of human rights involved the Japanese-Canadians. Most of the Japanese-Canadians lived in British Columbia. Thousands of them were rounded up and shipped to internment camps in the Rocky Mountains. Their property was taken and sold by the government. Families were split and left penniless. Some were shipped east to work in factories. Using books from your library, read an account of the treatment of Japanese-Canadians during World War II. Try to understand what happened in the context of the strong emotions of people, and the emergency powers exercised by the government during the war crisis.

USING YOUR KNOWLEDGE

29. Select any three of the listed powers exercised by the Canadian government during World War II. For each explain:
   a) how it takes away a normal right of citizens
   b) why this particular power was believed necessary during the war

THINKING IT THROUGH

30. Does a war emergency justify giving up basic rights and freedoms? Why or why not?

THE INVESTIGATIVE REPORTER

31. Find out what most Canadians thought about the government's action at the time.

THINKING IT THROUGH

32. How do you react to the idea of the internment of the Japanese-Canadians. Why?

33. Japanese-Americans were also interned during World War II. In 1979 the American government established a commission to investigate making some form of financial restitution. Do you think something similar should be done in Canada? Why or why not?

THE INVESTIGATIVE REPORTER

34. In 1755 the Acadians were removed from Nova Scotia and sent to other English colonies. Find out more about the story and note similarities and differences between their experiences and that of the Japanese-Canadians.

Fig. 19 A Japanese-Canadian family waits to be taken to a camp in the interior of British Columbia.

Although their property was not confiscated and sold, many Italian-Canadians and German-Canadians were also interned during the war. Some city and town governments refused jobs and social assistance to those who were not interned. In fact, the Alberta government passed a law preventing the sale of land to what they considered to be enemy aliens. Italian and German businesses were vandalized in some cities.

Conclusion:

The success of Operation Overlord, the triumphs of the Italian campaign and the victories on the eastern front reached their climax in 1945. In April of that year, Hitler committed suicide. In May, the Germans officially surrendered. The dropping of the atomic bomb on Japan in August led to the final surrender. The world was left to pick up the pieces from the emotional and physical destruction of war.

We remember World War II because it was such a terrible experience for so many people, not only in Canada but throughout the world. It is often easy, when studying the war from the distance of time, to overlook its horrors while enjoying its triumphs. A Canadian general who was badly wounded at Dieppe, reminds us of that other point of view. He said, "In war there are no winners. Wars have produced nothing but misery. I hate war."

World War II developed Canadian patriotism and showed Canada to be influential in world affairs. It also encouraged growth of the economy.

USING YOUR KNOWLEDGE

35. Look back through this chapter. Find examples of ways in which World War II changed economic and social life in Canada.

THINKING IT THROUGH

36. The Allies obviously won World War II. How could the Canadian general who contributed to that victory say that there were "no winners"?

7 Open doors (1945-1959): Canada and the North American way

Everything ahead is going to be wonderful

A Canadian soldier remembers his feelings on that day, in the fall of 1945, when he arrived home after World War II. Following many hours of air travel from Europe and a streetcar ride in his own city, he was within walking distance of his home. Suddenly he thought of his dog, Jim, which he had not seen for nearly three years. The soldier let out the yell he had always used to call his dog:

> . . . in about three seconds this brown streak comes racing out of the yard and heads for me. . . . (W)hen old Jim is about ten yards from me he takes off into the air. He just takes off, and "whomp", he hits me dead centre in the chest. I drop the (duffel) bag and nearly fall back and he's licking my face and whimpering and I'm ruffing his neck like I used to, and I think I'm crying a little.
>
> Now you've got to picture it. There's this beautiful day in October, warm and soft, and I'm coming home, back from the wars, in a manner of speaking, and I'm walking down the middle of the road with my duffel bag on my shoulder and on my chest, my arm wrapped around my little dog Jim, my wonderful little friend Jim, and I feel like a conquering army.
>
> I know nothing can go wrong. It's a new world, a new life, everything bad is behind and everything ahead is going to be wonderful.

> From *Six War Years, 1939-1945: Memories of Canadians at Home and Abroad* by Barry Broadfoot.

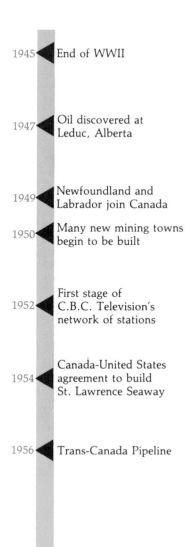

1945 — End of WWII

1947 — Oil discovered at Leduc, Alberta

1949 — Newfoundland and Labrador join Canada

1950 — Many new mining towns begin to be built

1952 — First stage of C.B.C. Television's network of stations

1954 — Canada-United States agreement to build St. Lawrence Seaway

1956 — Trans-Canada Pipeline

1960 — Trans-Canada Airlines begins jet service

Chapter overview

In the years after 1945, Canadians, like the soldier in the chapter opening, expected that "everything ahead was going to be wonderful." They had struggled through the Depression and the Second World War. Both "old" and "new" Canadians looked forward to a bright future. A special population of "new" Canadians was the people of Newfoundland and Labrador. Newfoundland and Labrador became a Canadian province in 1949.

The word "new" became one of the more commonly used ones in the Canadian vocabulary. New developments in mining, pulp and paper, agriculture, hydroelectric power and manufacturing brought new levels of prosperity to Canada. Major transportation projects were underway. Towns and cities were expanding and more and more Canadians were living in "suburbia." More people were making more money and spending it as never before. Many of the things they were buying were advertised on the new mass medium, television.

In the "Fabulous Fifties" American influence was growing everywhere. Most movies came from the United States. So did many of the books, phonograph records, clothing styles, fads and other products and ideas which Canadians consumed. Then there was American investment in, and often ownership of, Canadian companies and resources. The inflow of American money and ideas was a major reason for the boom in the Canadian economy. Canada in the 1950s was like a house with open doors. People, money and new lifestyles came in. If the "Canadian identity" was going out the door at the same time, the number who worried was small.

Signposts

Leaving the war behind ▷

FEATURE: The war brides ▷

Newfoundland and Labrador joins Canada ▷

Open doors: The way to the good life ▷

The American invasion ▷

FEATURE: Television: Window on the world ▷

Canadian identity ▷

Key words

veteran
referendum
social security

economic growth
resources
Americanization

fad
identity

Leaving the war behind

Of all the people in the world facing the challenge of switching from war to peacetime after 1945, Canadians were among the luckiest. Their country had been spared direct attack by heavy guns and bombers. Their factories and farms had been geared up to produce materials for war. With the return to peace, Canadians were able to change to the production of consumer goods for buyers at home and overseas.

Fig. 1 Peace celebrations in Ottawa, August, 1945

Canada escaped the kind of depression that followed World War I. The Canadian government continued its wartime direction of the economy until the changeover to peacetime had been accomplished. Former industrial nations, such as Germany and Japan, had been badly crippled by the war. As long as they remained this way, Canada would enjoy an unusual demand for its products, manufactures, as well as natural resources.

The boom continued through the 1950s. The Canadian economy experienced growth as never before. It was true that some regions of the country, such as the Maritimes, lagged behind the others. Yet most Canadians believed they lived in one of the "best of all possible worlds."

Old and new Canadians

With the end of World War II in 1945, Canada's doors were open to its veterans, Canadians of the army, navy and air force who were returning home. These "old" Canadians were given money payments and other benefits, such as the opportunity to attend university. Because they had fought in the war on Canada's behalf, the Canadian government wanted to help them make the change from war to peacetime living.

Fig. 2 Many veterans attended university or learned a new trade. The government paid their fees and living allowances, and also helped with salaries for trainees and loans for buying a house.

Canada's doors were also open to two groups of "new" Canadians. One was the "war brides," British and European women who had married Canadian servicemen and who came to join their husbands. The other was the Displaced Persons—"D.P.s"—the thousands of immigrants fleeing Europe in search of a new life in Canada.

The Displaced Persons filled a need for people power. During the 1930s, when jobs were scarce, the Canadian government blocked the entry of immigrants. Now, in a time of full employment, immigrants were welcome.

As a result of the inflow of "old" and "new" Canadians, Canada experienced a sharp increase in population. Correspondingly, there were numerous marriages and a "baby boom"—that is, a large increase in the number of babies born.

When they first came to Canada, immigrants were often forced to take less desirable jobs—that is, the jobs that Canadians did not desire. It is unfortunate that immigrants were exploited in this way, but through their own hard work and determination many immigrants have become leading citizens.

Fig. 3 Immigrant Arrivals, 1913-1977

YEAR	ARRIVALS	YEAR	ARRIVALS	YEAR	ARRIVALS	YEAR	ARRIVALS	YEAR	ARRIVALS
1913	400 870	1926	135 982	1939	16 994	1952	164 498	1965	146 758
1914	150 484	1927	158 886	1940	11 324	1953	168 868	1966	194 743
1915	36 665	1928	166 783	1941	9 329	1954	154 227	1967	222 876
1916	55 714	1929	164 993	1942	7 576	1955	109 946	1968	183 974
1917	72 910	1930	104 806	1943	8 504	1956	164 857	1969	161 531
1918	41 845	1931	27 530	1944	12 801	1957	282 164	1970	147 713
1919	107 698	1932	20 591	1945	22 722	1958	124 851	1971	121 900
1920	138 824	1933	14 382	1946	71 719	1959	106 928	1972	122 006
1921	91 728	1934	12 476	1947	64 127	1960	104 111	1973	184 200
1922	64 224	1935	11 277	1948	125 414	1961	71 689	1974	218 465
1923	133 729	1936	11 643	1949	95 217	1962	74 586	1975	187 881
1924	124 164	1937	15 101	1950	73 912	1963	93 151	1976	149 429
1925	84 907	1938	17 244	1951	194 391	1964	112 606	1977	114 914

Dept. of Employment and Immigration Statistic

The peak year for immigrants to Canada was 1913. The sharp rise in 1957 is accounted for by upheavals in Europe.
From *The 1981 Corpus Almanac of Canada Vol II* edited by Margot Fawcett.

GETTING THE FACTS

1. Explain in a paragraph why Canada did not suffer a major depression following World War II.

2. In a sentence or two for each, explain the following: a) veterans, b) war brides, c) Displaced Persons, d) baby boom.

USING YOUR KNOWLEDGE

3. Look at the chart in Figure 3. Compare the figures for the years

1951-1956 with any five-year period before and after. Suggest reasons why so many new Canadians arrived during this period.

4. Imagine you are a Displaced Person who is travelling to Canada in 1950. Write a conversation you might have on the trip with a returning Canadian veteran. You may want to include the following topics in your discussion: conditions in Europe during the war; hopes for the future in Canada; fears about adjusting to Canadian life.

Social security

Social security [seh-KYOOR-ih-tee] is a system of government help for the citizens of a country. Some people cannot provide themselves with basic necessities such as food and shelter. Unemployment insurance, for example, provides a certain amount of money for a person temporarily out of work. Other income from the government, such as family allowances and old age pensions, is available regardless of need. But an underlying idea of social security is improved living standards for people who cannot manage entirely on their own.

Since World War II, social security has become a big item in government spending. Before that time, it was thought of as "welfare" or "handouts," necessary only for small numbers of people in extreme need. The Great Depression of the 1930s changed that attitude. Great numbers of Canadians were reduced to poverty by conditions they could not control.

In 1940, the Canadian government had made the necessary arrangements with the provinces and passed the Unemployment Insurance Act. In 1946, the Liberals, led by Mackenzie King, were re-elected after promising voters more in the way of social security.

Fig. 4 Today, many people think of social security as a basic right. The federal government issues booklets like these to inform people of the benefits that are available.

The war brides

She was married during the war in her home city of London, England. As a volunteer at a reception for Canadian soldiers, she met her husband-to-be. When the war ended, her husband was sent home. Concerned with her baby's future as well as her own, she faced the choice of leaving home and country for Canada—a land about which she knew very little. For that matter, she knew little enough about her husband and what kind of a life to expect with him.

She was one of the "war brides." Nearly 50 000 of these women, mainly British, married Canadian servicemen during the Second World War.

Most of the war brides were willing to cross the ocean to join their husbands. The government of Canada was the first government in history prepared to help them do so. The Canadian Department of National Defense set up the Wives' Bureau to arrange their transportation to Canada. By January, 1947, 41 531 war brides and 19 737 children had made the ocean voyage.

The war brides' experiences were often heart-breaking:

It was August 1946 when I received my documents allowing me to leave Wales for Canada. At last, that very special envelope with my boat ticket and visa.

I well remember the look on my mother's face. And the heartbreak and excitement at the same time for me. I told my mother, "Don't worry, I'll be home in six months. I'll talk Alf into coming back to Wales with me."

We had to stay in London overnight, and I know a couple of war brides who went back home from the hostel. We were all so homesick that night in London and only the thoughts of seeing husbands and our new country kept the rest of us going.

When I got word to leave for Canada it was all very hush hush. I wasn't allowed to tell my family the name of the port of embarkation [departure] or the ship. My relatives all came to the station to say goodbyes to me and my one-year-old daughter. About a hundred war brides boarded the train along with soldier escorts and were locked in. As the train pulled out of Glasgow, one girl began singing "Bonnie Scotland I Adore Thee." That opened up the flood gates, and most of us cried until we were well out of the city.

From *The War Brides* by Joyce Hibbert.

THINKING IT THROUGH

5. a) Make a list of several problems and hardships that faced war brides who moved to Canada. Then make a list of the advantages they might enjoy.

b) How do you think the Canadians living in Canada at the time reacted to the coming of the war brides? Try to think of at least two different attitudes that people had toward these women.

Starting in 1945, family allowances ("baby bonuses") were paid out each month. In 1951, the old age pension plan was changed so that payments were made to all persons who had reached the age of 70 and had lived in Canada for 10 years. (Previously, since the 1920s, pensions were given only to those senior citizens who passed a "means test"—that is, proved that they were needy.)

By the end of the 1950s, social security was widely accepted as a right in Canada. In the years to follow, both federal and provincial governments would add to the system.

GETTING THE FACTS

6. Make a timeline, showing examples of social security for each of the following dates: 1927; 1940; 1944; 1951.

USING YOUR KNOWLEDGE

7. Compare and contrast attitudes to social security before and after the Depression.

THINKING IT THROUGH

8. Debate the question: "Is there a danger that social security can make people too dependent on government for their needs?"

Newfoundland and Labrador joins Canada

In 1949, Newfoundland and Labrador, a colony of Britain, became the tenth province of Canada. For nearly 400 years Newfoundland and Labrador had a political life apart from the mainland. Newfoundland and Labrador joined Confederation only after a hard fight. Joseph "Joey" Smallwood put his enormous energy and determined leadership into the struggle for union.

After World War II, the people of Newfoundland and Labrador were at a crossroads in their history. For the time being, they were governed by a commission of British civil servants. This arrangement dated from 1934, when Newfoundland and Labrador was close to financial disaster. By 1945-1946 the economy was considerably recovered since money had flowed into Newfoundland and Labrador during the war. The commission form of government could have continued in Newfoundland and Labrador. But other possible futures faced the colony. Two possibilities were a return to the status of a self-governing British colony as prior to 1934, or union with Canada.

Fig. 5 Lieutenant Governor Sir Albert Walsh about to address the House of Assembly on the day Newfoundland joined Canada

In 1946 the British government set up the election of a National Convention by Newfoundlanders. The National Convention's job was to study and debate the situation. Then it was to recommend the choices of government to be placed before the people of Newfoundland and Labrador in a **referendum** [rehf-er-EHN-duhm].

Two main groups formed. The anti-Confederates were opposed to joining Canada. They were led by important business people such as Chesley Crosbie and Peter Cashin, and many newspaper editors. On the opposite side were the pro-Confederates, in favour of union with Canada. Chief spokespersons were "Joey" Smallwood and the lawyer-businessman, Gordon Bradley.

In the early months of the struggle, the anti-Confederates had a natural advantage—union with Canada had been turned down before. Invited to join the original Confederation in the 1860s, Newfoundland and Labrador replied, "Not interested." Now, some 75 years later, the people of Newfoundland and Labrador were as proud and independent as ever. As a part of Canada, Newfoundland and Labrador would have less control over its own affairs than it

Fig. 6 Joseph Smallwood

From *Smallwood: The Unlikely Revolutionary* by Richard Gwyn.

would as a self-governing colony. As for the possible financial advantages of Confederation—perhaps a self-governing Newfoundland and Labrador would be able to make profitable trade agreements on its own with the United States.

Smallwood and his fellow pro-Confederates launched an energetic campaign to turn public opinion around. In his speeches, Smallwood talked about the charm of Newfoundland and Labrador:

> We all love this land. It has a charm, it warms our hearts . . . a magic, a mystical tug on our emotions that never dies. With all her faults we love her.

But he urged the people to face the facts:

> [Compared to Canada we] are fifty, in some things one hundred, years behind the times. We live more poorly, more shabbily, more meanly. Our life is more a struggle. . . .

> We might manage, precariously, to maintain independent national status. We can resolutely [firmly] decide to be poor but proud. . . .

> Our danger, so it seems to me, is that of nursing delusions of grandeur [living in a dream world]. We are not a nation. We are a medium-sized municipality. There was a time indeed when tiny states lived gloriously. That time is now ancient European history. We are trying to live in the mid-twentieth century, post-Hitler New World.

> We can, of course, persist in isolation, a dot on the shore of North America. Reminded continually by radio, visitors, and movies of the incredibly higher standards of living across the Gulf, we can shrug incredulously [not believing] or dupe ourselves into the hopeless belief that such things are not for us.

While Newfoundlanders debated their future, discussion began with the Canadian government. Prime Minister Mackenzie King was getting ready to retire after more than 20 years in office. He was persuaded that the joining of Newfoundland and Labrador with Canada would make him a kind of "Father of Confederation." The prime minister-to-be, Louis St. Laurent, strongly supported the union. By the late fall of 1947, Smallwood had an offer from Canada to tell the people of Newfoundland and Labrador about.

The pro-Confederates now had solid benefits with which to support their arguments. In addition to the expected increase in trade and business, the people of Newfoundland and Labrador could look forward to sharing in Canada's social security system; that is, family allowances, old age pensions and unemployment insurance.

Meetings between the pro-Confederates and the anti-

Confederates were often rowdy and almost violent. Disagreement between the two groups climaxed in not one referendum but two! The first, on June 3, 1948, resulted in the rejection of commission government—but not enough votes for a clear choice between Confederation and a separate Newfoundland and Labrador. The final decision came on July 22, 1948 when 52 percent voted for union with Canada.

The final terms of union were signed in Ottawa on December 11, 1948. "Joey" Smallwood was the first premier of Newfoundland and Labrador, Albert Walsh the first lieutenant-governor, and Gordon Bradley the first representative of the new province appointed to the Canadian Cabinet.

Minutes before midnight on March 31, 1949, Newfoundland and Labrador became the tenth province of Canada.

Fig. 7 Gordon Bradley

GETTING THE FACTS

9. Draw a timeline of the major steps that led to the union of Newfoundland and Labrador with Canada in 1949. Start your timeline at 1930 and be sure to include the different forms of government that Newfoundland and Labrador had throughout this period.

10. Examine Joey Smallwood's speech carefully and list the various reasons he gives in favour of the union of Newfoundland and Labrador with Canada. Then reread the section and list reasons that the anti-Confederates give against Confederation.

USING YOUR KNOWLEDGE

11. People with a certain point of view often use language that will persuade others to accept their views. Smallwood tries to convince Newfoundlanders to choose Confederation by painting a certain picture of Newfoundland and Labrador without Confederation.

   a) What picture does Smallwood present?

   b) List the words and phrases that Smallwood uses to create this picture.

   c) Do you think that Smallwood's speech would succeed in getting people to support Confederation. Give reasons for your answer.

Fig. 8 Why would Canada welcome union with Newfoundland and Labrador?

THINKING IT THROUGH

12. The debate between the anti-Confederates and the Confederates was a clash between two different sets of values or two contrasting views about what is important in life. Do you agree or disagree with this statement? Explain why.

Open doors: The way to the good life

The 1950s began as a decade of hope. Canada had struggled through the Great Depression and endured the Second World War. Now Canadians believed that the "good life" was just around the corner. Fifty years before, it had been predicted that the 1900s would be "Canada's century." The prediction seemed about to come true.

How did the 1950s turn out? Did Canadians finally get to enjoy the "good life"? For Canadians, of course, as for others, the quality of life includes more than money and possessions. Yet ownership of labour-saving devices and luxuries is one indication of progress. Consider the following facts and figures:

Fig. 10 Appliances in Canadian homes

	1948-1949 WITH/WITHOUT	1953 WITH/WITHOUT	1960 WITH/WITHOUT
Washing Machines	2 333 000/1 006 000	———	3 880 000/524 000
Refrigerators	977 000/2 363 000	———	4 010 000/365 000
Radios	3 247 000/ 257 000	3 511 000/ 130 000	4 236 000/168 000
Televisions	———	373 000/3 268 000	3 550 000/854 000

(Note: the figures in reports of the Dominion of Statistics were not complete for every year)

GETTING THE FACTS

13. From the chart on the previous page, what can you observe about the following examples of economic growth in the 1950s: a) the availability of washing machines? b) refrigerators? c) radios? d) television sets?

THINKING IT THROUGH

14. Based on the figures in the table, do you think that the quality of life improved in Canada in the 1950s? Why or why not?

15. Ownership of labour-saving devices is just one element of the quality of life. Suggest three other pieces of information that would help you to evaluate the quality of life in Canada during the 1950s.

The reports published by the Dominion Bureau of Statistics between the years of 1948 and 1960 show some of the incredible changes which, in general, took place in the lives of Canadians. The contrasts in the numbers at the beginning and the end of the 1950s are very revealing. So are the differences in the items on which statistics were kept. For example, car radios were so common by 1960 that apparently there was no point in reporting on them. It was quite the opposite in 1949 (see Figure 10). In that year, also, the question about washing machines was whether or not Canadian homes had one. By 1960, attention had shifted to the type of washer—that is, if the washer was automatic or not.

If we can judge from the increase in the number of household appliances, the 1950s was a time when more Canadians than ever before earned and spent more money than ever before. The following tables show some examples.

The Dominion Bureau of Statistics is now known as Statistics Canada.

	WITH REFRIGERATORS	WITHOUT REFRIGERATORS	TOTAL HOUSEHOLDS
Prince Edward Island	2 000	19 000	21 000
Nova Scotia	24 000	128 000	152 000
New Brunswick	19 000	94 000	113 000
Quebec	223 000	614 000	837 000
Ontario	498 000	688 000	1 186 000
Manitoba	41 000	165 000	206 000
Saskatchewan	26 000	206 000	232 000
Alberta	44 000	198 000	242 000
British Columbia	100 000	250 000	350 000
Canada	977 000	2 362 000	3 339 000

Fig. 11 Estimated number of households with and without refrigerators, by province

For the Dominion as a whole, only 29 per cent of the households have mechanical refrigerators.

From *Household Equipment* (November, 1948), Dominion Bureau of Statistics.

Fig. 12 Estimated number of households with and without car radios, by province

	WITH CAR RADIO	WITHOUT CAR RADIO	TOTAL HOUSEHOLDS
Newfoundland	2 000	71 000	73 000
Prince Edward Island	1 000	20 000	21 000
Nova Scotia	9 000	151 000	160 000
New Brunswick	10 000	111 000	121 000
Quebec	68 000	750 000	848 000
Ontario	125 000	1 105 000	1 230 000
Manitoba	14 000	191 000	205 000
Saskatchewan	23 000	209 000	232 000
Alberta	22 000	232 000	254 000
British Columbia	27 000	333 000	360 000
Canada	301 000	3 203 000	3 504 000

From *Radios and Household Electrification* (October, 1949), Dominion Bureau of Statistics.

The tables also show that the different regions of Canada did not share equally in the prosperity.

USING YOUR KNOWLEDGE

16. Examine Figure 11 showing households with refrigerators in 1948. Which province had the lowest percentage? The highest?

17. In 1949, which province had the lowest percentage of car radios? The highest? Compare your answers for questions 16 and 17. What conclusions can you make about this comparison?

Fig. 13 In the fifties more families than ever before owned cars. Many modern roads were built, and as a result, people began moving to hundreds of new suburbs on the outskirts of Canada's cities.

18. a) Native people living on reserves were not included in the surveys. If they had been, would they have affected the results very much? If so, in what way? Use books in your school or local library to find information on Native people's quality of life on reserves and answer these questions.

b) Do you think the Native people on reserves should have been included in the survey? Give reasons to support your opinion.

Economic growth

What caused the prosperity of the 1950s? The following is a simplified explanation:

> Jobs were plentiful in those days. In fact, Canada had so many jobs to fill that immigrants were welcomed for the first time since the 1920s. Canada opened its doors to people. And the country was opening up in so many ways. For example, it was taking advantage of its rich natural resources. That's how Canada seemed likely to prosper—by 'harvesting' its oil, silver, copper and uranium from below the ground and its vast forests on the surface. Companies handling these products had many countries to sell to.
>
> Meanwhile, the primary industries created the need for major projects in the energy and transportation fields. Thus the mining of iron was important to Canada's steel industry. And industries were often responsible for the expansion of cities and the need for more services, like supermarkets, dry-cleaning, auto repair shops, clothing stores and so on.

Fig. 14 Immigrants arriving from Scotland

The petroleum (oil and gas) industry is often singled out as the key to economic growth in the 1950s. The change in Alberta—and, to a lesser extent, in Saskatchewan, British Columbia and Manitoba—was great. Suddenly western Canada had another source of wealth besides farming and ranching.

The Leduc oilfields, discovered near Edmonton, Alberta, in 1947, were the first of several to boom in the 1950s. They provided much needed supplies of oil and natural gas for Canadian use. But Alberta had more than Canada could use. The extra production was sold to the United States and other customers.

In other parts of Canada, natural resources had long been seen as the key to prosperity. In the Canadian Shield of northern Quebec, Ontario and Manitoba, minerals had been discovered early in the century. The mining of nickel, copper, zinc and gold had, by the 1930s, made towns like Sudbury and Flin Flon important to the

Fig. 15 Leduc oil fields, on the day No. 1 well "blew in"—February 13, 1947

181

Canadian economy. The Depression, however, slowed the growth of mining.

The 1950s was the time when the "harvest" of Canadian natural resources became really important. Several conditions were responsible for this development. There was little competition from overseas after the Second World War. Thus Canada expanded its manufacturing industries and its need for raw materials. So had the United States, Canada's most important customer. Improved methods of locating and removing minerals made mining more efficient. Money, especially American money, was available for investment as never before. The result was an increase in the number of jobs for Canadians, as well as in the number of products they could buy with their earnings.

Canada in the 1950s was one of the world's leading producers of raw materials. Every region of the country benefitted from new and expanded ventures. Mining in particular was expanding. Examples include copper mines and asbestos in British Columbia, potash in Saskatchewan, and the Thompson nickel mines in northern Manitoba. In mineral-rich northern Ontario, Elliot Lake was the site of uranium mining and Timmins was known for its deposits of zinc-silver-copper. Northern Quebec was a regular news item because of copper in the Rouyn-Noranda region and the spectacular iron deposits in the Ungava district. The lead-zinc mines at Bathurst, New Brunswick were important to the Atlantic provinces.

American investors had shown particular interest in certain industries, such as the extraction [ehk-STRAK-shuhn] of resources important to manufacturing, the production of automobiles, pulp and paper, the manufacture of electrical products and supplies. Canadians enjoyed the benefits of this American investment. Yet

Extraction is the process of separating a metal from ore.

Fig. 16 Uranium City, a completely new town in Saskatchewan, 1954. What are the uses of uranium?

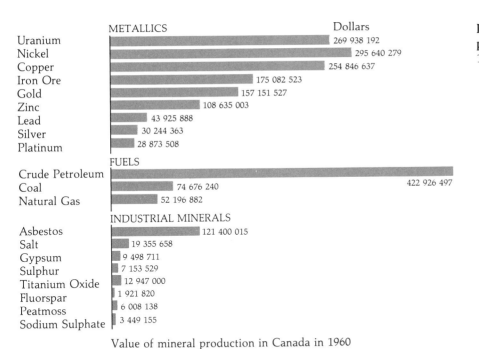

Fig. 17 Value of mineral
production in Canada in
1960

Value of mineral production in Canada in 1960

Fig. 18 Value of mineral
production in Canada by
provinces in 1960

PROVINCE OR TERRITORY	METALS	FUELS	INDUSTRIAL MINERALS	TOTAL FOR PROV. OR TERRITORY	PER CENT OF TOTAL
Newfoundland	78 925 679	—	7 711 444	86 637 123	3.5
P.E.I.	—	—	1 172 587	1 172 587	.02
Nova Scotia	102	44 981 257	20 472 172	65 453 531	2.6
New Brunswick	—	8 834 749	8 237 990	17 072 739	.28
Quebec	224 294 082	—	221 908 644	446 202 726	17.9
Ontario	817 803 023	9 724 055	155 577 334	983 104 412	39.4
Manitoba	29 904 851	10 690 384	18 107 462	58 702 697	2.4
Saskatchewan	84 187 425	112 950 194	14 955 606	212 093 225	8.9
Alberta	6 501	362 528 938	32 808 571	395 344 010	15.9
British Columbia	131 721 707	15 391 658	39 148 281	186 261 646	7.5
N.W. Territories and Yukon Territory	39 714 691	750 594	—	40 465 285	.6
Canada	1 406 558 061	565 851 829	520 100 091	2 492 509 981	100.0

From *Canada Year Book, 1962*, Statistics Canada.

some began to wonder about its drawbacks. The following item explains the mixed feelings among Canadians.

Investment in Canada

Investment means putting money into a business. For a business to grow, investment money—or capital—is essential. Investment can come from the people within a country. It can also come from outside.

Throughout Canada's history, growth of the economy has depended on foreign investment. Until World War I, money for business growth came to a large extent from Great Britain. From the 1920s on, United States' investors replaced those from Britain.

Basically, investment has two forms: portfolio [port-FOH-lee-oh] and direct. Both have been important to Canada. The difference between the two may not seem important. But portfolio investment means money in the form of loans and other debts that can be paid off. Direct investment, however, means ownership. And ownership is bound to mean control.

In the 1950s, only direct investment increased sharply in Canada. Canadians contributed some, but more came from foreign sources. The majority of foreign direct investment was American. Business people based in the United States had two ways of investing directly in Canada: (1) buying enough of a company's shares to control its operations; or (2) setting up a subsidiary [suhb-SIHD-ee-ahr-ee] or branch plant—a branch of the main United States plant fully owned by the parent company.

The benefits of foreign direct investment are many. Money flows in to increase economic growth, jobs, living standards and so on. New methods of production and new technology can lead to a greater number, variety and quality of products. Bigger, wealthier companies can take risks in developing resources and marketing products.

There are also many drawbacks to such investment. The goals of a foreign company may be good for the company or its home country—but not for the host country. A large foreign company may dominate an industry and even drive Canadian companies out of business. It may bring in values and ways of doing things that Canadians do not approve of. It may even lead to the influence of a foreign—e.g., American—government.

Canadians had good reason to wonder in the 1950s if the benefits of American investment outweighed the drawbacks. In the final analysis, was American investment bound to lead to United States' control of the Canadian economy and Americanization of the Canadian lifestyle?

19. In the West, particularly in Alberta, what was the most important natural resource in the 1950s? Explain how it helped raise the standard of living.

20. Make a chart showing major mining developments in the various regions of Canada in the 1950s. List them under the following headings: Atlantic Provinces, Quebec, Ontario, the Prairies, British Columbia, the North.

21. Explain the difference between "portfolio" and "direct" investment.

USING YOUR KNOWLEDGE

22. "The 1950s were years of great economic change in Canada." Reread the section on economic growth and find at least three facts which serve as evidence of the above statement.

23. For each of the actions below, list as many effects that the action had on Canada as possible. (You will find these effects in the section on economic growth.)
    i) The Leduc oilfields are discovered near Edmonton in 1947.
    ii) In the 1950s Americans invest heavily in Canada.

24. In which province or provinces would you expect, by 1960, to find
    a) towns and cities with high average incomes? Low average incomes?
    b) the most industrial pollution? The least?
    c) the best facilities for sports and other forms of recreation? the worst?
Suppose you were an immigrant arriving in Canada. In what province would you prefer to live? Why?

THINKING IT THROUGH

25. Imagine that you are an American business person whose company has developed a new fuel-efficient car.
    a) Write a conversation you have with a Canadian consumer.
    b) Write a paragraph summarizing the reaction of a Canadian car maker.
    c) Tell what you would say to a Canadian politician who has doubts about your setting up a "branch plant" in Canada.

26. Do you think it matters whether Canadian-based companies or foreign-based companies own (control) the larger part of a Canadian natural resource, such as petroleum or nickel? Why or why not?

27. Answer the following questions from the data provided in Figures 17 and 18.

a) For each of the three groups of minerals, tell which province was the leader in dollar value by 1960.

b) What mineral, other than petroleum, had the highest dollar value? What were the next three, in order of value?

c) What province led in total value of mineral production by 1960?

Major projects

Major projects, especially in transportation, went hand-in-hand with the expansion of the mining industry. The discovery of oil in Alberta led to the building of the trans-Canada pipeline. In one of the great national projects of the 1950s, pipelines were completed to carry crude oil and natural gas to markets both on the west coast and in eastern Canada and the United States. As a result, by the 1980s, petroleum was still one of the most important industries in Canada.

Railways were constructed, as well as new highways, to assist the opening of mines. Examples included the lines from the St. Lawrence River north into Quebec and Labrador, railways to Thompson and Lynn Lake in northern Manitoba, and routes from Edmonton, Alberta to the Great Slave Lake region.

A main transportation project of the 1950s was the St. Lawrence Seaway. Since the early 1900s, people in Canada and the United States had looked forward to the day when ocean-going ships could travel to the Lakehead, at Thunder Bay. In 1932, Canada

Fig. 19 The trans-mountain oil pipeline stretched 1150 km from Edmonton to Vancouver.

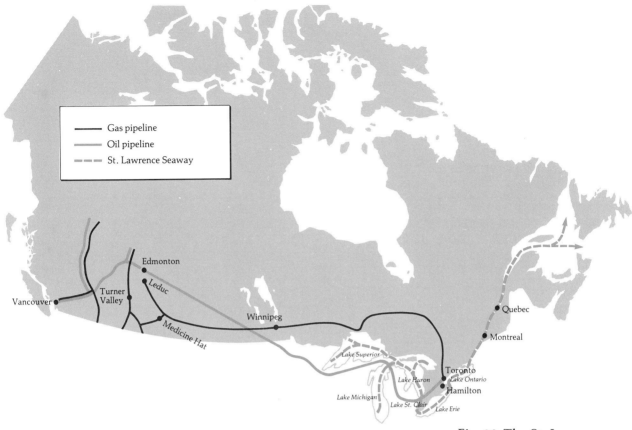

Fig. 20 The St. Lawrence Seaway and the trans-Canada pipeline were the major projects of the 1950s.

took the step of deepening the Welland Canal. However, discussions with the United States failed to produce an agreement for a cooperative building of the Seaway.

The Canadian government decided to go ahead on its own in 1951. The future was promising for the movement of minerals and grain to overseas markets. Hydroelectric power was another important pay-off. The United States was finally convinced to sign an agreement by 1954, and in 1959 the St. Lawrence Seaway was ready for operation.

The Seaway was only one of several important hydro projects. Others included the Columbia River in B.C., the Nelson River of Manitoba and the Churchill Falls of Labrador.

On land and in the air, other major projects were underway. The Trans-Canada Highway Act was signed in December, 1949. The plan was to build a highway, including new and improved sections, 8100 km long. Meanwhile, Trans-Canada Airlines (renamed Air Canada in 1964) and Canadian Pacific Airlines were expanding their services. Larger, faster and more comfortable planes were added. By 1960, these included ones powered by jet engines only.

The Trans-Canada Highway was officially opened in 1962.

28. List one important fact about each of the following: trans-Canada pipeline; new railways; St. Lawrence Seaway; Churchill Falls; air travel in Canada by 1960.

29. Find out about a major project of importance to your region of Canada in the past 10 years (for example, to do with power, transportation, a government facility, a business).

Collect information through reading and/or interviews. Prepare a report. Your teacher can assist you with decisions about the length of the report and other details.

The American invasion

Fig. 21 What effect do you think television had on family life?

Don Larsen was one of the best known names in Canada that September afternoon in 1956. It was World Series time, that time of the year when just about everybody is a baseball fan. The game went great for Don Larsen, pitching for the New York Yankees against the Brooklyn Dodgers. When he threw a third strike past pinch hitter Dale Mitchell, Larsen had the final out of his baseball masterpiece. He had pitched a no-hit, no-run, perfect game!

Not for 34 years—and never in a World Series—had a no-man-reach-base game been pitched. By supper time on that September day in 1956, millions of Americans knew it. So did Canadians from coast to coast. Baseball is the "great American game," but young Canadians play it as much as their short summers permit. Canadians follow the exploits of the teams in the "major leagues" with the same enthusiasm as do their American neighbours.

Baseball is only one of countless examples of United States' influence on Canadian life. Other sports, television programmes, clothing styles, comics, records, cars—you name it, the examples to imitate came from the United States. In the 1950s, the American lifestyle was the ideal.

In the 1950s, American influence invaded Canada as never before. It was a "peaceful invasion" and, by and large, it was welcomed. But it led to serious questions about how much American influence was too much American influence.

The age of the teenager

In the 1950s, Canada discovered "the teenager." Formerly, young people had been regarded as apprentice grownups, as adults-in-training. Now, youths were identified as a separate and distinct part

Television: Window on the world

Do you remember what it was like *not* to have a television set? Probably not; more than 90 percent of Canadians your age grew up in households where television was part of the furniture. But only recently has television been taken for granted. In fact, television was not generally available across Canada until the 1950s—and later in the less populated regions.

Developed in the 1930s, television was still in the experimental stage during the Depression. Then World War II postponed the making of many products not essential to fighting the war. Once the war was over, though, television sets were made and sold by the hundreds of thousands.

The spread of television was amazing. In the late 1940s, Canadian viewers along the United States border were already receiving broadcasts from stations in places like Buffalo, N.Y. In 1952, CBC-TV began broadcasting, with the first stations in Toronto and Montreal. By 1954, the chain had been extended to Halifax, Winnipeg and Vancouver. It included privately owned stations which carried some CBC programming. In 1958, the opening of microwave service from Vancouver to Sydney, Nova Scotia made the CBC-TV network the longest in the world.

Television caused great excitement. It brought images of the world into the homes of Canadians; it was like a "window on the world." We were entering a new era of information and entertainment.

Yet very early in the history of television, the debate over its advantages and disadvantages began. Critics of television feared it would cater to the lowest tastes of a mass audience. They said it would take people away from reading, conversation and other social activities. Instead of using their leisure time actively and creatively, people would waste their time in front of the "idiot box."

Defenders said that television would enrich us culturally, bring us the world's best in music and drama. It would heighten our interest in world events. It would enable educators to raise our levels of knowledge in a variety of ways. It would encourage international understanding and promote cooperation.

In Canada, the debate over television included a special question: Would television contribute to a Canadian identity—or would it open us up to Americanization?

GETTING THE FACTS

30. Television was invented in the 1930s. Why did it not become a popular part of Canadian life until the 1950s?

USING YOUR KNOWLEDGE

31. Under the headings "Possible Advantages" and "Possible Drawbacks," list at least three examples for each.

THINKING IT THROUGH

32. Do you prefer to watch television programmes made in Canada or in the United States? Give your reasons. Compare your answers with those of your classmates. You may have the chance to discuss the results in class.

Fig. 22 Elvis Presley, the "King of Rock 'n Roll" at Maple Leaf Gardens, Toronto

of society. Mothers and fathers had come through the Depression of the 1930s and World War II. In the 1950s, they had more money and more leisure; so did their "teenage" daughters and sons.

To mark their lifestyle as distinct from that of children or adults, teenagers adapted different kinds of clothing, hairstyles, slang and so on. For example, the "cool" male of 1953 sported a bogey cut—brush-like on top, long and slicked back on the sides—and drapes, which were slacks wide at the knee and curving sharply to a cuff barely large enough to pull over the foot.

Teenagers were a large and growing market, and manufacturers wasted no time catering to them. Besides clothing, there was a boom in comic books and magazines and popular recordings. Every year seemed to bring a new fad, like the hula hoop.

Where were all these products coming from? Mainly from the United States. Canadian teenagers welcomed the invasion of American products and American ways. Heroes, like the stars of "Rock 'n' Roll," invaded by way of "hit" records, LP's (long play records), radio, movies and television. Bill Haley and the Comets, Elvis Presley, Buddy Holly and the Crickets, Jan and Dean and many others became household names in Canada as well as in the United States.

Canadian identity

People have characteristics which distinguish them from others. When aware of these characteristics, people have identities, a sense of self. Without an identity, a person is likely to be confused, uncertain, lacking in confidence. How much of an identity did Canadians have in the 1950s?

Take the imaginary case of Nicole. If asked, "Who are you, Nicole?", she can give a fairly definite answer about herself as an individual. She may reply, "I'm Nicole Land and I'm 15 years old. I'm a Grade 10 student at Augustus E. Windheaver High. My favourite subject is computer repair and, in my spare time, I'm the page turner for the pianist in our school concert band. On weekends I do volunteer work for the food co-op my family belongs to. Of my friends, my favourites are Eva, Mario, John, Travis and Eleanor.

But Nicole is also a Canadian. If asked, "What does it mean to be a Canadian?", can she be as definite? Does she identify with the writings of Margaret Atwood, the music of the Canadian Brass, television coverage of the parliamentary debates, the Group of Seven, Hockey Night in Canada? Are Saskatoon pie, Arctic char, fiddlehead greens, tourtière and blueberry grunt at the top of her list of food preferences? Does she cross-country ski in the winter and take back-packing trips during the summer months?

If she has such a sense of being Canadian, she probably has a

Saskatoon pie—pie made of large, sweet purple berries called Saskatoons

Arctic char—a food and game fish

fiddlehead greens—young leaves of certain ferns

tourtière—a pork pie traditionally made in Quebec

blueberry grunt—a desert made of biscuit dough and blueberries

clearer idea of Canadian identity than most people in Canada had in the 1950s. Most Canadians of that time probably gave little thought to their Canadian, or national, identity. They were busy making a living, keeping up the payments on their refrigerators and cars and houses. If they were becoming absorbed by a lifestyle flowing across the border from the United States, they probably were not too worried—or aware.

Some Canadians, however, were concerned. The Canadian government appointed a commission to look into the situation. Headed by Vincent Massey, the commission presented a report in 1951.

The Massey Report on "National Development in the Arts, Letters and Sciences" recommended many ways to promote Canadian culture. One was to use the Canadian Broadcasting Corporation to encourage Canadian content in radio and television. Another led to the creation of the Canada Council, in 1957. Ever since, grants have been made to Canada's theatres, symphonies and other creative groups, as well as to individual artists.

Fig. 23 Vincent Massey was governor-general of Canada from 1952-59. He was a patron of education, arts and letters.

GETTING THE FACTS

33. In your own words, define the phrase "national identity."

THINKING IT THROUGH

34. In the 1980s many Canadians are worried about the Americanization of our country. In the 1950s, however, most people did not think it was a problem. Why do you think that the people of the 1950s were generally not as concerned as we are today?

Conclusion

In 1945, at the end of World War II, Canadians expected better times than they had known for many years. Fifteen years later, as the 1950s drew to a close, most Canadians were better off in many ways. Many people had better jobs, more money, more possessions.

Canada was known as one of the best countries in the world in which to live. It had "opened its doors" to new peoples, ideas, styles, technology and so on. The result had been a richer, more varied, way of life.

Yet there was a cloud on the horizon. That cloud was doubt about the future of a "Canadian identity." Was Canada on the way to being merely an imitation of the United States?

Such questions would be raised again and again in the years to come.

8 Canadians caught in a Cold War, 1945-1949

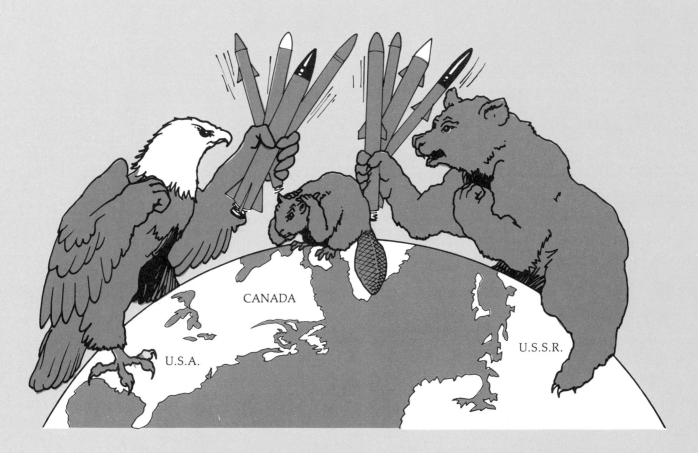

- Describe what each animal symbolizes and what is happening among them.

- This drawing illustrates the situation, especially as it affected Canada, in the world after World War II. What has happened, apparently, to the wartime alliance between the U.S.S.R. and the U.S.A.?

- What is significantly different about Canada's place in the world after World War II than before the war?

- The situation shown in the picture is referred to as a "Cold War." What do you think the expression Cold War means? How do you think this picture would have to be changed to make it a "hot war"?

The following is an imaginary account based on the letter exchange between two cousins, one living in Canada and one in Poland. They had been unable to write to each other during the war. With the war over, the two girls, now age fifteen, have started to write to each other again. Here are parts of their first letters to each other in the fall of 1945.

Dear Anna,

. . . I am so glad that the war is over and we can start writing to each other again. My dad is coming home from Europe with his army unit in the next few weeks. We sure are excited about the parades and welcoming celebrations that are planned. I hope that you have good news about your father and the rest of your family. My dad will be able to go back to his factory job because our government has a law which says that all veterans must be offered their old jobs back. We are looking forward to being able to buy the many clothes, bicycles and other things we have been unable to get during the war. Everyone has great hopes about the future. Our government leaders tell us that the United Nations, with all the countries cooperating, will prevent any more wars. Isn't that wonderful! Our future looks very good. . . .

Love, Your cousin,
Janice

Dear Janice,

. . . It is so nice to hear from you again. It is amazing that your letter actually arrived with the confusion in our country. I am so relieved that my father is alive and coming home. There are so many of my friends who have lost their fathers, brothers or uncles. Entire families have been killed by the shelling and bombing. Although everyone is happy the war is over, everyone is sad, too, about our ruined towns, homes, and countryside. It will be a long time before our factories and stores get going again. They will all have to be rebuilt. I don't know where my father will ever find work. Everything is either not available or in very short supply in the few stores that are open. Everyone is worried about the future. The Soviet soldiers are still in our country. We wonder when they are going to leave. We hear that there are going to be free elections so our parents can vote for their own government for Poland. But there are worries about this. Some rumours are around about what the Soviets might do about the elections. Many people are wondering if we will ever get our freedom.
I am jealous of your good luck in Canada. Everything sounds so different in your country than in mine. Even your view of the future of the world is different! . . .

Love, Your cousin,
Anna

- How do the views of the two cousins about the future of the world differ? How do you account for these differences? Do you think that Janice's view is *too* hopeful? Why or why not?

Chapter overview

The war of 1939-1945 was not even over when the Cold War began to take shape. The United States and the Soviet Union were partners or allies in the "hot" war. Before it ended, they were on opposite sides. Other countries began to choose sides, some with the Americans, some with the Soviets. Many people had pinned their hopes for a permanent peace on the new world organization—the United Nations. It was soon trapped in the post war conflict. The old-style alliances and rivalries emerged once more.

Like it or not, Canada was caught up in the resulting Cold War. Canada hoped to develop friendly relations with as many countries as possible. In this way, Canada believed it could play a role in preventing the development of new alliances and rivalries that could lead again to hostility and war among nations.

This ideal was not to happen as old patterns of friendship and hostility began to re-emerge. For example, because Canada is next door to the United States and because there were so many trade links between the two countries, close ties were bound to continue. In this chapter, you will see how events and issues in the Cold War brought Canadian-American relations closer than ever.

Signposts

From "hot war" to Cold War >

Soviet expansion in eastern Europe >

Capitalism and communism >

The United Nations—The world's hope for peace >

Canada's place in the post war world >

Igor Gouzenko: A spy ring in Canada! >

Canada and the Nuclear Age: The bomb and a "balance of terror" >

FEATURE: The Iron Curtain >

The Cold War terror continues—A tale of shattered expectations >

FEATURE: The Berlin Blockade and airlift >

NORAD: Defending North America >

Key words

Cold War	middle power	satellite	veto
power politics	arms race	guerilla war	bloc

From "hot war" to Cold War

Most countries had little to say about what was to happen with the post war world. Almost all the decisions were made by the three strongest countries to come out of World War II. These were the United States, the U.S.S.R. and Britain. Even while the war was being fought, they had begun to make some plans for after the war. Many of the most important decisions, however, were made at two major conferences in the closing months of the war. These conferences were held at Yalta in February and at Potsdam in July and August of 1945.

Yalta is a Soviet seaside resort town on the Crimean peninsula on the north shore of the Black Sea. Potsdam is a town in Germany close to Berlin.

Fig. 1 Churchill, Roosevelt and Stalin at the Yalta conference

The Yalta Conference

U.S.S.R.
Marshall Josef Stalin

U.S.A.
President Franklin Delano
Roosevelt

Britain
Prime Minister Winston
Churchill

The Potsdam Conference

U.S.S.R.
Marshall Josef Stalin

U.S.A.
President Harry S. Truman
(Replaced Roosevelt who died
in April 1945)

Britain
Prime Minister Clement
Attlee
(Replaced Churchill who lost
the July 1945 British election)

How might the outcome of
the Potsdam Conference
have been affected by the
change in leaders in Britain
and the U.S.A.?

Fig. 2 Harry S. Truman

At the conferences, each of the three countries was represented by its leader. The leaders soon discovered that, although they could be allies in war against common enemies, they could not agree on what to do when that common enemy was gone. Their differing views, aims and ambitions soon led to conflict among them. Their suspicions and disagreements helped to create the Cold War. The following information shows the suspicions and conflict that emerged at these conferences.

The following statements are not direct quotes of statements actually made by leaders at the conference but summarize the views of each country at the time.

Britain

> Britain suspects the U.S.S.R. has ambitions to gain more and more territory. We don't think Stalin is going to keep all the promises of cooperation he is making at these meetings.
>
> Our country is so badly drained by the war that we don't have the strength to keep the U.S.S.R. from taking what it wants.
>
> We must build up the power of war-ruined western Europe, especially Germany, to stop the Soviets from expanding westward.
>
> We must convince the Americans to agree with us and keep a strong presence in Europe, especially keep their armed forces here.
>
> Despite all this talk about international cooperation and the United Nations, we still believe the world is going to keep on operating according to power politics. The size and strength of military might is still going to be the big factor.

U.S.A.

> We are not nearly as suspicious as the British of the Soviets' motives. We think they will listen to reason.
>
> The U.S. believes we should get rid of military alliances. Through negotiations, we can re-establish the boundaries and governments of all the European countries. The United Nations will help us do this. It will preserve peace and prosperity.
>
> We are very optimistic about the cooperation of all the big powers, including the U.S.S.R., through the United Nations.

We are anxious to return to normal after the war; we want to bring our soldiers home and reduce the size of our armed forces.

We are the only country with the atomic bomb. This will certainly be an important factor in dealing with any possible trouble-makers.

The U.S.A. does not see the urgency that Britian does to rebuild western Europe.

U.S.S.R.

The U.S.S.R. does not trust Britain and the United States.

We want to prevent our country from being invaded again across the open plains of eastern Europe. We will make the security of our western frontier an important goal.

We are not prepared simply to hand over the eastern European countries our armies now occupy. We want to use them as a buffer zone to rebuild our country's devastated economy. We will also use those countries to help expand communism throughout the world.

The U.S.S.R. likes the idea of dividing Germany into zones for each of the big powers to run. This will keep Germany weak and will help keep all of it from falling under the "spell" of the Westerners.

These disagreements among the wartime allies developed rapidly in 1945-1946. Although the emerging rivals were not actually shooting at each other in a hot war, the tension between them created a near-war situation. This situation came to be called the Cold War.

The atmosphere of the Cold War—an atmosphere of fear and suspicion—affected everyone for many years after the war. In fact, it still affects our thinking today. Certainly, all the decisions made immediately after World War II were heavily influenced by Cold War tensions. These decisions involved such things as the United Nations, the peace treaties, defense and other alliances, and the development or purchase of armaments. At times, the conflicting views or actions left the world tottering on the brink of another war. In most cases, fortunately, the threats subsided into a war of words.

1. From the summaries of each country's views, select three issues on which there is disagreement. Construct a chart in which you present the issues and the different views of each country.

2. Which country was more suspicious of Stalin—Britain or the U.S.A.? Why?

3. Why does the future of Germany appear to be a major issue?

4. Why does the United States hope to see the end of military alliances? Why does Britain not agree?

Soviet expansion in eastern Europe, 1945-1949

The correct name for what is often called "Russia" is the "Union of Soviet Socialist Republics" (U.S.S.R.). Russia is actually only one of these republics, but since it is the largest and most important, its name is at times given to the entire country. In this chapter, "Russia" is sometimes used in this way.

At the end of World War II, Soviet armies had advanced far into eastern Europe. These armies did not leave promptly at the end of the war. Large numbers of Soviet soldiers remained. This enabled the Soviet political leaders to exercise a strong influence on events. During the war, several states along the Baltic Sea and parts of other countries had been taken over and added to the U.S.S.R.

In the years between 1945 and 1949 several more eastern European countries came under Soviet control or influence. In most cases these countries were suffering from economic and political confusion and weakness as a result of the war. Communist parties in these countries, with Soviet support, were able to take advantage of the lack of stability. They took over the governments and quickly turned these countries into one-party states, loyal to the U.S.S.R.

As a result, in a short period of time, the U.S.S.R. had brought under its control a series of what came to be called satellite countries in eastern Europe. Russia's former wartime allies in the west feared this communist expansion and became determined to try to stop further takeovers.

These former allies, led by the United States, were eager to have as many countries as possible in Europe supporting their point of view and on their side if hostilities ever broke out. This rivalry between the U.S.S.R. and its satellites and the U.S.A. and its allies was often described as a conflict between two very different styles of life. One style was the communist system as practised in the U.S.S.R. and the other, the capitalist system as practised in the United States and other countries. As we will read in this chapter, the struggle for military and economic power or supremacy was often just as basic an issue as the struggle over rival styles of life.

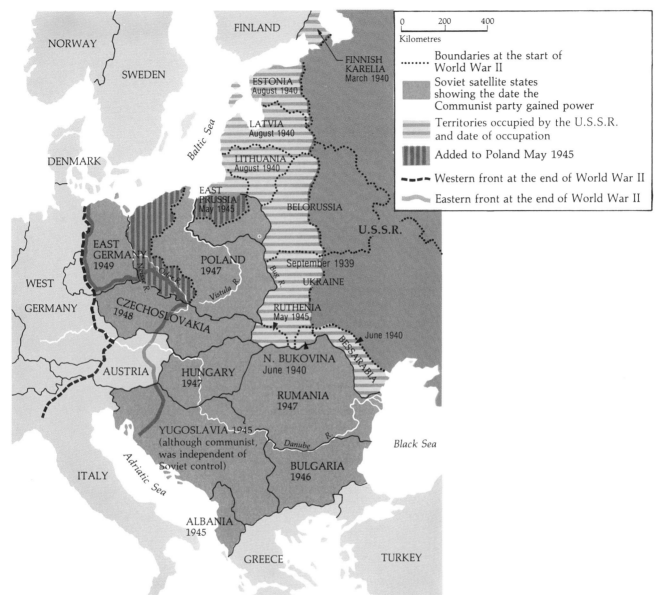

Fig. 3 Soviet expansion in eastern Europe, 1945-1949

Capitalism and communism

Although we see and hear the terms "capitalism" and "communism" quite often, they are difficult words to understand. The meaning of both terms is complex.

Over the years, the definition and usage of the words, capitalism and communism, has expanded. Below is a very brief explanation

of just some of the key parts of the meaning of these important terms.

1. Both terms are used to refer to very different ways of organizing the *economic* life of a country. Here are a few general features of the two economic systems.

   Capitalist Countries

   Communist Countries

   —term comes from "capital"—wealth that is used to produce more wealth—the money placed (invested) in a business to help it expand and make more profit is "capital"

   —since the mid-19th century this term has been identified with ideas of Karl Marx who wrote *The Communist Manifesto* in 1848

   —property, including factories, mines and other businesses, is privately owned

   —the community, or the people of a country as a whole, own all property and the means of producing and distributing all forms of wealth

   —decisions on investments and on what to produce on farms and in industries are made by the individuals and groups that own them

   —private property would be abolished

   —goods are sold at a profit with the price being determined by the free interaction of the supply of the goods and demand for them

   —all economic activity is planned and controlled by the people through their government which would operate in the interest of the working people

   —people's income is determined by the value of things they produce or value of services they perform

   —each person contributes (e.g. through work) to society based on his or her ability and receives material goods from society according only to his or her needs

2. Because the economic system of a country and its political system are closely related, the use of these two terms has expanded from

economics to include *politics*. Here are a few general features of the two political systems.

Capitalist Countries	*Communist Countries*
—have economic systems based on ideas of capitalism	—have economic systems based on ideas of communism
—the amount of govern- ment regulation or con- trol of the economy (e.g. trade, manufacturing, farming) will vary from country to country	—where communist revolu- tions have occurred (e.g. the U.S.S.R.) the govern- ment that emerged has taken full control of almost every aspect of the economy
—some capitalist countries are democracies with governments chosen in free elections and consti- tutions which protect the rights of individual citizens	—the governments are elected by the people but only one party—the Communist party—is permitted to run candidates
—there are some capitalist countries that have pow- erful leaders who have been placed in power by such influential groups as the armed forces—in such cases, civil rights for many citizens may not be protected	—there are constitutions guaranteeing civil rights although these rights do not always include rights that numerous capitalist countries would regard as essential (e.g. information reported by newspapers, television and radio is controlled by the government)

The Cold War after World War II developed into a conflict between the U.S.S.R. and its satellites, all of which were communist coun- tries, and the U.S.A. and its allies, all of which practise some form of capitalism. As a result, the use of the terms "capitalism" and "com- munism" has widened still further.

   Today, capitalism and communism mean not only differences in economic and political systems, but also a conflict between two dif- ferent ways of life. The terms are now used to represent the two sides struggling, in effect, for world supremacy. Hence, when "capital- ism" and "communism" are used today, they are often synonyms for "West" and "East" or "NATO alliance" and "Warsaw Pact." The two terms are used whether the issues are military, economic, political or

social. In fact, much of the history of the world since World War II is viewed or described as a struggle between capitalism and communism.

The United Nations—The world's hope for peace

Much of the world's hope for a permanent peace was placed in the United Nations. This organization was established in the closing days of World War II. Canada played a major role in the meetings that set up the United Nations and became an enthusiastic supporter of its activities. The countries that signed the U.N. Charter agreed that the main purpose of the United Nations was to work together to preserve world peace, to end poverty, disease and illiteracy, and to achieve basic human rights for all peoples.

When it was founded in 1945, the U.N. had 51 member countries. By 1981, the addition of many countries had raised its membership to 156. Most of these new members were from the new countries in Africa and Asia. The U.N.'s headquarters are in New York City, but many of its related organizations and agencies have their head offices in other parts of the world. The chart (facing page) describes four major parts of the U.N. organization.

You can observe from this chart that the main responsibility for keeping peace was given to the Security Council. You will also note that the major powers have the right to veto any proposed decision or action by the Security Council. This means that all five of the U.S.A., the U.S.S.R., Britain, France and China must agree for any action to begin. As we have begun to see, when the Cold War developed after 1945, this cooperation became virtually impossible. As a result, the great expectations at the end of the war that the U.N. would prevent future wars were not fulfilled. It was not long before nations began to become greatly concerned about their security in a threatened world and looked to means other than the United Nations to protect themselves.

The charter was the document that the founding members of the United Nations signed at a meeting in San Francisco in 1945. The Charter included the aims of the U.N., the structure of the organization and the rules by which it would operate.

Fig. 4 Lester Pearson experiences a moment of frustration at the United Nations in 1950.

GENERAL ASSEMBLY

- meets once each year and in special session when necessary
- all member countries equally represented and each country has one vote
- important issues require a 2/3 majority vote
- discusses world problems and decides U.N. budget
- elects Secretary-General on recommendation of Security Council
- votes on admitting members to U.N. on recommendation of Security Council
- elects members of the many U.N. agencies and related organizations
- elects its own President each year
- because any of the 5 permanent members of the Security Council can veto any efforts by the Security Council to settle international disputes, the General Assembly has become more involved in peace-keeping efforts because no country has a **veto** in the General Assembly

SECURITY COUNCIL

- consists of 15 member countries
  - 5 permanent (U.S.A., U.S.S.R., Britain, France, China)
  - 10 non-permanent (elected for 2-year terms)
- all 15 have one vote each, *but* each of the five permanent members has a veto over any action that the Security Council might decide to take
- the 15 countries take monthly turns chairing the meetings (the Council can meet at any time)
- major responsibility—discusses any dispute that might threaten world peace that is brought before it and makes recommendations for solving the dispute
- has power to use force to restore peace employing armed forces provided by U.N. members
- makes recommendations to General Assembly on admission of new members (and expelling of old ones) and appointment of Secretary-General

SECRETARY-GENERAL AND SECRETARIAT

- the administrative part of the U.N.
- includes thousands of employees who do the day-to-day work of the U.N.
- work under direction of the Secretary-General
- Secretary-General also serves as the spokesperson for the U.N. and plays a major role as a world diplomat attempting to bring about peaceful relations among all countries

ECONOMIC AND SOCIAL COUNCIL

- consists of 27 members—none permanent
- members elected for 3-year terms may be re-elected
- majority vote for decisions
- works to improve social, economic, education and health conditions for all peoples and encourages human rights and freedom throughout the world
- does much of its work through many specialized agencies and committees under it—for example—International Labour Organization (I.L.O.), U.N. Educational, Scientific and Cultural Organization (U.N.E.S.C.O.), Food and Agriculture Organization (F.A.O.), World Health Organization (W.H.O.), United Nations Children's Fund (U.N.I.C.E.F.)

Fig. 5 The United Nations building, New York, 1952

8. It has been argued that the real success of the U.N. is found in the work of the specialized agencies and not in the General Assembly or Security Council. Research one of the specialized agencies to discover what it does and what successes it has achieved and what difficulties it may have encountered.

Canada's place in the post war world

What was Canada's position in all of this? Two factors made Canada's place in this emerging Cold War very different from its status before World War II. In the 1930s Canada was still shaking off the last of the bonds as a colony of Great Britain. Canada had made an enormous contribution to the defeat of Hitler and his supporters during World War II. As a result, Canada had moved from its lowly role on the world stage to the rank of a middle power. Canada was not, of course, in the same category as the U.S.A., the U.S.S.R. and Britain. Few other countries, however, had the international prestige and military and economic strength of Canada in those first few critical years after the end of the war.

If Canada's war contribution had not pushed Canada on to the world stage at the end of the war, then geography certainly would have. The United States and the U.S.S.R. had emerged as the two dominant post war powers and their conflicting ambitions grew more threatening. During this, Canada's location between the United States and the U.S.S.R. took on ever increasing importance. It did not look like Canada was going to be permitted to stay out of international events even if it had wished to do so. Both the United States and the U.S.S.R. would, from now on, be vitally interested in Canada and its international attitudes and commitments.

In these changed circumstances, Prime Minister William Lyon Mackenzie King took his usual cautious approach. He strongly supported and participated in the creation of the United Nations and was prepared to take an active role in it to keep world peace.

However, when it came to the issue of arranging peace treaties and negotiating boundaries in war-torn Europe, King took a much less active role. He was prepared to let the big powers plan the settlement in Europe. Many Canadians were concerned about decisions which would, perhaps, affect the countries from which they came. However, the Canadian government's main interest was not in the many details of the settlement but in achieving peace and returning the world to economic prosperity as soon as possible. This would be good for Canada because its export trade was essential to its economic success. Only with international peace and stability would world-wide trade flourish.

To a great extent, relationships among countries for many years to come and the role of countries in world affairs would be established during this crucial period.

W.L. Mackenzie King was first elected prime minister of Canada in 1921 and served, with the exception of a few months in 1926, until 1930. He lost the 1930 election but returned to power in 1935. He sought compromise where possible and took the least controversial course of action when he could.

Although he *did not* expect to be involved in the detailed arrangements for peace, the Canadian prime minister *did* expect to have a voice in the general shaping of the post war world. One main objective of Canadian foreign policy in the years after 1945 was to be involved when important international decisions were being made. Canada hoped to play a role in shaping a peaceful world in which international cooperation through the United Nations would become the goal of every country. As we will see in this chapter, this goal soon became almost impossible to achieve.

GETTING THE FACTS

9. Which two countries emerged as the dominant powers after World War II? Why did these two countries have special significance for Canada.

10. Why was Canada a more important country in world affairs after World War II than it was in the 1930s?

11. What was Canada's main interest in international affairs after World War II? Why?

12. Why did Canada take a special interest in the United Nations?

Igor Gouzenko: A spy ring in Canada!

Although it is a date seldom recognized in Canadian history, on September 5, 1945, two events took place that played a very important role in changing the course of Canadian history. Both events pushed Canada into the emerging Cold War.

One of the two events on September 5, 1945 began in Ottawa with the action of one person. Within a few months, it became one of the most sensational events in Canadian history. It ended up involving many countries and led to changes in the course of world history.

The single individual was a short, young, blond Soviet who worked as a cipher clerk in the Soviet embassy in Ottawa. His name was Igor Gouzenko. When he left work on the evening of September 5, he had hidden several dozen top secret documents under his shirt. These documents included information on letter drops, passwords, forged passports and code names. This would soon prove the existence of a large Soviet spy ring in Canada—working out of the Soviet embassy. Knowing it would only be a short time before the Soviets would discover what he had done, the frightened Gouzenko, with his pregnant wife and daughter, fled to Canadian authorities with his story.

As a cipher clerk in the Soviet embassy, Gouzenko's job was to put messages into a code for sending back to the U.S.S.R. and to decode messages that were coming into the embassy from the U.S.S.R.

The initial reaction from government departments and newspapers to which Gouzenko went with his story was disbelief. It seemed that no one in September of 1945 could accept the fact that the U.S.S.R., Canada's wartime ally, would do such a thing. Like the others, Prime Minister King first dismissed Gouzenko as a crank. However, a check of the papers which Gouzenko had smuggled out of the Soviet embassy confirmed the presence of a spy network. King's diary for September 7 records that the documents,

> . . . disclose an espionage system on a large scale . . . things came right into our own country to a degree we could not have believed possible. . . . if publicity were given to this it might necessarily lead to a break in diplomatic relations between Canada and Russia and might also lead to that in regard to other nations as well, the U.S. and the U.K. . . . There is no saying to what terrible lengths this whole thing might go.

From *The Mackenzie King Record* vol. III by J.W. Pickersgill and D.F. Forster.

As a result, Canadians were not immediately told of the huge Soviet espionage ring at work in their country. It was not until February of 1946 that the information was made public. A number of

Fig. 6 Gouzenko had some success as a writer. His own story was published in a book, serialized in magazines, and later made into a movie. He also wrote novels, one of which won the Governor-General's Medal for the best Canadian novel in 1954. Here, he is reading from one of his books on television in 1966. Gouzenko's fear of Russian revenge was so strong that, until his death in 1982, he made all public appearances with his head covered.

people were arrested and eventually several were placed on trial. At least eight were convicted and sent to jail. From that time until his death in June, 1982, Igor Gouzenko, using an assumed name, lived with the protection and financial support of the Canadian government somewhere in Canada.

As a result of what Gouzenko had revealed, Canadians were shocked into the reality of the Cold War. The developing hostile split between the United States and its friends and the U.S.S.R. and its communist partners had been widened further. Canadians were now more aware that the international peace they cherished after World War II was far from a sure thing.

Among those convicted were the private secretary of the British High Commissioner in Ottawa, a member of the Canadian House of Commons, and a Montreal scientist who had developed a new way of making an important explosive. Also jailed was a British nuclear physicist. He was involved in nuclear research in Canada and had access to secret information regarding the Manhattan Project in the U.S.A. which developed the atomic bomb.

GETTING THE FACTS

13. What were two important results of the Gouzenko affair?

USING YOUR KNOWLEDGE

14. What did Prime Minister King mean when he wrote in his diary on September 7, "There is no saying to what terrible lengths this whole thing might go"?

THINKING IT THROUGH

15. One of the places Gouzenko went with his story when he fled the Soviet Embassy on September 5 was an Ottawa newspaper. Assume you had been a reporter in the newsroom of the Ottawa *Journal* when Igor Gouzenko arrived with his story. Would you have decided to try to have his story published? Why or why not? What would be the advantages and the risks of going ahead and publishing?

THE INVESTIGATIVE REPORTER

16. Find out how those arrested as a result of the Gouzenko revelations were taken into custody, held and questioned. What controversy arose as a result? Take a position on the controversy and defend it.

Canada and the Nuclear Age: The bomb and a "balance of terror"

The second event of September 5, 1945 which greatly affected the course of Canadian history and drew Canada further into the Cold War was actually a key event in a series which had begun a few years before. On September 5, 1945 in a top secret research lab at Chalk River, north of Ottawa, a team of scientists conducted a successful nuclear reaction. Canada entered the atomic age and became the second nation in the world, after the United States, to have a nuclear reactor.

For a number of years Canada had been one of several countries involved in research into nuclear energy. When the war began, however, research was concentrated on producing an atomic bomb. Canada worked closely with its allies on this project. Furthermore, Canada's cooperation became essential because it was the only source of uranium, the vital ingredient in the atomic bomb, available to the Allies. It was likely Canadian uranium that was used in the atomic bombs that were dropped on Japan. In 1942, the British research project, to get further away from the war zone, moved to Canada. There followed a period of close British and Canadian cooperation in nuclear research. But the top secret American research team was the first to develop a nuclear weapon. In July of 1945, the Americans exploded a test bomb in the New Mexico desert.

The world was shocked when, on August 6, 1945 a specially fitted American B-29 bomber dropped an atomic bomb on downtown Hiroshima, Japan. The city was levelled and almost 80 000 people killed. Thousands more were to die slower deaths from radiation and burns. After a second bomb destroyed the city of Nagasaki on August 9, the Japanese surrendered. Canadians at this time were especially surprised to learn that there was a secret nuclear research project underway in Canada and that within a month the Chalk River nuclear project would be in full operation. The world had entered a new and frightening era—the atomic age. Future decisions about relations among countries had to be made with the knowledge that, if war broke out, weapons now existed that could wipe out the human race.

Because of its role in wartime nuclear research and its uranium resources, Canada was in the thick of post war discussions on the future of atomic weapons and nuclear energy. Canada attempted to take a leadership role by both example and action. As an example to others, Canada, despite having the materials, know-how and equipment to manufacture nuclear weapons, adopted a policy of neither manufacturing nor possessing them. Instead, Canada would concentrate on developing nuclear power as a source of energy for peaceful purposes.

Control of the uranium supply became so vital that, in 1944, the federal government took over the previously privately-owned Eldorado Mining and Refining Company which controlled the uranium mines in the Canadian north and the refineries in Southern Ontario.

A Canadian scientist, Louis Slotin, was a key member of the American research team that developed the first atomic bomb. He built the explosive device for the bomb. In 1946, an accident in his lab exposed him to a massive fatal dose of radiation. His body was returned to his native Winnipeg in a lead coffin, but because of the top secret nature of his research, people were not told the cause of his death.

An illustration of the close cooperation among Canada, Britain and the United States in nuclear research is the fact that Prime Minister King and two government officials were among the very few in the world to know about the atomic bomb and that it was to be dropped on Japan.

Fig. 7 The huge mushroom cloud, characteristic of an atomic explosion. The atomic bomb dropped on Hiroshima released a quantity of energy equivalent to 18 kt of TNT.

Canada and most other nations believed that, as long as the United States was the only country with the atomic bomb, the chances of getting an international agreement were good. One of the greatest fears in the growing Cold War tension was that an agreement would be unlikely if the U.S.S.R. developed its own atomic bomb. Just about everyone assumed that there was lots of time for negotiations since most experts believed as late as 1947 that the Soviets would need at least five years and most likely twenty years to develop the bomb. It only took the Soviets two years.

The Soviets exploded their first nuclear device in 1949. From that point on, there was to be an arms race between the U.S.S.R. and its allies and the United States and its allies. The most important part of this race was a competition to determine which side could develop the largest number and the most advanced of these new and most terrible of weapons. The Cold War was no longer a struggle over a balance of power. The future of world security would now depend on a balance of terror!

There were no international controls on nuclear power immediately after the war so Canada also drafted plans for a system of such controls. Canada did much of this through the Atomic Energy Commission established by the United Nations. The Commission included the members of the United Nations Security Council plus Canada.

The Iron Curtain

While delivering a speech in May of 1946, Winston Churchill uttered a phrase which has become a basic part of the language of world affairs. Churchill, who had always warned of the threat of Soviet expansion, was describing the confrontation which had developed between East and West in Europe. He said that "... an *Iron Curtain* has descended across the continent."

The map shows where this imaginary Iron Curtain would be located by 1950. The term Iron Curtain is a very meaningful and apt description for what had happened between the U.S.S.R. and its eastern satellites and America and its western European allies.

Why was the word iron used? Why couldn't he have called it a cloth curtain? What is iron really describing?

What function does a curtain serve, whether it be on a window or on a stage? Why, then, is the word curtain a good word for describing the border between the eastern European states and the western European countries?

Having now dealt individually with the two words "iron" and "curtain," put them together to explain what Churchill meant by the "Iron Curtain." Was it a good description of the situation in Europe in and after 1946?

Find out what the status of the Iron Curtain is today. Are there places where the symbolic Iron Curtain has been replaced by something very real? Where? With what? Describe in some detail.

Fig. 8 The Iron Curtain

210

17. Why did the Allies believe there was such an urgency to develop the atomic bomb?

18. For what reasons was Canada guaranteed a role in international decision-making about the use of atomic energy?

19. What policy did Canada adopt in the post war negotiations on nuclear energy?

20. In what way did the Cold War change after the U.S.S.R. exploded its first atomic bomb?

THINKING IT THROUGH

21. Do you agree that an international agreement would be less likely if the U.S.S.R. developed its own atomic bomb? Why or why not?

THE INVESTIGATIVE REPORTER

22. a) It was President Truman of the United States who made the decision to drop the atomic bomb on Japan. Find out why he made that decision and explain his reasons in a paragraph.

    b) After you have the background information, put yourself in Truman's position. What would you have done? Why?

23. a) Is there still an arms race today? Consult a newspaper and clip one article about the building of nuclear weapons in the world. Write a summary of the article.

    b) Is an arms race necessary in today's world of conflicting world powers? Give reasons to support your viewpoint.

The Cold War terror continues

Canada emerged from World War II in 1945 with the hope that the United Nations would bring a fresh approach to international peace and cooperation. It was not long, however, before Cold War hostilities and a nuclear balance of terror began to change such hopes. Within four years, Canada found itself playing a leading role in the creation of an old-style military alliance such as those that had existed before World War I and World War II.

What follows is an imaginary story told by a Canadian who took a special interest in Canada's foreign policy and who shared the hopes for universal peace and international cooperation at the end of World War II. The story describes how Canada's expectations for the United Nations were shattered and how the breakdown of international cooperation led to the establishment of the NATO military alliance.

At the time of the discussions regarding the formation of NATO, St. Laurent was the Secretary of State for External Affairs. This meant he was the Cabinet minister in King's government in charge of Canada's foreign affairs. Lester Pearson was St. Laurent's top advisor as the under-secretary or deputy minister in the External Affairs department. By the time NATO was created, St. Laurent was prime minister and Lester Pearson was the Secretary of State for External Affairs.

A tale of shattered expectations

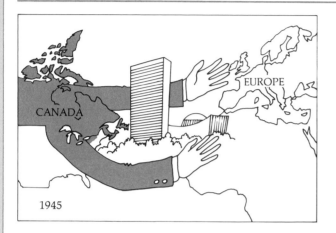

1945

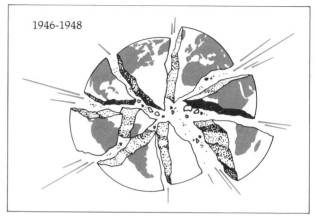

1946-1948

I have great hopes for the future of international relations. I am so pleased with this new organization—the United Nations. From now on, all countries will be able to talk to each other and solve their problems. We won't need all the old military alliances that have helped cause wars in the past. It is especially important that the friendship and cooperation between North America and Europe, that had grown so strong during the war, be continued. It is in Europe that any future problems are likely to start. The devastation and chaos left by the war has created a situation where the powerful countries of the world are trying to make sure that the new governments that emerge from this post war chaos support their point of view about the future course of the world. Rivalries for this influence or control are developing very quickly. There are already stories of difficulties with our wartime ally, the U.S.S.R. Since the U.S.S.R. is a member of the United Nations, perhaps we will be able to talk out our problems there.

I'm afraid that the idea of one world working together in a spirit of cooperation is rapidly being blown apart. Event after event has driven the world into two nervous blocs of opposing countries. Some of these events are:

(1) Soviet espionage activities uncovered.

(2) Soviets refuse to cooperate in U.N.

(3) Rival powers disagree over peace treaty with Germany.

(4) No success in control of nuclear arms.

(5) U.S.S.R. and U.S.A. fail to agree on Marshall Plan to rebuild economies of Europe. (U.S. assistance for European economic self-help)

(6) Soviets tighten control in eastern Europe.

(7) Local communist groups under Soviet leadership start a guerilla war in Greece.

(8) The Soviets try to force the western allies out of their sector of Berlin by blockading the city while the western allies strengthen their forces there.

(9) Local communist groups under Soviet leadership have taken over the government of Czechoslovakia. Which country is next?

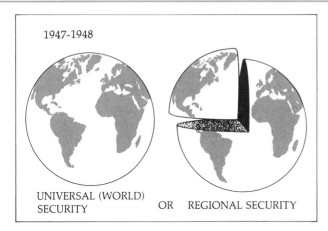

1947-1948

UNIVERSAL (WORLD)
SECURITY   OR   REGIONAL SECURITY

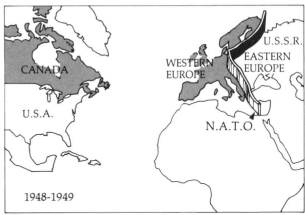

CANADA

U.S.A.

WESTERN
EUROPE

EASTERN
EUROPE

U.S.S.R.

N.A.T.O.

1948-1949

Our hopes for achieving world peace and security through the United Nations seem to have been broken. Although we have worked very hard at the United Nations and have joined in all its organizations and committees, we have become increasingly disappointed. It has failed in its important job of maintaining peace and security and preventing war. Our countries' leaders have begun to talk about this failure. It is little wonder that Canada, as well as other countries, is beginning to look around for other arrangements, especially with our friends to protect our security. That is why we have started to think of a regional military alliance with the Americans and our European friends.

1948 has seen increasing alarm among Canadians about the dangers of the Cold War. Our two top foreign policy leaders, Louis St. Laurent and Lester Pearson, are now at the head of a crusade to establish a regional military alliance. To do this would require Canadians to make a total break from past foreign policy. Never before had we entered into a military treaty.

Mr. St. Laurent said after the communist takeover of Czechoslovakia in February of 1948: "It is becoming increasingly necessary that the free nations form a united front to make it plain to Russia that she can go no further." Mr. King, who has never favoured Canadian entanglements with other countries, has also changed his mind in this time of crisis. He said in a speech in January that ". . . where force threatens, it can be kept at bay by superior force. So long as communism remains as a menace to the free world, it is vital to the defense of freedom to maintain a preponderance of military strength on the side of freedom, and to ensure that degree of unity among the nations which will ensure that they cannot be defeated and destroyed one by one."

The formation of NATO

The result of all these concerns was the formation of the North Atlantic Treaty Organization on April 4, 1949. At first, there were 12 members including Canada and the United States. Three later additions brought membership to 15. The stated objective of the NATO alliance was to promote "stability and well-being in the North Atlantic area." The real objective, however, was to have a collective defense against Soviet aggression. The treaty stated each member's responsibility—"an armed attack against one . . . shall be considered an attack against them all."

As a result of this treaty, large numbers of troops and weapons were stationed in western Europe facing the Soviet-dominated eastern European countries. Canada's initial commitment was to station an armoured brigade of 6500 soldiers and 12 fighter squadrons in Europe.

Although there have been and continue to be many controversies about NATO and even major disagreements among its members, NATO remains to this day the chief defense against Soviet aggression in the West. It is probably not surprising that, in response to the creation of NATO, the U.S.S.R. created, in 1955, an

Fig. 9 The countries of NATO and the Warsaw Pact, showing the dates they joined

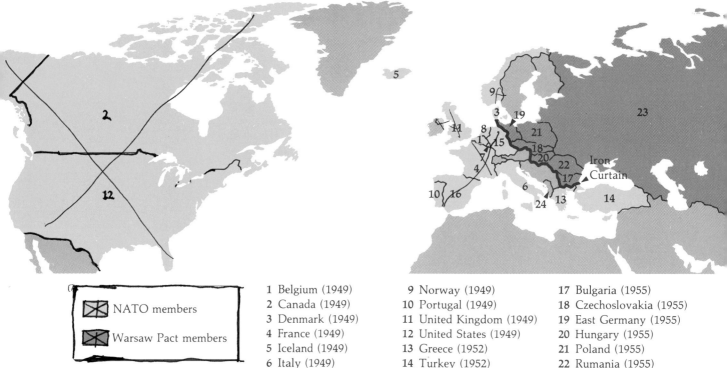

NATO members

Warsaw Pact members

1 Belgium (1949)
2 Canada (1949)
3 Denmark (1949)
4 France (1949)
5 Iceland (1949)
6 Italy (1949)
7 Luxembourg (1949)
8 Netherlands (1949)

9 Norway (1949)
10 Portugal (1949)
11 United Kingdom (1949)
12 United States (1949)
13 Greece (1952)
14 Turkey (1952)
15 West Germany (1955)
16 Spain (1982)

17 Bulgaria (1955)
18 Czechoslovakia (1955)
19 East Germany (1955)
20 Hungary (1955)
21 Poland (1955)
22 Rumania (1955)
23 U.S.S.R. (1955)
24 Albania (expelled 1962)

214

alliance of its eastern European satellites. This alliance is called the Warsaw Pact. The result was that these two rival alliances faced each other menacingly across the Iron Curtain. They did so with more weapons and military might than the world has ever known. The balance of terror was now all too real!

Spain joined NATO in 1982.

GETTING THE FACTS

24. a) Examine the speeches made by St. Laurent and King after the takeover of Czechoslovakia. Write down any words you do not understand. Look up their meanings in a dictionary and put the definitions in your notebook.

   b) In your own words, explain what each man is saying.

25. What was the purpose of the NATO alliance?

26. For what reasons does Canada support the organization of a NATO alliance?

27. What was the Warsaw Pact and why was it formed?

Fig. 10 Louis St. Laurent

USING YOUR KNOWLEDGE

28. List the advantages and disadvantages of regional security alliances.

29. In what way is the NATO agreement a great change in traditional Canadian foreign policy?

THINKING IT THROUGH

30. Decide: Is there a difference between a "balance of power" and a "balance of terror"? If not, why not? If so, what is it?

NORAD: Defending North America in the Cold War

The signing of the NATO alliance did not end Canada's efforts to protect itself in the increasingly tense Cold War. While NATO provided protection on its Atlantic side, Canada was still extremely vulnerable along its frozen northern frontier. Assuming that the U.S.S.R. was the most likely invader in these Cold War years, Canadians feared a Soviet bomber attack across the Arctic. These fears became even more pronounced as the Soviet-American confrontation grew more hostile. They were especially strong, after the U.S.S.R. developed its own atomic bomb in 1949.

NORAD was not created until 1958. It is included here because it was established in direct response to the Cold War. For the United States and Canada, NORAD extended the defense system established by NATO.

The Berlin Blockade and airlift

In the closing weeks of World War II, the Allied armies swept across the devastated German countryside. Soviet armies moved in from the east while the other Allied armies moved in from the west (see map, Figure 3; W.W.II chapter). The armies met in mid-Germany. Not only were the German countryside and economy in ruins, but also, with Hitler's death, the government had collapsed.

The wartime Allies now had to decide how Germany would be administered in the immediate post war period. None of the Allies wanted to be the first to remove its troops from Germany. With Germany's location in the heart of Europe and its past record as a major economic, political and military power, all of the Allies were very concerned about its future. Equally important was the suspicion that was developing between the Soviets and the other allies over each other's intentions and actions in trying to shape post war Europe.

As a temporary measure, Germany was divided into four zones. Each zone was to be administered by one of the great powers—the U.S.S.R., the United States, Britain and France. The city of Berlin was located over 175 kilometres inside the Soviet zone, and was divided into four similar zones. It was assumed in 1945 that within a short time all these zones would be ended and a treaty with Germany, which would include the creation of a new German constitution and government, would be negotiated. Yet this did not happen.

Germany, and especially Berlin, became the focus in the Cold War power struggle. Since the city was within the Soviet zone of Germany, access for the United States, Britain and France to their zones in Berlin depended on Soviet goodwill. It would be easiest for the U.S.S.R. to apply pressure on its Cold War foes in Berlin.

In April, 1948 the Soviets started the pressure. They began to disrupt road and railway transportation from the British, American and French zones to their "island" of West Berlin. In June, the Soviets blockaded all overland traffic to West Berlin. West Berlin's two million people had no more than a month's supply of food. What was to be done? The Americans and British were aware that any attempt to break through the blockade could start a full-scale war with the U.S.S.R. A bold decision was quickly made—rather than break through the blockade, they would fly supplies over it into Berlin.

The problem was that West Berlin each day needed at least 4000 tonnes of supplies for mere survival. In winter, thousands more tonnes of coal would have to be flown in to keep the population of two million people warm and alive.

Planes flew along three narrow air corridors from Western Germany, landing at one of three West Berlin airports every two or three minutes, twenty-four hours a day. The planes were so close to each other that if one could not land on the first try, it had to return home so as not to disrupt the others following behind. In eleven months over 2 300 000 tonnes of food, fuel, medicine and other supplies had been flown in by almost 278 000 individual flights. On the peak day of the airlift, almost 1400 flights brought in almost 13 000 tonnes of supplies. The people of West Berlin were remarkable. They showed no signs of weakening under the Soviet pressure.

In May, 1949, the Soviets lifted the blockade. The Berlin blockade had further increased Cold War tensions. The reunification of Germany into one country had become much less likely.

GETTING THE FACTS

31. Why was Berlin blockaded?

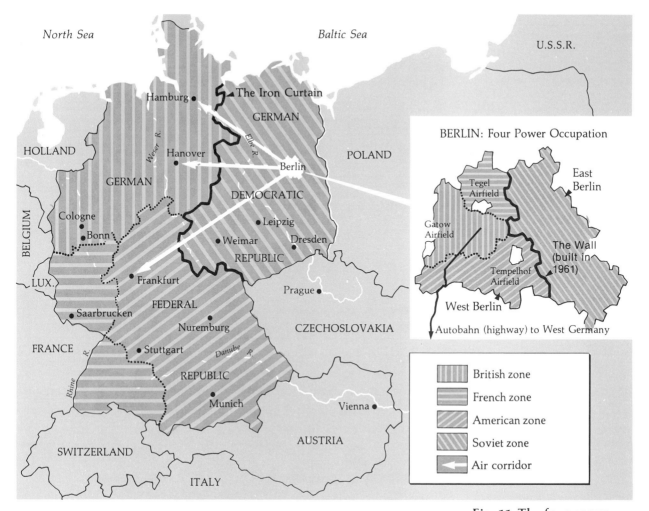

North Sea

Baltic Sea

U.S.S.R.

Hamburg

The Iron Curtain

GERMAN

HOLLAND

Hanover

POLAND

GERMAN

Berlin

DEMOCRATIC

Cologne

Leipzig

Bonn

Weimar

Dresden

REPUBLIC

BELGIUM

LUX.

Frankfurt

Prague

FEDERAL

Saarbrucken

CZECHOSLOVAKIA

Nuremburg

FRANCE

Stuttgart

Danube R.

REPUBLIC

Munich

Vienna

SWITZERLAND

AUSTRIA

ITALY

BERLIN: Four Power Occupation

Tegel Airfield

East Berlin

Gatow Airfield

The Wall (built in 1961)

Tempelhof Airfield

West Berlin

Autobahn (highway) to West Germany

British zone

French zone

American zone

Soviet zone

Air corridor

Fig. 11 The four power occupation of Germany. What do you think it would be like to live in the "island" of West Berlin? One Berliner wrote after the airlift, "... when we woke up, the first thing we did was to listen to see whether the noise of aircraft engines could be heard. That gave us certainty we were not alone ..."

The Americans, of course, shared the same concern. Thus in 1958 Canada and the United States made a defense arrangement called the North American Air Defense Agreement, or NORAD. This agreement created a single air defense system for the North American continent. The task assigned to NORAD was to search out enemy bombers and destroy them before they could get to major American or Canadian targets. Units of the air forces of both countries were placed under the command of NORAD and were on twenty-four hour alert. The commander-in-chief was an American and the second in command was a Canadian. The headquarters of NORAD were constructed inside a mountain in Colorado and almost all the regional command posts were in the United States. Much of the support in money, planes and labour was provided by the Americans. This was not surprising since the United States was so much larger, wealthier and had greater military strength than Canada.

Fig. 12 The NORAD agreement completed the defense of North America against Soviet attack, begun with the NATO alliance. When you examine NATO and NORAD together, what similarity do you see between them in the way they try to ensure Canadian security?

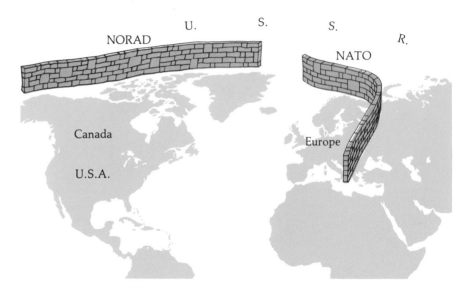

In order to give NORAD planes the earliest possible warning of a Soviet bomber attack, three radar detection lines were constructed: one near the Canadian-American border, one across central Canada, and one in the far north. All three were heavily financed, built by the United States and operated by Americans. The most important radar line, the Distant Early Warning (DEW) line in the far north, was entirely paid for and staffed by Americans although it was located mostly on Canadian territory.

This overwhelming American control of NORAD angered those Canadians who distrusted American influence in Canada. They believed that such unequal cooperation as that in NORAD was a threat to Canadian independence. These feelings were further aroused by other agreements arranged to make NORAD more effective and strengthen North American defense.

In the years after 1958, the NORAD agreement continued despite the controversy that surrounded it. In the 1960s and the 1970s new weapons led to changes in NORAD strategy. When missiles were added to military arsenals, their early detection and interception became a major purpose of NORAD. Some Canadians argued that this meant that Soviet missiles would be intercepted over Canada before they reached the United States. This would result in Canada facing most of the damage and destruction. There was also a great controversy over whether Canada should allow nuclear equipped American missiles to be stationed on Canadian soil as part of NORAD. Despite these controversies and others, the NORAD agreement has always been renewed and Canada continues to depend on it as the principal method of defense of its air space.

GETTING THE FACTS

32. Why were Canadians particularly concerned about their Arctic frontier during the Cold War?

33. What was the purpose of NORAD?

USING YOUR KNOWLEDGE

34. It is argued that very close cooperation between Canada and the United States in NORAD was essential. Why?

Fig. 13 This is the entrance to NORAD headquarters located deep inside Cheyenne Mountain near Colorado Springs, Colorado. The headquarters are three stories tall, but have a mountain roof of 520 m of solid granite. They were built at a cost of over $140 000 000 and are supposed to be strong enough to withstand a direct bomber attack. It would be from inside this mountain that all the NORAD air forces would be commanded in the event of a war.

THINKING IT THROUGH

35. a) Assume you are a strong Canadian nationalist. Write a one paragraph account of your reactions to NORAD.

b) Assume you are the Minister of National Defense for Canada. Write a one paragraph response to the nationalist's statement.

c) Which viewpoint do you agree most with? Give reasons for your answer.

FRINGE BENEFIT

Fig. 14 This cartoon is making a comment on one of the criticisms of the NORAD agreement. What does the rain represent? What is happening to the rain? Why is "Canada" looking so nervous?

Conclusion

Relationships among the countries of the world were very different in 1949 from what they had been at the end of World War II in 1945. Canada, like many other countries, became caught up in the growing tensions and divisions of the Cold War. Dreams of world peace and cooperation through the United Nations had been largely set aside. They had been replaced by the reality of regional military alliances and power blocs threatening each other with enormous military might and possible war.

Anna and Janice, the two imaginary cousins we met at the beginning of this chapter, have continued to write back and forth to each other from Canada and Poland since 1945. Here are parts of their letters written to each other late in 1949. Perhaps these letters will reflect the changes between 1945 and 1949.

Dear Anna,

. . . My, how things have changed in our country in the four years since the end of the war. Our economy is booming. There are jobs for just about everyone. One problem we keep hearing about, however, is the trouble between the great countries of the world. We even hear talk of another war. Our leaders speak of a "Cold War" which has developed between the U.S.S.R. and its satellites and the United States and its allies. Did you know that your country is considered to be one of the U.S.S.R.'s satellites? Our leaders are constantly warning us that this "Cold War" could turn into a real war.

We have become especially worried since we heard this year that the U.S.S.R. now has an atomic bomb. Our country has just helped make a big new alliance they call NATO. It is supposed to protect us from a Soviet attack. We have become even closer friends with the Americans as a result of our concern over our security. Some Canadians don't like this very much, but what are we going to do? People are so nervous they are even beginning to talk about building bomb shelters in their basements. I often wonder if our world's leaders have learned anything from World War II.

I read in the papers that things are not going well in your country. We hear that you have become a dictatorship under Soviet control. I hope everything isn't as bad as it sounds. Let me know in your next letter. . . .

Love, Your Cousin,
Janice

Dear Janice,

    . . . things have really changed in Poland but not like they have in Canada. Our government is now run by the communists. They call it a "people's democracy" but there are people in my country who say it is a dictatorship. In our elections, only one party, the Communist party, is allowed to exist. I hear rumours about what happens to those who speak out against the government. My dad often starts to mutter things at home but quickly stops himself. We still see and hear a lot about the Soviets. Whispers we hear suggest that they still have a lot to say about what happens here.

    Our factories have mostly been rebuilt and are working again. The government seems to have given industry in Poland a lot of attention since the war. We hear that life on the farms is difficult. There are efforts being made to break up the old large farms and create more government-controlled farms. The farmers are opposing the changes.

    It's strange that you write about the U.S.S.R. threatening war on your country. Here in Poland we are told that America and its friends are threatening to make war on us and that our armies must be constantly on the alert. We too, are worried about the future. Poland cannot stand yet another horrible war. Is there no end to all of these wars and threats of wars? . . .

Love, Your cousin,
Anna

USING YOUR KNOWLEDGE

35. Compare Janice's letter in the introduction of this chapter to this letter. In what ways are they different? What has caused the differences?

THINKING IT THROUGH

36. Do you think that the differences between the feelings and expectations expressed in Anna's first and second letters are as different as those between Janice's two letters? Why or why not?

37. Assume you could write a letter to Anna. How would you answer her question in the last sentence of her letter?

9 Canadians take on new global responsibilities, 1949-1959

This globe suggests that there were many major events in the world in the first fifteen years after the end of World War II. Not all of these events were discussed in the previous chapter. What world issues or problems are suggested by these pictures?

There are two faces on the map of Canada. What is suggested about the attitude of Canada toward the world issues by these faces? What does Canada seem to be concentrating upon in this diagram?

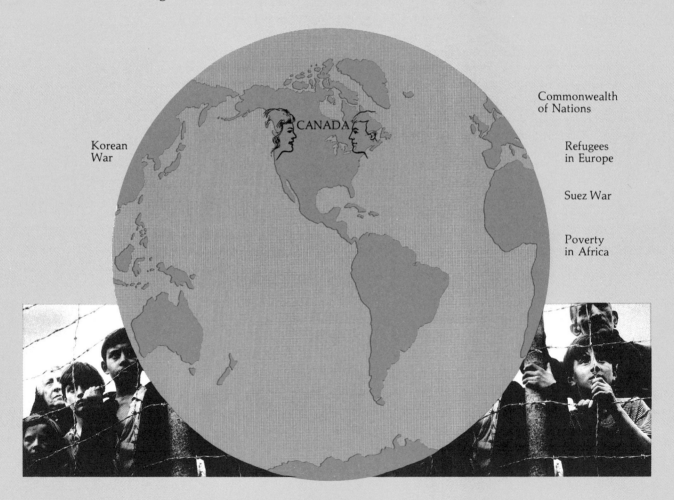

Korean War

CANADA

Commonwealth of Nations

Refugees in Europe

Suez War

Poverty in Africa

This globe suggests that Canada had another choice regarding world affairs. What is the difference between this choice and the one suggested in the other globe? What does this globe suggest about Canada's role in world affairs after World War II?

Canada had important decisions to make about world affairs. If Canada decided to get involved in world affairs, it had to make further important decisions about the number of commitments it wanted to make and the nature of these commitments.

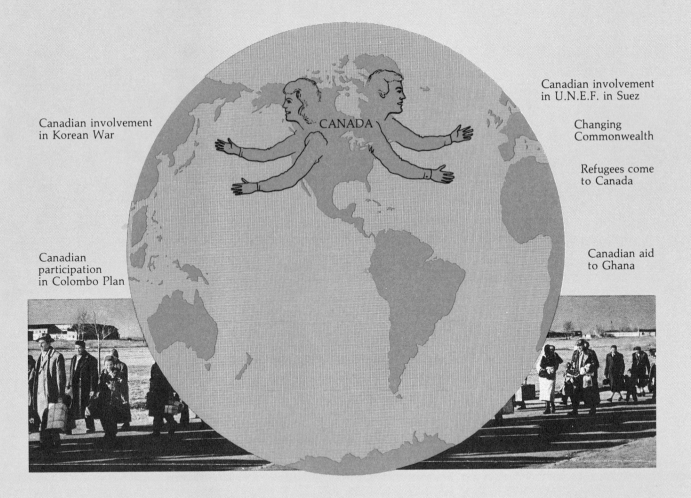

Canadian involvement in Korean War

Canadian involvement in U.N.E.F. in Suez

Changing Commonwealth

Refugees come to Canada

Canadian participation in Colombo Plan

Canadian aid to Ghana

CANADA

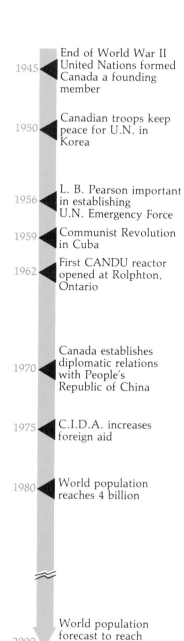

1945	End of World War II United Nations formed Canada a founding member
1950	Canadian troops keep peace for U.N. in Korea
1956	L. B. Pearson important in establishing U.N. Emergency Force
1959	Communist Revolution in Cuba
1962	First CANDU reactor opened at Rolphton, Ontario
1970	Canada establishes diplomatic relations with People's Republic of China
1975	C.I.D.A. increases foreign aid
1980	World population reaches 4 billion
2000	World population forecast to reach 6.35 billion

Chapter overview

We learned in the last chapter that Canada was concerned about its military security in the Cold War world. To protect itself, Canada had signed defense alliances with other countries. Yet important questions regarding Canada's relationship with other parts of the world remained. How much responsibility was Canada prepared to take for other people and their difficulties?

Canada had emerged from the Second World War not with its countryside and economy in ruins, but with a booming economy and a prosperous future. Many parts of the world looked to Canada for leadership and assistance. Canada had never had such prestige or such an opportunity to participate in global affairs and to help others less fortunate. Canada could also help to preserve the peace in the tense post-war world. In this chapter we will see how Canada took up these challenges, became a major participant in global affairs and made commitments to assist other peoples all over the world.

Signposts

Canada welcomes the world's refugees >

Refugees from the Hungarian Revolution: A case study >

Canada: Peace-keeper to the world >

FEATURE: Lester B. Pearson: A great Canadian >

The changing commonwealth >

Canada's relationship to new nations: Ghana— A case study >

Key words

refugees	stalemate
peace-keeping operations	nationalize

Canada welcomes the world's refugees

In 1945 scarcity was a way of life in Europe. Families lived in the cellars of bombed buildings: women and children grubbed for coal on the edge of railway yards. A bar of soap, a simple pad of writing paper, a box of matches or half a pound of coffee were prized possessions. Meat was often unobtainable. Medicines, particularly sulfa drugs and the new wonder drug penicillin, were in desperately short supply. Only one commodity was plentiful and that was homeless people.

From *A Time of Heroes* by S. Franklin.

Never in history had there been such huge numbers of homeless people as there were at the end of World War II. Many of the world's countries assisted the homeless people. Canada had escaped physical damage, with its economy intact. European countries could not feed, house, or employ refugees, and thus it was expected that Canada would assume considerable responsibility for helping these people. Canadians and their government soon showed that they were prepared to help the millions of desperate refugees.

As early as 1943, the governments of over 40 countries had cooperated to form the United Nations Relief and Rehabilitation Administration (UNRRA). This organization coordinated and financed the relief and resettlement of millions of Europeans left homeless and penniless by the war. Canada played a major role in the activities of UNRRA. The Canadian diplomat, Lester Pearson, was chairman of its Supplies Committee. In the summer of 1946 he

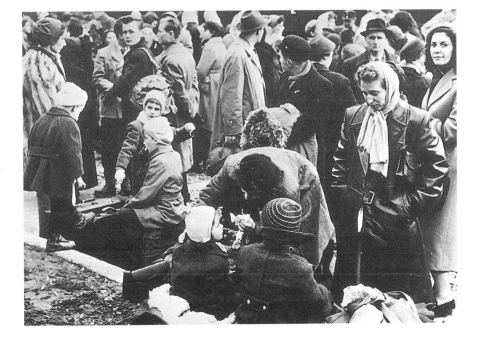

Fig. 1 What sort of problems would a homeless person in Europe in 1945 face?

toured the refugee camps on behalf of UNRRA. Many years later he described this experience in his memoirs:

> We went for a day into the country near Warsaw and watched the farmers cultivating recent battle-fields, often with dug-outs as their temporary homes. We talked to some. I shall never forget one old (at least she looked old) and stooped lady, who paused for a moment from her work and with moving sincerity and great dignity told us her tragic story, and also of her hope for a better future for those to come when war might be no more. She then quietly thanked us for visiting them and honouring their poverty and their work. It made one feel very humble.

From *Mike: The Memoirs of the Right Honourable Lester B. Pearson* by L.B. Pearson.

UNRRA's activities were very successful. Over 98 percent of the European war refugees were assisted in returning to their homes. In 1945, however, many refugees from the eastern European areas now under communist control refused to return home. The emerging Cold War conflict between East and West made any actions to help these people difficult. The U.S.S.R. demanded that all refugees be returned to their homelands, by force if necessary. The Western countries were unwilling to return these people forcibly.

UNRRA was replaced by the U.N.-sponsored International Refugee Organization (I.R.O.) in 1946. There were still over 1 000 000 homeless refugees, and most of them were from the eastern European states. Over the six year life of the I.R.O., Canada provided a large number of staff and approximately $18 000 000 for its work. Most important of all, by 1952 we had taken in 124 000 refugees as new Canadians.

The decision to accept large numbers of refugees was a major change in Canadian immigration policy. Since the early 1930s only a few immigrants had been admitted to Canada. Now, not only did regular immigration increase, but thousands of refugees poured into Canada. In 1947 and 1948, 20 000 refugees arrived in Canada. In 1949 almost 50 000 came. The refugee flow was so strong that one of every ten people who came to Canada in the twenty years after World War II was a refugee.

Among the first groups of refugees to come to Canada were 4500 Polish soldiers. They had fought as part of the First Canadian Army. At the end of World War II they refused to return to Poland since it was now under the control of the Soviet Union. These ex-soldiers signed contracts to work as farm labourers for two years in Canada.

A Liberal M.P., J. Ludger Dionne, received special permission to bring in 100 Polish refugees to work in his textile factory. They signed two-year contracts which paid them 25¢ per hour to start, yet other women in Quebec were paid 54¢ per hour, and other Canadian women were paid more than this. The resulting outcry was a major embarrassment to Mackenzie King's Liberal government.

Although there was a shortage of farm labour, their wages were well below those paid to Canadian farm workers. With a booming economy and a shortage of labour, the efforts to enforce

Fig. 2 Since the 1940s many organizations have been established to help refugees build new lives. "Operation Lifeline," whose office is shown here, is one of the more recent. What would be the main needs of refugees?

the contracts were weak. By the end of the first year many men had moved to the cities to take higher paying jobs.

The immediate post-war refugee crisis was resolved, but revolutions and civil wars in a number of countries created many new refugees. To deal with the continuing refugee crisis, the I.R.O. was replaced in 1952 by the United Nations High Commission for Refugees. Over the years Canada has responded to crises in other lands by opening its doors to refugees fleeing war and oppression in all parts of the globe. The following chart shows some examples of Canada taking on international responsibility.

When the U.N. proclaimed 1959 as World Refugee Year, Canada made special arrangements to take in refugees who were elderly or handicapped.

Fig. 3 The arrival of refugees in Canada

YEAR	APPROXIMATE NUMBER	NATIONALITY
1956-57	38 000	Hungarians
1968-69	13 000	Czechoslovakians
1970	228	Tibetans
1972-73	5 600	Ugandan Asians
1976	4 500	Chileans
1978-80	50 000	Vietnamese

GETTING THE FACTS

1. Why were the refugees from the eastern European countries especially difficult to re-settle?

227

2. Why was the decision to accept large numbers of refugees a major change in Canada's immigration policy?

3. Name three organizations designed to aid refugees. Explain the exact purpose of each.

USING YOUR KNOWLEDGE

4. How would someone become a refugee during World War II? Why was the number of refugees so high?

5. a) Imagine you are a 14-year-old living in a refugee camp in 1948. Write a diary entry about your thoughts both for and against the idea of going to Canada to start a new life.

   b) Imagine you are a 14-year-old Canadian in 1948. Write a diary entry about your thoughts on having a refugee family come to live in your neighbourhood.

THINKING IT THROUGH

6. a) Do you think Canada should have assumed responsibility for refugees at the end of World War II?

   b) Based on what you have read here, do you believe Canada did a good job of accepting responsibility for the plight of the refugees. Why or why not?

Refugees from the Hungarian Revolution: A case study

On a map in the chapter on the Cold War, find the location of Hungary. Based on its location, why would both the U.S.S.R. and its Warsaw Pact allies and the U.S.A. and its NATO partners be very interested in what happened in Hungary?

On October 23, 1956 a revolution broke out in Hungary. Although this event took place thousands of kilometres from Canada, it demonstrated Canada's willingness to take on major international responsibilities in a time of crisis.

The Hungarian Revolution had been building for some time. Many Hungarians disliked communist rule and especially the tight control exercised over the communist government by the U.S.S.R. They lived in an atmosphere of fear and persecution. Thousands of Hungarians had spoken out against the government, been picked up by the secret police and disappeared into jails. In addition, the standard of living of the Hungarian people was steadily declining. The Hungarians protested with street marches, demonstrations and the destruction of a gigantic statue of Stalin in the capital city of Budapest.

On November 4, the Soviets sent tanks and soldiers into Budapest. Several days of ferocious street fighting followed. The people of Budapest were caught in a hopeless mismatch. Using

Fig. 4 Refugees are interviewed by officials of the Canadian Embassy in a dancehall rented especially to process visa applications after the Hungarian Revolution.

broken paving stones from the streets or small homemade bombs, they tried to stop the huge Russian tanks. Booby-traps and sniper fire from windows and roof tops were of no use against cannon fire. By November 14, the Russian military might had crushed the Hungarian Revolution. The destruction of buildings and other property was enormous and over 20 000 Hungarians had been killed.

The Western world was outraged by the actions of the U.S.S.R. Prime Minister St. Laurent wrote to the Russian premier on November 13:

> I speak for the whole people of Canada in expressing our horror at the suffering of the Hungarian people as a result of their efforts to obtain the freedom to choose their own type of government....

One way in which the Western countries responded to the Hungarian Revolution was to try to deal with the plight of the 200 000 Hungarians who fled from their country during the revolution. Most of them had crossed the border into Austria hastily and with few possessions. In a brief twelve-week period, the largest number of refugees since the end of World War II had appeared. Of the countries of the world that responded to the plight of the Hungarian refugees, none made a greater contribution than Canada.

At first, the Canadian government was going to treat the refugees

This is an early example of television's impact on people's attitudes. Nightly newscasts brought to Canada and the rest of the world the shocking reality of the events in Hungary.

From *Canada in World Affairs, October 1955 to June, 1957* by J. Eayrs.

Because of the Cold War, the Western powers did not want to use military force to help the Hungarians. In addition, the great powers had to deal with the Suez crisis taking place at the same time.

Fig. 5 Hungarian refugees on their way to Canada. In what ways might they have found life in Canada different from life in Europe?

Hungarian refugees adjusted well to life in Canada. By December, 1958 only 3 percent were in need of government assistance.

as regular applicants for immigration. The processing of such applications is almost always slow and frustrating. Under pressure from the Canadian public, the Canadian government dropped almost all the usual regulations and procedures for immigration. Plans were swiftly made to look after, transport and settle large numbers of Hungarian refugees in Canada.

Provincial and local governments, churches, private clubs and organizations jumped in with offers of assistance. The federal government chartered planes and ships to bring the Hungarians over. The first Hungarians arrived in Canada before the end of November, 1956. By the end of December they were arriving at the rate of almost one hundred each day.

With the coming of spring the arrival of the Hungarians grew dramatically. By the end of 1957 over 36 000 had arrived. The final total was 37 565. The cost of the operation to the federal and provincial government was over $14 000 000. Canada accepted more Hungarian refugees than any other country in the world.

There are hundreds of success stories of Hungarian refugees who have not only adapted to life in Canada but also have made significant contributions to our country. Here is one of these stories:

Laszio Bastyovanszky was 15 years old, spoke no English and didn't have much of an idea what he was getting into when he landed in Halifax in January, 1957, on the MS Berlin from Bremerhaven, Germany, with about 500 other Hungarians.

"I got on a train," he said in an interview. "I was on it for three days and three nights and it gradually dawned on me what a big country this is."

"I was supposed to go to Vancouver but when I got to Winnipeg, it seemed like the right kind of place on the map, right in the middle of the country."

"I dreaded the thought of three more days on the train," he says.

So he disembarked, unexpected and ungreeted, and walked out into a –30 degree Winnipeg winter night looking for a policeman to arrest him and put him in a nice warm jail.

On Main Street he met a Hungarian.

His countryman took him to the Fort Osborne barracks, where the immigration department had set up a reception centre. Bastyovanszky lived there illegally for a week until an official, concerned about what was happening to missing extra meals, held a roll call and found him out.

A Winnipeg foster family took him in until he finished high school and found a job as a copy boy at the Winnipeg *Free Press*. He became a reporter, starting a career in journalism which took him to the Ottawa *Journal*, the Canadian Press and the CBC, where he now works as an executive to the corporation's head office.

From a C.P. article by Rob Bull which appeared in the Kitchener-Waterloo *Record* on October 24, 1981.

The Canadian response to the crisis of the Hungarian Revolution, combined with Canada's role in other international affairs, gave this country a strong image as a concerned nation, committed to assuming a share of the responsibility for the well-being of people in other parts of the world.

GETTING THE FACTS

7. List four reasons for the Hungarian Revolution.

THINKING IT THROUGH

8. At first the reaction of the Canadian government to taking in the refugees from the Hungarian Revolution was slow and cautious. Imagine it is 1956. Write a letter to the Minister of Citizenship and Immigration expressing your views regarding the admission of these people to Canada.

THE INVESTIGATIVE REPORTER

9. Identify people in your community who were refugees from Hungary or some other troubled area. Arrange an interview with one or more of them, and write down their story. How close was their experience to that of Laszio Bastyovanszky?

Fig. 6 Two members of a Canadian signals group in Lebanon, providing communications for United Nations posts. What sort of information do you think they would communicate?

Canada: Peace-keeper to the world

What is United Nations peace-keeping?

One of the U.N.'s most highly publicized activities has been its efforts to prevent or stop wars in many parts of the world. These activities are usually called peace-keeping operations. Units from the armed forces of several U.N. member nations come together in a peace-keeping operation as a special force under U.N. command. Countries asked to provide troops for each operation must be acceptable to all the nations that were involved in the fighting that led to the creation of the peace-keeping force. The big powers like the U.S.A., with one exception, and the U.S.S.R. have never been directly involved in peace-keeping because they usually have been closely involved with one of the sides.

In the years since 1948, Canada has been involved in every one of the U.N.'s peace-keeping operations. It is the only U.N. member to have done so. There are several reasons for Canada's remarkable record. They include:

1. Canada's willingness to serve. Canadians have believed that

In 1982 the U.S.A. became involved in a peace-keeping force sent into the war-torn Middle Eastern country of Lebanon. This peace-keeping activity was not, however, organized by the U.N., and involved only countries in the Western world.

232

the effort to prevent or end wars is a principal purpose of the U.N.

2. Although a member of NATO and a close ally of the United States, Canada has a strong international reputation for fairness.
3. Canada has highly specialized troops to handle important tasks such as communications and transportation.
4. Canada has never been an empire with colonies and thus is acceptable to third world nations as a member of a peace-keeping force.

Canada also served on an International Commission with India and Poland to supervise peace after a war in Indochina (Cambodia, Vietnam and Laos). This Commission was established, not by the United Nations, but by a special conference in Geneva, Switzerland in 1954.

Types of peace-keeping

There have been three types of United Nations peace-keeping operations:

1. A U.N. army enters an existing war on one side to try to defeat a country which has attacked another without a reason acceptable to the U.N. (It could be argued that this is not really peace-keeping. It has happened only once, in Korea.)
2. A U.N. force is placed between two warring countries to keep them apart.
3. The U.N. arranges a truce or cease-fire between rival groups within a country or between groups contesting control of a region where no stable government control exists or no claim of ownership is clearly accepted. A U.N. force observes and supervises the truce, often from a cease-fire line separating the rival sides. The peace-keepers report violations of the cease-fire agreement and try to prevent further hostilities.

As the following chart indicates, there has been a large number of United Nations peace-keeping operations. On the following pages we will examine one of each of the three types of peace-keeping operations.

Fig. 7 United Nations peace-keeping operations

Kashmir	1949
Palestine	1948
Korea	1950-1954
Egypt	1956-1967
Lebanon	1958-1959
Congo	1960-1964
West New Guinea	1962-1963
Yemen	1963-1964
Cyprus	1964-?
India/Pakistan	1965-1966

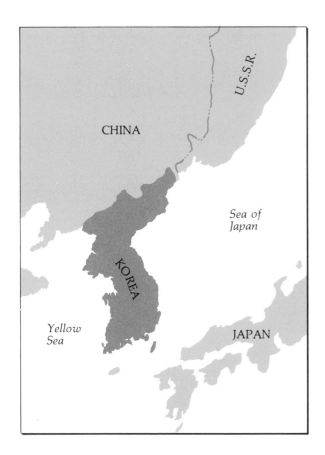

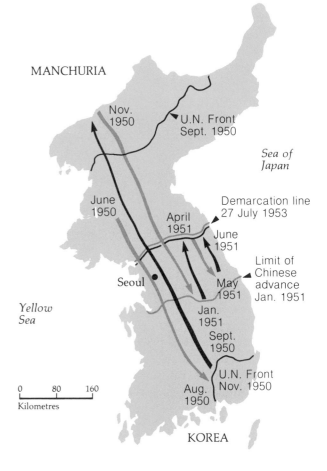

Fig. 8 These maps show the position of Korea, and the events of the Korean War. The arrows indicate the movement of the front line of fighting. Notice, from the dates on the map, how rapidly this line was pushed both north and south.

Russia was boycotting the Security Council because of the United Nations' refusal to recognize the new communist rulers in China as the official Chinese government.

1. 1950—Korea—The U.N. goes to war

Korea is a peninsula jutting into the Sea of Japan from the continent of Asia. Korea had been divided since the end of World War II. The north was under a communist government supported by the U.S.S.R. The area south of the 38th parallel of latitude was under a pro-Western government. All efforts to reunite the country had failed.

On June 25, 1950 North Korea invaded the south and rapidly pushed the southern forces back toward the sea. In an emergency session, the Security Council of the United Nations voted to establish a special U.N. army to stop the invasion. The U.S.S.R. did not use its Security Council veto to prevent the U.N. action.

More than 30 members of the U.N. responded with either troops or supplies or equipment. Over 300 000 troops served in the U.N. army. The overwhelming majority were American. Canada made the third largest contribution after the United States and Britain. Sailors and ships from the navy, planes and airmen from the air force and almost 8000 soldiers from the army made up Canada's

234

contribution. 27 000 Canadians served in Korea. Over 1000 Canadians were wounded and 400 killed in the Korean War.

Within a short time the U.N. forces had pushed the North Korean army close to the border of the Chinese province of Manchuria. Chinese forces joined the North Koreans and the U.N. army retreated southward once more.

By 1951 the war had reached a stalemate in approximately the same area it had begun. Fighting continued until 1953 when a truce was arranged. Negotiations to complete a permanent peace have never been successful. Canadian troops remained in Korea until 1957. Although the war had an inconclusive ending, the United Nations succeeded in preventing the conquest of South Korea by the northern aggressor.

2. 1956—The Suez crisis—Canada at the centre of the world stage

The Middle East required the U.N.'s close attention. Difficulties between the Arab states and the Jewish state of Israel and among rival Arab groups frequently broke out into armed conflict. Sometimes the big powers were involved. The President of Egypt, Colonel Gamal Abdel Nasser, had been quarreling with some of the major powers, especially Britain and France, for some time. Suddenly in July, 1956, Nasser nationalized the Suez Canal. This canal, which passed through Egypt, was an important link in the trade route from the Mediterranean Sea to the Middle and Far East.

The countries of the world were shocked and alarmed— especially Britain and France. Both were major investors in the canal and both were dependent on it for trade and access to their colonies and former colonies in the Far East. The U.S.S.R. encouraged Nasser and provided his army with weapons and equipment. In October, Israel, fearful of the Egyptian buildup of military power, launched a sudden invasion on Egypt across the Sinai Peninsula. At the same time to protect their own interests the French and British dropped troops by parachute at key positions along the canal. In response, the Egyptians sank several ships in the canal, effectively closing it. The U.S.S.R. threatened rocket attacks against the British, French and Israelis. Fighting raged along the canal while a jittery world feared the outbreak of a world war.

The United Nations went into a frenzy of activity. The most active and most important figure in the frantic days of late October and early November was Lester Pearson, Canada's Minister of External Affairs. Pearson worked out a compromise motion that the U.N., the major powers and Middle East combatants could accept. His motion called for an immediate cease-fire, the withdrawal of all foreign troops from Egypt, and the creation of a United Nations

Fig. 9 The Suez Crisis

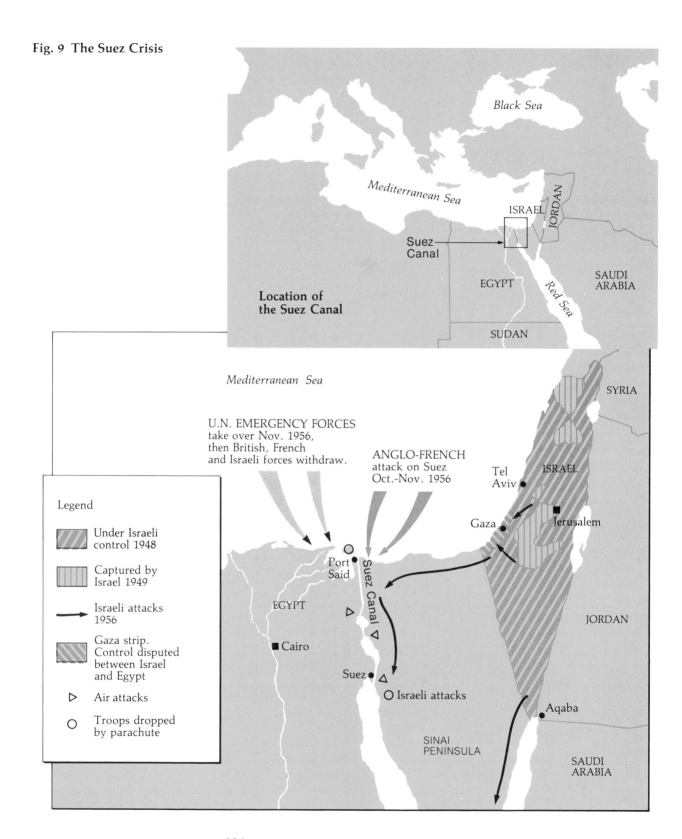

Black Sea

Mediterranean Sea

ISRAEL

JORDAN

Suez Canal →

EGYPT

SAUDI ARABIA

Red Sea

Location of the Suez Canal

SUDAN

Mediterranean Sea

SYRIA

U.N. EMERGENCY FORCES take over Nov. 1956, then British, French and Israeli forces withdraw.

ANGLO-FRENCH attack on Suez Oct.-Nov. 1956

Tel Aviv

ISRAEL

Gaza

Jerusalem

Legend

Under Israeli control 1948

Captured by Israel 1949

Israeli attacks 1956

Gaza strip. Control disputed between Israel and Egypt

▷ Air attacks

○ Troops dropped by parachute

Port Said

Suez Canal

EGYPT

Cairo

JORDAN

Suez

○ Israeli attacks

Aqaba

SINAI PENINSULA

SAUDI ARABIA

Emergency Force to supervise the cease-fire and be a buffer between the Egyptians and Israelis.

Once Pearson's plan was adopted, the fighting stopped. The first United Nations troops were in place within a couple of weeks. By the end of the year, the British and French had withdrawn. One of the most serious threats of full-scale international, and perhaps nuclear, war had ended.

A Canadian, General E.L.M. Burns, was given the challenging task of commanding the ten-nation United Nations Emergency Force. This was the U.N.'s first real "peace army" as it was intended to be placed between the combatants to keep the peace. It was not, like most other U.N. peace-keeping forces, a small observer group which only watched and reported cease-fire violations. Canada supplied the largest number of troops, about 800, to the Emergency Force. Canada's contribution included administrative, signal (communications), medical, transport and emergency personnel and equipment.

The United Nations Emergency Force remained in the Middle East for over ten years. In 1967, however, Egypt ordered the withdrawal of the U.N. force. War began once more in that troubled area.

Canada played a major role in the entire Suez crisis and was, for a time, at the centre of the world stage. It also had demonstrated its independence from the United States and Britain and assumed a leadership role among the middle and smaller nations.

Fig. 10 Canadian soldiers on patrol as part of the United Nations Emergency Force in Europe. How did the activities of this force differ from most other U.N. peace-keeping forces?

3. 1964—Cyprus—Controversy about Canada's peace-keeping role

The Mediterranean island of Cyprus had been troubled for years with conflict between the Greek and Turkish groups who lived there. In 1964 fighting broke out. After arranging a cease-fire, the U.N. quickly sent over 6000 military personnel to Cyprus from a number of nations. Canada contributed over 1000 men, as well as considerable military equipment. Canada also agreed to pay the costs involved in transporting its troops to Cyprus and maintaining them there.

The U.N. troops patrolled the lines dividing the hostile Greek and Turkish groups in Cyprus. They reported on violations of the truce agreement and generally tried to prevent fighting from breaking out again. Their efforts were successful for a number of years. The size of the U.N. force was reduced and by 1974 the number of Canadians was down to 500. In that year new fighting broke out. Concerned about an attempt by local Greek military officers to take control of the island, and join it with Greece, Turkey invaded Cyprus. The U.N. immediately increased its force and order was eventually restored. Over the next few years the U.N. force was again reduced, and once more the Canadian troops in Cyprus numbered around 500.

Fig. 11 Canadian soldiers in the U.N. peace-keeping force on lookout duty in the mountains. Put yourself in their place. What do you like about your assignment as a peace-keeper in Cyprus? What do you dislike? In each case explain why.

Lester B. Pearson: A great Canadian

Lester Pearson was one of Canada's most famous and most highly respected international statesmen. He was born in Toronto in 1897. He interrupted his education to serve overseas in World War I as a member of the Royal Flying Corps. After the war he graduated from the University of Toronto and from Oxford University in England. For several years he taught history at the University of Toronto. Always a keen athlete, he coached the university hockey team. He was also an avid sports fan and knew as much about sports, especially baseball and hockey, as he did about government and international affairs. He was known in later life to sneak out of Cabinet meetings to watch World Series baseball games on television in a nearby room.

In 1928, he left the university to join the Department of External Affairs. He rose steadily and became Canada's Ambassador to the United States in 1945. He played an important role in the establishment of the United Nations. He was nominated as the first Secretary-General of the U.N. but the U.S.S.R. refused to accept a Canadian in that post. (The Soviets believed that a Canadian would likely take the side of the West and especially the U.S.A. in an East—West or Soviet—American dispute.) After serving a year in 1952-53 as President of the General Assembly, he was again nominated for the post of Secretary-General, but again was vetoed by the U.S.S.R. Pearson also played a major role in the creation and design of NATO.

In 1948, Pearson had joined the Cabinet of Liberal Prime Minister Mackenzie King. As Minister of External Affairs and through his achievements at the United Nations, Pearson gained a reputation as one of the world's great diplomats. His friendly and modest manner and skilful powers of persuasion and compromise made him a major force in international affairs for many years. The high point of his diplomatic career came in 1956 when he played the central role in bringing an end to the Suez crisis and establishing the United Nations Emergency Force to maintain peace in the troubled Middle East. For this achievement he was awarded the Nobel Peace Prize in 1957.

In 1958, Pearson became leader of the Liberal party and in 1963 was elected as Canada's fifteenth prime minister. He was prime minister until his retirement in 1968. One of his accomplishments as prime minister was the establishment of the red maple leaf flag as Canada's national flag.

Even after his retirement, prestigious positions came his way. One of these was Chairman of the World Bank. Lester Pearson, a great Canadian, died in 1972.

Fig. 12 Lester Pearson and Mrs. Pearson display the Nobel Peace Prize medal.

Troops remain in Cyprus to this day because no permanent peace settlement has ever been worked out. Over the years, five Canadians have been killed and twenty wounded. In addition, because Canada agreed to pay the costs of Canadian participation when the operation began, the Cyprus commitment has cost Canada millions of dollars. In recent years it has been estimated that the Cyprus force is costing Canada between $2 000 000 and $3 000 000 a year beyond the normal expenses that would be involved in paying and equipping the Canadian troops no matter where they were stationed. The casualties and the length and the expense of the Cyprus operation have raised considerable controversy in recent years in Canada. Some want us to withdraw from Cyprus. Others are questioning the whole idea of Canadian participation in U.N. peace-keeping operations.

GETTING THE FACTS

10. Why are big nations not usually involved in peace-keeping?

11. List four reasons why Canada has been involved in peace-keeping operations.

12. Do you think the Korean War belongs in a discussion of peace-keeping? Why or why not?

13. The role of Canada in the Suez crisis is often regarded as the most important Canada has ever played in international affairs since the end of World War II. Why do you think some experts believe this to be the case? Suggest and discuss as many reasons as you can.

THINKING IT THROUGH

14. Canada's commitment to peace-keeping in Cyprus has lasted since 1964 at considerable cost to Canada in both money and casualties. Do you think Canada should put a time limit on its contribution to peace-keeping operations? Present arguments both for and against such a time limit.

The changing Commonwealth

Canada's growth as an independent nation is reflected in its changing relationship with Britain. Canada and other countries slowly gained independence from Britain yet retained some ties to each other through the unique organization of the Commonwealth.

—British Empire	—colonies under the "mother country" Britain
1926—British Commonwealth of Nations	—members of Commonwealth met as equals to discuss issues of mutual concern
	—British monarch was official head of state of each member country
	—maximum membership was 8 [Britain, Canada, Australia, New Zealand, South Africa, India, Pakistan, Sri Lanka (Ceylon)]
	—South Africa and Pakistan have since left the Commonwealth as a result of major policy differences with the other members
1949—Commonwealth of Nations	—changes necessary because of new nations emerging in Africa and Asia
	—British monarch became head of Commonwealth but not necessarily head of government of each member
	—members made own choice on head of government— some kept British monarch (Canada was one), some established own monarchy, others became republics with no monarch
	—examples of Commonwealth members with their own monarch include Malaysia, Tonga, Lesotho and Swaziland
	—membership grew to 42 by 1980
	—the 42 members of the Commonwealth have 25 percent of the world's population and 20 percent of the land area of the globe
	—Commonwealth now a

1971—Commonwealth Declaration	unique free association of countries of many different cultures and races
	—members strengthened their relationship by signing a declaration of goals:

1971—Commonwealth Declaration — unique free association of countries of many different cultures and races

—members strengthened their relationship by signing a declaration of goals:

   (1) international peace and support of the United Nations

   (2) elimination of racial prejudice

   (3) elimination of enormous differences in wealth around the globe

   (4) world-wide establishment of individual liberty and rights

As the Commonwealth changed and as Canada's role in it changed, our country was able to play a greater part in world affairs.

The remarkable growth in newly independent nations can be seen by examining the membership of the United Nations. When it was formed in 1945, it had 51 members. Thirty years later in 1975, it had 144.

Canada takes on responsibilities in the Commonwealth— The Colombo Plan

The Colombo Plan was discussed at a Commonwealth meeting in Colombo, Ceylon, (now Sri Lanka) in 1950. Seven members— Ceylon, India, Pakistan, Australia, New Zealand, Britain and Canada—agreed to future discussion and cooperation in economic development and growth. The economic development of the Asian members of the Commonwealth was emphasized. The initial plan was for a six year period, but it was renewed many times and later expanded to include non-Commonwealth countries.

The Colombo Plan in part resulted from the tensions of the Cold War and the victory of the communist forces in China in 1949. In 1950, John Diefenbaker stated that the financial commitment involved in strengthening the economies of other Asian countries ". . . would be cheap insurance for Canada . . . to halt Communism in Asia."

Countries receiving aid identified areas where they needed assistance with their own plans for economic growth. These countries then worked out an arrangement with one of the countries providing assistance. From 1951-1954, Canada provided over $25 000 000 of assistance each year. In the next two years, the total climbed to over $26 000 000 each year. By 1960 over $320 000 000 worth of assistance had been provided by Canada.

The assistance came in the form of material goods or technical teaching and advice. Projects to increase agricultural production were emphasized, but other projects included transportation, health care, power and industrial production. Specific examples of Canadian assistance were constructing the Warsak power and irrigation project in Pakistan, a nuclear reactor in India, and the Kundah hydro-electric power project in India, providing locomotives for India and

Ceylon's transportation systems, sending technical experts in agriculture, medicine and industry to Asia and bringing students to Canada for training in these technical fields. Such projects in economic cooperation show the strength of the changing Commonwealth.

Fig. 13 Canadian locomotives are loaded for shipment to Ceylon as part of the Colombo Plan.

15. What change was made in the role of the monarch in the Commonwealth after 1949? What did this change permit Commonwealth members to do?

16. While Minister of External Affairs, Lester Pearson commented on the value of the Commonwealth in a Cold War world: "Its value as a bridge of understanding between the West and Asia and Africa is very great in this age of suspicion and strain when there are few such bridges."
    a) Why did Pearson call the Commonwealth a "bridge"?
    b) Is this bridge valuable in a Cold War world? Explain.

17. If you were a leader of the Indian government at the time of the formation of the Colombo Plan, what would you like about it? What fears or concerns might you have about it?

18. The second Monday of March each year has been declared Commonwealth Day by its member nations. Prepare a wall poster for this day that would illustrate its goals and achievements.

Canada's relationship to new nations: Ghana— A case study

Ghana was chosen as the name for the new nation because it had been the name of one of the great empires from West Africa's glorious past.

In 1939 there were only 3 independent nations in Africa—Liberia, Ethiopia and Egypt. By the end of 1949 there were 9. In 1960 there were 5 more and in 1961 another 4 more.

Many new nations emerged in Asia and Africa as the result of the dismantling of the old colonial empires of Britain, France, Spain and others. With their independence, the new nations gained the freedom to decide on their own form of government and future. Ghana was formerly a British colony in Africa called the Gold Coast. On March 6, 1957 it won its independence. It was the first of the many new nations to do so.

Canada had not taken an active role in African affairs. With the emergence of Ghana, Canada took a greater interest in Africa. There were several reasons for this: Canada could 1) offer help to new Commonwealth members; 2) develop new trade partners; and 3) prevent the U.S.S.R. from gaining influence in these new nations.

Canada established diplomatic offices in Ghana in 1957. Ghana

244

needed techical experts and technical training for its own people. In 1958, Canada provided $135 000 for technical assistance. In succeeding years this amount was greatly increased. The plan begun with Ghana was expanded to other new Commonwealth countries under what came to be called the Commonwealth Technical Assistance Programme. In 1960, the Canadian government established the Special Commonwealth Africa Assistance Plan for all Commonwealth nations in Africa. In the first eight years of this program almost $35 000 000 in assistance was provided.

In the case of Ghana the assistance took many forms—technical experts and teachers sent from Canada to Ghana, the establishment of scholarships for students from Ghana to study in Canada, a $1 000 000 contribution to the construction of a technical training centre in the capital city of Accra, the construction of hydro power transmission lines and assistance in the training of Ghana's armed forces.

As the 1960s began, Canada had come a long way from a policy of inactivity in Africa. Canada had assumed major responsibilities in helping to ensure the success of the new, independent nations of Africa.

Fig. 14 The location of Ghana

USING YOUR KNOWLEDGE

19. What similarities were there between Canadian assistance to Ghana and to India, Pakistan and Ceylon under the Colombo Plan? How do you account for these similarities?

Conclusion

Canada takes on global responsibilities—The controversy

Taking on new global responsibilities marked an important new direction in Canadian policy toward the rest of the world. This new direction did not become policy without some controversy. Look back to the picture and map display at the beginning of this chapter and then examine the quotations below.

1. A Member of Parliament asked, during the influx of refugees to Canada from the Hungarian Revolution

... what is the difference between a refugee from the maritime provinces or some other part of Canada, and a war-scared refugee from Europe? One can get just as hungry as the other.

245

Fig. 15 Refugees register at a United Nations camp, 1980. Look at the list of countries on the board. Do you think these countries have many features in common, apart from their willingness to accept refugees? Give reasons for your answer.

2. A New Brunswick Member of Parliament said, when he saw the budget for some Colombo Plan projects, that he was

> ... astonished ... by the ... financial assistance for various projects which this government is giving outright to foreign countries, while in the same breath denying the very same kind of projects to our own people in New Brunswick. ...

3. A Member of Parliament from Cape Breton Island, a region of high unemployment in the 1950s, commented on the Colombo Plan.

> Why don't you get a Colombo Plan in Canada for us?

THINKING IT THROUGH

20. Analyze the above quotations by answering the following questions:

a) With which of the two displays are these comments most closely associated? Why?

b) Explain what each Member of Parliament is saying. What is common to all three? Using the knowledge you have gained in your study of this chapter, write two paragraphs in which you respond to those comments. Use as many examples from the chapter as possible in defending the actions of the Canadian government.

c) Did you find yourself agreeing with the comments of the Members of Parliament quoted above or with the response you have written to them? Why? Or, did you find merits on both sides? If so, what advice would you give to the Canadian government to try to satisfy both sides?

d) Are there any examples in more recent times of the same type of controversy? If so, how is the example you have found similar to and different from the issues of the 1950s?

M, President Discuss Plan

Joint Cabinet Committee
New Proposal for Defense

How to Meet Red Threat Parley Theme

By HARVEY HICKEY
Globe and Mail Staff Reporter

Ottawa, July 9—Establishment of a joint cabinet committee on defense

Colorful Reception At Capital

From the Ottawa Bureau of The Globe and Mail

Ottawa, July 9—In an atmosphere of excitement, heightened by a smart military display, President Eisenhower arrived at Uplands Airport today on a threeday visit to the capital.

After circling the airport for a few minutes his aircraft, Columbine III, touched down sharp on the stroke of 11 a.m. A moment later, amid a salute of 21 guns boomed, he and his party were being warmly greeted by Governor-General Massey and Prime Minister Diefenbaker and Mrs. Diefenbaker.

"I am very happy to see you here," Mr. Diefenbaker said, grasping the president's hand. Mr. Eisenhower, tanned and looking the picture of health, returned the greeting with equal warmth.

About half the crowd were the children of RCAF officers and men stationed at the two stands overlooking the scene. After he had inspected the guard of honor, Mr. Eisenhower began to ensemble the black limousine to proceed to Government House.

Mrs. Eisenhower, immediate.

North American Defense Discussions
...possibility of a joint cabinet committee to con...

P.M. Feels 'Isolated
On Crisis Over Cu

Mr. Diefenbaker rose the House of Commons terday and in weary, tones explained that he not casting any dou President Kennedy's c that there were So fensive missile bases island

...ARS
...iter

...anadian
...ing the
...Soviet
...is of
...g of

PEARSON YESTERDAY
At Rideau Hall

By VAL SEARS
Star Staff Writer

OTTAWA—A new Liberal government, headed by Prime Minister-to-be Lester Pearson, takes office ...day to begin '60 days of decision.'

...wearing his old diplomatic uniform ... hombarg, walked out of ...bedroom yester ... Deme

'60 Days Of Decision'

PEARSON TO SEE MAC
THEN MEET KENNEDY

CUT FOREIGN OWNERSHIP
GORDON'S BUDGET PLA

By VAL SEARS
Star Staff Writer

OTTAWA — Liberal Finance Gordon set three main goals in budget presented to Parliame employment, increased revenue of Canadian control of Canadi

The budget left the mod but planned to tap big busines plugging corporation tax lo on "expense account livin

The 57-year-old speech drew one of the in years.

Mr. Gordon, read fully between sips of mons he expected to gree by nearly

...BOWS TO ROBARTS
...lling Hotel

10 The 1960s set the stage for a new Canada

In the 1960s television took on a greater role in the spreading of news and the providing of entertainment. A Canadian thinker, Marshall McLuhan, first recognized and described the way television was influencing society. Television made the world seem smaller. Distant events were brought closer to people. McLuhan used the phrase "global village" to describe this tendency. During the 1960s, McLuhan wrote four best-selling books—*The Gutenberg Galaxy*, *Understanding Media*, *The Medium is the Massage*, and *War and Peace in the Global Village*.

The following excerpt refers to the tragic assassination of President Kennedy, seen over and over on television.

> The Kennedy assassination gave people an immediate sense of the television power to create depth involvement, on the one hand, and a numbing effect as deep as grief, itself, on the other hand. Most people were amazed at the depth of meaning which the event communicated to them.
>
> From *Understanding Media* by Marshall McLuhan.

- What impression do you think some of the major events mentioned in this chapter would have had on you if you had seen them on television? In one or two sentences for each, describe how you would react to these events.

- Do you think your reactions would be different if you read about these events in a newspaper or heard about them on the radio? Why or why not?

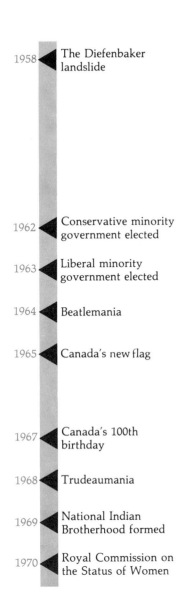

1958	The Diefenbaker landslide
1962	Conservative minority government elected
1963	Liberal minority government elected
1964	Beatlemania
1965	Canada's new flag
1967	Canada's 100th birthday
1968	Trudeaumania
1969	National Indian Brotherhood formed
1970	Royal Commission on the Status of Women

Chapter overview

In many parts of the world, the 1960s was a decade of protest and unrest. Because of the media, particularly television, Canadians were aware of world issues and events. Many Canadians came to share in the mood that was sweeping the world. Some world issues and events that affected Canadians were:

—baby boom of the 1950s
  —expansion of colleges and universities
  —changes in education
  —student protests and sit-ins
  —hippies
—folk and rock music
  —Woodstock
  —Beatlemania
—Vietnam War
  —draft dodgers
—assassination of President Kennedy
—civil rights movement
  —Martin Luther King
—women's movement
—first astronaut on the moon

This chapter will focus on selected events of the 1960s. The youthquake and the reform movements of Native people and women are featured. In addition, we will look at some of the Canadian political issues of the time.

Signposts

> Some problems in studying recent history

> The youthquake

> Reform movements

> The Diefenbaker-Pearson feud

> FEATURE: "Third Parties" in Canadian politics

> The Yankee dollar

Ottawa and the provinces >

Trudeaumania >

Key words

perspective	generation gap
sources	Red Power
bias	outmigration
social history	cooperative federalism

Some problems in studying recent history

The 1960s may seem like ancient history to you. Historians, however, are used to dealing with events much further back in time. To them, the 1960s seem like only yesterday. This can create problems when historians attempt to study the decade.

Why is recent history always a challenge to explain? Because we are so close to it, we have trouble "telling the forest from the trees." That is, we lack perspective. Something happens that seems important at the time. Yet perhaps in fifty years people will realize that it wasn't important at all. Or something happens and people don't pay much attention. Years later, we find out that this event changed the course of history.

Sources are another difficulty in handling recent history. Historians dealing with events of hundreds or thousands of years ago often have little information to work with. Discovery of a new fact means adding another piece of an incomplete picture. In contrast, historians describing the 1960s have many sources—newspapers, magazines, television, film, public opinion polls, autobiographies and other records. Some of these records are more difficult to find than other information. Perhaps they are buried in the files of governments, businesses and other organizations, or in the memories of individuals who took part in important events. First historians must locate these sources. Then they must decide which are significant and which are not.

Bias is another problem in explaining recent history. Historians may try very hard to be objective—"to tell it like it was." However, personal experiences, feelings, and viewpoints affect the way they see things and record them. Without realizing it, they can portray history in a biased way.

Fig. 1 In the sixties the whole world was shocked by the death of two men in the United States: President John F. Kennedy, assassinated in 1963; and Martin Luther King, the black civil rights leader, assassinated in 1968. Do you think the course of history can be changed by a single person?

Fig. 2 During the sixties, public protests often made news. How might the policeman report this event? Would the protesters see it in a different way?

A quick look at the stories in the newspapers and on radio and television news reveals another problem in the writing of recent history. How often do they involve people like yourself? How much "good news" is reported? Journalists are attracted to the dramatic, the unusual, the wierd, the spectacular event—so are other observers, writers, record-keepers and historians.

In dealing with recent history, we must keep these problems in mind and try to overcome them. Also we should keep our minds open for new facts and ideas that could improve our understanding. We hope that students will always look cautiously and critically at explanations of recent *and* ancient history.

1. In your own words, define each of the following: perspective, sources, bias, spectacular event.

USING YOUR KNOWLEDGE

2. Have you ever looked back on something that happened to you when you were younger and wondered, "Why did I ever get so upset about a little thing like that?" Explain why you feel differently about the incident now. In your answer, refer to historical perspective.

THE INVESTIGATIVE REPORTER

3. Suppose you are a historian in the year 2001.
   a) What four or five events of the past year do you think you will be including in your write-up of history?
   b) For one of these events, collect pictures from magazines. Put them together as a collage, or picture-history, that explains the event as objectively as possible. Do you have problems in trying to present a fair or objective picture of the event? Explain your answer.

The youthquake

If you look for young people in most historical accounts, you are likely to be disappointed. In general, young people have not filled roles, like running governments, businesses, or armies, that are often highlighted in history books. However, in an account of the social history of the 1960s, young people play an important part.

After the end of World War II in 1945, Canadians could settle down and have families. The birthrate increased sharply in the late 1940s. By the 1960s, the "baby boomers" were in their teens.

The "baby boomers" generally grew up in a time of prosperity. More and more Canadians felt secure about their basic needs—food, shelter, clothing. When these needs can more-or-less be taken for granted, people have time and energy for thinking about the pros and cons of their way of life. Many Canadians became aware of the problems and shortcomings of their country's way of life. Some concerns were pollution, the ongoing danger of another world war, and the limited rights of women and minority groups. Widespread education and the growth of television helped draw people's attention to controversial issues. Many young people became interested in trying to understand and change these conditions around them that

Fig. 3 The young wore buttons to proclaim their feelings. Choose two slogans from these buttons and explain what you think they mean.

Fig. 4 Many adults were outraged by the new mini-skirt fashion. Why do you think this was so?

From "Requiem for the '60's," *Macleans* (January, 1975) by Philip Marchand.

seemed unacceptable. Their involvement ranged from simply becoming informed to holding protest marches, "sit-ins," and other dramatic activities.

According to the mass media, a "youthquake" was underway. Television, radio, newspapers, magazines and books reported that the young were rebelling against the values and authority of their elders. Such statements were true for many young people, although not all of them. Nevertheless, throughout the sixties a certain set of values became linked to young people in general. These values included peace, brotherhood, freedom and equal rights. Among the values rejected by the young were overconcern with money and possessions such as houses, cars and clothes.

The following statement reveals some of the attitudes for which young Canadians of the sixties became known:

> One wonders if any other generation will ever experience the thrill we did at discovering we were truly a separate, distinct nation living on this continent. . . . Our nation would soon take its rightful place, after a genial [friendly] revolution. We would make this continent clean and habitable [liveable] for the first time since the Indians.

During the sixties people spoke of the conflict in attitudes between some members of the younger generation and some

254

members of the older generation. This conflict or split came to be called the generation gap. The split was further highlighted by the fads, styles and music of young people in the sixties.

One group of young people who seemed to symbolize the "youthquake" was the hippies. Their trademarks were long hair, casual clothes, sandals, and coffee houses where they might listen to the folk music of Ian and Sylvia, Joni Mitchell, Gordon Lightfoot and others. Through their unconventional dress and behavior, the hippies showed their indifference to conservative, middle-class values. The experimental use of drugs was one of the features of the hippy sub-culture which drew negative media attention in the sixties. Positive features, such as hope for universal peace and goodwill and concern for the environment, did not receive as much attention from the media.

Fig. 5 Canadian singer, Joni Mitchell, whose songs are still popular today

How did the older generation react to the "youthquake," the apparent rebelliousness of the young? Comments like the following editorial in *Macleans* (November, 1965) appeared in Canadian newspapers and magazines:

> . . . Today's generation of rebels seems to be especially difficult and numerous. Some experts believe they are quite different from any who went before. Their estrangement from adults is almost complete. They are unique in having a youth subculture. They have their own literature, their own music and films, and a host of expert marketers who have created a mythology [set of beliefs] for them by which they live and buy.

> . . . Most adults could tolerate [put up with] the rejection more easily if only the young people would wash and shave and get their hair cut and work more regularly. But this is part of the protest against conformity to which they rigidly conform. . . .

How deep was the generation gap? How serious was the division between young people and adults? These questions are still difficult to answer. By the end of the sixties the styles and attitudes of young people had spread to the population in general. Many adults well beyond their teens and twenties adopted longer hair, more casual clothing, behaviour and concerns. Yet very often members of both groups failed to understand or refused to tolerate each other's values.

What was the best way to deal with the gap between generations? The following paragraph concluded the *Macleans* editorial. It offers one possible answer to this complex question asked very often during the sixties. What answers can you suggest?

> But there they [the young] are. We produced them, and they reject the values we profess. It will do no good to fuss about it.

Fig. 6 Some Canadians protested against the United States' involvement in the Vietnam War in south east Asia. Often they were joined by "draft-dodgers," Americans who had been "called up" to the armed forces, but who came to live in Canada to avoid fighting in a war in which they did not believe.

What we need to do is examine the values we claim to believe in and reject the elements which an honest appraisal shows to be false. Then we may be able to start communicating with our children again.

GETTING THE FACTS

4. Use each of the following terms in a sentence: youthquake, basic needs, hippies.

5. What is your understanding of the term "values"? Give two examples of values that appeared to divide young people from adults in the 1960s.

USING YOUR KNOWLEDGE

6. Look over the November, 1965 editorial in *Macleans*.
   a) In your own words, summarize the main idea of the editorial.
   b) Do you think the author is biased? Explain your answer.
   c) What advice for adults does the editorial contain? Does this make the editorial seem less biased?

7. Suppose you were a 15-year-old in the 1960s. Write a letter to the editor giving a reply to the editorial.

THINKING IT THROUGH

8. Many people in the sixties felt that the young people who wanted to change the world were troublemakers with nothing to contribute to Canada. Many young people, on the other hand, felt that adults had made a mess of the world and that it was up to the young to clean it up. Imagine that you are an historian in the 1980s who is trying to decide which point of view was more valid. You want to do research to see whether there are more facts to support one point of view than the other point of view.
   a) Suggest at least two facts that would support the young people's point of view. Then suggest at least two facts to support the adult point of view.
   b) What sources of information would give you the facts you are looking for? Are some sources more reliable than others? Explain your answer.

Reform movements

The 1960s was a decade in which many questions were raised about life in Canada, and there was much talk of change. Even as they celebrated their Centennial, Canadians wondered about their "identity." In Quebec, a way of life was being examined and altered. Young people questioned old values, and dreamed of a different

future and women and Indian peoples were beginning to take a stand for an equal place in Canadian society.

Women

The women's movement was one of the main forces for change in Canada in the 1960s. A major step was the formation, in 1966, of the Committee for Equality of Women. It brought together representatives of dozens of Canadian women's organizations. At the first meeting of the Committee, spokesperson Ms. Laura Sabia called for immediate pressure on the Canadian government to look into the status of women.

Concern for their status, their place in Canadian society, had been growing among Canadian women since the beginning of the decade. In 1960, they generally had the right to vote and were eligible to be elected, but they lacked many other rights and opportunities taken for granted by men. The place of women was still widely regarded to be the traditional one—married, busy at home raising the children and running the household. Canadian women were not expected to have careers outside the home.

Yet one of every three people in the labour force was a woman, and more than half of working women were married.

Among working women, the desire for change was growing. They had jobs, but, in most cases, they were the ones traditionally held by women—nurses, hairdressers, elementary school teachers, secretaries and receptionists. Rarely did they become doctors, principals, business managers or electricians. Through television, improved education and the growth of women's organizations, Canadian women—and men too—were made more and more aware of the inequality between the sexes.

The inequality of women went far beyond the limitations of career choices. Women doing the same job as men were commonly paid less. The tax system and the laws of Canada worked to the disadvantage of women. Schools and universities, the mass media, even governments, helped maintain the unequal position of women in society. Perhaps the biggest problem was the attitude, among many women as well as men, that this situation need not be changed.

Women active in the 1960s in the campaign for equal rights faced an enormous challenge. In the early 1900s, the suffragettes had shown courage and determination in achieving the right for women to vote. However, they were disappointed in their hopes that women would obtain their fair share of political power. Between 1917 and 1970, Canada had 134 elections, including federal and provincial. The number of people elected was 6845. Of these, only 67 were women. In 1970, following the "Trudeaumania" election two years before, Grace McInnis was the only woman among the 264 members of the House of Commons. When Thérèse Casgrain

Fig. 7 Thérèse Casgrain

Fig. 8 Judy LaMarsh

was named to the Canadian Senate, also in 1970, only six of the 102 members were women. In 1967, the year of Canada's Centennial, Brenda Robertson made history in New Brunswick by becoming the first woman ever elected in her province. She was its first female Cabinet minister three years later.

If women were not gaining power within the system of government, they had to apply pressure on government from outside. This is exactly what they did. The Committee for Equality of Women prepared a report demanding a study of the many forms of inequality facing Canadian women. Women's organizations from all over the country gave their support. They were encouraged by a member of the federal Cabinet, Judy LaMarsh, to confront the Canadian government. Meetings followed, and the result was the appointment, in February, 1967, of the Royal Commission on the Status of Women.

The report on the Status of Women was presented on December 7, 1970. It included 167 recommendations. Some of the main ones were:

—a network of day-care centres, to assist mothers working outside the home
—a Canadian council to promote improvements in the status of women in Canada
—the same salaries for women doing the same work as men
—an increase in the number of women holding top level jobs in government, business, education
—longer maternity leave for women away from their jobs to have babies, combined with improved unemployment insurance benefits

Fig. 9 What do you think the advantages of day-care centres are for both parents and children?

It remained to be seen how many of the Report's recommendations would be put into effect by governments. However, by the time the Report was completed, interest in the status of women had been stirred up across the country. The stage was set for a continuing look at the part played by women in Canadian life. In the 1970s and beyond, continuing change in the status of women was likely. Many features of society—marriage, family, use of leisure time, to name only a few—were bound to be affected.

GETTING THE FACTS

9. In a sentence or two, identify: Laura Sabia, Brenda Robertson, Thérèse Casgrain, Judy LaMarsh.

USING YOUR KNOWLEDGE

10. Imagine you were Anne Francis, the broadcaster who headed the Royal Commission on the Status of Women. In a paragraph or two, give what you consider to be the most important facts about the inequality of Canadian women in the 1960s.

THINKING IT THROUGH

11. a) What was the Royal Commission on the Status of Women?
    b) Which of the recommendations in its report do you think are most important? Give reasons for your viewpoint.

THE INVESTIGATIVE REPORTER

12. a) For the recommendations you selected in question 11, find out what action has been taken to reduce or solve the problem since 1970.
    b) Do you think that more should be done to improve the status of women on those matters? Give reasons to support your viewpoint.

Red Power

In 1969 *The Unjust Society* was published. This book was written by Harold Cardinal, a 24-year-old Indian leader from Alberta. It told of Canada's treatment of Native peoples. It was the latest example of what some referred to as Red Power

What was Red Power? What forms did it take? What were its effects?

Red Power refers to organized efforts by Canada's Native people to deal with their problems. Native people were trying to gain control over their own lives. No longer were they willing to accept

Fig. 10 What sort of programmes would this radio station broadcast?

the decisions of politicians, civil servants and other "bosses." It was as though the Native people were saying, "We are treated unfairly by other Canadians, and we are sick of it!"

Red Power surprised many Canadians. Because of the reserve system, they often had little contact with Indians, for example, and assumed most of them would continue to live indefinitely on reserves. For some 75 years, in fact, the Indians of Canada had lived for the most part on reserves. All of a sudden in the 1960s, a growing number of Indians became part of the movement known as outmigration. They were abandoning life on reserves and moving into cities like Winnipeg, Regina and Edmonton.

Why were Indians leaving the reserves for the city? They wanted to make a decent living. They wanted jobs and education and other benefits that were not available on isolated reserves. The cities seemed the only hope for getting a job and sharing in the general prosperity available to other Canadians.

Outmigration resulted in many problems. In the cities, Indians faced discrimination, unemployment, poor housing and inferior education. Another serious problem was that Canadian Indians found themselves in danger of losing their cultural identity and customs. Some individuals adapted to their new surroundings. For many, however, moving to the cities in the 1960s was an unhappy, even tragic, experience. They found themselves shut out by white society and attitudes and customs.

Indians responded in a variety of ways. Some turned to the Native traditions kept alive on the reserves. Others formed organizations to cater to social and cultural needs in the cities. Still others

got involved in political groups that led the struggle for Native rights.

Political action—Red Power—had many obstacles to overcome. Native people from different parts of Canada often had little in common except the unfriendly attitudes and discrimination of non-Natives. Many had lost their traditional languages, arts and customs. Long years of enduring non-Native control—and attempts at assimilation—had robbed Natives of their confidence.

A serious problem was division and conflict among Indians themselves. The needs of Indians on reserves were different from those who had moved to cities. Indians anxious to be accepted by non-Natives in the cities sometimes denied their Native background. Indeed, under Canadian law, many people of Native ancestry were not considered to be Indian.

Indians were also divided on methods to improve the conditions of their people. Members of the older generation often wanted to trust the Canadian government to bring about changes gradually. The young, on the other hand, were inclined to confront non-Native society with demands for immediate improvement. Nothing seemed to get results like a public demonstration that attracted the mass media, especially television.

The key to Red Power was organization. By the end of the 1960s, the National Indian Brotherhood and the Native Women's Association of Canada were active. They brought Native people together to share their common concerns. Much effort was needed to build a foundation of Indian pride and identity. Now, in the 1980s, Indian reformers are making real gains.

The work of Indian painters and other artists was a valuable contribution. Norval Morrisseau, Jackson Beardy, Odjig and a host of other creative Indian men and women were becoming known across Canada. So were writers and performers like Alanis Obomosawin, Duke Redbird, Wilfred Pelletier and David Campbell. The latter, for example, wrote "pride songs," such as "Pretty Brown," from which the following lines are quoted.

Pretty Brown you're a song
that I can't keep from singing
Pretty Brown as you move
you don't know that you're winning
And your eyes say you're lost
like an autumn leaf spinning
Turn around, dry your eyes, Pretty Brown

From *Pretty Brown* by David Campbell.

Indian languages and practices concerning religion, medicine, family and other traditions have survived in many parts of Canada. This is so in spite of efforts—for more than 100 years—by governments, churches, schools, etc. to assimilate Indians.

For more information on the definition of "Indian," use the index to find the pages telling about the Indian Act.

Fig. 11 Norval Morrisseau became known for the expression of his Ojibway heritage. He was called the "grandfather of Canadian Native Art," and received the Order of Canada in 1978.

13. Explain, in your own words, the following: Red Power, outmigration.

14. List at least three problems that Native people faced when they moved to the city.

15. Native peoples in the 1960s chose organization as one way of starting to improve their lives. In your opinion was this a good way to deal with their problems? Give reasons for your answer.

16. Why do you think David Campbell wrote *Pretty Brown*?

17. What conditions were Harold Cardinal and other Native people protesting? Using *The Unjust Society* and other sources, select and write a one-page report on one example of unfair treatment of the Native peoples. Do you feel that there was a need to protest this treatment? Explain your answer.

18. Make a report on modern achievements in the arts by Canadian Native people. You can either present brief descriptions of the work of several Native artists, musicians, etc., or do an in-depth study of one particular person.

The Diefenbaker-Pearson feud

In 1967, Robert Stanfield, former premier of Nova Scotia, was chosen as the new leader of the Progressive Conservatives.

From 1958-1967, two politicians waged a battle for control of Canada's government. John Diefenbaker was the leader of the Progressive Conservative party. Lester Pearson was the head of the Liberals. Not only did they lead opposing political parties, they were opposites in personality and style. Diefenbaker, the Prairie lawyer, rivaled Pearson, the central Canadian career diplomat. The aggressive and outspoken Diefenbaker opposed the shy and softspoken Pearson. How did this confrontation come about?

The Diefenbaker magic

In June, 1957, one of the most stunning upsets in Canada's political history took place. John Diefenbaker led the Progressive Conservatives to victory in the federal election and ended 22 years of Liberal rule.

Who was Diefenbaker, this "man from the West"? A lawyer, he had defended many people accused of serious crimes, including

murder. Because he rarely lost a case, his name was a household word in Saskatchewan. In politics, however, Diefenbaker had failed in several attempts to get elected. Yet the image of underdog did not dampen his ambition. The voters of Prince Albert finally elected him as their Member of Parliament. Next, he set his sights on the leadership of the Progressive Conservative party. The Conservatives had a history of favouring eastern Canadians for the position. Nevertheless, in the fall of 1956, the Conservatives chose John Diefenbaker as the person most likely to lead them to victory over the Liberals.

In the late fifties, plans were being made to build a trans-Canada pipeline. It would carry natural gas from Alberta to the growing markets in Ontario, Quebec, and the United States. The Liberal government granted a company the right to build the pipeline. This company was financed in part by American investment. However, the Canadian government was asked to provide loans to cover the high costs of getting started.

The Liberals, led by Prime Minister Louis St. Laurent, agreed to this proposal. In the House of Commons, Diefenbaker and the Conservatives disagreed. To deal with the opposition, the Liberals used "closure." This was a way of severely limiting any discussion of the issue.

Diefenbaker and his colleagues accused the government of acting like a dictatorship. The Liberals went ahead anyway and used their majority in Parliament to pass a pipeline bill. The Liberals counted on Canadians to forget the whole affair. But the newspapers reported it in detail. More dramatic was the coverage given in

Fig. 12 John Diefenbaker

Fig. 13 Diefenbaker jokes with a worker on a tour of a factory.

the news by the new medium—television. Canadians were evidently convinced that the Liberal government was ignoring their concerns. The result was the surprise victory of Diefenbaker and the Conservatives in the election of 1957.

Even more surprising was the 1958 election campaign. Campaigning over television and at massive rallies across Canada, Diefenbaker captured the imagination of Canadians in every part of the land. He declared a "vision" of a country, including its mineral-rich north, growing in prosperity.

In the Conservatives' landslide victory of March 31, 1958, Mr. Diefenbaker's party won 208 seats of the total of 265 seats in the House of Commons. The "Diefenbaker phenomenon" was born. In Quebec, the Conservatives won a majority for the first time since Sir John A. Macdonald had done so back in 1891. Elsewhere, Conservatives were swept into office "on the coattails" of the leader.

The Pearson challenge

Meanwhile, in 1958, Lester Pearson had become leader of the Liberal party of Canada. This was surprising news to many people, since Pearson had spent much of his life living outside Canada, working overseas. He had little experience in politics at home, and he was a newcomer to the House of Commons. But Pearson was well-known. He had been awarded the Nobel Prize in 1957 for helping to bring about peace between Egypt and Israel.

Pearson lost in the Diefenbaker landslide of 1958. Yet within four years, he was in a position to drive Diefenbaker from office. The Conservatives had been plagued by problems. The postwar boom had ended. Relations with the United States had gone sour, especially concerning defense. In the election of June 18, 1962, the Conservatives won enough seats—118 to the Liberals' 100—to cling to power. Gone was the huge majority of 1958. In its place was a

Fig. 14 Lester Pearson

Fig. 15 As part of the 1962 election campaign, the Liberal party issued the "Diefendollar." What effect do you think it was intended to have?

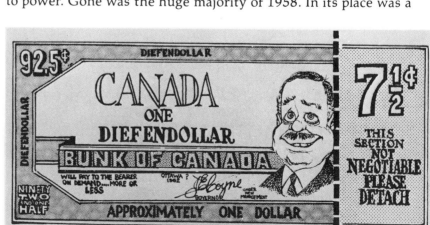

minority government, with fewer than half the seats in the House of Commons.

Another election followed on April 18, 1963. This time Pearson's Liberals won 129 seats, and took over, also as a minority government. Prime Minister Pearson's new government pushed forward with a programme of change, including greater recognition of the rights of French Canadians, a new flag, increased social security, and changes in Canadian defense.

The next three years were dark ones for both Liberals and Conservatives. Charges of scandal flew back and forth between the two parties. Rumours spread about members of both sides being associated with "shady" characters. The House of Commons became a kind of battleground for personal quarrels.

The Liberal government named November 8, 1965 as the date for another election. It appealed to Canadians to vote in a majority of Liberals. The Conservatives accused the government of bungling and wrong-doing and called on the voters to "throw the rascals out." The Liberals came out ahead in the election, with 131 seats to the Conservatives' 97—another minority government. John Diefenbaker had failed in his attempted comeback. Lester Pearson, though still prime minister, was denied a majority government once again.

Fig. 16 The issue of a new flag for Canada caused heated debate throughout the country. A parliamentary committee, representing all parties, considered almost 2000 designs. Canada's new flag came into use on February 15, 1965.

GETTING THE FACTS

19. What was the "Diefenbaker phenomenon?

20. In what sense was Lester Pearson a newcomer to politics when he became leader of the Liberal party?

21. Summarize the following paragraph in your own words. Before you write your summary, define the following words: endowed, strategist, tactician.

Seldom has there been so strange a contrast as exists between Mr. Pearson and Mr. Diefenbaker. The Liberal is richly endowed with good sensible ideas about the direction of Canada's future. He is also, perhaps, the worst strategist and tactician who has ever held high place in this country. Mr. Diefenbaker is utterly absorbed with these latter matters but has few glimmers about policy. . . . If our two leaders could be placed in a blender—and thoroughly shaken up, we might get an ideal prime minister—unless of course, what emerged was the worst in both of them.

From *Canadian Annual Review*, 1965.

THINKING IT THROUGH

22. a) According to the author of the quotation in question 21, what are the qualities of the ideal prime minister?

b) Do you agree that these are the most important qualities? Give reasons for your answer.

23. Debate the statement: "Voters are influenced more by the personalities of leaders than by the political parties and what they claim to stand for."

24. Reread the section dealing with the closure issue. This issue did not blow over as the Liberals had hoped because of the great amount of newspaper and television coverage. Do you think that the media can help shape political events and influence people's opinions? Explain your answer, giving specific examples.

The Yankee dollar

In the summer of 1963, the farthest thing from the minds of most Canadians was trouble with the United States. The United States was our neighbour and friend. The border between us was no real barrier to the spread of American ways, ideas, styles—and money—and our country. How could there be trouble?

Yet the news headlines showed that the United States was angry with Canada. The reason was the Canadian government's decision to limit United States' investment and ownership of our businesses and industries. Why was this decision taken?

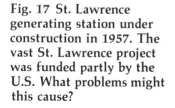

Fig. 17 St. Lawrence generating station under construction in 1957. The vast St. Lawrence project was funded partly by the U.S. What problems might this cause?

Third Parties: Choices for Canadians

A big reason why neither Diefenbaker nor Pearson could win a majority in the 1960s was the existence of the New Democratic party (NDP) and the Social Credit party. In the election of 1962, for example, the NDP elected 19 Members of Parliament and the Social Credit elected 30.

How did these third parties manage to deny victory to the two old or traditional parties? Many reasons have been given, mainly to do with Canadians' loss of faith in the Liberals and Conservatives. According to this negative view, Canadians were unwilling to trust either of those parties with a majority government. But T.C. "Tommy" Douglas, leader of the NDP, and Réal Caouette, leader of Social Credit in Quebec, were two individuals who greatly influenced politics in the 1960s.

Réal Caouette's success in the 1962 election was spectacular. He had established Le Ralliement des Créditistes de Québec in 1958, the year of the Diefenbaker "landslide." By 1962, however, support for the Conservatives had declined sharply in Quebec. Caouette had become widely known, particularly in rural and small-town Quebec, through his skillful use of television. An automobile dealer from Rouyn-Noranda, he knew how to appeal to people who felt ignored by the big city politicians. Caouette spoke simply but forcefully to drive home his main point: "You have nothing to lose by voting Social Credit."

Thanks to the personal popularity of Réal Caouette, Social Credit won 26 seats in Quebec in the election of 1962.

The success of Tommy Douglas was of a very different kind. In fact, in the election of June, 1962, he was personally defeated in Regina. Not until a by-election in November did he enter the House of Commons, as the representative of the British Columbia riding of Burnaby-Coquitlam. But he had contributed to the election of 19 NDP members by

Fig. 18 Tommy Douglas

criss-crossing Canada for 18 months, attending countless meetings and making countless speeches.

Mr. Douglas was the first leader of the New Democratic Party (NDP), formed in 1961. This was not really a new party, but a reborn version of the C.C.F. (Cooperative Commonwealth Federation). The NDP differed from its forerunner in that it had the official backing of organized labour—the unions of Canadian workers.

Tommy Douglas had long been known on the Canadian political scene as the dynamic premier of Saskatchewan. First elected there in 1944, he led the only socialist government in North America for 17 years. During that time, he had brought in many reforms. Perhaps the most important was medicare, a plan to provide the people of his province with free health and medical care.

Tommy Douglas was convinced that the kind of government he had led in Saskatchewan would be the best kind for all of Canada. When he retired from the leadership of the NDP, Douglas handed his successor a well-organized party, especially in the West. And Tommy Douglas continued to serve Canadians as a witty political speaker.

Both Douglas and Caouette remained active in politics after the 1960s. Réal Caouette continued as the head of Social Credit until the fall of 1976. Tommy Douglas retired in 1971 from the NDP leadership.

Walter Gordon was the finance minister in the new Liberal government, elected in April, 1963. His number one concern was the growing influence in Canada of business people from the United States. Gordon believed that Canadians must take a stand or they would lose control of their land, its resources and their way of life. The means of taking a stand, in Gordon's view, was action by government. So the budget which Gordon announced in June, 1963, proposed taxes to slow down foreign investment (80 percent of which came from the United States) in Canada.

Did Canadians have good reason to worry about the influence of the "Yankee dollar"? Consider the facts shown by the following table:

Fig. 19 How much of Canada is foreign-owned?

INDUSTRY	PERCENT CANADIAN	PERCENT FOREIGN
Agriculture and Forests	94	6
Book Publishing	5	95
Chemical Products	12	82
Communications	99	1
Construction	85	15
Credit Agencies	57	43
Electrical Products	32	64
Financial Industry	87	13
Investment Companies	71	29
Machinery	26	72
Manufacturing	42	58
Mining	31	67
NHL Teams	14	86
Paper and Allied Products	60	40
Petroleum and Coal	1	99
Primary Metals	45	55
Public Utilities	81	19
Retail Trade	69	21
Rubber Products	6	93
Transportation	91	9
Transportation Equipment	12	87
Wholesale Trade	58	31

The figures given above, compiled under CALURA (Corporation and Labour Union Returns Act), show the percentage of foreign investment in Canada. U.S. investors were responsible for 80 percent of all foreign investment in Canada.

From *Canada and the U.S.—Continental Partners or Wary Neighbours* by R.P. Bowles et al.

Not only the reaction of the United States to the "Gordon budget" was swift. Within Canada, business leaders, premiers of provinces and others anxious to keep American friendship criticized

the Canadian government. Gordon was left with no choice but to drop the "anti-American" features of his budget.

How did Canadians in general feel about the question of American economic influence? Opinions were sharply divided, but the following scenarios suggest three main viewpoints:

(1) **Nationalist:** These people believed in "Canada for Canadians." Among their members were university professors, writers and broadcasters, some publishers of books and magazines. As far as they were concerned, the Canadian government should give leadership. It should pass laws to encourage Canadian businesses—or, in some cases, actually take over foreign-owned companies.

(2) **Middle-of-the-Roaders:** Some Canadians believed that governments should stay out of business. In their view, a company, whether Canadian or foreign-owned, should be allowed to succeed or fail on its own. While they thought of themselves as Canadians, they saw no reason why their "Canadian identity" should be a handicap. They were entitled to goods and services at the best price, whether Canadians or foreigners provided them.

(3) **Continentalists:** These were Canadians who saw their country as part of North America. They were not afraid of closer ties with the United States. In fact, the continentalists welcomed the chance for business opportunities in the United States as well as in Canada. Even if they did not welcome closer economic ties with the United States, they believed they were bound to come. The attitude of the continentalists was to make the best of a probable situation.

Canada seemed to be a crossroads as the 1960s were coming to an end. More Canadians than ever before seemed to be concerned about American economic influence. How would the government respond? Canadians watched with keen interest as Pierre Elliott Trudeau began his first term (1968-1972) as prime minister. The 1970s were likely to be the decade in which important decisions would be made about the role of the "Yankee dollar" in Canada.

USING YOUR KNOWLEDGE

25. Examine Figure 19. In which industry was foreign ownership greatest? In which industry was it smallest? How do you account for these features?

a) Which of the opinions—nationalist, middle-of-the-road or continentalist—most appeals to you? Why?

b) Do you think most Canadians of the 1960s would have agreed with you? Why or why not?

Ottawa and the provinces

In 1963, the Royal Commission on Bilingualism and Biculturalism was appointed to study and make recommendations for improving relations between French Canadians and English Canadians.

"What does Quebec want?" was a familiar question in the rest of Canada in the 1960s. The Quiet Revolution and the activities of separatists in Quebec were constantly in the news. The government of Quebec seemed to be generally in conflict with the Canadian government. Was Quebec the only province in this situation?

No, the 1960s was a decade of "tug o' war" between the provinces and the government in Ottawa. The problem was not new. Ever since Confederation, power had shifted back and forth between the two levels of government. Then, during World War II, the Canadian government had taken on extra authority over the country in order to manage the war effort. In the years after the war ended, the provinces—particularly Ontario and Quebec—were anxious to regain power. By the 1960s, Quebec was leading the way. All provinces, however, were insisting on more say in the running of the nation's business.

Canada, remember, has a federal system of government. This means that a central government, located in Ottawa, has the

Fig. 20 Pierre Trudeau at the federal-provincial conference of 1969. What point might he be making by linking his fingers?

responsibility—and supposedly the power—to look after matters concerning the whole country. Such matters include the money system, the post office, dealings with other countries, defense and many others. Yet each province also has a government. Each of these, singly and together with the others, is interested in exercising as much power as possible.

A federal system is hard to operate. When there are eleven governments, such as Canada has, the chance of disagreement is fairly high. When governments grow in size and take on more responsibilities to serve the public, the division of powers is often less clear. Sharing the money from taxes between governments is likely to be difficult.

By the 1960s, annual federal-provincial conferences had become a regular part of Canada's system of government. Representatives of the federal and provincial governments met many times a year to sort out disagreements and make decisions.

As prime minster, Lester B. Pearson encouraged the idea of cooperative federalism. He hoped to promote good will instead of conflict, and to convince the provincial governments that they had a fair share of power. A series of federal-provincial agreements were made. An important example was the pension plan for senior citizens. For this and for many other programmes, including the promotion of bilingualism, the Canadian government "shared costs" with the provinces.

The Pearson years ended in 1968, when Mr. Pearson retired. Cooperative federalism was still more a promising idea than an established fact. The real test was still to come, after the new prime minister, Pierre Elliott Trudeau, took office.

GETTING THE FACTS

27. In your own words, explain a federal system of government, and give at least one reason why this kind of a system is difficult to keep running smoothly.

USING YOUR KNOWLEDGE

28. Examine the statement, "The 'tug o' war' between the provinces and the government in Ottawa was not new." Give at least two facts that show this to be true.

THINKING IT THROUGH

29. Consider this hypothesis: "Even if there had been no Quiet Revolution in Quebec, Canada would have been a difficult place to govern in the 1960s." Give evidence to support or disprove this hypothesis.

Fig. 21 Pierre Trudeau at the Liberal leadership convention, Ottawa, 1968

"Trudeaumania": The beginning of the Trudeau era

Pierre Elliott Trudeau, formerly a law professor and journalist in Quebec, assumed the position of prime minister of Canada in April, 1968. Lester Pearson had retired. The Liberal party held a leadership convention to choose a new leader. Mr. Trudeau had only entered the Liberal party and the House of Commons in 1965. Before long, however, Liberals recognized him as a leader. He was the overwhelming choice as the new leader of the party. Once in power, Mr. Trudeau called an election.

In the election of June, 1968, Mr. Trudeau proved to be popular with Canadian voters too. Reporters invented the term "Trudeaumania" to describe his effect on people. Wherever he appeared—on television and radio, in auditoriums, at whirlwind visits to shopping centres—he was received with cheers and applause. Canadians of all parts of the country, regardless of age or background, reacted in much the same way.

"Trudeaumania" was too much for the opposing parties. The Liberals elected 155 members and achieved the first majority government in Canada since 1962.

Canadians had high hopes for their country under the leadership

of their new prime minister. Mr. Trudeau had made few specific promises, but he had spoken repeatedly about working toward a "just society." He seemed to stand for a new age of fair and equal opportunity for all Canadians. The 1960s would end before they could judge how well he met their expectations.

THINKING IT THROUGH

30. Ask an adult what he or she remembers about Trudeaumania. After talking to him or her, explain why you think Trudeau was so popular in 1968.

Conclusion

The 1960s illustrate many of the difficulties of studying recent history. We can safely conclude that it was an important time in Canada's history. Some events stand out because of their influence on life in Canada up to the present. Yet it may be too soon to tell which developments will be long-lasting—and which will be studied by future generations of history students.

Nevertheless, the 1960s may be said to have "set the stage for a new Canada" in many ways. The Trudeau era of majority government began, and the New Democratic party emerged as the enduring third party. Young people brought social issues, particularly those relating to individual rights and freedoms, to the attention of the Canadian public. The women's rights movement gained momentum in the 1960s. So did efforts by Native peoples to improve their status. Concern about foreign influence and control in the Canadian economy was raised by individuals and groups within and outside governments. The Centennial celebrations of 1967 highlighted the age-old question of identity, "What is a Canadian?" Confederation became more complicated than ever, as federal-provincial conferences took on a key role in the power struggle between levels of government. It would be hard to deny that Canada after the 1960s was a place far different from what it had been before.

Fig. 22 In 1967 Canada celebrated its 100th birthday. Centennial events took place all over the country, but the one which captured most attention was Expo 67. Sixty-two nations exhibited at the Montreal fair which was visited by almost 50 000 000 people.

THINKING IT THROUGH

31. Consider the hypothesis: "Life in Canada improved in the decade of the 1960s."

Read through the chapter and find evidence which supports or disproves the hypothesis.

THE INVESTIGATIVE REPORTER

32. Look back at the list of world issues and events in the chapter overview. Research one of the points and prepare a report for presentation to the class.

11 Quebec: A time of change

Music, especially folk music, has always played an important part in the life of the Québécois. A chansonnier (folk song) movement, led by Félix Leclerc, revived the interest of the Québécois in their own music. Two of Quebec's most popular chansonniers are Gilles Vigneault and Pauline Julien.

Julien is well-known for the political statements that her songs make. She often sings of the working-class and their problems. During the October crisis, Julien was jailed for a short time, yet no charges were ever laid against her. (See this chapter for more information on the October crisis.)

The following excerpt is taken from a song recorded by Pauline Julien and written by Réjean Ducharme and Robert Charlebois. (Charlebois is well-known for his contribution to rock music in Quebec.)

Déménager ou rester là (To move or to stay?)

The ceiling is falling on my shoulders and head
    in thousands of pieces
The janitor said he would try to repair it.
I'm going to tell the owner.
I've been waiting for too long.
I don't know whether to move or stay.

- "She [Pauline Julien] often sings of the working class and their problems." How would you interpret the excerpt from *Déménager ou rester là?*

◀ Quebec singer, Pauline Julien

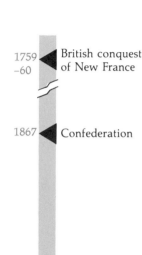

1759–60	British conquest of New France
1867	Confederation
1960	Quiet Revolution begins
1970	October Crisis
1976	Parti Québécois forms Quebec government
1982	Canada's new constitution

Chapter overview

In 1967, Canada celebrated her 100th birthday. Special events took place all across the country. This was a proud and happy time for most Canadians.

Yet there was reason to worry about the state of the Confederation. The "Quiet Revolution" had begun in Quebec. The 1960s were to shatter the myth of Quebec as a traditional, rural province where nothing really changed.

The government and people of Quebec were the central figures in the drama of the Quiet Revolution and the developments that followed, but its effects were wide-reaching. By the end of the decade, Canadians would be much more aware of the frustrations and demands of the Québécois.

Signposts

The first two hundred years ▷

FEATURE: The Asbestos strike ▷

The Quiet Revolution ▷

Independence or death: The FLQ ▷

Lévesque and the Parti Québécois ▷

FEATURE: The arts in Quebec ▷

Federal government reaction ▷

FEATURE: Francophone communities outside Quebec ▷

Key words

maîtres chez nous	referendum	sovereignty-association
je me souviens	la survivance	backlash
la révolution tranquille		

Fig. 1 The French general, Montcalm, lies mortally wounded on the Plains of Abraham. Although the English general, Wolfe, was also killed in the battle, his troops were victorious. Thus, in 1759, English rule of the colony began.

The first two hundred years

It can be argued that no other issue in Canada's history has been as significant as French-English Canadian relations. This relationship has at times been far from friendly. To understand why there has been conflict between the two groups, we need to understand French Canadian history.

The early French, of the seventeenth century, settled mainly in Nova Scotia, New Brunswick and southern Quebec. They developed their own way of life, or culture. In 1759, on the Plains of Abraham in Quebec City, the French forces were defeated by the British. Soon afterwards all of French Canada fell to the British.

Many French colonists were deeply upset by the defeat. Nonetheless, Quebec still developed along its own French Canadian cultural lines. The francophones (French-speaking people) made every effort to guarantee la survivance (survival) of their own culture. Their motto became je me souviens (I remember). Respecting their heritage is still very important for most French Canadians.

Early Quebec was mainly a rural, agricultural society. Farming was the main occupation. Most farmers were self-sufficient, that is,

they supplied their families' needs from what they grew or made on their own farm. But the small farms did not bring in a lot of money and farming families were large. Ten or twelve children in a family were not uncommon.

A very important person in each community was the parish priest. The Roman Catholic Church was not concerned only about the religious beliefs of the people. It also influenced politics and education. For example, the subjects taught in French schools in Quebec were largely determined by the Church. Many subjects involved studying the works of ancient scholars, religion and French history—the traditional classics courses.

By the 1860s, many politicians in British North America felt that they should work together to establish a new nation—Canada. Although Confederation was achieved in 1867, there was much disagreement over the issue in Quebec. Two leading Quebec politicians at the time were George Cartier and A.A. Dorion. Their feelings represent the split attitudes of the Québécois over Confederation.

> "In our Confederation there will be Catholics and Protestants, English, French . . . each will add to the prosperity of the Dominion, to the glory of the new Confederation . . . to work together for the common welfare."
>
> —Cartier during the Parliamentary Debates on Confederation

> "I am opposed to this Confederation in which . . . our most important civil rights will be under control of a General Government, the majority of which will be hostile to Lower Canada (Quebec)."
>
> —Dorion during the Parliamentary Debates on Confederation

In the years following Confederation, francophones became very suspicious of the federal government. Most Members of Parliament were anglophones (English-speaking). As a result, anxiety arose in Quebec that the French Canadian culture could not survive in a country controlled by anglophones.

Certain events were to further worry the Québécois. Let us briefly examine some of these key events.

1. Many French Canadians believed that Louis Riel was trying to protect the French language and Roman Catholic religion. Riel was hanged after the failure of the Northwest Rebellion. To the francophones, this seemed to be an example of English Canadians crushing the interests of French Canadians.

2. Education became a source of dispute as well. In Manitoba, Alberta, New Brunswick, Saskatchewan and Ontario, the provincial

In this text, Québécois refers to all citizens of Quebec. The term Québécois is sometimes used to refer only to the francophones of Quebec.

One example of bitter educational conflict occurred in Ontario in 1912. The Ontario Department of Education adopted "Regulation 17." This act made English the only language of instruction in elementary schools. Regulation 17 created serious distrust between anglo- and francophones. Also see the Manitoba Schools Question, in "The uncomfortable union," in the *Discovering Canada* series.

Fig. 2 Rural Quebec c. 1700. What can you tell about life at this time from the picture?

governments passed laws limiting the educational rights of the French-speaking citizens.

3. French Canadians were angry with the federal government because it did not use its power of disallowance. This is the federal power to repeal, or cancel, any provincial law thought to be unconstitutional, or illegal.

4. There were other events in which anglophone demands won over francophone demands. For example, refer to the chapter on World War I for further discussion of the conscription issue.

GETTING THE FACTS

1. Write a brief description of Quebec society in the late seventeenth or early eighteenth century. Include the role of the Church in your description.

2. In your own words, state the views of Cartier and Dorion about Confederation.

3. a) Imagine you are a francophone living in a mainly French community in Ontario in 1913. How would you react to Regulation 17?

   b) Imagine you are an anglophone living at the same time. You support Regulation 17. Explain the reasons for your viewpoint.

4. Many French Canadians question whether Ottawa and the other provincial governments are willing to assist in the protection of Québécois culture and rights. Do you think this attitude is justified by the history of the French in Canada? Explain.

The roots of change

In the twentieth century, tremendous social changes took place in Quebec. Earlier we saw that the province was a rural society greatly influenced by the Church. This was to change dramatically.

Ringuet's book, *Thirty Acres*, examines some of the social changes taking place in Quebec and their impact on the Québécois in the early twentieth century. In the following scene, the father, Euchariste Moisan, is talking with his two sons about their cousins. The cousins had left Quebec some years earlier to live in an American city and work in a factory.

> "You never know, perhaps they're fed up with the States and want to come back and live here. Specially if they've money to buy a good farm."
>
> "Come back and live here!" exclaimed Ephrem with a jeer. "The hell they will! They'd have to be awful damn fools to leave Lowell, where they get good wages—regular too—all year round, to come and work their guts out on a farm."
>
> But this was going too far. Euchariste snatched his pipe out of his mouth to reply:
>
> "In the first place, you're just guessing. And you ought to be ashamed of yourself, Ephrem, talking that way. The Moisans are farmers. Farming's always been good enough for the Moisans and they've always been pretty good at farming. Farming never lets you down."
>
> "Except when there's no rain and the wheat gets burnt up or else . . ."
>
> "You shut your mouth! I can't hardly believe it's you talking that way. And you was there last spring, wasn't you, when the Bishop came to visit the parish? Don't you remember what he said? Didn't he say it was us, the people of the country, who are

Fig. 3 "Ringuet" was the pen name used by the writer and doctor, Philippe Paneton. *Thirty Acres*, **his best known novel, was published in 1938 and won four awards in Canada and France. It has been translated into English, German and Dutch.**

the real Canadians, the real folk? He said when a man loves the land it's just like loving God, Who made it and Who takes care of it when we deserve it . . . And he said if you desert the land you're practically headed straight for hell."

In the above quotation, Euchariste Moisan and his son express conflicting views about change. Euchariste wants the traditional farm life of the Québécois to continue. Ephrem, however, has no such desire.

Quebec society was changing. There was not enough good farm land to support all of the people. As more industries opened up, great numbers of young people left the farms for the cities and the new factories which offered regular work and salaries.

The Québécois quickly discovered that these factories were almost always owned and managed by English-speaking Canadians and Americans. Francophones were often forced to speak English on the job. They were rarely promoted to management positions and were usually given low pay.

In the mid-1930s a new political party emerged in Quebec—the Union Nationale. The Union Nationale was founded and led by Maurice Duplessis, a very colourful and powerful speaker. His speeches dealing with Quebec nationalism won much support for him in the province. From 1936-1939 and from 1944-1959 Duplessis was premier of Quebec.

Duplessis was a traditionalist. He liked to say that the Union Nationale was the people's party. By this he meant that the chief concern of the government was the well-being of the ordinary citizen. But since Duplessis did not want change, he used the power of the government and the law to suppress it. In addition, Duplessis liked to reward the individuals and companies that supported him. Corruption, unfortunately, was a frequent result of this practice of rewarding supporters and crushing opposition.

Despite Duplessis, the demand for change was taking root. The educational system, for example, was changing. The influence of the Roman Catholic Church was not as great as it had been. French schools were beginning to offer more courses in mathematics and the sciences. These subjects were more practical than the traditional religion and classics courses. Yet as more francophones received a higher education, their anger and frustration increased. This was largely because they still could not get high level management jobs in their own province—even when they had received the same education as the anglophones.

In 1959, Duplessis died. Within one year, the Union Nationale was voted out of office. In its place came the Liberals, led by Jean Lesage. Little did he suspect that he would lead his province through one of the most significant periods of change in its history.

Fig. 4 Quebec Premier Maurice Duplessis (with scissors) and Archibishop Charbonneau at an official function

281

Fig. 5 Formed in 1950, the "Rassemblement pour l'Independence Nationale" (R.I.N.) was one of the largest separatist parties in Quebec. After the Parti Québécois was founded in 1968, the R.I.N. voted to disband itself and join the P.Q.

5. State one important change taking place in Quebec in the early 1900s.

6. Why was the demand for change in Quebec taking root in the mid-twentieth century?

USING YOUR KNOWLEDGE

7. The excerpt from *Thirty Acres* presents a conflict in values in Quebec in the early twentieth century.
   a) Identify the two sets of values that are evident in the conversation.
   b) From what you know about Quebec society, would changes in lifestyles and attitudes be easily accepted in the early 1900s?
   c) Do you feel that these changes were necessary? Explain.

8. In earlier chapters you learned what a stereotype is.
   a) Do you think there are stereotypes in the passage from *Thirty Acres*? Explain.
   b) Are stereotypes sometimes useful, or usually harmful? Give reasons for your answer.

THE INVESTIGATIVE REPORTER

9. Maurice Duplessis was a colourful and powerful figure in twentieth century Quebec. Look in your school or local library to find out more about him. Then write a report entitled "Duplessis: Saviour or Tyrant?" Be sure to use facts to support your arguments.

Fig. 6 Trucks arriving with food for strikers at Asbestos

The Asbestos strike

With the growth of industry in Quebec, unionism also developed. Disputes between management, largely anglophone, and workers, largely francophone, were often bitter and long. The most dramatic example of such a dispute occurred in 1949.

In that year, the miners in the Quebec town of Asbestos went on strike. They were asking for higher pay, safer working conditions and the right to form a union. The strike became a major turning point in Quebec history. It reminded French Canadians that there were problems within their society. Business and society in general were largely controlled by non-francophones.

The strike was important for another reason as well. It showed that francophones could bring about changes themselves. The Asbestos strike became a symbol for French-speaking Québécois breaking out of their "foreign" controlled past.

The provincial government considered the strike illegal. It did not recognize the authority of the union. Nonetheless, the strikers picketed and marched in protest. Although the strikers acted peacefully, Premier Duplessis sent 75 carloads of heavily armed police to Asbestos. The strike created great tension, especially when the police severely beat some strikers whom they had arrested.

For weeks the strike dragged on. The Church had come out in support of the strikers. In May, Monseigneur Joseph Charbonneau, the Archbishop of Montreal, preached a dramatic sermon in support of the strikers.

> ... There is, today, a conspiracy on the part of the government and foreign-owned industry, to crush the workingman into a state of economic slavery. And when there is a conspiracy to crush the worker ... it is the duty of the Church to intervene and speak out against tyranny. ... We wish to pray for social peace. We do not wish and pray for economic slavery. That is why we, the clergy, have decided to intervene and take a stand in the Asbestos strike. We want the government and industry to respect the basic principles of justice and charity. We ask them to pay more attention to the human element in work, and less importance to the interest of money.
>
> From this day on ... a special collection for the striking Asbestos workers will be taken at the door of every Church in my dioceses ... I ask you, in the name of Lord Jesus Christ, to raise money, food, and clothing for these families. I ask you to organize in order to meet their material needs. This, my brethren, is a Christian duty ... this is simply Christian charity.

From *Charbonneau et le chef* by John McDonough.

Because of the Archbishop's successful call for aid to the strikers, Duplessis was determined to use his influence to discredit the priest. As a result Charbonneau was pressured into resigning from his position.

After 142 days, the strike finally ended. It had been a costly and often brutal affair. The workers received a 10¢ an hour raise and two more paid holidays. More importantly, the strike united many francophone groups in their battle against foreign control of their industries.

GETTING THE FACTS

10. What was the significance of the Asbestos strike?

THINKING IT THROUGH

11. Do you agree with the Church's decision to intervene in the strike? Explain.

Fig. 7 Jean Lesage, Liberal premier of Quebec, 1960-66

The Quiet Revolution

A period of great social and political change took place in Quebec during Jean Lesage's leadership. This period in Quebec's history is often referred to as la révolution tranquille or the Quiet Revolution.

Lesage was determined to reform the political system and solve the many problems facing his province. The major problems that Premier Lesage had to deal with included:

1) Poor hospital and health care: Infant mortality rates were approximately 50 percent higher in Quebec than in the rest of Canada.
2) Population: As the birth rate dropped and non-French immigration to Quebec increased, the continuing existence of the French culture and language was threatened.
3) The economy: The unemployment rate in Quebec was among the highest in the country.
4) Social structure: Most businesses were owned by anglophones who forced their workers to speak English on the job.
5) Social structure: Almost all of the top executive positions in large businesses were held by anglophones.
6) Social structure: Francophone workers were among the lowest paid workers in Quebec.

In 1962, Lesage called a provincial election. The Liberals won by a wide margin. Their campaign motto was maîtres chez nous (masters in our own house). This slogan summed up the spirit of the Quiet Revolution. The francophones wanted to control their own future.

The Lesage government made many successful reforms. The reforms were possible partly as a result of the change in attitude that took place slowly throughout the twentieth century. Here are some of the reforms:

1) Laws were passed which resulted in increased wages and loans for francophones who wished to set up their own businesses. Also, the General Investment Corporation was established. It offered loans to small businesses to assist in expansion. This encouraged greater employment.
2) Old age pensions were increased and more hospitals were built.
3) Improvements in government offices and policies were made in order to try to eliminate the cases of corruption and bribery that had occurred under the leadership of Duplessis. For example, government employees were hired and promoted according to their skills and not their political connections.
4) Numerous hydroelectric companies were taken over by the province. The government-owned Hydro Quebec company was

Fig. 8 Average income in Quebec, by ethnic origin, 1961

	Dollars
All Origins	$3469
British	$4969
Scandinavian	$4939
Dutch	$4891
Jewish	$4851
Russian	$4828
German	$4254
Polish	$3984
Asiatic	$3734
Ukrainian	$3733
Other European	$3547
Hungarian	$3537
French	$3185
Italian	$2938
Native Indian	$2112

From *Royal Commission on Bilingualism and Biculturalism*, Report, Vol. III.

established, giving the Quebec government direct control of the province's vast hydroelectric power and related natural resources. Hydro Quebec's creation also resulted in more electricity at a cheaper rate.

5) A Department of Education was established. Thus the Catholic Church no longer controlled education. The Lesage government believed that education was a form of job training. Skills important to modern industrial Quebec were taught and less emphasis was placed on religion and classical subjects. More and more francophones were receiving technical and business education that would prepare them to take over management positions.

The Lesage government was defeated in the 1966 election. Naturally people asked why this government, which had fought so hard for reforms, was defeated. Had Lesage gone "too far too fast"? Although the reforms had helped to solve the problems of the Québécois, they had been costly in two ways. First, they resulted in higher taxes and prices. And second, the more traditional Québécois thought that the "old ways" had been changed too much. For example, many did not like to see the influence of the Church decreased.

Yet other Québécois felt that the changes brought about during the Quiet Revolution were not radical enough! These were the separatists, mainly young French-speaking Québécois. They wished to see changes in Quebec. But they also wanted to see Quebec break away from the rest of Canada.

Separatism had always existed to some degree in Quebec. But separatism meant different things to different people. For some it simply meant that Quebec should be able to keep its separate language and culture. For others, separatism meant political independence from Canada but with the continuation of economic or business union. For others, separatism meant total independence from Canada. Some supporters of this last view have been willing to use violence to try to achieve a separate Quebec.

GETTING THE FACTS

12. In your own words explain the following terms: la révolution tranquille, maîtres chez nous, separatist.

USING YOUR KNOWLEDGE

13. Compare the list of problems that Lesage faced with Lesage's reforms. Which problems were dealt with by these reforms?

14. Examine Figure 9 closely.

a) What percentage of francophones held professional and technical jobs in Quebec in 1961? What percentage of francophones held managerial positions?

Italian   British
French   Jewish

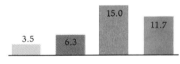

Professional and technical

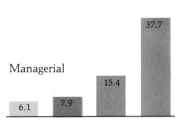
3.5   6.3   15.0   11.7

Managerial

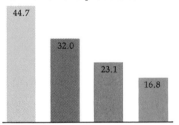
37.7
6.1   7.9   15.4

Craftsmen and production workers

44.7   32.0   23.1   16.8

Labourers

17.4   7.2   3.0   0.9

Others

28.3   46.6   43.5   32.9

Total
100.0   100.0   100.0   100.0

Number
34 211   999 798   151 852   21 998

Source: *Census of Canada*, 1961

Fig. 9 Occupation in Quebec, by ethnic origin, 1961 (in percentages)

b) The majority of Quebec citizens were francophones. How do you think they would react to the percentages which you have noted?

15. One Canadian historian said that "Quebec's Quiet Revolution did not begin quietly in the year 1960. It began violently in the year 1949 in the little mining town of Asbestos." What do you think this historian meant? Do you agree with this interpretation? Why or why not?

16. Debate: How successful was Lesage in improving conditions within his province? Be sure to back up your arguments with facts.

THINKING IT THROUGH

17. When we think of the term "revolution," we usually think of the violent overthrow of governments.
a) Can you suggest why the term "Quiet Revolution" is often used in relation to the years of the Lesage government?
b) Do you think it is a good choice of terms? Explain.

Terrorism is the use of fear and violence as a political weapon—that is, to achieve a political goal.

Fig. 10 In July, 1967, the French president, Charles de Gaulle, visited Canada. In a public speech in Montreal, he exclaimed, "Vive le Quebec libre!" Quebec's separatists were overjoyed by the statement. The federal government was not. Prime Minister Pearson declared his action "unacceptable" and de Gaulle shortened his stay in Canada.

Independence or death: The FLQ

The most violent of Quebec's separatist organizations was the Front de Libération Québécois (FLQ). The FLQ was structured along military lines. It was divided into small groups, or cells, which were independent of each other. It was set up in this way so that if a member of one cell was arrested, this person could not inform on members of other cells.

The aim of the FLQ was independence for Quebec. They felt this could only be achieved by violent revolution. FLQ terrorism began in March, 1963, when a bomb was thrown against the wall of a wooden Canadian Railway building in Montreal. The words "Vive le Quebec libre" were painted on a nearby wall.

After several bombings in the Montreal area, the FLQ released a written declaration of their views. It was called the FLQ Manifesto and it included the following statements.

A Message to the Nation by the Front de Libération Québécois.

Patriots,

Ever since the Second World War, the various enslaved peoples of the world have been shattering their bonds to acquire the freedom which is theirs by right. . . .

Like so many others before us, the people of Quebec have reached the end of their patience with the arrogant domination of Anglo-Saxon colonialism.

We are a colonized people, politically, socially, and economically. Politically, because we do not have any hold on the political instruments necessary for our survival. Ottawa's colonial government has full powers in the following fields: economic policy, foreign trade, defence, bank credit, immigration, the criminal courts, etc. Moreover, any provincial legislation may be repealed by Ottawa if it so decides. . . . It [Quebec] is also economically a colony. A single statement will serve to prove it: over 80 percent of our economy is controlled by foreign interests. We provide the labour, they bank the profits.

Socially, too, Quebec is a colony. We represent 80 percent of the population, and yet the English language prevails in many fields.

. . . Wrench off the colonial yoke, get rid of the imperialists who live off the toil of our Quebec workers. Quebec's tremendous natural resources must belong to Quebeckers!

. . . Quebec Patriots, To Arms! The Hour of National Revolution Has Struck! Independence Or Death!

Between 1963 and 1970, many more FLQ bombings occurred in Quebec. Banks were robbed, weapons and explosives stolen and several innocent people killed.

But the FLQ demand for a popular uprising by the francophone workers and students failed. The vast majority of Québécois were opposed to violence.

Fig. 11 While attempting to dismantle a terrorist bomb, Sergeant-Major Walter Leja was seriously injured, May 17, 1963.

The October Crisis

In 1970, FLQ members carried out what proved to be their last desperate act of violence. The October Crisis was one of the most publicized and despised violent actions in Canada's history. This crisis affected all Canadians. It resulted in the temporary loss of the democratic rights of every citizen!

On October 5, a cell of the FLQ kidnapped James Cross. Mr. Cross was the British Trade Commissioner to Canada. His offices and home were in Montreal. The kidnappers issued a list of demands. Included was the demand to release a number of FLQ members in prison.

Shortly after the first kidnapping, another cell kidnapped Pierre Laporte. He was the Minister of Labour in the provincial Liberal government of Robert Bourassa.

Wild rumours of an uprising spread throughout Quebec. Premier Bourassa was so concerned that he temporarily transferred the provincial government from Quebec City to Montreal, the centre of the anglophone population of Quebec.

In this atmosphere of violence, rumours, and for some, panic,

The Quebec Liberals, led by Robert Bourassa, were elected in April, 1970.

The War Measures Act was first passed near the beginning of World War I. Before 1970, the War Measures Act had been proclaimed only two times—during World Wars I and II. Simply speaking, this Act takes away our democratic rights and gives extra power to the government. For example, persons can be put in jail temporarily without being formally charged with a specific crime.

the federal government took action. On October 16, Prime Minister Trudeau issued the War Measures Act. Both the governments of the city of Montreal and the province of Quebec had requested that the Act be issued.

With the passage of the War Measures Act, some five hundred Québécois were jailed with no official charges laid. The end result was that less than twenty-five were tried and convicted of criminal offences. The Québécois were generally angered by this abuse of police power. In fact, it was to serve as a further argument for the separatists in their ongoing debate with Ottawa.

The same day that the Act was passed, the FLQ was outlawed and Canadian Armed Forces were called out in Quebec. To see armed troops patrolling Quebec City and Montreal upset many Canadians. The following day, October 17, 1970, the body of Pierre Laporte was found in the trunk of an abandoned car near the Montreal airport.

Almost sixty days after James Cross had been kidnapped, the authorities discovered the whereabouts of James Cross and his kidnappers. In return for his safety, the FLQ terrorists demanded safe passage to Cuba for themselves and their families. Their demand was agreed to. The exchange was viewed by millions of Canadians on national television.

In the same month, those who had kidnapped and murdered Laporte were captured. They were eventually tried and imprisoned. It was not until 1982 that all of Cross' captors had returned to Quebec to face justice.

The overwhelming majority of Québécois, including separatists, was opposed to violent, terrorist action. It was not surprising to see a separatist, but non-violent, party arise in the late 1960s. This party, the Parti Québécois, wanted political separation from Canada, to be achieved by democratic means. Their leader was René Lévesque.

Fig. 12 Prime Minister Trudeau calls out the army

THINKING IT THROUGH

18. In the FLQ Manifesto, Quebec is referred to as a colony. Is this term accurate? Explain.

19. a) Why do you think a terrorist group emerged in Quebec?

b) Is violent action ever justifiable in a society that is ready for change? Consider the question carefully and give reasons to support your views.

20. Read carefully the section of the BNA Act which deals with the division of federal and provincial powers. Was the FLQ correct in claiming that Quebec does not have the political authority to protect the survival of the French Canadian culture? Explain.

21. Obtain a copy of the War Measures Act and examine it closely.

    a) What democratic rights are lost when this Act is enforced?

    b) Do you think this type of law is justifiable in peacetime in a democracy?

    c) Why do you think many Canadians so easily accepted the Act in 1970?

Lévesque and the Parti Québécois

In the 1976 Quebec provincial election Lévesque led his Parti Québécois to victory against the Liberal government of Robert Bourassa. During the election campaign, Lévesque attacked Bourassa's handling of the Quebec economy. Quebec was approximately $1 000 000 000 in debt. Unemployment was high. Many industries were on strike. The Parti Québécois leader did not stress the separatist issue in the campaign. Thus Québécois who did not strongly support separatism in Canada would not be afraid to vote for the Parti Québécois.

Fig. 13 René Lévesque

Joe Clark of the federal Conservatives and Ed Broadbent of the federal New Democratic party, like many other Canadians, were surprised by the election results. They publicly stated that they felt that the Parti Québécois won not because people supported separatism, but because the people did not want to vote for the Liberals. Look at the accompanying newspaper clipping. What was the prime minister's reaction to the election results?

René Lévesque was born in Quebec in 1922. During both the Second World War and the Korean War he was a press correspondent. During the 1950s, Lévesque became a popular television figure in his home province.

In 1960, he was elected as a Liberal to the Quebec National Assembly. He became a Cabinet minister in the government of Jean Lesage. Over the years he became more and more a strong Quebec nationalist. In 1967, he left the Liberal party. Soon thereafter he helped create the Parti Québécois.

Mainly the federal government and non-francophone interests control communications, immigration, criminal law and certain business regulations in Quebec, as in the other provinces. Because of this, Lévesque says the Québécois "are not masters in our own house. This is why I am separatist."

Since 1976, the Quebec government has attempted to improve both economic and political conditions. Public opinion polls within the province seem to indicate that the majority are happy so far with the Lévesque government.

However, within the first four years of this government, two

Trudeau: Canada one nation and will remain so

OTTAWA—. . . Quebec is still part of an "indivisible Canada". . . .

"In the democratic election, Quebec voters have given the Parti Québécois enough seats to form the next provincial government. . . . Mr. Levesque and his party . . . [may] form a government in the province, not . . . separate the province from the rest of Canada," Trudeau said.

issues have created a great deal of controversy. These issues were Bill 101 and the Referendum.

BILL 101

"The Charter of the French Language"

1. All business in the Quebec government and courts will be carried out in French.

2. French is the only official language of Quebec.

3. The people of Quebec have the right to:
   a) speak French at work,
   b) be served in French in stores,
   c) be taught in French. The following children may be taught in English:
      i) if one parent was educated at an English school in Quebec;
      ii) if one parent went to an English school anywhere, and the parent was living in Quebec before August, 1977;
      iii) if the child's other brothers or sisters went to English school.

BILL 101

Bill 101 made French the only working language in Quebec. Premier Lévesque said this about it: "Let me admit that Bill 101 in Quebec in some important ways is restrictive legislation [cuts back people's rights]." Nonetheless, he went on to say that the Bill was necessary because: (1) 90 percent of immigrants entering Quebec did not speak French; (2) Quebec's birthrate is the lowest in the country and therefore fewer francophones are being raised in the province; (3) before, most businesses in Quebec had insisted that English be used; and (4) people feared that the francophone culture, including language, was being swamped by the English, Canadian and American cultures.

The Québécois were split over Bill 101. Most francophones gave their support. They saw the Bill as a major step in preserving their culture and gaining control of their economy. The reaction of Edmond B. is typical of a great many francophones.

You ask me why I support Bill 101, well I'll tell you. All big business was controlled and run by the English. It was impossible for a francophone to get a top management position in a large business in Quebec. You had to be English-speaking.

I know anglophones who were born in Quebec, whose parents were even born in Quebec, and have refused to speak French. They look down on the French language and culture. These same people might go to Spain for a vacation. And when they return they would try to impress others with the amount

Edmond B. is an actual individual who recently transferred from Quebec to take up a position in his company in Ontario. His concerns are real and reflect the concerns and frustrations of a great many francophones.

290

of Spanish they learned. And yet they won't even try to learn French. You must remember that most people who live in Quebec speak French. Can you imagine how francophones react to such people?

You see we have had a small minority, "les anglais" [English], controlling the French majority in my province. This is really frustrating and maddening.

So if you ask me if I support Bill 101, of course I do! Things have to change; they finally are changing.

On the other hand, some Québécois, especially the anglophones, are opposed to Bill 101. They say that it goes too far. They feel that their rights as Canadians in a bilingual country are threatened. The accompanying newspaper article illustrates one such case.

The Quebec referendum

The other issue which created so much controversy was the referendum or vote on sovereignty-association. Simply speaking, sovereignty-association means independence from Canada but with economic ties to Canada. That is to say, the Parti Québécois government wants to control and manage their own affairs within Quebec. At the same time, however, they wish to keep certain business ties with Canada, such as using the same money.

Being a separatist, Premier Lévesque wants to negotiate with Canada for his province's independence. Before starting such negotiations, Lévesque promised to hold a referendum in his province to see if the majority of Québécois desired such talks. The first referendum was on May 20, 1980.

The referendum campaign was heated. Premier Lévesque and the Parti Québécois wanted the Québécois to vote "Oui" in the referendum. The Liberal opposition leader, Claude Ryan, asked the people to vote "Non." (Ryan had replaced Bourassa as leader some two years after the first Parti Québécois victory.) He told the people of Quebec that reforms were necessary, but that it would still be best for Quebec to remain in Confederation.

Arguments for both sides appeared on television, billboards, radio and newspapers. Huge rallies were held. Often the Parti Québécois used popular francophone entertainers to attract people to their rallies. The Liberals called in federal politicians like Pierre Trudeau to attract support. Within Quebec many families were divided on the referendum issue.

This was what the referendum asked:

The Government of Quebec has made public its proposal to negotiate a new agreement with the rest of Canada, based on the equality of nations; this agreement would enable Quebec to

Even if the results of the referendum had been reversed, the other provincial premiers and the Canadian prime minister were not interested in negotiating with Quebec for independence.

Approximate breakdown of the referendum results:

	Oui	Non
francophones	60%	40%
anglophones	9%	91%
non-franco/ anglophones	16%	84%

acquire the exclusive power to make its laws, administer its taxes and establish relations abroad—in other words, sovereignty—and at the same time, to maintain with Canada an economic association including a common currency; any change in political status resulting from these negotiations will be submitted to the people through a referendum; on these terms, do you agree to give the Government of Quebec the mandate to negotiate the proposed agreement between Quebec and Canada?
Oui_____   Non_____

The results of the referendum proved to be a major disappointment for the Parti Québécois government. There was a record voting turn-out of 82 percent with 59.4 percent voting "NON" and 40.6 percent "OUI." By far the majority of voting anglophones had voted "NON." Among the francophones, who comprised the majority of voters, the vote was closer with a majority voting "OUI." Although the majority of the Québécois had supported Lévesque in the provincial election, it seemed that they would not go so far as to support separation from Canada.

GETTING THE FACTS

22. Define the following terms: sovereignty association, referendum.

23. Quebec Provincial Elections—1970-1980:

PARTY	1970 NUMBER OF SEATS WON	% OF POPULAR VOTE	1973 SEATS	%	1976 SEATS	%	1981 SEATS	%
Liberal	72	41.8	102	54.8	26	33.8	41	45.5
Parti Québécois	7	23	6	30.3	71	41.4	81	49.5
Creditistes	12	11.1	2	9.9	1	4.6	—	—
Union Nationale	17	19.6	—	4.9	11	18.2	—	—
Other	—	4.5	—	—	1	2	—	—

Péquistes is a term used to refer to the supporters of the Parti Québécois.

a) From the above election statistics how many more seats did the Péquistes win in the 1976 election than in the 1973 election?

b) How many did the Liberals lose? What reasons can you suggest for the Liberal loss in 1976?

c) Make a list of observations about the other parties in the 1981 election.

The arts in Quebec

Since the 1960s, there has been a great surge in artistic output in Quebec. Many of the singers and writers involved have received international recognition. The common theme of Quebec survival and identity runs throughout much of their work. In the opening spread of this chapter, you were introduced to a number of chansonniers Québécois. Now you will meet a number of écrivains (writers) Québécois.

In the field of writing, Gabrielle Roy was one of the first francophones to become well-known and published outside Quebec. Another continually popular writer is Anne Hébert. She began writing in the 1930s. Her 1970 novel, *Kamouraska*, has been translated into many languages and was made into a successful movie. Her most recent book, *Héloïse*, was published in 1980. Other recognized writers include Hébert Aquin and Gérard Bessette.

Theatre in Quebec has undergone great changes. One of the most influential people in this field is Michel Tremblay. His plays have been internationally acclaimed. Recently, Jean Claude Germain's play, *Un pays dont la devise est je m'oublie*, has received a great deal of attention. The play's title in translation means "A nation whose motto is I forget." You know that the motto of Quebec is "je me souviens." What do you think the theme of Germain's play would be? Another popular Québécois playwright and feminist is Denise Boucher, whose most recent play is entitled *Les fées ont soif*.

It is interesting to note that despite the widespread recognition that these artists have received in Quebec, parts of Europe and the United States, many Canadians do not recognize them. What might this suggest about the anglo-francophone relations in Canada?

THE INVESTIGATIVE REPORTER

24. Find out about a novel or play by a French-Canadian author and report on the work. Be sure to explore the work's theme in your report.

THINKING IT THROUGH

25. a) List Lévesque's reasons for introducing Bill 101.

b) How do you think francophones living in Quebec at the time reacted to Bill 101? How did anglophones in Quebec react?

c) What do you think about Lévesque's reasons for Bill 101? Imagine you are writing Lévesque a letter about the Bill. Give your reactions to it, with reasons to support your arguments.

26. Examine the referendum results carefully. What do you think they say about the feelings of the Québécois?

THE INVESTIGATIVE REPORTER

27. Throughout Canada's history there have been a number of

separatist movements in various parts of the nation. Research and write a report on:
    a) a past separatist movement
    b) a current one

Federal government reaction

During the the 1960s and 1970s, the people of Quebec were very concerned about the survival of their culture, surrounded as they were by mainly English-speaking neighbours. As a result, the Québécois wanted more authority over their own affairs. At the same time it had become obvious that the federal government had to re-examine the relationship between French and English-speaking Canadians. In 1963, Prime Minister Lester Pearson appointed the Royal Commission on Bilingualism and Biculturalism. It consisted of an equal number of franco- and anglophone members. For thirty months they travelled across the country interviewing Canadians. In 1967, they released a six volume report on bilingualism and biculturalism.

A Royal Commission is a committee appointed by either the federal or a provincial government. The committee tries to study a problem in a fair manner. Since Confederation there have been hundreds of Royal Commissions such as the Rowell-Sirois, Status of Women, and Massey commissions.

"Bi and Bi" Commission

Objective

To study the problems of French-English relations in Canada

Conclusion

"Canada is passing through the greatest crisis in its history." If Canada is to survive, improved relations between Canadians are necessary.

Suggestions

Anglophones must accept francophones as their equals. Canada should be a bilingual nation with French and English the official languages. The federal government and courts should operate in both French and English. Anglophones should be encouraged to learn French.

Francophones must forget about past injustices. Rather, they should be more interested in working towards a better Canada. French-speaking Canadians should try to learn English.

In 1969, Prime Minister Pierre Elliott Trudeau took most of the language suggestions of the "Bi and Bi" Commission and placed them in a new act.

> The Official Languages Act
>
> 1. English and French are the two official languages of Canada. Either language can be used in the Parliament of Canada, federal courts and federal government offices.
> 2. Bilingual districts will be officially recognized. These are areas where there are large minorities of either anglophones or francophones. In such areas both languages will be recognized.
> 3. Much of Canada's civil service is to become bilingual.
> 4. The Ottawa area is a bilingual district and all schools in this area must offer French and English instruction.

The "Bi and Bi" Commission Report and Trudeau's bilingual policies have not been favourably accepted by all Canadians. In Quebec, most separatists and the Parti Québécois are concerned about protecting and encouraging the French language in Quebec and certain francophone areas across Canada. They are not as concerned about anglophones speaking French outside of Quebec. Anglophone back-lash (negative reaction) toward the Liberal government's policies was evident. It appeared to some anglophones that Quebec was

Fig. 14 Left to right: Jean Marchand, Pierre Trudeau, Gerard Pelletier. When these three influential and popular Québécois entered federal politics, John Diefenbaker nicknamed them "the three wise men." In 1968, five years after arriving in Ottawa, Trudeau replaced Lester Pearson as Liberal prime minister.

obtaining special status, or powers and rights. In fact, this was not the case. The mutual understanding and cooperation mentioned in the "Bi and Bi" Report was apparently lacking.

When the Royal Commission on Bilingualism and Biculturalism released its report, official bilingualism was quickly adopted. However, biculturalism was not. In its report, the "Bi and Bi" Commission made special note of the multicultural nature of our country. Especially since World War II, there has been a great increase in the different races and nationalities of people entering Canada. In 1971, a federal policy of multiculturalism was adopted.

For further information, see "Canada: land of many cultures."

In 1977, the federal government established "The Task Force on Canadian Unity." It had two main objectives: first, to obtain the views of Canadians on the state of unity in Canada; second, to make recommendations to Ottawa concerning unity issues.

This quotation is taken from the Task Force's recommendations:

For further information, see "Can the Canadian constitution protect everyone's rights?"

We believe, therefore, that there should be a new Canadian constitution to meet the aspirations [hopes] and future needs of all the people of Canada. . . . Quebec is distinctive [different] and should, within . . . Canada, have the powers necessary to protect and develop its distinctive character. . . . assign to Quebec formal law-making powers, denied to other provinces, over such matters as culture, language, immigration, social policy, communications and some aspects of international affairs.

Fig. 15 Distribution of language groups in Canada

CANADA AND PROVINCE	TOTAL POPULATION	ENGLISH NUMBER	FRENCH NUMBER	OTHER NUMBER	NOT STATED NUMBER
CANADA	22 992 600	14 122 170	5 887 205	2 537 615	445 020
Newfoundland	557 725	545 340	2 760	3 965	5 665
Prince Edward Island	118 230	109 745	6 545	935	1 005
Nova Scotia	828 570	768 070	36 870	13 625	10 010
New Brunswick	677 250	435 975	223 780	6 925	10 565
Quebec	6 234 445	800 680	4 989 245	334 055	110 470
Ontario	8 264 465	6 457 645	462 070	1 178 670	166 080
Manitoba	1 021 510	727 240	54 745	218 875	20 645
Saskatchewan	921 325	715 685	26 710	163 935	14 995
Alberta	1 838 040	1 482 725	44 440	272 395	38 480
British Columbia	2 466 610	2 037 645	38 430	325 610	64 930
Yukon	21 840	18 940	525	1 630	745
Northwest Territories	42 610	23 085	1 095	16 995	1 435

Note: Calculations based on rounded data.
From *1976 Canada Census.*

Francophone communities outside Quebec

Although most French-speaking Canadians live in Quebec, there are francophone communities throughout Canada. The people of these communities are not transplanted Québécois. Instead, they have long and colourful histories of their own.

For most of the non-Quebec francophones, the threat of losing their culture is a very serious one. There are various reasons for their concern. For example, most provinces do not offer official status to the French language.

Although the loss of their culture and language is a real danger, there are, nonetheless, signs that all is not lost. For example, in New Brunswick there is a political party, Le Parti Acadien, which is struggling to ensure the survival of the Acadian way of life. (For more information on the history of the Acadians, see *Discovering Canada, Settling a land*.) A few francophone newspapers and other media help promote their cause. As well, francophone associations exist across Canada.

Ensure French education, Davis urged
By ROBERT MATAS

Ontario should recognize the right of French-speaking students to education in their mother tongue from junior kindergarten to the end of secondary school, a group of francophones and provincial Government officials says.

[A recommendation was made to require school boards] to provide instruction in French or provide transportation to schools where French instruction is available.

Uphill fight for Manitoba bilingualism

WINNIPEG—[In] . . . 1979 . . . the Supreme Court . . . declared that . . . the Manitoba legislature . . . had [no] authority to remove [its] French-language provisions. . . . [Manitoba] began to do what it could to provide French-language service. . . . Birth certificate forms have been bilingual since June. . . . Drivers' licenses . . . [since] October.

. . . .[T]ranslation of . . . government statutes and regulations, however, . . . will take at least seven years.

In the past, the Québécois tended to feel somewhat "responsible" for their French Canadian compatriots. Now each of the francophone communities is feeling more responsible for its own fate. What would happen to them if Quebec separated from Canada?

THE INVESTIGATIVE REPORTER

The following section lists some other reasons for concern:
- The greater the number of francophones who move into the larger cities with people of numerous ethnic backgrounds, the greater the threat that their traditional culture will be lost.
- French may be spoken in the home, but the working environment is usually English.
- Francophone communities are surrounded by anglophone communities.
- English is used more than French in most of our mass media.

28. Find out about the history of a French Canadian community in your province, with the help of books in your school or local library or by interviewing a member of the community. Write a one-page report on the subject.

Fig. 16 French speaking students from Essex County, Ontario demand an education in their native language. How would schooling for these students have been affected by government policies?

USING YOUR KNOWLEDGE

29. Look at Figure 15. Why do you think that the federal government suggested that the governments of New Brunswick and Ontario recognize two official languages in their provinces.

30. Prime Minister Trudeau has always felt that the provincial governments should have equal powers with each other and that the federal government should be stronger than the provinces. In view of this, how do you think he felt about the Task Force recommendation quoted in this chapter? Explain.

THINKING IT THROUGH

31. a) List the objectives of (a) the Royal Commission of Bilingualism and Biculturalism and (b) the Task Force on Canadian Unity.

b) Which objectives do you agree with? Disagree with? Give reasons for your answers.

c) Based on your opinion, describe your own vision for Canada.

32. As a result of the "Bi and Bi" Commission report, the federal government officially adopted a policy of multiculturalism.

a) Define the term multiculturalism. How did the government support this policy?

b) Why do you think the government did not adopt a policy of multilingualism?

Conclusion

Canada, without being fully conscious of the fact, is passing through the greatest crisis in its history.

The source of the crisis lies in the Province of Quebec . . . but . . . it has become a Canadian crisis, because of the size and strategic importance of Quebec, and because it has inevitably set off a series of chain reactions elsewhere.

If it should persist and gather momentum, it could destroy Canada. On the other hand, if it is overcome, it will have contributed to the rebirth of a richer and more dynamic Canada. But this will be possible only if we face the reality of the crisis and grapple with it in time.

The above quotation appeared in 1965 in the "Preliminary Report of the Royal Commission on Bilingualism and Biculturalism." Basically the report stated that Canadians must understand and come to terms with the frustrations and needs of French Canadians. If we do not, Canada may cease to exist as an united nation. Do you think Canadians have come to understand the feelings of the francophone Québécois?

If Quebec separated from the rest of Canada, we would have to answer some very serious questions. For example:
What would happen to the approximately 900 000 French Canadians living outside Quebec?
What would happen to the approximately 900 000 anglophone Québécois?
Would Quebec independence result in other provinces breaking away from Confederation?

These questions presently remain unanswered. There is, however, one thing of which we all should be aware. Without greater understanding and cooperation between French- and English-speaking Canadians, Canada may well cease to be a nation "from sea to sea."

THINKING IT THROUGH

33. Based on your knowledge of French-English relations throughout Canada's history, make two reasonable predictions about the future of the relationship between Quebec and Canada. Be sure to support your predictions.

34. Debate the following questions:
Should Quebec receive special treatment in Canada?
Should other provinces be entitled to special status also?

12 Canada: Land of many cultures

Cultural origin of Canadian population

	1901	1931	1971
British	57.0%	51.9%	44.6%
French	30.7%	28.2%	28.7%
Other European	8.5%	17.5%	23.1%
Asian	0.4%	0.8%	1.3%
Native Peoples	2.4%	1.1%	1.5%
Black	0.1%	0.1%	0.3%
All Others	0.9%	0.4%	0.5%
TOTAL	100%	100%	100%

Source: *Census of Canada*

Birthplace of Canadian population

	1901	1931	1971
Canada	87.0%	77.8%	84.7%
United Kingdom	7.5%	11.0%	4.3%
United States	2.4%	3.3%	1.4%
Other Commonwealth	0.3%	0.4%	0.8%
Europe	2.3%	6.9%	7.8%
Asia	0.4%	0.6%	0.6%
Other	—	—	0.4%
TOTAL	100%	100%	100%

Source: *Census of Canada*

Polish dancers at a festival of multiculturalism

Canadian population by mother tongue

	1971		1981	
	NUMBER OF PEOPLE	PERCENTAGE OF POPULATION	NUMBER OF PEOPLE	PERCENTAGE OF POPULATION
English	12 973 810	60.2	14 918 460	61.3
French	5 793 650	26.9	6 249 095	25.7
Baltic	43 385	0.2	38 610	0.1
Celtic	24 630	0.1	12 135	0.1
Chinese	94 855	0.4	224 030	0.9
Croatian/Serbian	74 190	0.3	87 870	0.4
Czech/Slovak	45 145	0.2	42 825	0.2
Finnish	36 725	0.2	33 385	0.1
German	561 085	2.6	522 850	2.1
Greek	104 455	0.5	122 955	0.5
Indo-Pakistani languages	32 555	0.2	116 990	0.5
Inuit	15 295	0.1	18 840	0.1
Italian	538 360	2.5	528 780	2.2
Japanese	16 890	0.1	20 135	0.1
Hungarian	86 835	0.4	83 725	0.3
Native Indian	164 525	0.8	147 730	0.6
Netherlandic languages	159 165	0.7	156 645	0.6
Polish	134 780	0.6	127 960	0.5
Portuguese	86 925	0.4	165 510	0.7
Romanian	11 300	0.1	12 945	0.1
Russian	31 745	0.1	31 485	0.1
Scandinavian languages	84 335	0.4	67 720	0.3
Semitic languages	28 550	0.1	58 900	0.2
Spanish	23 815	0.1	70 160	0.3
Ukrainian	309 855	1.4	292 265	1.2
Yiddish	49 890	0.2	32 760	0.1
Other/Unknown	41 830	0.2	158 415	0.7
TOTAL	21 568 310	100.0	24 343 180	100.0

Source: *Census of Canada*

Sir John A. Macdonald said "A British subject I was born, and a British subject I shall die." He tried to make Canada as British as possible. Pierre Trudeau said "Every ethnic group has the right to preserve and develop its own culture and values" in Canada. He worked to provide as varied a culture for Canada as possible. Read the following statement:

> Sir John A. Macdonald's view made sense in his time, when one looks at the Canadian population figures for 1901. Pierre Trudeau's view made sense in his time because of the changes which had taken place in the population by 1971.

- Examine the charts on these two pages. Do they provide support for this statement? Write a paragraph in your notebook, agreeing or disagreeing with the statement. Use figures from the charts to defend your view.

Chapter overview

The population charts on the previous pages show that Canada is a nation whose people come from many different backgrounds. People of British and French origins have always made up a majority of the Canadian population, but their share has been declining since the beginning of the twentieth century.

There are two ways of looking at the variety of our population. One view says that variety is a source of strength. It makes our life richer to hear many languages being spoken and to see the festivals of different peoples being celebrated. The other view says that variety could weaken our nation. The differences among our people prevent a strong sense of Canadianism from emerging. The first view suggests that it is possible to retain one's own ethnic background and still be fully Canadian. The second view states that one has to make a choice between the two.

This chapter will look at some of the differences in the Canadian population. Its purpose is to decide whether these differences add to, or detract from, our nation's strength. You will look at the question of language. How many languages should Canada have? One, two or many? You will look at government policy. Should it try to preserve the ethnic differences among Canadians, or to eliminate them? You will also look at some documents from our history, to see how policies on this subject have changed over the years. Finally, you will have to decide which view you take—are differences a source of strength or of weakness?

The term "British" includes people from England, Scotland, Wales and Northern Ireland.

Signposts

What is culture? >

How many cultures should we have? >

The federal government adopts a policy of multiculturalism >

FEATURE: Canada then: How black immigrants were kept out >

A case study in multiculturalism: The heritage language issue >

Key words

ethnic	uniculturalism	official language	mosaic
ethnic group	biculturalism	heritage	heritage
culture	multiculturalism	melting pot	language

What is culture?

Culture is a way of being, thinking and feeling ...
a driving force (guiding) a significant group of
individuals united by a common tongue, and sharing
the same customs, habits, and experiences.

Royal Commission on Bilingualism & Biculturalism, 1967.

Does the above statement help you to understand the meaning of
the term "culture"? What factors does it include, and what factors
cannot be considered part of culture? Let us explore the term
further.

Try to think of the term
"youth culture" and all it
involves. ("Pop" music, jeans,
hot dogs, soft drinks, etc.) To
be part of this, one must
adopt many of these items.

**Fig. 1 Native tongue by
province, 1976. How might
the variety of languages
influence government
policies?**

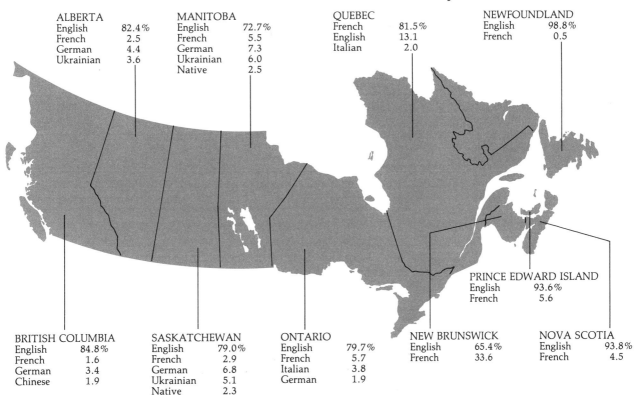

ALBERTA
English	82.4%
French	2.5
German	4.4
Ukrainian	3.6

MANITOBA
English	72.7%
French	5.5
German	7.3
Ukrainian	6.0
Native	2.5

QUEBEC
French	81.5%
English	13.1
Italian	2.0

NEWFOUNDLAND
English	98.8%
French	0.5

PRINCE EDWARD ISLAND
English	93.6%
French	5.6

BRITISH COLUMBIA
English	84.8%
French	1.6
German	3.4
Chinese	1.9

SASKATCHEWAN
English	79.0%
French	2.9
German	6.8
Ukrainian	5.1
Native	2.3

ONTARIO
English	79.7%
French	5.7
Italian	3.8
German	1.9

NEW BRUNSWICK
English	65.4%
French	33.6

NOVA SCOTIA
English	93.8%
French	4.5

To begin, let us take an example, the largest ethnic group in our country—English Canadians. We can say that they have enough common features to allow us to talk of an English-Canadian culture. Look at the following list of features. Re-read the above definition of culture, and then decide which of these features can be considered part of English-Canadian culture.

—the English language
—farming and agriculture
—the cold, northern climate
—steel plants
—the belief in individual
  freedom
—fishing boats
—the Christian religion
—labour unions

—"fast food" outlets
—railway stations
—ice hockey
—Boeing 747s
—free and easy lifestyle
—the stock market
—casual style of dress
—Denmark

Now we need to identify some headings under which each feature can be placed. Look at the following list of features. Each pair is part of English-Canadian culture. Write the list in your notebook, and try to identify a heading for each pair.

Fig. 2 Features of English-Canadian culture

FEATURES	HEADING
split pea soup	
apple pie with Cheddar Cheese	food
ice hockey	
drive-in movies	
the Presbyterian Church	
the Roman Catholic Church	
all people should be free	
Canada is a great country	
apartment buildings	
warm, comfortable houses	
fur-lined parkas	
cut-off jeans	
celebrating birthdays	
going to church	
making pine furniture	
knitting sweaters	

Of course, not all English-Canadians share all of these features. You will notice, too, that many of these features could be typical of other cultures. However, your entries in the "Heading" column should help you identify what *sort* of elements make up a culture.

When you have completed the exercises in this section, you should be able to define the term culture for yourself. But an interesting question remains. How is culture learned?

Fig. 3 Two Dutch-Canadians in traditional dress prepare a Christmas tree. Note the wooden shoes and ornaments on the table. Dutch Christmas is celebrated on December 6.

One feature of culture is language. In many ways, language is easy to learn. One can learn to speak French or Spanish in school. However, it is much more difficult to learn what people in France or Spain think funny, or beautiful. Think of yourself—how did you learn what our society thinks funny or beautiful? Did someone tell you? Probably not. It is likely you just picked up these ideas from others, your parents and friends perhaps. You probably learned the rest of our culture in the same way. You share most of your ideas and **customs** with family or friends. This is the value of a culture. It binds a group of people together and gives them a common outlook on life.

GETTING THE FACTS

1. In your own words explain how culture is learned.

2. Using the information contained in the first chart at the start of this chapter, make a bar graph which shows the size of each ethnic group, for 1901 and 1971. Use the following example to guide you.

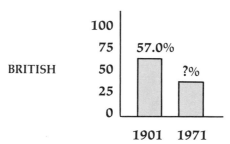

Be sure to include a title and all necessary figures.

USING YOUR KNOWLEDGE

3. Examine your bar graph. Which groups have grown in size? Which have fallen? Which groups show the most change? The least change?

4. Examine each of the charts in turn. For each chart, write down in your notebook three observations on the changes in our population over the years.
Suggestion: Write a conclusion about the *overall* change, the area of greatest change and the area of *least* change over the years, in each chart.

5. Make a copy of the following diagram:

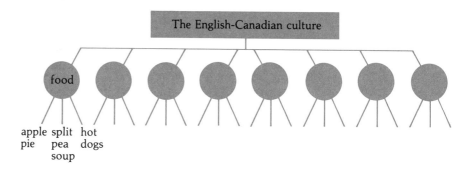

In each circle, write one heading which you made up from the list of paired features in Figure 2. Below each line, write a feature which belongs under that heading, and think of a third one of your own. One example has been provided for you.

6. To test whether you fully understand the term "culture," make a diagram, similar to the one above, for the French-Canadian culture or any other cultural group listed in the charts at the opening of the chapter. Be sure to put in the headings and individual features.

How many cultures should we have?

Should Canada have one, two or many cultures? There have been different answers to this question over the years. Discussion has frequently centred on language.

Throughout our history, we have tried to decide whether Canadians should speak one, two or a variety of languages. We have had to decide how many languages should be used by our governments in their daily business. From the following extracts you will see that the answers to these questions have varied through history. Uniculturalism, biculturalism and multiculturalism have all been tried at various times.

Uniculturalism—having a single culture in one nation
Biculturalism—having two cultures
Multiculturalism—having many cultures

Lord Durham's Report

Following the rebellions of 1837, Lord Durham was asked by the British government to investigate Canada's problems and to report

Fig. 4 These Toronto street signs, in Greek and Chinese, show how both population and attitudes in Canada have changed since Lord Durham's time.

on ways to solve them. He believed that French Canadians were a problem, and this is what he said of them:

> The French residents of Lower Canada are lacking in culture. Their language is peculiar, and they have no history and no literature. I believe that the best solution is to give all power to the English Canadians, and that in this way, the French Canadians would change their ways.

The British North America Act (1867)

Canada's original constitution outlined the uses of the English and French languages, in government and the courts.

> Either the English or French language may be used by any person in the debates of the Parliament of Canada and of the Legislature of Quebec . . . and either of these languages may be used . . . in all or any of the Courts of Quebec.

The B.N.A. Act did not permit the use of English *and* French in all the courts and governments in Canada. English could be used anywhere, but French was to be used only in Parliament or where French Canadians were a majority. Over the next century, however, attitudes towards French language rights changed.

The Royal Commission on Bilingualism and Biculturalism (1965)

> We recommend that the provinces of New Brunswick and Ontario declare that they recognize English and French as official languages . . .

> We recommend that the provinces other than Quebec, New Brunswick and Ontario declare that both English and French may be used in the debates in their legislatures and that these provinces provide appropriate services in French for their French-speaking minorities.

As a result of the Commission's recommendations, the federal government passed the Official Languages Act. This permits the use of English and French by any citizen in dealings with the federal government. This Act has effect in any part of Canada.

Some people feel that this emphasis on English and French ignores other groups of people in Canada. So, while only English and French are official languages, the federal government has come to support a policy of multiculturalism.

Fig. 5 **People of various ethnic origins have played important roles throughout Canada's history. The first Canadian to be awarded the Victoria Cross was a Nova Scotian black, William Hall. He won the medal for his bravery during fighting with the British at Lucknow, India, in 1857.**

Since people of English-speaking (anglophone) and French-speaking (francophone) backgrounds made up the majority of the Canadian population in 1867, only these two languages are recognized as official ones. Of course, a person may speak any language at all.

Prime Minister Trudeau

Although there are two official languages, there is no official culture, nor does any ethnic group take precedence over any other ... A policy of multiculturalism within a bilingual framework (is) the most suitable means of assuring the cultural freedom of Canadians.

House of Commons Debates, October 8, 1971

These extracts show major changes to our attitudes towards culture and towards language in particular. Biculturalism was unthinkable to Lord Durham; multiculturalism is now the official policy of our federal government.

Fig. 6 Two Scots in formal evening dress.

GETTING THE FACTS

8. What is an "official language?"

9. Read each of the extracts in this section (from Lord Durham, the British North America Act, the Royal Commission, Prime Minister Trudeau). Which of the three policies does each recommend— uniculturalism, biculturalism or multiculturalism?

USING YOUR KNOWLEDGE

10. You have read the views of Lord Durham and Pierre Trudeau. Imagine that each was writing a letter to a friend about the views of the other. What would they say? Write two imaginary letters— Durham commenting on Trudeau and Trudeau commenting about Durham.

11. If it were possible for Durham and Trudeau to have a televised debate on the subject, who would win? Why?

THINKING IT THROUGH

12. a) Consider each of the extracts again. Select one with which you particularly disagree. Write a paragraph explaining why you disagree with the ideas expressed.

b) Ask a classmate to compare your paragraph with the extract. Which view (yours or the extract's) does your classmate agree with? Why?

13. The Canada Act (1982) is our new constitution. Here is an extract from it on the subject of official languages.

English and French are the official languages of Canada and have equality of status and equal rights and privileges as to

Despite section 16(1), there is only one province which is officially bilingual—New Brunswick. Despite strong pressure on the governments of Ontario and Quebec, both provinces remain unilingual—Ontario in English, and Quebec in French.

their use in all the institutions of the Parliament and government of Canada.

Section 16(1)

a) Compare this with the extract from the British North America Act (1867). What similarities are there between the two? What differences?

b) Do you think that the changes made by the 1982 Act are good or bad ones? Give reasons to support your viewpoint.

The federal government adopts a policy of multiculturalism

If people do not know much about each other, it is easy for them to develop distrust and even dislike. Sometimes people in a majority group know very little about various minorities. It is easy for them to see only those things about a minority that are different—for example, its style of dress or its food. Unless they make an effort to understand these differences, bad feelings can quickly result.

In October, 1971, the Canadian government adopted a policy of multiculturalism. It accepted the idea that we would all remain Canadians first, but various peoples and cultures should retain their heritage. Prime Minister Trudeau explained the purpose of multiculturalism in the House of Commons when he said:

> I wish to emphasize the view of the government that a policy of multiculturalism . . . is basically the conscious support of individual freedom of choice. We are free to be ourselves but this cannot be left to chance. It must be fostered and pursued actively. If freedom of choice is in danger for some ethnic groups, it is in danger for all.

The government supports the idea that cultural variety is a major part of Canadian life. It also believes that no group should have the right to force another group to change its culture.

The Cabinet minister responsible for putting Canada's multiculturalism policy into effect is the Secretary of State. The policy has four goals.

> First . . . the government will seek to assist all Canadian cultural groups . . . to grow and contribute to Canada.

> Second, the government will assist . . . cultural groups (to enjoy) full participation in Canadian society.

> Third, the government will (encourage cultural groups to learn more about each other) in the interest of national unity.

All Canadian.

Fourth, the government will continue to assist immigrants to acquire at least one of Canada's official languages in order to become full participants in Canadian society.

House of Commons Debates, October 8, 1971

The policy is carried out by Multiculturalism Canada, a branch of the Department of State. Since 1971, when the policy began, this branch has been given approximately $10 000 000 each year to help multicultural growth. It runs a variety of programmes to do this. For example, it provides funds to help authors writing about ethnic groups in Canada. It assists schools and universities to establish courses on multiculturalism, and it promotes festivals which involve all sorts of ethnic groups. In addition, it has set up the Canadian Council on Multiculturalism. This council has 100 members who examine problems related to multiculturalism. They advise the government on its policies in this area.

Fig. 7 The federal government's policy of multiculturalism is supported on a provincial level. This poster was produced by a provincial government to further "intercultural understanding and racial harmony."

There is no doubt that multiculturalism has grown in Canada since 1971. Glance at the yellow pages of the telephone book of any big city. Under the heading "restaurants," you will see evidence of a great variety of cultures. Annual festivals show the strength and vigour of multiculturalism in Canada. The Calgary Stampede, Edmonton's Klondike Days and Vancouver's Pacific National Exhibition all contain displays from various ethnic and multicultural groups. Toronto has a television station—Channel 47—geared to multiculturalism. Three-quarters of its prime-time broadcasting is in languages other than English or French. Cars, soap powder and breakfast cereals are advertised in over a dozen languages. Clearly the federal government's multicultural policy is being put into effect at all levels.

GETTING THE FACTS

14. Read the first extract from Prime Minister Trudeau's speech. What is the basic reason he feels that a policy of multiculturalism is a good idea?
    a) Explain the meaning of "heritage."
    b) In a short paragraph, describe your own heritage.

USING YOUR KNOWLEDGE

15. Look at the four major goals of multiculturalism. Rewrite them in your own words in your notebook.

16. Look at the following list of headlines. Of which goal is each an example? Write each goal and the headlines which go along with it in your notebook.

Government Aid to Multicultural Festival Increased

Board of Education Provides English Classes for Senior Citizens in Chinatown

T.V. Station Provides News in German

New Multiculturalism Minister Promises Action to Make Programmes Higher Profile

Government Bill Outlaws Discrimination Based on Ethnic Origin

Ethnic Groups Discuss Common Problems At Government-Sponsored Conference

Ukrainian Folk Dance Troupe Given Travel Grant To Perform In Vancouver

Canadian Council on Multiculturalism Discusses Concerns of Various Cultural Groups

Government Programme Introduced To Provide Aid To "Deprived" Cultural Groups

Funds For New Italian Club Being Raised

17. Obtain a copy of the Yellow Pages for one of Canada's cities. (Your Public Library may be able to help you if you do not live in a city.) Under the heading "Restaurants," how many businesses are listed? How many of these advertise food from a particular culture? How many cultures are represented? Does the city appear to be multicultural, based on this evidence?

Fig. 8 Chinatown, Victoria, B.C. Using a dictionary, look up a definition of the word "community."

Canada then: How black immigrants were kept out

Between 1896 and 1907, 1 300 000 immigrants came to Canada. Of these, less than 900 were black. It is one of the more shameful parts of Canadian history that there was such a strong effort to keep black immigrants out. The reason given for this effort was always that black people could not adapt to Canada's cold climate. But, of course, this is untrue. Many people simply did not want black immigrants. Here are some examples of the methods used to keep them out.

Chicago Daily News, 1911
Winnipeg—A black man was Perry's sole companion when he reached the North Pole. Yet the Winnipeg Board of Trade is protesting against the taking up of homesteads in Alberta and Saskatchewan by blacks on the ground that they are not adapted to the climate.

Kansas City 1910. The Canadian government's agent wrote to the superintendent of Immigration in Ottawa.
Replying to yours of the 22nd . . . re black people moving to Canada . . . When I have known of black parties applying (for information about immigration to Canada), I have declined to forward literature.

Of course, there were already some black people in Canada at this time. In Nova Scotia, especially around Halifax, there was a community descended from the slaves. They had settled there with their Loyalist owners during the American Revolution. Chatham, Ontario, had served as a Canadian terminus for the "Underground Railroad," so a significant black population had settled there. These people were descended from American slaves smuggled into Canada before the American Civil War.

Some had been successful. For example, Mary Ann Shadd of Chatham ran an anti-slavery newspaper during the 1850s. She was probably the first woman newspaper publisher in Canada. Delos Rogest Davis of Amherstburg, Nova Scotia became a qualified lawyer in Ontario in 1885. In 1910, he was appointed a King's Counsel, and was the first black to hold such a position in all of Canada. ("King's Counsel" is the title given to senior and experienced lawyers, who are permitted to represent the Crown in legal cases.)

Such cases were unusual, however, and Canadians continued to discriminate against black immigrants. The situation began to change in the 1960s. Since then, blacks from the United States, Africa and—most often—the Caribbean, have joined the many immigrants who come to Canada each year.

USING YOUR KNOWLEDGE

18. a) Compare the examples of methods used to keep blacks out of Canada with the charts at the beginning of this chapter. Does it appear that the methods were successful? At what point did the black share of the population begin to increase?

   b) Is the black population of Canada significantly large today when compared with other groups?

19. Discuss: Why do you think societies are often unwilling to accept certain groups of people? You may want to refer back to the first part of this chapter for some ideas.

THE INVESTIGATIVE REPORTER

20. Using books from your school or local library find out about the "Underground Railroad."

Fig. 9 Children of early black settlers, Athabasca, Alberta

Two views of multiculturalism

Views on the subject of multiculturalism differ enormously. Some people favour a multicultural Canada, others oppose it. Here are two views on the subject, together with the reasoning behind them.

Canada as a melting pot

When you look at Canada, you can see that it is made up of people from widely different backgrounds. Living here we have people of many different religions, languages, skin colours and cultures. It is impossible to form a truly strong nation unless a common culture emerges. In the United States the "melting pot" approach has helped to form a strong and united nation.

During the period between 1880 and 1910, large numbers of people from eastern Europe fled to the United States. They spoke little or no English, and understood nothing of American culture. Their children had no choice but to go to English-language schools, so they rapidly adopted American culture. Within two generations, these east European families became as American as the descendants of the original settlers.

The lesson of history suggests that if a nation is to succeed, it must have a single culture. People must think of themselves first as American, not as Polish or Italian–Americans; or as Canadians,

A melting pot was the pot in which different metals used to be heated and melted to form another metal. The term is used to mean the process through which different groups are made part of one majority culture.

315

rather than Polish or Italian–Canadians. People will still retain links with their cultural past, but this should not be as important to them as the present. If each group retains its original culture, the nation will remain divided.

For these reasons, multiculturalism is not the answer. The federal government should reduce its spending in this area in order to eliminate some of the differences among Canadians.

Canada as a mosaic

A mosaic is a picture made up of small, distinct tiles or beads. The term is used to mean a society in which minority groups are encouraged to retain their separate features.

People who disagree with multiculturalism like to compare Canada with the United States. The U.S. is a melting pot and a strong nation in world affairs, they say. They are suggesting that a melting pot Canada would be stronger internationally. However, there is really no evidence to support this argument.

Canada is different from the United States in one very important way. In the U.S., a single culture, English, dominated the development of the country. In Canada, two cultures, English and French, existed side by side from the beginning. In the U.S., therefore, non-English-speaking immigrants were forced into the melting pot. In Canada, if two cultures could co-exist, why not twenty-two? So we become, not a melting pot, but a mosaic. English and French remained official languages, but a host of others were spoken here too.

Opponents of multiculturalism say that it emphasizes the differences among Canadians. But one must remember that if we understand these differences, we are likely to be more tolerant of

Fig. 10 Filipino Canadians perform the Tinikling dance. They dance between the bamboo poles which are beaten together at an increasing speed. The dance represents the cry and movement of a bird common in the Philippines. It is a popular dance at all Filipino get-togethers.

each other. We are also more likely to be interested in each other, because one group can learn from another.

Canada should not try to imitate the United States. We should not regard our multicultural history as a source of division. Instead, we should take pride in the spirit of tolerance it has encouraged in our nation. We should do all we can to encourage and stimulate our multicultural heritage.

GETTING THE FACTS

21. In your own words, explain the "melting pot" and "mosaic" views of society.

THINKING IT THROUGH

22. a) Make a copy of the following chart. Provide at least four statements in each column.

STATEMENTS SUPPORTING MULTICULTURALISM	STATEMENTS OPPOSING MULTICULTURALISM

b) Which viewpoint do you most agree with? Give reasons for your answer.

A case study in multiculturalism: The heritage language issue

Should a student of Greek or Chinese background be able to take classes in his or her heritage language at High School? Should these classes count towards a High School graduation diploma? Should classes in heritage languages be paid for out of taxes? These are some issues of dispute between the Toronto Board of Education and the Ontario Ministry of Education.

In recent years, cultural groups in the city have put pressure on the Board of Education, which runs the city's public school system, to provide heritage language instruction. At first, the Board agreed to provide such classes for interested students at the end of the school day. While some students were involved in clubs and school sports, others would take instruction in their heritage language.

But this did not satisfy many of the cultural groups. Many students, faced with a choice of playing basketball or taking extra classes, would prefer the sporting activity. So mounting pressure

A heritage language is the language of a cultural group before coming to Canada. In some cases, families still speak this language at home. In other cases, individuals no longer speak it.

was put on the Board to permit heritage language classes as a regular part of the school day. In May, 1982, the Board agreed. This immediately touched off a dispute with the Ministry of Education. The Ministry is responsible for supervising local school boards, and deciding education policy in the province. The positions of the Board of Education and the Ministry are outlined below.

The Toronto Board of Education's position

The Board wishes to introduce heritage language classes at some, but not all, high schools in the city. Classes would be set up in schools where there are enough students of different cultural backgrounds. The families of such students are taxpayers, and deserve a

Fig. 11 The head priest of a Sikh Temple, Vancouver. In what ways might a student's education be enriched by his or her cultural heritage?

school system which meets their needs. Heritage language classes would help these families retain their cultural identity, by teaching their children more about their background. In addition, these classes would assist understanding among cultural groups. Interested students could take classes in languages other than their own and learn more about different people. Such a development would strengthen our society.

If there is sufficient demand for such classes, they should be offered in school time, and they should be paid for out of taxes. Moreover, they should count towards a high school diploma. Students should not be asked to choose between sports and extra classes after school. Nor should they be expected to pay for such classes out of their own or their family's pocket.

The Ontario Ministry of Education's position

The Ministry is not opposed to heritage language instruction itself, but it is opposed to such instruction during school time. The Minister of Education, Dr. Bette Stephenson, outlined her Ministry's position to a newspaper reporter. She told him that the Ministry has three basic reasons for taking this position.

First, according to Ontario's Education Act, heritage languages are classified as continuing education subjects. This means that they cannot be taught as part of a regular school program. They can only be taught outside the school day. The Act could be changed, but the Ministry is opposed to this.

Secondly, the Ministry is worried that a variety of heritage language classes might divide student groups. Students might tend to become separated into smaller groups according to their cultural backgrounds. This would obviously be harmful to school spirit.

Finally, the Ministry is worried about cost. If heritage language classes became part of the school day, demand for them might well increase. Taxpayers are already complaining about high education taxes. The Ministry feels that it would be unfair to ask them to pay even more in order to run heritage language classes.

GETTING THE FACTS

23. What are the issues in the heritage language dispute? Summarize, in point form, the positions of the Board of Education and the Ministry on the subject.

24. a) What do *you* think? Which position comes closer to your views on the subject? Write your views in your notebook, along with your reasons.

b) Compare your views with those of some of your classmates. Do you generally agree or disagree on this issue? Can you think of any reasons for this?

Conclusion

In 1981, the federal government spent approximately $52 000 000 000 to run its various programs. In the same year, it spent approximately $12 000 000 to promote multiculturalism. To put it another way, multiculturalism accounted for only 0.02% of the government's total spending.

There is a division among Canadians on whether the federal government's spending on multiculturalism is worthwhile. In the previous section of this chapter, you have seen different views on the subject. Now it is up to you to decide what should be done to the government's multiculturalism spending. Should it be increased, remain the same, be reduced or eliminated?

Fig. 12 Students from different cultural backgrounds. What problems could arise in organizing heritage language instruction for students like these?

Fig. 13 You might think that this is a group of Canadian Indians. In fact, the picture was taken in Rzeszow, Poland in 1972, and the people are all Polish-Canadian. They are showing people the traditions of Native Canadian groups. This picture suggests that cultural groups have not remained isolated, and shows the effect they have on each other.

USING YOUR KNOWLEDGE

25. Review all the material presented in this chapter. What do you think are the advantages and disadvantages of a policy of multiculturalism for Canada? Explain your answer fully.

THINKING IT THROUGH

26. Imagine you were a senior member of the federal government, with the power to increase, reduce, eliminate or maintain at present levels spending on multiculturalism. Which of these choices would you pick? Prepare a news release in which you explain your decision and the reasons which lie behind it.

13 Canadian-American relations

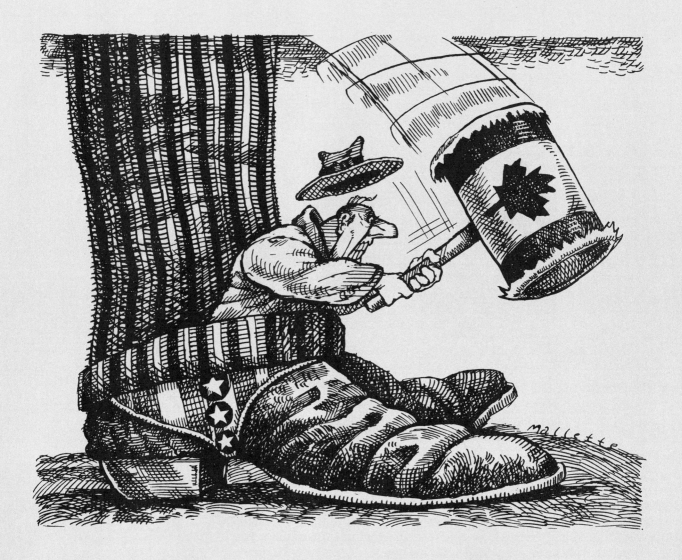

Imagine that you and your family share a house with another family that is larger, older and wealthier. The house has no walls, so you draw an imaginary line down the centre to separate your space from the larger group's space. Your family lives side by side with the other family in a peaceful and friendly way. In fact, your family benefits a great deal from the wealth and experience of the others. For example, the larger family buys all kinds of records that you cannot afford. You soon develop a taste for the other group's music. The others have fancy garden equipment. They offer to let you use some of their tools and share some gardening tips that they have picked up over the years. When you buy clothes, you shop at stores where the other family has special discounts. This way, you can get good quality clothes for a better price than if you shopped by yourself.

Life is rolling along smoothly and everything is fine—or is it? One day you begin to feel overwhelmed by the other group's tastes, wealth, and power. You want to develop your own ideas and interests. Where do you start? How do you avoid offending the other group?

- Suggest two of the first steps that should be taken by the smaller group to establish its own identity.

- What problems do you think the smaller group will face?

- Examine the cartoon closely. What does the man symbolize? What does the foot symbolize? What message is the cartoonist presenting?

- Is Canada's relationship with the U.S. similar in any way to the relationship between the two families in the story? Explain your answer.

Chapter overview

Earlier chapters show how Canada grew from a young country tied to Britain to be a stronger, more independent nation. The struggle to establish a Canadian identity has been slow. Events outside of Canada, such as the two world wars, have affected the shaping of Canada's identity.

U.S. influence also greatly affected the shaping of Canada's identity. There are no physical barriers between Canada and our enormously powerful neighbour. Increasingly, we have tried to control U.S. influence in Canada, and thus shape our identity.

This chapter will focus on four important areas in Canadian-American relations: culture, economic growth, resources, and defense. While studying this chapter, keep in mind two questions:

What are Canadians doing to control U.S. influence? How will these Canadian actions affect Canadian-American relations?

Signposts

Should Canadians protect and develop a distinct Canadian culture?

Economic independence: Should Canada control U.S. investment?

FEATURE: The National Energy Programme: A case study in Canadian ownership

Can we work together to protect our resources and the environment?

FEATURE: The Peloquin family—Victims of acid rain

Defense: Should Canada have a voice of its own?

1967 — Canadian Film Development Corporation established

1968 — Canadian Radio-Television Commission (CRTC) established

1970 — Committee for an Independent Canada formed

1971 — Canadian Development Corporation (CDC) established

1972 — Canadian-U.S. agreement to clean up the Great Lakes

1973 — NORAD crisis Foreign Investment Review Agency (FIRA) established

1975 — Petro-Canada established

1979 — Canadian Book Publishing Development Programme established

1980 — Acid Rain Memorandum signed by Canada and U.S. National Energy Programme (NEP) established

1981 — Petro-Canada purchases Petrofina

Key words

cultural domination energy   defense
cultural survival   resources
foreign investment   acid rain

Should Canadians protect and develop a distinct Canadian culture?

By the time you graduate from high school you will have watched something like 20,000 hours of television. That's about twice as many hours as you will have spent in classrooms since you started school. If you are typical of all Canadians, 15,000 of those hours will be spent watching American programs.

Watching television appears to be a major cultural activity for many Canadians. The average Canadian adult watches 25 hours of television a week. Recent studies suggest that 74 percent of this time is spent watching foreign (mainly U.S.) programmes. How many of your favourite television programmes are American? Do

From *Canada and the World* by Rupert Taylor.

Fig. 1 Dancers of the National Ballet of Canada perform *Newcomers*. The choreography, music and design are all by Canadians.

Culture is complex, but can be defined simply as the characteristics of a group of people that make that group distinct from other groups. Do you think that Canadians are culturally distinct from Americans?

you think the number of American television programmes we watch affects Canada's cultural identity?

Canada is a large but sparsely populated country. Many Canadians are concerned about maintaining a distinct Canadian identity, located as we are beside the heavily populated, very rich and powerful U.S. Canadians feel that without a common and distinct cultural identity Canada may not survive as a separate nation.

Most Canadians agree that Canada must actively protect its cultural industries—music, the arts, film, radio, television and publishing—from U.S. cultural domination. Like the smaller family in the opening story, we feel overwhelmed by the tastes, wealth and power of the U.S. Over the years the government of Canada has established agencies and programmes which encourage the growth and development of the arts, music, film, radio, television and publishing in Canada. Some of these agencies and programmes are listed in the following chart:

Fig. 2 Canadian agencies and programmes

Canadian Broadcasting Corporation, 1936 Provides a national broadcasting service that is mostly Canadian in content and character. In 1980 the federal government gave the CBC $477 400 000 for the production of Canadian television programmes.

National Film Board, 1939 Established to produce documentary films about Canadian life and culture for Canadian and international audiences. Many National Film Board productions have won international awards.

On private AM radio stations, for example, meeting Canadian content means that at least 30 percent of all recorded songs presented daily from 6:00 to 12:00 are Canadian. According to the CRTC, to be Canadian, a recording must meet at least two of the following four standards:
1) the music is written by a Canadian;
2) the lyrics are written by a Canadian;
3) the recording artist is Canadian;
4) the recording is produced in Canada.

Canada Council, 1957 Established to promote the arts such as dance, music, and theatre. Each year the Canada Council provides grants and awards to deserving Canadian artists, writers and performers. The Council also sponsors exhibits of the Canadian arts inside and outside the country.

Canadian Film Development Corporation, 1967 Promotes the development of a feature film industry in Canada through such activities as investing in Canadian film productions and making loans to producers of Canadian films.

Canadian Radio-Television and Telecommunications Commission, 1968 Established to supervise and regulate all aspects of the Canadian broadcasting system, including radio, television and telecommunications carriers. The CRTC issues and renews broadcast licences if radio and television stations meet Canadian content and other programming requirements.

Canadian Book Publishing Development Programme, 1979 A $20 000 000 programme sponsored by the Department of Communications to assist the Canadian book publishing industry in the following areas: textbook development, publishing and marketing research, professional development, foreign book fairs and export sales assistance.

Despite government programmes to encourage our cultural industries, Canadians buy many U.S. recordings, television shows, movies, books and other cultural imports. Why do Canadians buy

American rather than Canadian cultural products? For some answers to this question, we will look at the music and recording industry in Canada.

Canadian recording industry

Eight major record companies dominate record sales in Canada. All eight companies are multinational business corporations (with branches in a number of countries). Six of the eight are U.S. owned. The major multinational record companies sell three types of recordings in Canada:
1) foreign records they have produced using non-Canadian artists, technicians and production facilities;
2) Canadian records they have produced using Canadian artists, technicians and production facilities;
3) Canadian records produced by independent Canadian record companies.

Statistics Canada reports total record sales in Canada of $270 000 000 in 1980. Foreign recordings produced outside of Canada accounted for over 90 percent of that $270 000 000. Figure 4 shows how the multinational record companies dominated the top 100 selling albums in Canada in 1982.

Over the years there have always been independent Canadian record producers who have developed Canadian artists and provided consumers with high quality Canadian music products. There are a

Successful Canadian artists, such as Joni Mitchell, Gordon Lightfoot, Anne Murray, and Neil Young, often sign contracts with the major multinational companies who can afford to produce more copies of each album and advertise and market records internationally.

Fig. 3 Two members of the Canadian group Saga, their producer and engineer mix the sound track of a new record in a Toronto studio. What might be the advantages or disadvantages of recording in Canada?

Independent Canadian record companies generally discover the talent, provide the financing to produce the record and oversee the production of the recording on 24 track or 32 track tape. About 25 independent Canadian record companies have succeeded in gaining distribution agreements for their recordings with major multinational companies. However, the vast majority of independent Canadian record companies sell their own records without the marketing support of a multinational record company.

number of success stories among independent Canadian record companies. Independent companies such as Attic, Anthem, Aquarius and True North have developed Canadian musical talents who compete successfully on a national and international level. However, most independent Canadian record companies struggle for existence in a market controlled by the major multinational record companies and dominated by successful foreign records. Many are forced to withdraw from the Canadian music scene. Of the 122 independent Canadian music companies that were charted on RPM listings between 1965 and 1980, 99 are no longer in business. Although particularly serious in the Canadian music industry, the problem of foreign domination is common to all of Canada's cultural industries.

An interview with John Harris

John Harris has been involved in artist management, music publishing and record production since 1966. Between 1977 and 1980 John Harris and Bob Hahn founded and operated Rising Records, an independent Canadian record company.

Interviewer: Why do Canadians buy so many foreign records?

John Harris: For two very simple reasons. First, most Canadians are influenced by and attracted to foreign (particularly American and British) artists. This is largely due to the excellent international marketing of the multinational record companies. Second, the vast majority of records available in Canadian retail stores are foreign in origin. This is due also to the marketing expertise and control of the record industry in Canada by the multinational record companies.

Interviewer: Why do the multinational record companies dominate the Canadian recording industry?

John Harris: A multinational record company is able to share production costs with the foreign producer of the record. As a result, the foreign record costs less to produce than comparable Canadian produced records. In addition, these major record companies are most often selling a record that is already internationally successful. The result is that their promotion expenses are substantially lower. These two advantages mean profits are excellent and as a result the major companies have the financial and human resources necessary to market their records on a national scale.

Interviewer: Under those circumstances, why did you and Bob Hahn found Rising Records in 1977?

John Harris: I was in the business of managing Canadian artists. My experience with the major multinational record companies was that they would prefer to import internationally known artists

Fig. 4 Record companies ownership and number of albums in the top 100 in 1982 (Canada only)

COMPANY	OWNERSHIP	NUMBER OF ALBUMS IN TOP 100	
WEA Music of Canada	U.S.	WEA Canadian produced	— 0
		WEA foreign produced	— 28
		*Independent Canadian produced	— 0
		TOTAL	— 28
CBS Records Canada	U.S.	CBS Canadian produced	— 3
		CBS foreign produced	— 19
		*Independent Canadian produced	— 0
		TOTAL	— 22
Polygram Limited	Germany	Polygram Canadian produced	— 0
		Polygram foreign produced	— 12
		*Independent Canadian produced	— 2
		TOTAL	— 14
Capitol Records— EMI of Canada	U.S.	Capitol Canadian produced	— 1
		Capitol foreign produced	— 7
		*Independent Canadian produced	— 15
		TOTAL	— 23
A & M Records of Canada	U.S.	A & M Canadian produced	— 1
		A & M foreign produced	— 6
		*Independent Canadian produced	— 4
		TOTAL	— 11
RCA Records (Division of RCA Limited)	U.S.	RCA Canadian produced	— 0
		RCA foreign produced	— 6
		*Independent Canadian produced	— 1
		TOTAL	— 7
MCA Records Canada (Division of MCA Limited)	U.S.	MCA Canadian produced	— 0
		MCA foreign produced	— 2
		*Independent Canadian produced	— 0
		TOTAL	— 2
Quality Records Limited	Canada	Quality Canadian produced	— 2
		Quality foreign produced	— 0
		*Independent Canadian produced	— 1
		TOTAL	— 3

*Independent Canadian record company that has a distribution agreement with the major company identified.
From RPM Weekly, December, 1982

Fig. 5 John Harris, founder of the independent Canadian record company, Rising Records

rather than risk the development of unknown Canadian talent. Even when a major company did take such a risk, I found they lacked the expertise to launch and develop new Canadian artists.

The main goal of the individuals working for the major record companies was to develop an artist who would sell internationally. Often this meant artists were expected to imitate and model themselves on successful foreign artists. This experience convinced me that it was essential to my artists' careers that I have control over the recording part of their professional development.

Last, but definitely not least, I expected Rising Records to make a profit for me and my artists.

Interviewer: Where did Rising Records expect to find the musical talent necessary to build a successful independent Canadian record company?

John Harris: Because of the major record companies' dependence on foreign records, a large number of very talented and creative Canadian artists have been ignored. Rising Records intended to provide a recording outlet for that talent. Most independent Canadian record companies have similar goals.

Interviewer: If there are so many Canadian artists and talented record producers, why have so many independent Canadian record companies failed?

John Harris: Most independent Canadian record companies have failed because they have started without enough financial support or they were unable to earn profits quickly enough to continue production and sale of new records.

Interviewer: Do you think it is easier now for independent Canadian record companies to be successful than it was when you founded Rising Records?

John Harris: It will never be easy to produce successful Canadian records. However, I think new opportunities for Canadian artists and recordings are available. Recently there has been a substantial increase in the sale of Canadian records outside of Canada. The success of Rush, Triumph, Chilliwack, Saga, Bruce Cockburn internationally will have the effect of attracting much needed financing to Canadian record companies. At the 1981 Juno Awards, four of the top five albums were produced by independent Canadian record companies. This kind of recognition will also help. Finally, I think the major multinational record companies will become even more conservative in who they record in the latter part of the 1980s. This will continue to leave many new artists without an outlet for their talent. This situation provides golden opportunities for independent record producers who can overcome the lack of adequate financing.

In response to the persistent threats to Canada's cultural survival, the Canadian government started a major study of Canada's cultural life in 1981. A Federal Cultural Policy Review Committee travelled across the country to hear and study Canadians' views about Canada's cultural life and future. The Committee struggled with many questions. Is there a distinct Canadian cultural identity to protect? In what ways can Canadians build a strong cultural identity? How can the development, distribution and marketing of Canadian cultural products be improved? Should there be stricter control on all U.S. cultural products (T.V., records, films, books, magazines) that come into Canada?

Canadians will continue to struggle with these questions, especially as pay T.V., broadcast satellites, satellite dishes, computers and other telecommunications systems increase the exchange of culture.

GETTING THE FACTS

1. List at least four of Canada's cultural industries. Name one agency or programme that has been designed to protect and develop each industry.

2. In your own words, explain how the U.S. tends to dominate Canadian culture.

3. According to John Harris, what is a major goal of independent Canadian record companies?

4. List two of the reasons why independent Canadian record companies have failed.

USING YOUR KNOWLEDGE

5. In your own words, explain how the following differ from each other:
—Foreign records produced by a multinational company
—Canadian records produced by a multinational company
—Independently produced Canadian records

6. The CRTC regulates that local Canadian television stations must provide Canadian content for 60 percent of their programming time between 6:00 and 12:00. Examine the T.V. listings for your local television station. How does the station distribute its 60 percent Canadian content throughout the day? What are the results of this programming schedule for the viewers?

THINKING IT THROUGH

7. Agree or disagree with this statement: As satellites, computers, and other forms of communication technology improve, it will be

harder for Canadians to maintain a unique cultural identity. Be sure to give reasons for your opinions.

THE INVESTIGATIVE REPORTER

8. Besides the CBC, CRTC and other agencies discussed in this chapter, there are many other government bodies set up to help protect Canadian culture. The National Arts Centre, National Library, National Museums, Public Archives, Social Science and Humanities Research Council are a few. Find more information about one of these agencies, and write a one page report explaining what it is and how it assists in protecting the Canadian identity.

Economic independence: Should Canada control U.S. investment?

As you read in the chapter opening, the smaller family began to feel overwhelmed by the larger family's tastes, wealth and power. They seemed to have lost control of their own lives. Most likely, all of us have felt at one time or another that we do not have real control of our life. Perhaps because of your part-time job you do not have the time to study music or play school sports. Perhaps you cannot find a job and therefore cannot afford the music lessons or sports equipment you want. For many of us, being in control often means having economic independence.

The above examples are very simple illustrations of an important issue facing Canadians today. Who controls Canada's economy? Does Canada have economic independence? Is economic independence important?

We have seen in earlier chapters that in the past Canada has welcomed foreign investment. Over the years, British, American and other foreign investors have financed the development of Canada's rich resources. Foreign investment has directly contributed to economic growth and a high standard of living in Canada. In turn, Canada has provided the investing countries with an opportunity to strengthen their own economies.

Foreign companies have shared their technology, improved our productivity and created jobs for Canadians in many economic sectors such as the automobile, chemical, oil and gas industries.

Most of the direct foreign investment in Canada is from the United States. Direct investment and U.S. companies establishing branch plants in Canada have resulted in American ownership and control of many Canadian industries. The ownership and control of Canadian industries by foreign corporations is outlined in Figures 6 and 8.

United States investment in and control of Canadian industries grew rapidly after World War II. This was a time of economic

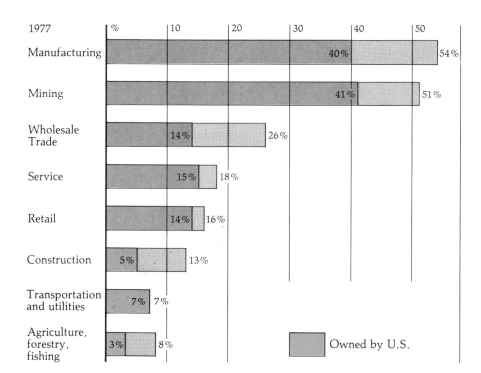

1977

Manufacturing	40%	54%
Mining	41%	51%
Wholesale Trade	14%	26%
Service	15%	18%
Retail	14%	16%
Construction	5%	13%
Transportation and utilities	7%	7%
Agriculture, forestry, fishing	3%	8%

Owned by U.S.

Fig. 6 **Foreign-owned assets in Canada**

growth and prosperity, and the benefits of foreign investment seemed obvious. However, some Canadians became alarmed that our economy was increasingly controlled by non-Canadian companies. In 1968 a small group of influential Canadians formed the Committee for an Independent Canada (CIC).

Among other things the CIC encouraged government to limit foreign investment in Canada. During the 1970s many Canadians were particularly concerned that U.S. economic control of Canadian industry limited Canada's independence in economic, political and cultural matters. They suggested that the U.S. owned multinational corporations served their U.S. parent company's interests first and were not concerned with Canada's economic interests. They believed corporate decisions about production, expansion, employment and profits were made in the U.S. often at the expense of Canada's needs.

Fig. 7 In your own words, explain the captions on this poster issued by the Committee for an Independent Canada.

let's keep it Canadian

The survival of Canada as an independent nation is one of the most important issues facing Canadians today.

The time for mere talk is past; action is very urgently needed.

Let us join together in urging our elected representatives to commit themselves honestly and enthusiastically to Canadian independence.

COMITÉ POUR L'INDÉPENDANCE DU CANADA
COMMITTEE FOR AN INDEPENDENT CANADA

Fig. 8 Foreign control of corporate assets in manufacturing

SECTOR	PERCENTAGE	
	U.S.	TOTAL
Tobacco Products	27	100
Rubber Products	72	94
Petroleum & Coal Products	68	92
Transportation Equipment	72	77
Non Metallic Mineral Products	16	70
Electrical Products	59	69
Chemical Products	54	68
Machinery	51	64
Textile Mills	48	58
Metal Fabricating	33	40
Food Products	31	39
Paper & Allied Industries	29	39
Beverages	20	31
Wood Industries	15	21
Leather Products	18	20

From 1977 Stats Canada, Corporations and Labour Unions Returns Act 61-210

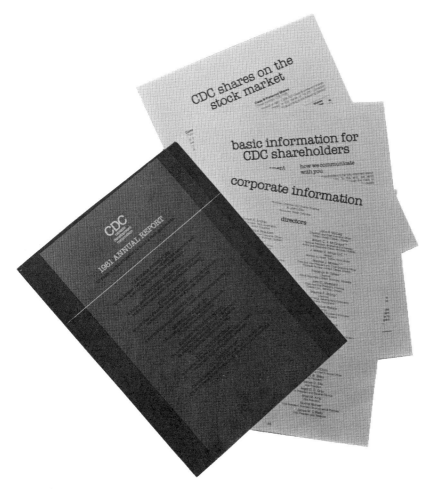

Fig. 9 How could an
organization like the CDC
help Canadians gain more
control over their own
economy?

In the 1970s and 1980s, the Canadian government responded to
these concerns about U.S. influence in the economy. Among the
steps it has taken to try to regain some control are the following:

- 1970—*Denison Mines*, a Canadian company, was put up for sale
  to a foreign company. About 40 percent of the uranium sold in
  Canada was produced by Denison. If the sale went through,
  then 90 percent of Canadian uranium would be produced by
  foreign companies. The sale was stopped by the federal
  government.

- 1971—*Canada Development Corporation (CDC)* formed by the Canadian federal government. CDC set out to develop and
  strengthen Canadian controlled corporations and to give Canadians greater opportunities to invest in the economic development of the country. By 1982 CDC had invested in a wide
  range of companies from gas to mining to fish processing. The
  federal government now owns less than 50 percent of CDC's
  voting shares. The remainder of the voting shares are owned by
  private Canadian investors.

Fig. 10 Do you think it is more important for some industries, rather than others, to be controlled by Canadians? If so, which industries are they? Give reasons for your answer.

For further discussion of multinational corporations in Canada refer back to the section on the recording industry.

- 1974—*Foreign Investment Review Agency (FIRA)* formed. FIRA's purpose is to review all foreign investment proposals and advise the government as to whether or not the investment would "be of significant benefit to Canada." FIRA makes recommendations to the federal Cabinet which makes the final decision. FIRA reviews every foreign investment application for its benefit to Canada in the following areas:
  1. employment in Canada;
  2. use of Canadian parts or services;
  3. Canadian participation in management or ownership;
  4. research and development in Canada;
  5. Canadian exports;
  6. productivity, product variety and innovation in Canada;
  7. capital investment;
  8. compatibility with national economic policies.

From May, 1974 to August, 1982 approximately 3865 foreign investment applications were screened by FIRA. Of those applications, 293 were rejected and 3572 were judged to be of significant benefit to Canada.

- 1975—*Petro-Canada* formed. Petro-Canada was created to increase Canadian presence in the oil and gas industry and give the federal government some first-hand experience in the workings of the oil and gas industry. Petro-Canada is completely government owned.

- 1980—*The National Energy Programme (NEP)* established. The NEP was created in part to bring about 50 percent Canadian ownership of the oil and gas industry by 1990. The NEP encourages Canadian control of a significant number of larger oil and gas firms as well as increased ownership in the oil and gas industry by the government of Canada.

The National Energy Programme: A case study in Canadian ownership

World developments in energy during the 1970s pointed to some serious problems for Canada. In 1979, 17 of Canada's 25 largest petroleum companies were foreign owned controlling over 70 percent of Canadian oil and gas sales. Due to the fact that so many of our petroleum companies were foreign-owned, Canadians felt helpless in the face of the increased cost of energy and the lack of oil supply security in Canada.

In response to these concerns the federal government formulated the National Energy Programme in October, 1980. A main goal of the NEP was to make sure that by 1990, 50 percent of the oil and gas industry would be Canadian owned:

—Larger government incentive grants were given for exploration to companies with at least 50% Canadian ownership.
—Companies with at least 50% Canadian ownership were given preference to explore on Canada Lands (owned by the federal government in the North and off-shore).
—Petro-Canada would retroactively take a 25% interest in any discovery (not in commercial production), on Canada Lands.
—Petro-Canada would purchase several of the large oil and gas firms at a fair market price.

The United States government reacted angrily to the NEP. U.S. Ambassador to Canada, Paul H. Robinson, attacked the programme as being unfair to U.S. oil companies in Canada. He claimed Canada was changing the rules of the game in the middle of play with its retroactive policy of taking a 25 percent interest in any discovery on Canada Lands. U.S. oil companies feared the Canadian government's plan to purchase foreign-owned Canadian companies through Petro-Canada. They claimed the incentives given to Canadian-owned firms decreased the value of their branch plants.

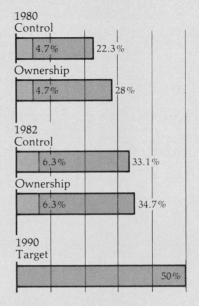

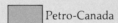 Petro-Canada

Fig. 11 Canadian ownership and control of the oil and gas industry

GETTING THE FACTS

9. With the help of a dictionary, write short definitions for "retroactive" and "incentive."

10. What is the main goal of the NEP?

11. List three actions taken by the federal government to encourage Canadian ownership of the oil and gas industry.

THINKING IT THROUGH

12. a) What positive effects might the NEP have on Canada's oil and gas industry? Why?

b) Describe the U.S. reaction to the NEP. Why do you think the U.S. reacted in this way?

c) In your opinion, is the NEP worth the risk of creating conflict with the U.S.? Give reasons for your opinion.

d) In what other areas of Canada's economy might the government consider passing similar legislation? Why?

Fig. 12 In what ways would the NEP help develop new oil fields?

GETTING THE FACTS

13. Construct a timeline that shows some Canadian steps to limit U.S. control of the economy. Start your timeline at 1968 and write a one sentence explanation of what took place on each date.

USING YOUR KNOWLEDGE

14. a) Examine Figure 8 and list the five industries with the highest amount of foreign ownership.

b) Choose one of the five industries and explain why you think the amount of foreign ownership is so high. Try to give two reasons.

Should Canada limit foreign investment?

Action was taken by the Canadian government in the 1970s and early 1980s to limit foreign investment and increase Canadian participation in the economy. This greatly increased the tension between Canada and the U.S. The U.S. government complained that Canadian investment policies discriminated against American investors. Scarcely an item—lumber, potatoes, fish, steel, water, oil, cars, television—escaped the conflict. Despite being each other's biggest customer, the two countries seemed to be locked into an economic collision course.

	ENOUGH NOW	LIKE TO SEE MORE	DON'T KNOW
National			
1975	71%	16%	13%
1977	69	20	12
1978	69	23	9
1980	64	20	17
1981	67	21	12
1982	56	36	8
By Region 1982			
Atlantic	56	38	7
Quebec	48	39	14
Ontario	60	33	7
Prairies	61	34	5
Br. Columbia	54	41	6

Fig. 13 Poll on U.S. capital invested in Canada

From the *Toronto Star*, Aug. 28, 1982.

Canadian attitudes towards foreign investment and economic independence vary. Some people feel that Canada should be more flexible in its attitude to U.S. investment. As one official has said, "one pound of economic benefit is better than one pound of Canadian ownership." Other Canadians feel that Canada must have greater control over the economy. Figure 13 shows the variety of attitudes Canadians have towards U.S. investment and Canadian ownership.

THINKING IT THROUGH

15. In the 1980s Canada should be more "flexible" in its attitude to U.S. investment.

a) Give one argument to support this statement. Then give one argument against it.

b) Which position do you agree with? Give reasons for your answer.

16. Do you think that the government should actively intervene to control the economy? Should it leave the economy in the hands of private industry? Or is there a middle-of-the-road solution? Give reasons for your viewpoint.

THE INVESTIGATIVE REPORTER

17. Canadians have many different opinions about foreign ownership, but they can be put into three main categories: economic nationalist; laissez-faire ("middle-of-the-roaders"); continentalist.

Reread the section in the 1960s chapter that refers to these three categories, and write a paragraph explaining the main beliefs of each viewpoint. Look at your answer to question 16. Which category does your viewpoint fall into?

Can we work together to protect our resources and the environment?

We are worried—and you *should* be worried—because it is not only a Canadian problem. Acid rain impacts are extending and deepening in the eastern half of the United States as well. It is *our joint* problem—we create it together and, if we are to respond to it successfully, we must respond to it together.

Speech by John Roberts, Minister of the Environment, to the National Wildlife Federation, Milwaukee, March 20, 1982.

In the twentieth century, the volume of these pollutants has become of concern to environmentalists and the government in Canada and the U.S. As early as 1909, the two countries signed the Boundary Waters Treaty, which called for each country to prevent "injury to health or property on the other side of the boundary." In 1972 and 1978 came the Great Lakes Water Quality Agreement.

The Canadian-American border is not a physical boundary. Water and air move freely between the U.S. and Canada whether diplomats and border police like it or not. Many pollutants that are emitted by the industries of one country have shown up in the air and water of the other. This situation continues to cause problems for both countries and has resulted in tension between the United States and Canada. In recent years, a new environmental challenge faces Canada and the U.S.—acid rain. Some environmentalists have labelled it the most deadly crisis of the decade.

What exactly is acid rain? It starts as the nitric or sulphic oxides that are emitted into the air from car tailpipes, smokestacks of power plants, smelters and refineries. When they reach the high

Fig. 14 Canadian officials and members and aids of the U.S. Congress inspect an Ontario lake affected by acid rain. Why is cooperation between Canada and the United States vital in dealing with the problem of acid rain?

The Peloquin family—Victims of acid rain

In 1925 the Peloquin family settled on Lake Chiniguchi about 60 km northeast of Sudbury, Ontario. Peter Peloquin was attracted to the area by the abundant mink and otter population that assured a profitable trapline. In addition, the lake was rich in fish life. In 1953 the Peloquin family opened Camp Chiniguchi as a small tourist operation for fishing. Camp Chiniguchi thrived and expanded. The Peloquins constructed sleeping cabins, a main lodge and invested in boats, motors and all the equipment for a successful fishing camp.

The camp's success was shortlived. By 1963 Lake Chiniguchi's deterioration as a fishing lake was obvious. About 68 km away, Inco (formerly the International Nickel Company) had been pumping sulphur dioxide into the air for over thirty years. The resulting acid rain was gradually turning Lake Chiniguchi into an acidified lake. The Peloquin's guests could no longer catch any fish. The business declined rapidly.

In 1971, Ontario Lands and Forest officials netted in the lake for 58 hours without catching a single fish. In 1974 the lake was officially declared dead . . . a victim of acid rain.

Chiniguchi is a large lake (7 miles [11.7 km] long) and has not been heavily fished. Peloquin's camp is the only one on the lake. However, there are no fish in the lake and even the lily pads and water grasses are disappearing.

From *The Sudbury Pollution Problem: Socio-Economic Background* (unpublished) Department of the Environment, Ottawa, 1974.

Who is responsible for acid rain and what is being done about it? It is estimated that the amount of pollution produced in North America that leads to acid rain is about 60 000 000 tonnes. Of this, Canada produces 6 000 000

Fig. 15 Smokestacks in Falconbridge pump pollutants into the air.

tonnes. It is also believed that 4 000 000 tonnes of sulphur dioxide and unknown quantities of nitric oxides blow from the U.S. to eastern Canada each year.

With this vast amount of pollution travelling across the border, both Canada and the U.S. recognized that acid rain was a mutual problem. On August 5, 1980, Canada and the United States signed a memorandum of intent on transboundary air pollution. The two neighbours would study the problem and take steps to reduce the air pollutants that led to acid rain.

Since then, Canada has taken actions to reduce the acid rain problem. Here are some examples:
1) Ontario has the largest emissions of sulphur and nitrogen oxides. Concern led to action against INCO's Sudbury smelters. In September, 1980, INCO was ordered to reduce emissions to 2500 tonnes of SO_2 (sulphur dioxide) per day. By 1983 this was reduced to 1950 tonnes per day. Technical specialists have been assigned the task of designing *scrubbers* to prevent as much sulphur as possible from escaping through smokestacks.

2) Ontario Hydro, another major polluter from its coal-fired generating stations, has taken action to reduce SO_2 emissions by 43 percent by 1990.

3) In December, 1980 the Canadian Parliament passed Bill C51 giving the Ministry of the Environment the authority to regulate air pollutants affecting another country. The Canadian Clean Air Act now could work in harmony with the United States Clean Air Act and a vigorous public awareness programme was initiated with buttons, folders, stickers and exhibits.

According to many analysts, acid rain is far from under control. Industry has been reluctant to reduce oxides emitted by factories. While it is possible to extract much of the sulphur and nitrogen at source, most companies claim the costs are too high to make it realistic. These companies also claim that not enough is known about acid rain yet and it may not be worth the expense of trying to clean up emissions. Some environmentalists are concerned that governments on both sides of the border have softened their positions about acid rain for economic reasons.

It seems that while both countries have agreed to deal with the acid rain problem, they are moving more slowly than many people would like. The U.S. government seems to be moving even more slowly than the Canadian government, and this has caused further tension in Canadian-American relations.

Fig. 16 **Measuring the acidity of snow**

GETTING THE FACTS

18. Why is environmental pollution a joint concern of Canada and the U.S.?

19. Give two examples of Canadian-U.S. cooperation over environmental issues in the past.

USING YOUR KNOWLEDGE

20. Imagine you are a member of the Peloquin family in the late 1950s. Write a letter to your federal M.P. about the growing problem of acid rain and how it is affecting your life.

21. a) Suggest reasons why the governments of both Canada and the United States may be softening their position on acid rain.

b) What evidence is there that the U.S. position is less than satisfactory from the Canadian standpoint?

THINKING IT THROUGH

22. According to one U.S. official, Canada should put "so much pressure on the U.S. it won't be able to refuse to clean up . . . your government will have to stop playing nice guy."

a) What kind of pressure do you think would change the U.S. government's position?

b) What actions do you think Canada should take to help solve the acid rain problem? Explain why you think these actions would work.

atmosphere they combine with water vapour in the air to form sulphuric and nitric acids. These drop back to earth in the form of rain or snow.

The deadly effects of acid rain are felt by large areas of Canada and the United States. How much damage is done by acid rain? The following facts give us some idea of the problem.

—By the end of the century, 48 000 lakes in Ontario will be dead (no longer able to support fish life) if acid rain continues at its present level. Approximately 140 lakes have already been declared dead.

—According to the U.S. Council on Environmental Quality, acid rain eats through paint and metal and causes half the corrosion on North American cars. It also eats away at buildings, causing an estimated billion dollars of damage each year to historic buildings in Canada alone.

—Nova Scotia has lost 9 salmon rivers already and may lose 22 more. This means that about a third of the province's $2 000 000-a-year salmon industry may disappear.

—Human lungs can be eroded by the acid-filled air we breathe. According to one U.S. scientist, up to 5000 Canadians die each year from acid rain related lung problems. The U.S. Council on Environmental Quality estimates that acid rain related health care costs $2 000 000 000 annually.

Defense: Should Canada have a voice of its own?

If a nation's strength and independence is measured by its military power, then Canada in the late twentieth century would likely be considered weak. Canada's military contribution to the two world wars was large for a young nation. However, as of 1945, Canada's voice in defense matters has been overpowered by the military, economic and political power of the United States. Defense is a major issue affecting Canada's relationship with the U.S.

The powerful position of the United States in the postwar period led to Canada's increased dependence on the U.S. in defense matters. Although Canada was a founding member of the North Atlantic Treaty Organization in 1949, Canada played only a minor role in deciding its military strategy. By the late 1950s Canada could no longer manufacture complete weapons systems without importing key parts. In 1981 Canada had one percent of its labour force in the armed forces compared to a NATO average of 2.8 percent. By the early 1980s Canada had become a minor military partner in NATO.

For example, the U.S. president encouraged the increased use of coal fired generators to help the U.S. become energy self-sufficient. The U.S. is also seriously considering whether or not to relax some present air pollution controls. One of the largest contributors of sulphur and nitrogen oxides to the air in Canada, Ontario Hydro, and the Ontario government, have refused to install scrubber systems because of the high cost involved.

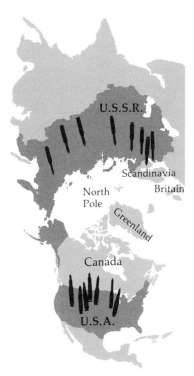

Fig. 17 Canada holds sovereignty over vital air space. Explain why.

Fig. 18 Over recent years, there have been heated debates over the testing of the U.S. Cruise missile in Canada. What are the main arguments of Canadians both for and against the missile?

Canada's participation in NORAD further reinforced Canada's status as a minor military partner of the United States. NORAD developed during World War II when it became clear that the defense of Canada and the U.S. was a single problem. Canada is situated between the two world super-powers, and thus Canada's air space is important to the defense of the U.S., as well as Canada (see Figure 17).

Canada and the U.S. signed the North American Air Defense Command Agreement in 1958 to achieve a single continental defense policy. NORAD was to provide a continental defense system at reasonable cost and ensure Canada played a significant role in this system. In part NORAD was created to make sure that the U.S. would not simply act in Canadian air space without consultation.

NORAD was never really an equal partnership. Radar detection and surveillance systems were constructed at high cost. Many of these were built and run by U.S. military personnel in Canadian territory. The U.S. contribution to NORAD's costs was much greater than Canada's, and with the growing importance of intercontinental ballistic missiles (ICBMs) and submarine launched ballistic missiles, U.S. dependence on Canada's participation in NORAD decreased.

In 1973 a crisis developed in the underground headquarters of NORAD. The U.S.S.R. appeared to be preparing to intervene in the war between Israel and several Arab states. In response to this threat, the president of the United States put all American forces on world-wide alert. The nuclear bombers controlled by NORAD were immediately prepared for war. Many of these bombers were flying over Canadian air space during the alert period. Unfortunately, Canadian forces in NORAD were not informed of the alert until eight hours after the crisis had begun despite the assurances of the NORAD agreement. In response to criticism of the U.S. action, U.S. military experts claimed that when alerts were called in the past Canada either acted extremely slowly or not at all.

This incident seemed to point out the reality of Canada's junior partner role in NORAD. The U.S. domination of both NATO and NORAD has contributed to Canada's dependent position in both these alliances.

Many Canadians are questioning what Canada's defense policy should be in the late twentieth century. The choices Canada might make about its future defense and military programmes are critical to our future relationship with the United States. Although by no means a complete list of choices, some of Canada's future options are outlined below.

These missiles are capable of travelling thousands of kilometres to predetermined targets, and thus U.S. defense was not totally dependent on long-range bombers and fighter planes stationed in Canada or patrolling in Canadian air space.

1. *Junior partner option*
   Canada remains in NATO and NORAD and its financial participation remains minor. Canada allows NORAD to use the airborne warning and control systems (AWACS) over Canadian air space.

2. *Increase participation option*
   Canada remains in NATO and NORAD and increases its financial commitment by buying new military hardware and participating in space based surveillance and defense systems.

3. *Armed neutralism option*
   Canada withdraws from NATO and NORAD and declares its territory a nuclear free zone. Canada launches a non nuclear weapons development programme to ensure self-reliance in producing its own armaments and to defend its territory from a conventional armament attack.

4. *National protection option*

   Canada remains in NATO and NORAD but declares its first priority to be the protection of Canadian territorial sovereignty in the Arctic and at sea. Canada launches a military and naval armament industry aimed solely at enforcing its territorial claims in the Arctic and at sea.

5. *No defense option*

   Canada withdraws from NATO and NORAD and reduces its armed forces and defense budget drastically from present levels.

GETTING THE FACTS

23. Suggest as many reasons as you can for the fact that Canada's voice in matters of defense has been overpowered by the voice of the U.S.

24. Why is Canada in an awkward position in relation to the U.S and U.S.S.R.?

25. What is the purpose of NORAD? Why was NORAD never really an equal partnership?

USING YOUR KNOWLEDGE

26. Review the five policy options on defense mentioned. In your notebook explain the following for each of the options:

    a) What effect the policy option might have on Canada's independence;

    b) What effect the policy option might have on Canada's relationship with the U.S.;

    c) What effect the policy option might have on Canada's relationship with other countries in the world.

27. Should Canada have a voice of its own in matters of defense? Why or why not? Which of the policy options would you choose for Canada? Prepare a news story that explains and defends your position.

THINKING IT THROUGH

28. One possible solution to the problem of increasing tension between the U.S. and Canada is the formation of a special committee. The committee would examine each situation over which the two countries disagree and advise on solutions that would be acceptable to both countries.

    a) What would be the benefits of such a system? The disadvantages?

    b) Would you want to see such a committee formed? Give reasons to support your viewpoint.

Fig. 19 How would Canada be affected if the United States were to follow the advice on this banner?

THE INVESTIGATIVE REPORTER

29. Examine your newspaper to find one issue that involves American influence. You can choose a cultural issue such as television programming, an economic issue such as foreign investment, an environmental issue such as acid rain or a defense issue such as the F-18 fighter interceptor. Research the issue using as many other sources as you can find. Define the issue clearly. Suggest several *options* that could be taken to resolve the issue. Suggest the option that seems most desirable from your point of view.

Conclusion

"Whatever has happened to good old neighbourly ways across the world's longest pretended border?", questions journalist Roderick McQueen (*Maclean's 1982*) as he detected tensions in Canadian-American relations. The concern about Canada's cultural survival led the government to protect Canada's cultural industries. Actions taken by the Canadian government through FIRA, CDC, NEP and the CRTC combined to cool the usually friendly relations between Canada and the United States. Environmental problems seemed on the path to a resolution but were seriously hampered by the oil crisis which prompted a return to coal as an energy source in the U.S.A. with the result that SO_2 emissions would increase. The NORAD crisis of 1973 and the changing needs of continental defense caused a further 'frostiness' in Canadian-American relations during the seventies.

14 The new technology: Changes and choices

Would many people in 1920 have believed that we would reach the moon?

Scenes of Change

Necessity is the mother of invention.

Build a better mousetrap—and the world will beat a path to your door.

If at first you don't succeed, try, try again.

These are well known sayings. They may remind us that the twentieth century has been a time of inventions. As a result, young Canadians in the 1980s know a world very different from the ones their parents and grandparents grew up in. See if the following scenes apply to you and your family. If not, do they apply to another family you know?

(1) The 1920s: The world of grandparents

I am a Canadian growing up in the 1920s. Born in a house on my parents' farm, I still live in the same place. In winter, we get our heat from a coal-burning furnace. In summer, we depend on our shade trees for relief from the hot sun.

One of my many chores is to cut and haul wood for the kitchen stove. On that stove, we cook our meals. When the meal is over, we "play the game" of washing and drying the dishes.

Yet life is not all work. When the sun goes down, we read our newspapers and books by the light of a kerosene lamp. We play checkers or cards or chess. Neighbours and relatives often drop over to visit, to talk, or to sing songs while someone plays the piano. Sometimes we crank up the gramophone. The telephone rings often, since we share a party line with four other families.

Some families do have cars. However, we usually travel by horse-drawn buggy and in winter by sled. For longer distances we travel by boat or train.

(2) The 1950s: When parents were young

I am a Canadian growing up in the 1950s. Born in a hospital, I still live in the same small city where I was born. When I was small, my family moved to the suburbs. Our house is kept warm in winter by oil heat, and cool in summer by electric fans.

My chores around home are few—mainly keeping my room tidy—but I earn money from babysitting, mowing the neighbour's lawn in summer, and cleaning snow from the walks in the winter-time. My paper route is my steadiest job.

We have electric lights, of course. Electricity runs many things in our home, such as the stove, the vacuum cleaner and the radio.

Like most Canadian families, we own a car. It's second-hand and five years old, but it's one of the most important things we own, next to our house. Gasoline is so cheap that we often cross town or travel to another town. We use the car to go shopping, go to a movie, or to visit friends and relatives.

We listen regularly to our favourite radio programmes. Some people we know even have television sets—black and white, of course.

- State three differences between life in the 1920s and life in the 1950s.

- Describe two ways that life in the 1980s has not changed since the time of your grandparents or parents.

- Describe at least two ways life has changed for your grandparents or parents.

Chapter overview

The period from the 1940s onward has been referred to as the Age of Science and Technology, the Television Age, the Space Age, and the Computer Age, to mention a few. These labels are quite appropriate when you consider the rate at which technology has advanced. Invention has followed upon invention. We have been living in a time of remarkable and rapid change. Never before in history have young people grown up in a world so different from the one their parents knew as young people.

Technology is the word often used to describe the avalanche of changes. It is a word that is difficult to define to everyone's satisfaction. Technology can be used to describe the invention and development of tools, machines and ways of using them. Technology can also refer to improvements in sports equipment, medical breakthroughs in treating disease, new devices for exploration in space, or even equipment for improving the quality of popular music.

News of the latest technology seems to be a daily event. No sooner do we know about the "latest thing"—a discovery, an invention, a product appearing in the stores for the first time—than we

Fig. 1 One example of new technology: the "Canada Arm" of America's space shuttle can remove a satellite from the cargo bay and put it into orbit. The camera at the "elbow" of the arm allows the viewer to examine and check the exterior of the space shuttle.

find our knowledge out of date. Something even newer has come along.

In this chapter, you will survey examples of old and new technology. You will see how technological change has an impact on almost every part of our daily lives. You will examine some of the effects of technology on Canadian life, and explore some of the related questions and issues.

Signposts

New technology: A parade of inventions

FEATURE: "Brought to you by satellite...."

Computers in the home: The micro-chip revolution

Technocrats versus technophobes: Coping with change

Key words

technology	micro-computer	technocrat
satellite	revolution	technophobe
computer	videotext	scenario

New technology: A parade of inventions

In the past forty years or so, Canada and much of the rest of the world have been faced with change as never before. In that time, ball-point pens, transistor radios, polyester clothing, pocket calculators, microwave ovens—you can easily add to the list—have become common items in the lives of Canadians. Anti-polio vaccine, heart transplants, plastic surgery and countless other advances have been made in the field of medicine. Vehicles and equipment for space travel and research have become more sophisticated with each passing year.

Look at the following visuals of items from recent years. All of these illustrate advances in technology.

Fig. 2 A parade of
inventions

352

Why is it so important to understand what is meant by technology? Well, the rate at which our lives are affected by technology is increasing. New forms of technology—radio, automobiles, stereos, video recorders, nuclear power plants, weapons geared to mass destruction—usually have far-reaching effects. They can set off patterns of changes in the way that people and nations live.

GETTING THE FACTS

1. The following is a list of inventions of the past 50 years or so, together with the dates when they became generally available to the public.

ballpoint pen (1945), frozen food (1920s), transistor (1948), vacuum cleaner (1908), "miracle" rice (1966), long-playing records (1948), hearing aid (1935), colour television (1951), zipper (1913), aerosol spray can (1941), dry soup mix (1962), solar energy (1950s), antibiotics (1940), roll-on deodorant (1955), over-size tennis racquet (1970s), laser (1960)

Make a timeline.

USING YOUR KNOWLEDGE

2. Pick at least four of the above items.
   a) Tell how each has been an advantage for Canadians.
   b) Suggest a drawback of each of the four items.

THINKING IT THROUGH

3. Debate the statement: "Every invention has both advantages and disadvantages."

THE INVESTIGATIVE REPORTER

4. Consult your school or local library. Identify, and record the dates of at least three items not mentioned so far in the chapter but which can be found in your home. Would you be willing to get along without these items? Why or why not?

"Brought to you by satellite. . . ."

Listen carefully the next time you watch a special news programme, or sports event. The announcer will probably introduce the programme with words like "Brought to you by satellite from. . . ." Satellite programming is a method of broadcasting programmes that cannot be transmitted by ground.

A satellite, that is, a communications satellite, works like a mirror in the sky. Signals are sent to it and it sends them back to television sets over thousands of kilometres. The satellite revolves around the earth in twenty-four hours—exactly the time it takes the earth to rotate. Therefore, the satellite, in its orbit 37 241 kilometres above the equator, appears from the earth to be fixed in the sky.

A television satellite operates on electricity from the sun. Even one satellite can handle a large quantity of information, and it is far enough up in the sky to beam signals to almost half the earth.

The first North American domestic satellite was launched in 1972 by Canada. It was first intended to be a way of keeping in touch with the far North. Therefore, it was called "Anik," meaning "brother" in Inuit. However, it was soon realized that "Anik" satellites could also provide cheaper television service than could existing ground-level means of broadcasting.

Both northern and southern Canada are affected by communications satellites. In southern Canada, satellites meant increased choices, including Pay TV. In northern communities, colour television appeared almost overnight. Thus Flin Flon hockey fans could watch a live broadcast of "Hockey Night in Canada" in colour along with people in Vancouver or Winnipeg or Halifax.

Advances in satellite technology raised some difficult political questions. By way of Anik, the Canadian Broadcasting Corporation (CBC) provided television programming under

Fig. 3 The Anik satellite

government supervision. The Canadian Radio and Television Commission has, for more than a decade, been responsible for maintaining a certain amount of Canadian content aimed at Canadian households. Satellites other than Anik, however, have been placed in orbit. With the proper receiver, a "dish" like the one shown in Figure 3, people could pick up programmes unavailable via ground transmission.

Political questions had to be faced. Would

Canadians be swamped by television from foreign countries? Would the Canadian government take steps to ensure Canadian content on the nation's television screens? Should Canadians have the right to choose their programmes regardless of the source?

GETTING THE FACTS

5. What is a communications satellite?

6. How does the Anik satellite show that Canada has played a leading role in the development of telecommunications technology?

7. What is the main job of the CRTC?

USING YOUR KNOWLEDGE

8. Explain why satellites have had more impact on Canada's North than on southern Canada.

9. Put yourself in the place of a person living in Flin Flon. State your view about the Canadian government controlling what programmes are available on your TV screen.

THINKING IT THROUGH

10. Debate the statement: Canadians should be protected against a flood of non-Canadian television programming.

Computers in the home: The micro-chip revolution

By the 1980s, computers were a familiar part of factories and businesses and were beginning to appear in Canadian homes. Many of them were small enough to carry. These micro-computers were expected to be as common in the home as television sets.

Predicting the future importance of any form of technology is a risky business. Consider the following examples:

—In 1939, television was dismissed as a "passing fancy," unlikely to be taken seriously as a rival to radio.
—In the 1940s, Canadians assumed that railways would continue indefinitely to be the main form of travel across the country.

Families buy home computers for a variety of reasons; for example, handling the family bank account, organizing the collection of money for a paper route, shopping, doing homework, planning the use of family money and—of course—playing video games.

Have micro-computers become the central appliance in the households of your area? If not, can you forecast when they may be widely used?

Micro means very small.

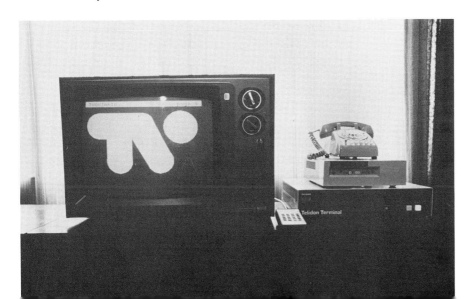

Fig. 4 Many businesses, and even some families, own terminals that provide a range of information.

—In the 1950s, motion pictures (movies) were not expected to survive the growing popularity of television.

—In the 1960s, books—especially textbooks for schools—were declared to be a thing of the past. Some people seemed certain that books were being replaced by the electronic media; that is, television.

—In the 1970s, Canada's National Energy Board forecast that Canada had all the petroleum (oil and natural gas) supplies that the country would need in the foreseeable future.

The potential use of computers in homes and businesses is not really surprising when you contrast the "generation" of computers available now with those of the 1950s. According to a leading writer on the subject:

> Early computers cost millions of dollars, consumed many kilowatts of power, required large rooms with special cooling equipment to house them, and were notoriously unreliable. Hardly the sort of beast one would invite into one's home. The price of executing an instruction on a computer has declined by a factor of about 1,000,000 since the early 1950's. It is as though you saw a beautiful mansion for sale in 1950 at a price of a million dollars and came back today to find it for sale for about a dollar. Not only that, but you would discover that unlike the mansion of thirty years ago which required many servants to maintain it, and which was continuously experiencing failures in the heating, plumbing and electrical systems, the mansion today would cost only pennies to maintain while its essential systems were so reliable that you would not expect to experience a failure during your lifetime or that of your children.

From *Gutenberg Two* by David Godfrey and Douglas Parkhill.

Such a change could not have been predicted in 1950 of course. Like so many things we now take for granted, computers are the result of a long history of invention. Consider the case nearly 350 years ago of the 20-year-old Frenchman, Blaise Pascal. His father was a collector of taxes who needed a faster way of dealing with numbers than counting on his fingers. The dutiful son proceeded to invent a machine that could count, add and subtract much faster than an individual could.

Twenty years after Pascal, the German genius, Leibniz, came up with a machine that could also divide and multiply. A century passed before the Englishman, Charles Babbage (1791-1871) made the next great advance on the road to the modern computer. A co-founder of the Royal Astronomical Society, he hit upon the idea of harnessing power—steam power, the most important form of energy at the time—to the business of making calculations. Like so many inventors, he died before people were convinced he was on to something.

Fig. 5 Charles Babbage's differential engine used steam power to make calculations. Why would the use of energy for this purpose be an advance towards the modern computer?

A host of inventors—English, German, French—made various improvements on Babbage's discovery before the Americans got into the act. This brings us to the story of Herman Hollerith (1860-1929). He was working on the United States' census of 1880. With the population growing rapidly, he realized that people working without the aid of machines would be unable to complete the 1880 census before the next one was due in 1890.

Hollerith made two advances in the development of a computer. One was the punched card, which could be coded so as to sort and record information. The second was to use electricity to process the cards. With Hollerith's system, the total population of the United States was calculated within a month after the 1890 census had been carried out.

In the twentieth century, computers became much more than machines for rapid calculation and information storage. Inventions in the field of electronics made possible the design of fully automatic computers. Computers could now be given "instructions" in the form of "programmes" to carry out a host of operations in a fraction of the time they could be done by hand. For example, they could process cheques, go through tax returns, keep track of business decisions and guide vehicles in space.

Since the 1950s, a new generation of computers has entered the lives of Canadians in ways we are scarcely, if at all, aware of. What was science fiction a few years ago has become routine in the 1980s.

What is a micro-computer?

You have probably seen micro-computers in stores, offices, schools and an increasing number of homes as a piece of equipment with a keyboard and a TV-like screen.

The basis of the micro-computer is the micro-chip. This is a piece of silicon, perhaps the size of a fingernail, containing electronic circuits; that is, miniature transistors. Where a radio or television set requires a handful of such circuits, a computer uses thousands. This helps explain the generally higher cost of computers as compared to radio and television sets. However, consider what computers can do that radio and television cannot.

Silicon is a crystal-like element; a semi-conductor of electrical current. It is valuable in the making of transistors.

A transistor is a device for controlling or increasing the flow of electricity. Because transistors can be made very small, they have made possible the reduction in size of radios and all kinds of other equipment.

Fig. 6 The micro-chip held in the tweezers contains the electronic circuits on which this telecommunication equipment depends.

The long list of uses includes controls for jet planes, factory assembly lines, space flights, weapons systems, the temperature in buildings; the printing of bank statements and newspapers and magazines, sorting mail and all kinds of business and government decisions and information, talking cash registers in supermarkets; and, of course, video games.

Even if home computers are less common than optimistic forecasters have expected, micro-computers had become widespread by the late 1970s. Whether you knew it or not, a big change has been underway for years. What uses of micro-computers are more and more Canadians able to see firsthand and take part in? A partial list includes: electronic mail; access to news about current events, sports, weather and many other forms of information; shopping; working at home; education; entertainment. All of these have been available to some Canadians for years. The question is: Are we in the midst of a revolution, meaning the widespread use of micro-chip technology by the average Canadian?

GETTING THE FACTS

10. State four examples of predictions about technology in the past 50 years that have *not* come true.

11. What is a micro-computer? Give three or four examples of its use in the world around you.

THE INVESTIGATIVE REPORTER

12. Find out about a person involved with micro-computers in his/her daily life. Interview that person, and make a brief report.

The sending, receiving and sharing of *information* is the main function of micro-computers. Video games are becoming increasingly popular as a recreational activity. More serious and financially important functions are, however, the reason for all the talk about a technological revolution.

Teletext is a form of one-way communication to the viewer. Words and pictures—or a combination of both—can be sent by way of cable, or over the air, to any household having a TV set equipped with an adapter. News, announcements and advertising, for example, are familiar items "broadcast" in this way.

Videotext, though, is more dramatic. It provides for *two-way* communication. Rather than just being a receiver of information, the consumer is a sender as well. By way of two-way cables or telephone lines, a person has access to databases (sources of information).

A home computer is, therefore, both a receiver and memory bank and a device for sending information.

What are the possibilities for home computers hooked into an information network? Consider the following examples:

Electronic mail: For as long as most of us can remember, Canadians have been able to send mail or telephone calls to almost anywhere in the world. Messages can be sent to any TV set with a special receiver or computer terminal. Messages can be stored until the receiver is able to check his/her "electronic mail box."

Public access: Various databases (sources of information) are becoming available to the general public. With their home computers, Canadians can request news, background information, sports scores, weather, stock market reports and other types of data.

Shopping: Without leaving the comfort of their homes, Canadians can buy groceries, clothing and all other items that are "plugged into" the system. In fact, they can pay for purchases by notifying their bank to transfer money from a personal account to the company supplying the goods.

Working at home: Many jobs, in offices and factories, can be handled—at least part of the time—by a person just as well at home as at a central location. With a home computer, people can keep in touch with "headquarters." They can also prepare memos, forward decisions, and even make products.

Education: A micro-computer can enable a student to maintain contact with teachers and databases. Rather than "going to school," a student can bring the school into his or her home.

GETTING THE FACTS

13. What is the basic difference between Teletext and Videotext?

14. List four possible uses for a home computer hooked into an information network.

USING YOUR KNOWLEDGE

15. a) Tell about the difference in shopping before and after the popularity of home computers.

b) In what other ways could family life be changed by the widespread use of micro-computers?

Technocrats versus technophobes: Coping with change

New technology often leads to changes in people's lives. For example, the automobile was once a new kind of transportation. Only the rich could afford the high prices of the early models. With mass production underway, lower costs meant many more cars sold. The growth of the automobile industry led to the investment of huge amounts of money, the employment of thousands of auto workers, business people and office staff. Automobile dealerships, service stations, improved roads, parking lots and other related services were developed.

As has been the case with automobiles, other new technologies have led to patterns of change. Examples include radio, television, plastic products and plastic surgery, antibiotics, frozen food and micro-computers.

In the early years, some people resisted the automobile "revolution." These technophobes felt that cars were a threat to a way of life they were comfortable with. Some went so far as to spread tacks and broken glass on roads and to put up barriers. Others simply refused to buy and to learn to drive a car.

Eventually, automobiles became a normal part of the environment. People grew up with them. They appreciated the mobility, independence and other benefits the automobile had to offer. On the other hand, they regretted the injuries and deaths caused by automobile accidents. They worried about air pollution and noise and junkyards piled with rusted cars. They cursed the costs of gasoline, insurance, repairs and complained about the shortcomings of other means of travel. But they had a hard time imagining their world without automobiles.

Fig. 8 The cars on this assembly line are being put together by "robots". What might a technophobe think of this assembly line? What might be the view of a technocrat?

The widespread use of automobiles raised all kinds of questions and arguments and problems. Is the same thing happening in the case of micro-computers? We cannot know for sure; predicting the future is a chancy business. But we can make some careful guesses—in the form of scenarios—based on our observations of recent developments, and of the history of other technological changes. Consider the following scenarios.

(1) *New occupations* Micro-computers, as they become part of the furniture in more and more offices and homes, are being mass produced. A growing computer industry attracts investors looking to make a profit. Jobs are opening up for skilled workers in manufacturing, sales and service. Tremendous demands exist for people to develop programmes—the "software"—for the many uses being found for computers.

(2) *A nation of electronic hermits* Busy interacting with their home computers, people may increasingly become "loners." Instead of relating to people, many may prefer computers, which are always ready to obey. If we can make a living by working at home, perhaps we will be less and less obliged to deal with people. With an assortment of video games, movies and other entertainment, perhaps we will lose interest in public events.

(3) *Invasion of privacy* If we are plugged into a computer network, how can we protect our privacy? Every time we use the system, our activity is recorded and filed in some "memory bank." A centralized record could be compiled on our household members,

showing ages; size and appearance; financial situations; education; tastes in clothes and food and entertainment. How can we guard against our records becoming available to businesses and advertisers? Suppose a government wants to check into our political views and activities? How might they use such information to our disadvantage?

(4) *Computer crime* Suppose Canadians become accustomed to shopping, banking and paying bills by home computer. They could key in their password or number to buy a major appliance. But what are the dangers of eavesdropping by criminals? A "computer" criminal might be able to use your password or number to order something you would end up paying for. In a computer revolution, can the "good guys" keep ahead of the "bad guys"?

GETTING THE FACTS

16. List five changes resulting from the widespread use of the automobile.

17. What is a scenario? How may this be a useful way of thinking about the future?

USING YOUR KNOWLEDGE

18. In your notebook, make a chart like the following and fill in the requested information.

PURPOSE: To form an opinion on the effect of the computer "revolution" on the lives of Canadians	
BENEFITS	DRAWBACKS

CONCLUSION:

Conclusion

THINKING IT THROUGH

19. Pick at least two scenarios in the section called "Technocrats versus Technophobes." Based on your own experiences do you disagree with any of the ideas presented? If so, explain.

20. To employers, the value of employees might be determined by their success at adapting to the "computer revolution."
    a) Do you think employees' jobs should be protected in some way from this kind of employer attitude? If so, explain.
    b) How might employers try to protect their job security in the "computer revolution."

15 Our legal system in action

The shipwrecked sailors

In 1883 an English ship was wrecked on the high seas some 2000 km from land. The only survivors were three sailors and a cabin boy, huddled together in a small lifeboat. After 20 days their food ran out and their water supply was exhausted soon afterward.

After a week without food and three days without water, they knew that they could not survive much longer. Dudley, the ship's captain, suggested that the only solution was to kill one person in the lifeboat so that the other three could eat him. The captain wanted to draw lots. The loser would sacrifice his life. The others would not agree to this. Two days later, the cabin boy lost consciousness. He was obviously weak and probably dying. The next day, the three sailors agreed that the only way for them to survive was to eat the cabin boy. The captain said a prayer, and the sailors slit the cabin boy's throat.

The sailors fed on the cabin boy's blood and flesh. This kept them alive until they were rescued by a passing ship four days later.

The captain and the senior sailor, a man named Stephens, were eventually charged with murder. Their trial took place in 1884. In their defense, Dudley and Stephens said that the act of killing was justified in these circumstances, for it had led to the survival of three others. The prosecution stated that there are no circumstances in which the killing of a human being is justified, and that the act was clearly murder.

The jury could not agree on the subject. Saying that they believed that Dudley and Stephens had killed the cabin boy, the jury left it to the judge to say whether the act was murder or not. The judge stated that the duty of a shipwrecked captain is to preserve the life of the crew, and that deliberate taking of life cannot be justified. Dudley and Stephens were sentenced to death by hanging.

After considerable outcry about the case and the decision, the sentence was reduced to life imprisonment. Even this sentence was not carried out. Dudley and Stephens were released from prison after six months.

- The above story is true. Do you think that Dudley and Stephens should have been charged with murder? What are your reasons?

- Do you think that the law should be strictly applied in all cases? (Two people killed another, which is against the law.) Or should each case be dealt with according to its own facts? (The circumstances were very unusual, and should perhaps be considered.) Explain your view.

- What would be the advantages for each of us, if there were no laws governing the things we do? What would be the disadvantages? Are the advantages or the disadvantages more important? Why?

Chapter overview

In order for its citizens to enjoy freedom, a nation must have a clear-cut set of laws. The law provides a code for citizens to live by. The law also protects citizens and keeps order and peace. This chapter examines our legal system and the way it works.

The two major divisions of law—criminal and civil law—have different features. This chapter outlines both a civil and a criminal trial. Thus, you will see how the procedures in court differ between the two divisions of law. You will also look at the various penalties which can be imposed on lawbreakers.

The citizens of a country should know about the law and the way it works. After studying this chapter, you will understand how effective our legal system is in protecting our freedom.

Fig. 1 Inside the Supreme Court, Ottawa. This is the highest court in Canada. It hears final appeals against judgements passed in lower courts.

Signposts

The two divisions of law >

The three elements of a crime >

Criminal offences: From the minor to the serious >

How cases are decided in court >

The use of evidence in court >

FEATURE: How should juvenile offenders be treated? >

Punishment for lawbreakers >

Legal terms

You may be unfamiliar with many of the legal terms used in this chapter. These terms appear in bold type the first time they are used and are defined below.

criminal law	The division of law which deals with crimes such as theft or murder.
civil law	The division of law which deals with disputes between people.
rights	The freedom of the individual and his/her property from harm by another.
suing, sue	The legal action taken by someone to bring another person to court.
damages	Payments made by one person to another for violating their rights.
plaintiff	The person taking legal action. (In a criminal case, the Crown is the plaintiff.)
defendant	The person against whom legal action is being taken.
insane	Not responsible for an action because of mental illness.
sanity, sane	Of sound mind, and therefore responsible for an action.

summary offences	Less serious offences. The maximum penalty for summary offences is two years' imprisonment and/or a $500 fine.
preliminary hearing	A pre-trial held in indictable offence cases. The purpose of a preliminary hearing is to see whether enough evidence exists against the accused person to hold a full-scale trial.
prosecution, prosecutor, prosecute	The side in a criminal case which represents the Crown and tries to prove that the accused person is guilty.
defense	The side in a criminal case which represents the accused person, and which generally tries to prove that the accused is not guilty.
Crown Attorney	The chief lawyer representing the Crown in a criminal case.
verdict	The decision of the court in a criminal case; whether the accused is guilty or not guilty.
deterrent	A punishment which discourages citizens from committing a crime.
probation	A period of time during which an offender must not commit further crimes, and must meet regularly with a social worker.
rehabilitate, rehabilitation	Reforming and educating an offender; providing him or her with the necessary skills to prevent committing a further crime.
penitentiary	A federal prison for more serious offenders. Such prisons are located in New Westminster, B.C., Kingston, Ont., and Dorchester, N.B.
parole	Early release from prison before the complete sentence is served for those prisoners the authorities consider to have reformed. A paroled prisoner who commits another crime has to serve the remainder of the original sentence as well as any new one.

The two divisions of law

The law contains two major divisions.

1. Criminal law

Criminal law is designed to protect society from wrongdoers. Governments pass laws against certain actions (such as stealing) in order to preserve peace and order. Anyone who commits such an action is taken to court and, if found guilty, is punished for it. The court can imprison, fine or otherwise punish the guilty.

2. Civil law

Civil law is designed to make sure that people honour contracts (legal agreements) they have made with others. It makes sure that everyone's rights have been protected. Court cases usually involve someone suing someone else, and the court acts as a referee. The court does not have the power to punish anyone. However, it can order someone to pay damages to someone else for failure to live up to an agreement, or for violating another person's rights.

Lawyers frequently specialize in one division of law. Courts are specialized too. With few exceptions, they deal with criminal or civil cases, but not both.

Court cases are known by the names of the people involved. For example, Jane Herman sues Tom Lapointe for selling her a car which he knew to have major defects but did not tell her about. This civil case is known as Herman vs. Lapointe. Note that only family names are used, and that the name of the person suing comes first. If Ranjit Singh sues his neighbours, Peter and Molly MacLeod, for building a fence on his side of the property line, the case is known as Singh vs. MacLeod and Macleod. The person suing, Mr. Singh, is known as the plaintiff. Mr. and Mrs. MacLeod are being sued. They are known as the defendants.

If a law has been broken, the matter is a criminal case. All laws are written in the name of the Crown. Thus, in criminal cases, the Crown is always the plaintiff. The Crown is referred to as R., from the Latin words Regina for Queen and Rex for King. If, for example, Davis O'Neill punches Louis White one night in a bar, the case is known as R. vs. O'Neill. The Crown—not Mr. White—is the plaintiff in this case because assault is a criminal matter. O'Neill is the defendant.

Sometimes an incident involves both criminal and civil cases. For example, if Louis White wants to sue David O'Neill because of

Many lawyers accept cases in only one area of the law such as real estate sales or divorce. Others are experts in complicated drug or personal injury cases. An example of a specialized court is a surrogate court which only handles cases involving the wills of dead people.

In law, the term Crown means executive authority. The Crown is symbolically represented by the Queen or King.

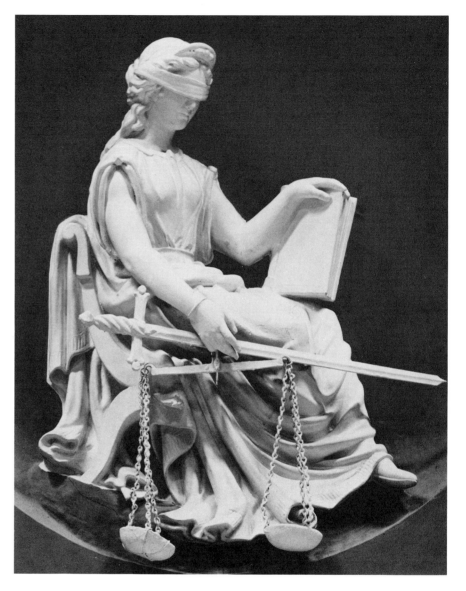

Fig. 2 This figure is the symbol of justice. What do you think the book, the sword and the scales represent? Why is the figure blindfolded?

the dental expenses resulting from O'Neill's punch, he may sue for damages. The criminal and civil cases will be heard in different courts before different judges at different times. O'Neill might even have different lawyers in the two cases.

GETTING THE FACTS

1. In your own words, explain the differences between criminal and civil law.

2. In your own words, write definitions of the following terms: damages, plaintiff, defendant, R.

3. Remember the way in which court cases are known and referred to.

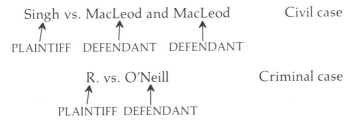

Singh vs. MacLeod and MacLeod   Civil case

PLAINTIFF   DEFENDANT   DEFENDANT

R. vs. O'Neill   Criminal case

PLAINTIFF   DEFENDANT

Write the title of each of the following cases as they would be known and referred to. (Remember that, as in the White-O'Neill incident, there could be both a criminal and civil case arising out of a single event.)

a) Brian Himmeldorf is stopped for exceeding the speed limit in his brand-new car.

b) Linda Barker buys herself a flashy new sports car. She writes a cheque for the $2500 deposit to Martin O'Reilly and drives off in the car. She knows there is only $231.81 in her bank account.

c) Wasim Abbas wants his car repainted. Arthur Cherzski agrees to do the job, using top-quality acrylic paint for $375. Abbas later discovers that Cherzski used only a low-quality paint and believes he has been overcharged by $190.

4. Use back copies of a newspaper to find stories dealing with legal cases. Find two examples of Canadian criminal cases and two of Canadian civil cases.

a) How would each case be known and referred to?

b) What are the main facts of each case as described in court?

c) What differences can you observe between the way in which the plaintiff's lawyer and the defendant's lawyer presented their evidence in court?

The three elements of a crime

You have been looking at the differences between criminal and civil law. This section of the chapter deals with criminal law only.

In general, any action against the law is a crime. However, it is possible to break the law but still not be guilty of a crime. In order for an action to be considered a crime in Canada, it must meet the three conditions on the next page.

1. The action must be forbidden by federal or provincial law.
2. The accused person
   a) must have intended to commit the offence; or
   b) could have been able to see that such an action would reasonably result in the breaking of a law.
3. The accused person must be of sound mind. (The legal test for sanity is quite straightforward. If an accused person can understand that the act is wrong, and that it could lead to punishment, that person is legally sane.)

Only one of conditions 2(a) and (b) need apply in order for an action to be considered a crime.

No person in Canada can be found guilty of a crime unless all three of these conditions are met. It is the duty of the Crown to prove that all three conditions are met, and that the accused person is therefore guilty. If an accused person's lawyer can prove that even one of the conditions is not met, that person must be found not guilty.

USING YOUR KNOWLEDGE

5. Carefully read the three conditions which must be met in order for a crime to take place. Which of the following incidents do you think would be judged by a court to be a crime? Explain your reasons for each incident.

a) In the early hours of the morning, Margaret Wilson hears a prowler in her house. Getting out of bed, she picks up her son's rifle from the hall closet, loads it and noiselessly descends the stairs. By the light of the street lamp she sees a man outlined against the living room window. The man is taking her expensive tape recorder and putting it inside a large suitcase. Margaret orders the man to "freeze." The man acts calmly and tells her that she will not use the rifle, and he intends to leave. In order to convince the man, Margaret fires the rifle into an unlit corner of the room, where the man's accomplice (partner in crime) stands unseen by Margaret. He is severely wounded in the leg. A passing policeman, hearing the rifle shot, stops to investigate.

b) The *Criminal Code of Canada* is the document which states what actions are considered crimes. Section 234 states:

The Criminal Code is written in the male gender, using words like "he" and "his." It applies, however, to both males and females alike.

Everyone who, while his ability to drive a motor vehicle is impaired by alcohol or drug, drives a motor vehicle, or has care or control of a motor vehicle, whether it is in motion or not, is guilty of an ... offence.

Read the following case study and decide whether Henry Chen has broken Section 234.

Henry Chen has just received a raise of $5000 a year on his promotion to area sales manager for the large publisher for which he works. After work, Henry takes all his office sales personnel to

372

Fig. 3 Have you seen other posters aimed at preventing crime, to reduce the need for punishment? How effective do you think such posters are?

a local tavern for a few drinks to celebrate. Henry has too much to drink. Going back to his car, he realizes that he is not in a fit state to drive. Inserting the key in the ignition so that it will not fall out of his jacket, Henry climbs into the back seat and goes to sleep. A policeman has been watching all this and approaches Henry's car to investigate.

c) Paul Rossini has just returned from Hawaii where he has been enjoying a mid-winter holiday. As he picks up his luggage from the carousel at Vancouver Airport he is approached by a woman whom he vaguely knows, as she works for the same company he does. She tells him she has brought two cartons of cigarettes

back from the U.S. by mistake, while Canada Customs will only allow her to bring in one carton duty-free. She asks Paul if he will carry one of the cartons through Customs for her as he has no cigarettes to declare. Reluctantly, Paul agrees, as he doesn't want to seem a "spoilsport." The Customs Officer looks suspiciously at Paul's carton. On closer examination the Customs Officer finds the duty free seal has been broken. Paul is handed over to the RCMP. Their examination of the carton shows that it contains heroin mixed in with the tobacco. The heroin is calculated to have a street value of $15 000. By this time the young woman has disappeared.

THE INVESTIGATIVE REPORTER

6. Use back issues of the newspaper to find a report of a Canadian case where the accused person was found not guilty. Which of the three conditions was not met? Explain how it was shown in court that this condition had not been met.

Fig. 4 Summary offence or indictable offence?

A magistrate is an official qualified to supervise trials for less serious offences. A judge has a wider range of training and experience. Only a judge can supervise a trial for more serious offences.

Criminal offences: From the minor to the serious

If you obtained a copy of the Criminal Code, you would see that it forbids a wide range of actions such as stealing or kidnapping. Such actions are called crimes or offences. Some are considered to be less serious than others, and have lesser penalties for those found guilty of them. For example, speeding in an automobile is a less serious offence than murder.

The Criminal Code recognizes such differences and divides offences into two classes. Less serious offences are called summary offences. More serious ones are called indictable offences. The differences between the two are illustrated in the following chart.

Fig. 5 Differences between summary and indictable offences

	SUMMARY	INDICTABLE
Examples	common assault; impaired driving	drug trafficking; murder
Maximum penalty if found guilty	less than two years prison and $500 fine	life imprisonment
Usual way the accused comes to court	police issue summons (notice of court date) and accused promises to appear	arrest by police; accused held in jail until trial or released after paying money (bail) as promise to appear
Trial held by	magistrate	magistrate or (for very serious offences) a judge

This chart shows that the Criminal Code considers indictable offences to be more serious than summary ones. However, indictable offences range from serious to extremely serious. In fact, the Criminal Code divides indictable offences into three groups and lays down different procedures for dealing with each one. The following chart shows you the way in which all criminal cases are handled by the courts.

Fig. 6 Method of trial for all criminal cases

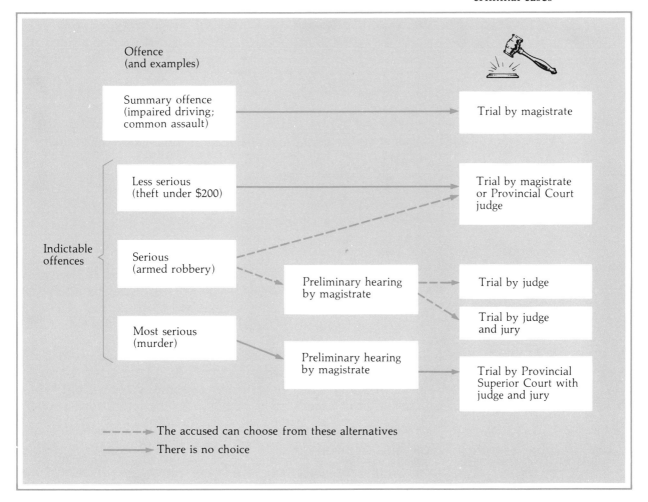

As the chart indicates, in some cases the accused person has a choice in the method of trial, while in others there is no choice. For example, a person accused of a serious indictable offence may choose to have a preliminary hearing before the trial. The evidence relating to the case would be presented to a magistrate. Then the magistrate would decide if sufficient evidence existed to send the accused to trial. On the other hand, the accused could by-pass the preliminary hearing and proceed directly to trial. Similarly, such a person could

Evidence presented at a preliminary hearing may be reported in the media. This might cause people serving on juries to decide on the accused's guilt or innocence before the trial begins. Sometimes, therefore, the accused will decide to by-pass the preliminary hearing.

375

Lawyers often feel that juries are less likely to find the accused guilty than judges are. They therefore recommend trial by jury.

choose to be tried by a judge, or by a judge and jury. In trial by judge, the judge decides the accused's guilt or innocence and passes sentence if necessary. In trial by judge and jury, the accused's guilt or innocence is decided by the jury and the judge passes sentence on an accused person found guilty by the jury.

The methods of trial are complex. Thus it is wise for the accused person to have a lawyer. A skilled trial lawyer can advise the accused on the best way to present his defense, pointing out to the court any weaknesses in the prosecution's evidence about the accused. A good trial lawyer also can help the accused with the complicated legal process.

GETTING THE FACTS

7. Review all the materials contained in this section. How many different facts can you discover which show that the Criminal Code regards indictable offences as more serious than summary ones?

USING YOUR KNOWLEDGE

8. Read the following case study and answer all the questions which follow it.

Joe Golini, owner of the famous restaurant "Millie's Beanery", was shot to death by his former friend and business partner, Arthur Dietrich.

a) Is this a summary or indictable offence? Explain your reasoning.

b) What choices, if any, does Arthur have regarding his method of trial? Explain your answer.

c) What purpose will be served by a preliminary hearing? Will Arthur's guilt or innocence be decided there? Explain your answer.

THINKING IT THROUGH

9. For an offence punishable by more than five years in prison, an accused person usually loses the right to choose the method of trial. Trial by judge and jury is laid down as the only method of trial. What reasons can you suggest for this?

THE INVESTIGATIVE REPORTER

10. From back issues of a newspaper obtain news stories of Canadian criminal trials. Make sure that some cases are summary and others indictable. Also, make sure that some indictable cases are of the most serious variety (punishable by more than 5 years in prison).

Fig. 7 Some defendants choose to conduct their own cases in court, but most people prefer to rely on the services of a lawyer. Why do you think this is so? (Picture posed)

a) Which case do you find most interesting? Why?

b) What differences do you note between the summary case and the most serious indictable case? Are there any differences you note which are not mentioned in this section?

How cases are decided in court

One of the most interesting features of the law is the way in which legal cases are argued and decided in court. Numerous television series have been made about criminal lawyers and their clients. Such programmes frequently involve trials in court. Television viewers are familiar with witnesses being questioned by lawyers for the prosecution and the defense. Courts hear both civil and criminal cases and so we will examine one of each. Both cases are imaginary.

This refers to criminal lawyers—those who specialize in criminal cases—as opposed to civil lawyers.

CRIMINAL CASE	CIVIL CASE
Richard Johnson and Susan Swerski have been charged with bank robbery.	Roland Hughes is suing the Saskatoon Salamanders, a professional hockey team, for $17 500 which he claims they owe him because he scored sufficient goals to qualify for this salary bonus.
R. vs. Johnson and Swerski	Hughes vs. Saskatoon Salamanders Hockey Club, Ltd.

Preliminary hearings are not held right away. This allows lawyers for both sides time to interview witnesses and gather information relating to the trial.

CRIMINAL CASE

Having been brought before a magistrate on January 5, the accused were instructed to appear again for preliminary hearing on March 16. Their lawyer requested that they be released on bail until the preliminary hearing. The magistrate refused, and they were held in jail by the police.

At the preliminary hearing, the Crown called witnesses who identified Johnson and Swerski as being in the bank. The witnesses told how they saw the accused rob a teller of $15 000 while holding everyone at gunpoint.

The defense lawyer could have asked questions of the witnesses but did not choose to do so.

The magistrate decided that there were reasonable grounds for a trial. The defense chose trial by judge and jury. The magistrate set the trial date for June 14.

At the opening of the trial, a jury of 12 citizens was chosen, and the charges against the accused were read. Johnson and Swerski were asked if they pleaded "guilty" or "not guilty." They both pleaded "not guilty."

The Crown's lawyer, known as the Crown Attorney, spoke to the jury explaining how the Crown would show the accused to be guilty. The defense lawyer then spoke to the jury, explaining how the defense would show that the accused were out of town on the day of the robbery and were therefore not guilty.

The Crown Attorney called a series of witnesses who identified Johnson and Swerski as being the two who held up and robbed the

CIVIL CASE

Hughes' lawyer obtained a Writ of Summons from a court. This document contained a brief outline of Hughes' case. It ordered the Saskatoon Salamanders to appear in court on March 4 to answer the case. If they did not appear, they would automatically lose the case.

The Salamanders' lawyer appeared in court and requested an Examination for Discovery. This is where both sides have an opportunity to question the other side. This was set for May 6 and was to be held in the office of an official qualified to hold it. The official is known as a Special Examiner.

In Examination for Discovery, both Hughes and the President of the Salamanders answered questions about Hughes' contract with the club. Each side produced a copy of the contract. Because they could not agree on the meaning of one clause in the contract, they agreed to have the whole case heard in court on July 15.

At the opening of the hearing the judge reminded both sides that there was no jury. The judge would make the decision.

The lawyer for the plaintiff (Hughes) outlined the evidence which would be brought to court to show why Hughes should be paid the $17 500. The lawyer for the defendants (Saskatoon Salamanders) outlined the evidence which would be brought to show why Hughes should not be paid.

The plaintiff's lawyer asked him (Hughes) questions about the contract and why he felt he was owed $17 500. Hughes said he

bank. They described what they saw and heard during the robbery. The defense lawyer tried to show, by asking questions, that these witnesses were unreliable. Since the two robbers wore Hallowe'en masks to hide their faces, they could not be easily identified. Since they spoke very little, their voices were difficult to recognize.

The Crown Attorney called two police officers who arrested Johnson and Swerski. They told the jury how they found the accused with $4300 in bills. From the serial numbers these were identified as being stolen from the bank. The defense lawyer did not choose to question the officers.

The lawyer for the accused called witnesses into court and asked them questions. They said that Johnson and Swerski had been with them at the track to see the horse races in another town when the robbery took place. The Crown Attorney tried to suggest that these witnesses who had long criminal records were lying.

Johnson and Swerski were then called to give evidence. They said they had won $4300 by putting money on the winning horse in each of the eight races. Answering questions from the Crown Attorney, they admitted they could not remember the clerk who had paid them their winnings. They admitted that the betting authority had no evidence of their winnings in its records.

The defense lawyer, in a final address, spoke to the jury outlining the evidence which cast doubt on Johnson's and Swerski's guilt. He reminded the jury of

had a bonus clause in his contract which said he would get $17 500 if he equalled or bettered the league's scoring record of 77 goals in a season. He scored 77 goals and was therefore entitled to the bonus. The defense lawyer asked him questions about the contract, suggesting that Hughes needed 78 goals to collect the bonus. Hughes said this was incorrect. The plaintiff's lawyer then called an expert in contract law to give evidence. The expert read the contract and agreed that Hughes' understanding of it was correct. The defense lawyer asked no questions.

The defendant's lawyer gave a final outline of the case to the judge, reminding the judge of the verbal agreement between Hughes and the President.

CRIMINAL CASE	CIVIL CASE
the difficulty in recognizing the robbers and the witnesses who testified that the accused were with them at the time of the robbery.	
The Crown Attorney, in a final address, spoke to the jury and outlined the evidence which suggested that the accused were guilty. She reminded the jury that there was not a scrap of evidence to support Johnson's and Swerski's statement that they won the $4300 at a horse race.	The plaintiff's lawyer gave a final outline of the case, reminding the judge that there was only the President's word about the verbal agreement. The contract contained no mention of it.
The judge then gave final instructions to the jury. They were reminded that the Crown Attorney had to show that the accused were guilty beyond all reasonable doubt. If there was any doubt at all, they must find the accused not guilty.	
The jury went out to another room. They discussed the case together. At first ten members believed the accused guilty and two believed them not-guilty. But in order to find the accused guilty, all twelve jury members must agree. After further discussion, all twelve agreed that the accused were guilty.	The judge then left the court to consider the verdict. Realizing that the side with the strongest case must win, the judge decided that Hughes was correct.
The jury returned to court. They told the judge they found the accused guilty.	The judge returned to court, announcing that the plaintiff (Hughes) had won his case.
The judge, who until this time had to be unbiased, said he agreed that the jury had made the right decision. The judge then sentenced the two accused to a fine of $5000 and six years in prison.	The judge, who until making the decision had to be unbiased, said that Hughes had a strong case. The judge had no power to sentence anyone to prison in a civil case, and ordered the Saskatoon Salamanders to pay Hughes $17 500 plus $5000 for his lawyer's and other costs.

Even if the judge felt that the jury's decision was wrong, it would still be necessary to find the accused guilty. The judge has no power to overrule the jury.

11. What role is played in a trial by each of the following?

    a) Criminal case: preliminary hearing, Crown Attorney, defense lawyer, jury, judge.

    b) Civil case: Writ of Summons, Examination for Discovery, plaintiff's lawyer, judge.

12. Summarize the similarities and differences between the criminal and civil cases under the following headings: (a) proceedings before main trial; (b) role of lawyers; (c) role of witnesses; (d) which side must prove its case; (e) decision and sentence of the court; (f) role of the judge.

13. In a criminal case, if there is any doubt about the accused's guilt, the jury must find the accused not guilty. (See the judge's final instructions to the jury.) In some countries, in order to be set free, the accused must prove his/her innocence. If there is any doubt, the jury must find the accused guilty. Which system do you think is better? Explain your reasons.

14. In the civil case, the judge has no power to sentence anyone to prison or to fine them. (The judge's verdict can only order one side to pay the other money.)

    a) Do you think that this is a good or bad idea?

    b) Do you think that the law should allow the directors of the hockey club to be placed in prison?

    c) Do you think they are guilty of a crime, or was it a case of genuine difference of opinion? Explain your reasons fully.

The use of evidence in court

In a court of law, lawyers for both sides question people who have some knowledge of the case. These people are called witnesses. In a bank robbery trial, for instance, the bank workers and customers present during the robbery would tell the court what had happened.

Courts are very strict about the evidence witnesses give. Generally witnesses may only tell what they saw, heard, smelled, tasted or touched. They must only talk about the circumstances relating to the crime itself. A judge or magistrate will not usually allow a witness to give an opinion in court. For example, if a witness clearly saw the driver of a car before an accident, he or she could answer questions about who was driving the car. If too far away to identify the driver, the witness could not say whom he or she thought was driving. Nor could the witness say that the accused was probably

Evidence consists of what witnesses say to the court, and sometimes documents or items connected with the witnesses' statements.

driving the car, because that was the only person the witness had ever seen driving it on previous occasions.

Both sides may call witnesses into court. However, each side has the chance to question the other side's witnesses. This is known as cross-examination. In cross-examination, lawyers frequently try to show that the witness is unreliable, and not to be believed. In a murder trial, for instance, the defense lawyer might bring in a doctor who has examined the accused, and believes the accused to be not guilty because of insanity. The prosecution would probably try to show that the doctor is not to be believed. Perhaps the examination was very brief. Perhaps the doctor is not very experienced in dealing with insane people. This will all come out in cross-examination. The jury will have to decide whether to believe the doctor or not.

Another possibility is that witnesses are lying. This is a crime, but occurs from time to time. In cross-examination, the lawyer will try to show this. The jury will then decide that the witness' evidence is questionable, and ignore it. By carefully controlling what witnesses may and may not tell the court, the truth is more easily arrived at. It is the responsibility of the judge or magistrate to see that witnesses do not give evidence which they are not supposed to give.

15. a) In general, what are the only things which witnesses are allowed to tell the court?
    b) What may they not tell the court?

16. What purpose do you think is served by carefully limiting what witnesses may tell the court?

Punishment for lawbreakers

When a person is found guilty of a crime, it is normal for the court to impose some penalty or punishment. This may range from a small fine for a minor traffic violation all the way up to life imprisonment for a serious crime such as murder. The punishment should achieve three things. First, it should act as a deterrent—it should persuade the person not to commit further crimes for fear of the punishment which would result. Second, it should reform the person and remove the desire to commit further crimes. Third, it should protect society, encouraging others not to turn to crime.

The Canadian Charter of Rights and Freedoms states in Section 12: "Everyone has the right not to be subjected to any cruel and unusual punishment and treatment." The Canadian Charter of Rights and Freedoms is part of the Constitution Act of 1982. This means, in general, that the degree of punishment must not be more severe than the crime itself. For example, it would be illegal for a court to impose a penalty of life imprisonment on someone found guilty of jaywalking. A good deal of thought lies behind our system of punishment for lawbreakers. The following section looks at some of the sentences which a court can impose on a lawbreaker.

Suspended sentence. This is the lightest sentence normally imposed by a court. Young people and first offenders will normally be placed on probation for a period of time, generally to a maximum of two years. This means that they must meet regularly with a social worker and, providing they do not break the law again during this period, will not be punished further. If they do commit a second crime while on probation, they will be punished for both the original crime and the second one.

Fines. Some offenders, such as those charged for motor vehicle offences, are required to pay money to the court. If they do not or cannot pay the fine, such offenders must serve a prison sentence instead.

How should juvenile offenders be treated?

The *Criminal Code* requires special treatment for juvenile offenders. In 1908, the Juvenile Delinquents Act established special family courts where juveniles could be dealt with privately, away from the publicity of adult courts. In February, 1981, the federal government announced that it intended to replace the 1908 Act with a new Young Offenders Act. There were important differences between the old Juvenile Delinquents and the proposed Young Offenders Acts. The following chart summarizes these differences.

THINKING IT THROUGH

17. Which method of dealing with juvenile offenders (the 1908 Act or the 1981 Act) do you think would have more success in each of the following cases? Explain your reasons.

a) a 13 year old boy from a stable home, with no previous record of crime, charged with shoplifting.

b) a 17 year old girl, who has lived in group homes since the age of 13, with a long history of offences, charged with trafficking in (selling of) illegal drugs.

c) a 14 year old boy, abandoned by his parents when two years old, who has lived in 14 foster homes since then, has three previous convictions for theft, and is now charged with stealing a car.

SUBJECT	JUVENILE DELINQUENTS ACT (1908)	YOUNG OFFENDERS ACT (1981)
Minimum age at which one can be charged with a federal offence	7 years old	12 years old
Method of holding a trial	Trial held in private. Media not allowed to report name of any juvenile charged with an offence.	Trial held in public. Media may report proceedings but may not identify a young offender by name or description.
Rights of the accused	The accused's rights are protected by the judge, so the juvenile does not need a lawyer present in court. Similarly no prosecution or Crown Attorney is necessary.	The accused should have the right to have a lawyer present in court to protect his or her rights. Similarly, Crown Attorneys may prosecute young offenders in court.
Reasons behind what the Act says	Juvenile Delinquents are not criminals. They are misguided individuals. In court, by talking informally to the accused's family, probation officer, etc., the judge can find out the best way to help the accused. In this way the judge can encourage the accused not to get into trouble with the law again.	Any youngster who is old enough to be held criminally responsible for his or her actions should be treated in a manner appropriate to an adolescent. A young offender should have the same rights and responsibilities as anyone else. They should be punished for their actions if found guilty.
Age at which a person becomes an adult and tried in adult court	16-18 years old, depending on province or territory.	18 years old anywhere in Canada.

Fig. 9 One member of the jury, the foreman or forewoman, is chosen to deliver the verdict. (Picture posed)

Imprisonment. Prison sentences range from a few days to life imprisonment, depending on the offence. Less serious offenders are kept in low or medium-security institutions. Here they will be encouraged to increase their education, learn a trade, etc. By providing them with such skills it is hoped that they will abandon crime entirely—in other words, that they will be rehabilitated. Offenders serving prison terms of two years or more must do so in a federal penitentiary. These are higher security prisons. Although offenders can still learn trades and improve their educations there, the emphasis is more on protecting society, and inmates of penitentiaries have few freedoms. Prison inmates may be released at any time after they have served one-third of their sentence, if the prison authorities feel they have been rehabilitated. This is known as release on parole. Although only about half of all prison inmates qualify for parole, it provides a reason for prisoners to reform.

Some offenders in low security institutions work outside the prison during the day at a regular job. Their wages are kept and given to them when their sentence is complete.

Death penalty. 150 years ago, the death penalty was imposed for a number of crimes, such as stealing farm animals or forgery of money. Today only one crime is punishable by death in Canada—treason. To be guilty of treason, one must betray Canada to an enemy country in wartime. Until 1976, certain types of murder were punishable by death. At present, life imprisonment, with a minimum of 25 years before release, is the penalty for first degree murder. (First degree murder is murder planned in advance by the accused, or in order to further an additional crime, such as a bank robber shooting a teller.)

No executions have taken place in Canada since 1962.

Other penalties. There are a variety of other penalties available to the courts. People convicted of motoring offences may have their driver's licence suspended. People convicted of violence against elderly people or minority groups may be required to do volunteer work in their community as part of their sentence.

In imposing penalties on lawbreakers, courts try to do two things. They try to protect society by making the guilty pay for their actions. They also try to give less serious offenders lighter sentences. This encourages them not to repeat their offences when a heavier sentence would result. It is not easy to protect society against criminals and at the same time give offenders a second chance by imposing a light sentence. As a result, members of the public often complain that stiffer sentences are needed.

GETTING THE FACTS

18. Explain, in your own words, the meaning of Section 12 of the Canadian Charter of Rights and Freedoms, which states that "everyone has the right not to be subjected to any cruel and unusual punishment and treatment."

19. Identify and explain the three things which should be achieved by any penalty imposed by a court.

THINKING IT THROUGH

20. Make a copy of the following chart headings.

CRIME AND PENALTY	DETERRENT	REFORM OFFENDER	PROTECT SOCIETY	REMARKS

Now copy the following crimes and sentences imposed by Canadian courts in the CRIME AND PENALTY column:

   a) Possession of marijuana; suspended sentence, two years probation

   b) Assaulting an elderly person; 50 hours volunteer work in home for elderly, $200 fine

   c) First degree murder of a relative; life imprisonment (minimum 25 years)

Under the next three headings indicate how effective you think the penalty will be. Use the following numbers:

   1 = not effective at all
   2 = little effect
   3 = somewhat effective
   4 = generally effective
   5 = very effective

Last, in the remarks column, state how effective overall you think the penalty will be in dealing with the crime.

21. Prisoners who have served at least one-third of their sentences may be released on parole if prison authorities believe they have reformed.

   a) Do you think that such early release offers the prisoner an encouragement to reform and protects society against lawbreakers? Explain your views.

   b) What changes, if any, would you make to this system of early release? Explain.

Fig. 10 The symbol of the Supreme Court of Canada. What is the meaning of the motto "Dieu et mon droit"?

Fig. 11 Supreme Court, Ottawa. As well as hearing appeals on criminal or constitutional matters, the Supreme Court advises the federal government on proposed laws when asked to do so.

Conclusion

Canada's legal system is designed to protect society. Laws are made and anyone found guilty of breaking one knows that some form of punishment is likely. At first, you might think that if sentences were more severe, people would be less likely to commit crimes. For example, if the penalty for impaired driving were life imprisonment, you might think that very few people would drink and drive. However, history shows that even the most severe penalties do little to reduce crime if there is a reasonable chance that offenders will not be caught. For example, in England in the seventeenth century the

penalty for pickpockets was death by hanging. Pickpockets were publicly executed before large crowds which had assembled for what they considered entertainment. Can you guess the most likely place in which you might have had your pocket picked? At the executions! Pickpockets knew about the severe penalty which awaited them if caught, but they considered it worth the risk. If they were good at their trade, the chances of being caught were small.

Severe sentences will help to reduce crime, but only if the chances of detection are great. For this reason it is necessary to provide police forces with the resources they need to do their job effectively. Severe sentences alone are generally ineffective.

The purpose of punishment is to deter criminals and to protect society. Yet many law officials feel that unless criminals are offered the chance to reform, they have no incentive to abandon crime. First offenders usually receive light sentences. Even repeat offenders can have their sentences reduced, if it is felt that they genuinely desire to reform. Executing criminals has been rejected in Canada, because it is felt that this does not deter crime, nor does it offer offenders a chance to reform. On the other hand, however, if the penalties for crimes are too light, people may commit them more frequently. Even if caught, it might still be worth the risk, and society would quickly become lawless. Clearly, the law must be firm and at the same time fair.

THINKING IT THROUGH

22. From what you have read in this chapter, what changes would you make to our legal system in order to protect society while at the same time being fair and just to criminals? Think particularly about court procedures and penalties.

23. The death penalty for murder has been abandoned in this country. However, those convicted of first degree murder must serve a minimum sentence of 25 years before being released. Do you think that it is fair that someone convicted of this crime, no matter how much they might have reformed in the meantime, must serve such a complete sentence? Would you allow fully rehabilitated murderers earlier release than this, if you had the power to do so? Explain your reasons fully.

16 How our government works

What do governments do?

Study the accompanying picture closely. It shows a scene which could take place in many Canadian cities. If you look closely, you will see that it contains numerous items which are controlled by, operated by, owned by, or forbidden by government.

- With a partner, make four lists of things shown in the picture which involve or concern government in some way. Use these following headings: Enforcing the law; Services; Regulation of society; Issuing licences. Try to put at least 15 items on your chart.

Chapter overview

Some of us tend to think that government and politics have little effect on our daily lives. However, decisions made by our governments have a great deal to do with what we do every day. If sales tax rises from 7 percent to 10 percent, this immediately adds $300 to the price of an average car. If our police forces are given greater powers to give breathalyzer tests to those they suspect of impaired driving, any of us might be stopped for such a test. If government agencies require greater Canadian content on cable TV, this could mean that you could no longer watch your favourite American station. From such examples you can see how greatly government decisions affect all of us.

In this chapter you will learn about the different roles governments play in our lives and the way in which governments function in Canada. You will examine the differences between the powers of our national government and our provincial governments. This chapter also looks at how people are elected to our House of Commons, and what they do as members of it. Remember, you will soon be 18 and qualified to vote in national elections. In order to do so properly, you should know something about government and politics. This chapter is designed to help you in this regard.

Signposts

The three functions of government $>$

FEATURE: But what has government to do with me? $>$

Federalism: The key to our political system $>$

The legislative powers of the federal and provincial governments $>$

FEATURE: Parliament: The core of our government $>$

If I have a problem, can the government help me? $>$

How are laws made? $>$

Elections: High point in political life >

What do politicians do? >

Key words

legislature   federal
executive   municipal government
judiciary   democracy
constitution   ballot

The three functions of government

Regardless of their size, beliefs and strengths, all governments carry out three basic functions: the making of laws, putting laws into effect, and the interpreting of the legal code and constitution. In some countries, these three functions may be carried out by one person or group of people, while in other countries there is strict separation between the parts responsible for each of the three functions.

The part of government responsible for making laws is generally termed the legislature. The legislature's primary role is to pass laws and taxes suggested to it by its leaders. In addition, the legislature provides a place for the informed discussion of public issues before a decision is taken, and a place where the representatives of the people can state their views. It also provides an opportunity to make voters aware of issues confronting the country so that they can vote in an informed manner.

The executive part of a political system suggests new laws and taxes to the legislature. It also puts into effect or "executes" the laws passed by the legislature. The Cabinet (part of the executive) writes new laws, which the legislature may pass, suggests ways of raising money through taxes to the legislature, and generally manages the affairs of government.

The third part of government is the judiciary or court system. This is normally separate and independent from the executive and legislative parts of government. The purpose of law is to keep order in communities of people, and to protect the rights of citizens. It is the business of the courts to interpret the laws where there are disputes about legal rights. These disputes may involve conflicts between the citizen and the government or even conflicts between

governments. The courts therefore act both as referees of private rights and as interpreters of the constitution.

The following chart illustrates the three functions of Canada's government, and the name we give to each part.

Fig. 1 The functions of Canada's government

FUNCTION	GOVERNMENT TERM	NAME(S) USED IN CANADA
To suggest new laws To put new laws into effect	Executive	Governor-General prime minister Cabinet Civil service (government workers)
To make laws To impose taxes	Legislature	House of Commons Senate
To decide if a law has been broken To impose punishment on the guilty	Judiciary	Courts

GETTING THE FACTS

1. Write the heading "Dictionary of government terms" at the top of a new page in your notebook. Write definitions of the following terms: legislature, executive, judiciary. You will be asked to add to your dictionary throughout the chapter.

USING YOUR KNOWLEDGE

2. Write each of the following headlines in your notebook. Beside each one, write which part of government (executive, legislative or judiciary) would be responsible.

NEW SEATBELT LAW PASSED: $28 FINE FOR NON-WEARERS
YOUTH FOUND GUILTY OF RECKLESS DRIVING
CAPITAL PUNISHMENT ABOLISHED
CABINET SUGGESTS CHANGES IN FAMILY LAW
VOTING AGE REDUCED TO 18 IN FEDERAL ELECTIONS
ORDER SIGNED: POST OFFICE BECOMES CROWN CORPORATION
FINANCE MINISTER SUGGESTS RAISING INCOME TAX
WOMAN FOUND INSANE IN HUSBAND MURDER CHARGE
PRIME MINISTER SUGGESTS RAISING RAIL RATES IN PARLIAMENT
ARGUMENTS HEARD IN NEWFOUNDLAND *VS.* QUEBEC ENERGY
   DISPUTE

3. Make up three headlines of your own to add to the list. Each headline should represent a different function of government.

Fig. 2 Some of the ways in which government affects our daily lives

4. Read the following story and answer the questions which follow it.

THE ROBBIE HAMILTON STORY

The citizens of the area became concerned with alcohol consumption among young people. Motor accidents involving young people and alcohol were increasing, and the citizens as a group demanded that the government take action. Responding to these complaints, the Cabinet proposed raising the legal drinking age from 18 to 19, and the Members of Parliament approved this change. The law came into effect in early September, and the police—as agents of the government—were instructed to enforce the new law.

In October of that year, Robbie was found with some bottles of beer in his sports bag by a policeman searching people on their way into a football game. Robbie was only 18, and therefore charged with possession of alcohol while under the legal age.

When his case came up in court, Robbie was found guilty of the offence and fined $100.

In the above story,
   a) what actions were performed by the legislature?
   b) what actions were performed by the executive?
   c) what actions were performed by the judiciary?

5. In your school or local library, search back issues of a newspaper. Find three news items which would serve as an example of the three functions of government—one item for each function. Examine each example carefully and think of one more example of each function. Then discuss the following questions: Which function do you think is more important? Or do you feel that all are equally important? Explain your answer.

But what has the government to do with me?

If you look back to the opening exercise in this chapter, you will see that the government affects the lives of all citizens in a variety of ways. These can be summarized under three major headings. First, the government makes laws to protect our society. Second, it provides services such as schools or welfare for its citizens. Third, it decides what the citizens must pay to maintain the services it provides.

At first, you might think that all of the above concerns only adults. You might think that, as a student, the government has little effect on you. This is simply untrue, for almost every day you are affected by the government. What is the minimum age you can leave school in your province or territory? What taxes do you pay when, for example, you buy a pair of running shoes? Do you have to pay fees for attending a public school? Why not? These are three examples of how government is affecting you now.

As you get older, of course, the government may affect you even more. You may qualify for special privileges, such as the right to vote, to apply for a beginner's automobile licence, and eventually, to collect a government pension. It is also likely that you will have to pay far more in taxes than you do now. You will have to pay tax on money you earn from your job, and on certain items you buy, especially imported items. You will probably make use of more services offered by government. For example, you might collect unemployment insurance while temporarily unemployed, or an operation you had in a hospital might be paid for by a government health plan. Even your salary could be paid for by the government if, for example, you became a firefighter, teacher or an employee of Air Canada. If you look at the total value of wages and services in Canada produced in a single year, you will find that for every $100 of wages paid to Canadian workers in total, over $40 is paid to government workers. All the other employers in Canada account for less than $60 of the total.

As you have seen, the existence of government greatly influences your life even now. As you get older, it is likely that this influence will increase.

GETTING THE FACTS

6. Make a timeline of your life. On the timeline, write the different ways in which government is involved in your life and will be involved in your life later on. To help you, a number of examples have been put in for you.

0 —	**Need to obtain birth certificate**
10 —	
20 —	**Can obtain driver's licence**
30 —	
40 —	
50 —	
60 —	**Eligible for Canada Pension**
70 —	
80 —	

THINKING IT THROUGH

7. As you can see, government plays an active role in the life of Canadians. Does it, perhaps, play too large a role?

a) Can you think of any dangers for the citizens if the government were to play too large a role?

b) Do you think it does in fact play too large a role now? Or is it about right? Explain your reasons.

Fig. 3 A fire department is one service provided by government. What other services does the government provide for the benefit of citizens?

Federalism: The key to our political system

The Canadian political system is a federal one. This means that we have two levels of government. There is a national government, whose laws apply anywhere in Canada. In addition, each of the ten provinces has its own government, whose laws apply only in that province. This means that if you live in any province, you are subject to the laws of two governments, and must pay taxes to two governments. This is not as unusual as you might at first think. Look at the following item.

Rules and Regulations

1. You must be in home room at 8:55, or sign in at the office in the late book.
2. You must be in bed by 22:30 on week nights.
3. You must arrive in class with all homework complete.
4. You must at all times obey the laws of Canada.
5. You must wash the dinner dishes on weekends.
6. You must not use any locker which has not been assigned to you by your home room teacher.
7. You must not make unnecessary noise when your brothers or sisters are doing their homework.
8. You must take out the garbage every Tuesday night.
9. You must not make noise outside any classroom and disturb other students.
10. You must make sure that your bicycle is securely locked when not in use.

GETTING THE FACTS

8. Write each of the above rules in your notebook. Beside each one, note whether the rule is likely to be made by parents (P), school (S) or both (B). Now consider the following questions.
a) Why are there two separate authorities?
b) Do their powers overlap?
c) How would it be decided who should make rules about, for example, your bed-time or weekends?

Consider similar questions about our government.
1) Why are there two separate governments? The country is so large and complex, no single government could deal with all aspects of the nation's life.
2) Do their powers overlap? Sometimes they do. Each government has sole power to make laws about some things, but both governments make laws about other things as we shall see.

3) How is it decided which government has the power to make laws about a particular item? This is written down in a constitution to reduce disagreements between governments. A constitution is a legal document which sets down the basic rules for the running of the country.

What a constitution does

Many people belong to some kind of club or organization. Perhaps you belong to a sorority or fraternity, a youth group at your church, Students' Council at your school, the Scouts, Guides or Junior Achievement. Many parents belong to clubs like Chamber of Commerce, the Lions or Rotary. Whenever people come together to achieve a common purpose, it is necessary to have rules and regulations. These help to provide organization for the club, reduce the chances of disagreements among members, and provide an orderly atmosphere for people to work in and enjoy.

Rules and regulations generally cover a large number of subjects. For instance, most clubs have rules governing how the leader is chosen, how long the term of office will be, qualifications for club membership, frequency of meetings, fees, duties and responsibilities of members. All rules and regulations are generally written down and made available to all members. The term used to describe an organization's rules and regulations is a constitution.

In many ways, a country is similar to the kind of club or

Fig. 4 The first parliament of Lower Canada, 1792. The word "parliament" comes from the French word "parler." Can you say why?

organization described here. Like a club, a country needs rules and regulations to provide organization and orderliness. Can you imagine what it would be like to live in a country where there were no rules to tell its citizens how, when and where its leaders would be chosen? Imagine the time involved if people had to think and decide what procedures to use every time they wanted to choose a leader.

The constitution of a country will normally describe the parts which make up the government, the duties and responsibilities of the government to its citizens, and the duties and responsibilities of citizens to the country.

The British North America Act of 1867 (B.N.A. Act) was our first constitution. In 1982, the B.N.A. Act of 1867 was renamed the Constitution Act of 1867. The 1982 Constitution Act revises certain clauses in the Constitution Act of 1867. It contains 146 sections, dealing with a variety of topics. Among these are the sections dealing with the form of government Canada has and the sections which state the powers of the federal and provincial governments. These have remained almost unchanged since 1867.

GETTING THE FACTS

9. Define the following in your dictionary of government terms: federal, constitution.

10. Make a copy of the following diagram.

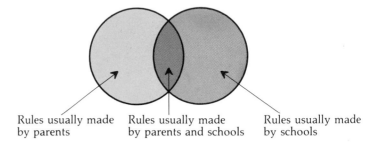

Rules usually made by parents   Rules usually made by parents and schools   Rules usually made by schools

Read over the list of Rules and Regulations. List each rule in the correct place in the diagram, using the number for each rule.

USING YOUR KNOWLEDGE

11. Read the three questions and answers following the Rules and Regulations. In your own words, explain how the Rules and Regulations exercise is similar to the position of a citizen living in a federal system. (Suggestion: You may have to reread the definition of "federal" first.)

12. Imagine that we had no constitution which states the powers of the federal and provincial governments. What sorts of arguments and disputes might arise? Write an imaginary news story for a newspaper—complete with headline, date and reporter's name—describing an imaginary dispute. You might choose from the following list of ideas:
—Any government (national or provincial) could issue its own money.
—Any government could maintain its own army.
—The national government could try to take over responsibility for issuing all licences—including small business and dog licences.

The legislative powers of the federal and provincial governments

The Constitution Act of 1867—formerly known as the British North America Act of 1867—outlines the powers of the governments. Section 91 describes the powers of the federal government, while Sections 92 and 93 describe those of the provincial governments. The following lists are based on Sections 91 to 93.

Section 91: Legislative powers of the federal government

2.	Regulation of trade and commerce.
2A.	Unemployment insurance.
3.	Raising money through taxes.
4.	Borrowing money for government purposes.
5.	Postal service.
6.	Keeping statistics about Canada.
7.	National defence.
9.	Navigation aids for ships.
10.	Shipping.
12.	Sea coast fisheries and inland fisheries.
13.	International or interprovincial ferries.
14.	Money.
15.	Banking.
16.	Savings banks and trust companies.
17.	Weights and measures.
21.	Bankruptcy.
24.	Native affairs.
26.	Marriage and divorce.
27.	Criminal law.
28.	Penitentiaries (prisons for serious offenders).
29.	All other matters not mentioned anywhere else.

If an item appears in Section 91, the federal government does not necessarily own it. For example, it does not own all ships although Clause 10 lists shipping as a federal power. Clause 10 means that the federal government has the power to make laws about ships and their operation. Similarly, according to Clause 7 of Section 92, the provincial government makes laws about hospitals, although it does not necessarily own them all.

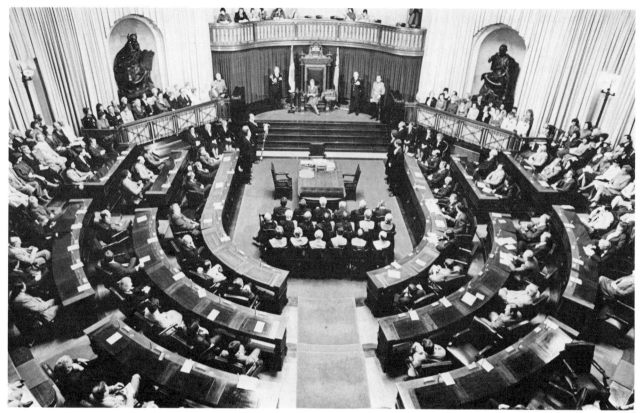

Fig. 5 Opening of the Manitoba Legislature. Who is the Member of Provincial Parliament for the riding in which you live?

Section 92: Legislative powers of the provincial governments

2. Raising money through taxes for provincial purposes.
3. Borrowing money for provincial purposes.
6. Prisons for young offenders and less serious offenders.
7. Hospitals, charities, mental institutions.
8. Supervision of local city and county governments.
9. Licences for shops, taverns, auctioneers, *etc.*
10. All local works are provincial with the exception of the following federal powers:
    a) ships, railway, telephone projects, *etc.*, which extend beyond one province;
    b) shipping lines extending beyond Canada;
    c) any item which the federal government claims is in the interest of Canada. Such items may be removed from provincial control.
11. Licensing of companies which operate in only one province.
14. Operating the court system to hear criminal and civil cases.
15. Punishing people convicted of offences.
16. Local matters.

Fig. 6 Toronto City Hall. What are the responsibilities of a municipal government?

Section 93: Legislative power of the provincial governments

Provincial governments make laws about educational affairs, although the national government is given the power to protect the educational rights of minority religions.

In addition to the federal and provincial governments, there is a system of local governments across the nation. You will see that Section 92 (16) makes the establishment and maintenance of local governments a provincial responsibility. As a result, their structure varies from province to province. In general, towns and cities have municipal governments (from the Latin word for "free town"), while rural areas have township, parish or county governments. Whatever the form of the local government, it is responsible, under the direction and supervision of the province, for building permits, streetlighting, "no parking" signs, garbage collection and other such matters. Local government responsibilities are mainly technical (how large should building plots be?) or administrative (what is the most efficient way to provide fire protection services?). Such responsibilities may seem less glamorous than those of the federal or provincial governments, but they are still vital to the smooth operation of the nation.

As we have already seen, it is necessary to have a clear understanding of the powers of government to prevent disputes between federal and provincial governments. Sections 91-3 provide this understanding and help to ensure harmony among our governments.

13. Make a copy of the following diagram.

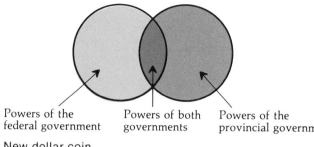

Powers of the federal government   Powers of both governments   Powers of the provincial government

New dollar coin

Using the extracts from Sections 91-3, make a list of the following newspaper headlines beside the correct place on the diagram and draw arrows from the list to the proper section of the diagram, as shown. To make it easier, one item has been placed for you.

NEW DOLLAR COIN CELEBRATES CONSTITUTION
P.E.I. FERRY INCREASES SUMMER SAILINGS
NEW LOCAL BABYSITTING COMPANY FORMED
INDIAN RESERVE POPULATION INCREASING
JAPANESE CAR IMPORTS RISE 2%
NEW GOVERNMENT BONDS ISSUED
HALIFAX HARBOUR EXTENSION PLANNED
MASTER CRIMINAL TRIED IN COURT
CHEQUE ISSUING REGULATIONS TIGHTENED
TAXES TO BE RAISED NEXT YEAR
NOW OVER 1 000 000 UNEMPLOYED
GAS STATIONS ALLOWED TO OPEN ON SUNDAYS NOW

14. a) When you look at the division of powers as set out in the Constitution Act of 1867, do you think that the division is clear cut? Or could there be disagreements among governments regarding which level was responsible for a particular item? Be sure to explain your answer, giving examples if necessary.

b) If such disagreements arose, what do you think would be the best way of solving the problem?

15. Some countries, such as Great Britain, have only one level of government—a national one. In Canada there are two levels.

a) What advantages can you see in having two levels in a country like ours?

b) What disadvantages can you see?

c) Do the advantages outweigh the disadvantages? Explain your answer.

Parliament—The core of our government

You will remember that at the beginning of this chapter you learned about the executive, legislature and judiciary—the three functions of government. These are not the names, however, that Canadians generally use in talking about them. People generally talk about the Cabinet, which is the name we give to one part of the executive branch of government. Does it all sound confusing? Perhaps the following diagram will help you.

Canadian name	Part of government
The Crown (Queen/King) or Governor-General	Executive
Parliament	Legislature
House of Commons (elected) / Senate (appointed)	
Cabinet	Executive
The court system	Judiciary
Voters	

The main business of government is carried out in Parliament. It is divided into two houses—the House of Commons and the Senate. The 282 members of the Commons are elected by the voters while the 104 members of the Senate are appointed by the Governor-General. As you will see in a later section of this chapter, the Commons and Senate are not equally powerful. Because they are elected by the voters, and therefore represent the people more directly than the Senate's members, members from the Commons are given almost all of the Cabinet positions. The prime minister is always a member of the Commons. As leader of the government, this is the most important politician. The prime minister is responsible to the House of Commons for the government's actions.

At the provincial level of government, the pattern is basically the same, although some of the names might be different.

Canadian name	Part of government
The Crown (Queen/King) or Lieutenant-Governor	Executive
Legislative Assembly (elected)	Legislature
Cabinet	Executive
The court system	Judiciary
Voters	

The most important difference between the structure of the national and provincial governments is in the legislature. In the provincial government there is only one House, while the national government has two. But the similarities are striking. The government party—the one which won the most seats at the last election—chooses a group of people (the Cabinet) to make suggestions for new laws. The other parties criticize the government where necessary, and offer alternative suggestions for running the government. In the next section, you will see how this is done. The point to remember for now is that the national and provincial governments are basically the same in structure and proceedings.

GETTING THE FACTS

17. Add the definitions for each of the following terms to your dictionary: municipal government, Legislative Assembly, House of Commons, Senate, Parliament, opposition party, prime minister, Cabinet.

18. List the ways in which the national and provincial governments are similar. Then list the ways in which they are different.

16. Using back issues of a newspaper, find three stories relating to matters regulated by the federal government. Find three which are provincial matters.

a) Which set of stories (federal or provincial) do you think would most affect the lives of the citizens living under that government? Give reasons for your answer.

b) Can you find any evidence in your stories and in the division of powers section of this chapter to show that one level of government has more important powers than the others? Explain.

If I have a problem, can the government help me?

We all have problems from time to time. Should we look for a new job? Is this a good time to buy a new house? Governments do not generally get involved in such personal problems as these. It is up to the individual to decide. Yet citizens frequently have problems with which governments should help them. Am I entitled to unemployment insurance? Can I have "no parking" signs put up on my street? Can I attend a school closer to home? These are the sorts of problems with which we expect government help.

The first question to ask is which government can help—the national, provincial or local government? You would not ask your teacher if you could stay out till 23.00 on the weekend. This is a decision for the home, not the school. Nor would you be able to get help from the federal government to build an extension on an overcrowded school. That is a matter for the province.

Having decided which government can help, the next thing to do is to identify the department or office of that government to contact. This is not always an easy matter. For example, the Toronto telephone book lists over 400 numbers for the various offices of the government of Canada. Similarly, the government of Ontario and the local government account for another 400 numbers between them.

It is sometimes fairly easy to identify the proper office to contact, and a quick telephone call or two can help to get advice or action on the problem. On other occasions, however, the problem may be just too complicated for a quick answer. On these occasions, it often pays to contact the local Member of Parliament or Member of the Legislative Assembly, depending on which level of government is involved. Of course, these people are very busy and should be approached only on larger problems. If you do have a significant problem, contacting your M.P. or M.L.A. is often the best way to get help. Their experience and knowledge of government will quickly

Fig. 7 Federal Parliament in session. Who is the Member of Parliament for the riding in which you live?

Fig. 8 How would you apply to receive welfare payments or unemployment insurance?

put you in contact with the correct department or office. Additionally, their influence and reputation often make it easier for you to have your problem solved to your liking, if this is possible.

Read through the list of problems below. Canadians would require the help of the government to deal with these problems. You will be asked to analyze them in the questions that follow.

a) Your unemployment insurance cheque is two weeks late and you have no money to buy food.

b) You want a stop sign put up at an intersection near your house to slow passing traffic in your street.

c) A relative has been found guilty of a serious offence and sentenced to seven years' imprisonment in a federal penitentiary. You have just uncovered some new evidence which you believe will prove your relative's innocence.

d) There is a rumour that the interchange to and from a nearby expressway may be permanently closed because of a number of serious accidents which have taken place there. This would cut off two-thirds of the customers from your service station, and you would be forced to close your business.

e) You have lost contact with a relative. You know that this person is serving with the Canadian Armed Forces and wish to find an address to which you can send a letter.

f) You have two cousins living in eastern Europe and wish to sponsor their coming to live in Canada.

g) You want to find out how much duty you will have to pay if you bring back a video-cassette recorder on your forthcoming trip to Japan.

h) You live in a part of Canada where English-speaking people are the majority. Since your grandparents are French-speaking and you do not want to lose your French ties, you would like to attend French immersion classes. Unfortunately, your local school board does not provide such classes.

i) You would like to have "No Overnight Parking" signs placed on your street to prevent a nearby truck haulage firm from parking its trucks outside your house and blocking the light.

j) Your retirement pension turns out to be 10 percent less than you think it should be. This is because of a mistake on your birth certificate which shows that you are 65 years old. In fact, your correct age is 68 years old.

k) You would like to open a video games lounge in an empty store you own. You cannot be granted a licence to do so, and therefore cannot open the lounge, as the store is only 350 m from a school. A local law states that no such lounge can be opened or operated within 500 m of a school.

USING YOUR KNOWLEDGE

19. By referring back to the section dealing with the powers of the federal and provincial governments, identify which of the above problems fall under which government.

20. Look at the list of problems which you have identified as falling under the federal government's responsibility. Which of the problems do you think you might be able to solve yourself? Which problems might need the help of your Member of Parliament?

21. Look at the following extract from the blue pages of the Toronto telephone directory, which lists the numbers of the government of Canada. If you lived in Toronto, which number would you call first to try to get help for each of these problems?

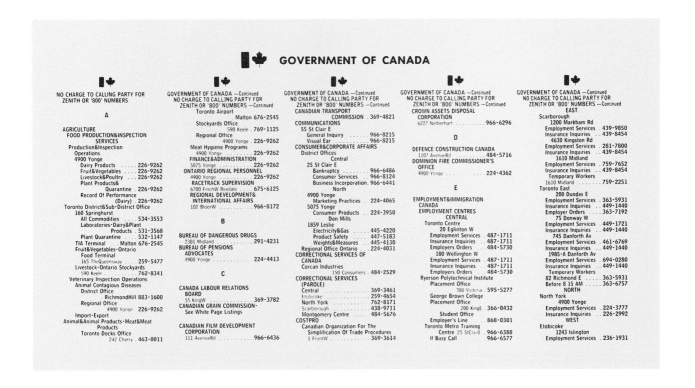

GOVERNMENT OF CANADA —Continued
NO CHARGE TO CALLING PARTY FOR
ZENITH OR '800' NUMBERS —Continued
Insurance Inquiries . . 231-4151
1620 Albion
Employment Services . 745-9410
Insurance Inquiries . . 231-4151
3253 Lake Shore Bl W
Employment Services . 236-1931
Insurance Inquiries . . 231-4151
High Park
2968 Dundas W
Employment Services . 763-3611
Insurance Inquiries . . 766-6431
909 Jane
Employment Services . 766-8131
Insurance Inquiries . . 766-6431
1335 Dundas W
Employment Services . 535-7534
Insurance Inquiries . . 766-6431
1384 St Clair W
Employment Services . 763-3611
Insurance Inquiries . . 766-6431
Temporary Workers
391 Keele 763-3611
Before 8 15 AM 763-2781
CNE Grounds Office
Dufferin Gates 595-0495
If No Answer Call . . . 763-3611
Weston
1315 Finch W
Employment Services . 638-5115
Insurance Inquiries . . 245-8213
1747 Jane
Employment Services . 247-8261
Insurance Inquiries . . 245-8213
1267 Weston 247-7881
Temporary Workers
Westdale Shopping
Centre . 247-8261
York University
Placement Office
4700 Keele . 667-2417
EMPLOYMENT CENTRE FOR
STUDENTS
Toronto Centre
Apr-Sept 1 FrontW . . . 868-0301
EMPLOYMENT DEVELOPMENT
BRANCH
55 StClairE 966-5844
TORONTO DISTRICT
OFFICE . 966-6279
DISTRICT ECONOMIST . . . 966-6313
Record Of Employment Centre
1919 LawrenceAvE . 757-3653
IMMIGRATION CENTRES
Toronto
Inquiries 598-4444
Central 480 University . 598-4444
East 130 BloorW 598-4444
West 1243 Islington . . 598-4444
Mississauga
165 DundasW
. Cooksville 270-7400
Toronto International Airport
Terminal 1 . . . Malton 676-3911
Terminal 2 . . . Malton 676-3690
Adjudication
6900 AirportRd . Malton 675-6373
Enforcement
6900 AirportRd . Malton 675-2730
IMMIGRATION APPEALS OFFICE
130 BloorW 966-5620
DISTRICT ADMINISTRATOR
IMMIGRATION
Mississauga
6205 AirportRd . Malton 671-1800
ONTARIO REGIONAL OFFICE
4900 Yonge 224-4888
ENERGY MINES&RESOURCES
2242 Lake Shore Bl W
Canada Oil Substitution
Program (C O S P) . 252-5866
Conservation&Renewable
Energy Office . 252-5866
25 St Clair E
Survey&Mapping Branch
Regional Surveyor . . . 966-7503
ENVIRONMENT
Atmospheric Environment
Services
National Headquarters
4905 Dufferin
General Inquiries 667-4882
Media Relations 667-4554
Ontario Regional Headquarters
25 StClairE 966-5624
Scientific Services . . . 966-5554
Climate Services
. Malton 676-3024
Ontario Weather Centre
. Malton 676-3019
Toronto Weather Office
General Weather Inquiries
. Malton 676-3066
Marine Weather . Malton 676-4567
Out-Of-Town Weather
. Malton 676-4567
Aviation Weather
. Malton 676-3026
If Busy Call . . Malton 676-3027
General Aviation Briefing
Office . Malton 676-3085
Environment Protection Service
25 St Clair E
Environment
Emergencies . 966-5840
Pollution 966-5840
General Information . 966-5840

GOVERNMENT OF CANADA —Continued
NO CHARGE TO CALLING PARTY FOR
ZENITH OR '800' NUMBERS —Continued
EXTERNAL AFFAIRS
Passport Office
General Inquiries 369-3251

F

FEDERAL BUSINESS
DEVELOPMENT BANK
Financial&Management Services
Regional Office
250 University 593-1144
Toronto Metro Branch
204 RichmondW 598-0341
Etobicoke Branch
Valhalla Executive Centre
304 TheEastMall . 239-4804
Scarborough Branch
2978 EglintonE 431-5410
Oshawa Branch
22 KingW . . . . Oshawa 576-6800
Oakville Branch
345 LakeshoreRdE
. Oakville 844-0911
Toronto-North Branch
4430 Bathurst 638-0823
C A S E (Counselling Assistance
To Small Enterprises) Offices
Regional Office
204 RichmondW 593-1143
Toronto Branch
204 RichmondW 598-0341
Toronto-North
4430 Bathurst 638-1340
Oshawa Branch
22 KingW . . . . Oshawa 571-1355
FISHERIES&OCEANS
590 Keele 763-1161

G

GOVERNMENT OF CANADA
PENSION COMMISSION
Sunnybrook K Wing 486-4747

H

HEALTH&WELFARE CANADA
Public Relations
789 DonMillsRd . 966-5535
Area Personnel Manager
789 DonMillsRd . 966-5635
Staffing&Training
789 DonMillsRd . 966-5589
Health Promotion
102 BloorW . 966-6483
Health Protection
Food&Drugs
2301 Midland . 291-4231
Medical Services Directorate
General Inquiries 966-6241
Quarantine Immigration
Toronto 966-6245
Malton 676-2840
Prosthetic Services
Sunnybrook Hospital
2075 BayviewAv . 486-3556
HUMAN RIGHTS COMMISSION
55 StClairE 966-5527

I

IMMIGRATION APPEAL BOARD
102 BloorW 966-6261
Members 966-6035
INCOME SECURITY PROGRAMS
Canada Pension Plan
Family Allowances
Guaranteed Income Supplement
Old Age Security
Spouse's Allowance
Don Mills
789 DonMillsRd . 423-6900
Etobicoke 1243 Islington . 231-5683
North York 4900 Yonge . 224-4403
Scarborough
2401 EglintonE . 752-6480
Toronto Central
60 StClairE . 966-6580
Francophone Services 966-8336
INDIAN&NORTHERN AFFAIRS
Indian Minerals (Mining)
1 FrontW 369-4615
Ontario Regional Office
55 St Clair E
General Inquiries-
Library . 966-6234
Information Services . 966-5544
Education 966-6203
Reserves&Trusts
(Lands) . 966-8110
Local Government (Band
Support) . 966-6516
Socio-Economic
Development . 966-6223
Technical Services . . . 966-6227
Student Counselling
25 StClairE . 966-6211
INDUSTRY TRADE&COMMERCE
1st Canadian Place
Regional Office 369-4951
Business Information
Centre . 369-4941

GOVERNMENT OF CANADA— Continued
NO CHARGE TO CALLING PARTY FOR
ZENITH OR '800' NUMBERS —Continued
Tourism 369-4951
Small Business
Assistance . 369-4951
Export Assistance 369-4951
INSURANCE DEPARTMENT . . 369-4280

J

JUSTICE
Toronto Dominion Centre . 369-4241

L

LABOUR CANADA
4900 Yonge
General Inquiries 224-3850
Conditions Of Work
Federal Labour
Standards . 224-3850
Employment Relations
Union-Management
Services . 224-3850
Federal Mediation&
Conciliation Services
Conciliation&
Arbitration . 224-3845
Occupational Health&
Safety . 224-3850
Regional Safety
Officers . 224-3823

N

NATIONAL DEFENCE
REGULAR FORCE
Canadian Forces Base Toronto
Downsview . 633-6200
Canadian Forces Command&
Staff College
215 YongeBl . 484-5624
Canadian Forces Recruiting
Centre
Inquiries 4900 Yonge . . . 224-4015
If Busy Call 224-4016
Canadian Forces Staff School
1107 AvenueRd . 484-5640
Defence&Civil Institute Of
Environmental Medicine
1133 SheppardAvW . 633-4240
DND Regional Audit Group
25 StClairE . 966-6560
3 Canadian Forces Technical
Services Agency
4900 Yonge . 224-4958
DND Public Affairs Office
4900 Yonge . 224-4087
Canadian Forces Technical
Services
305 Detachment
4900 Yonge . 224-4085
306 Detachment
4900 Yonge . 224-4983
307 Detachment Dehavilland
Aircraft Downsview . 633-7310
308 Detachment Hawker-
Sidley Orenda Division
. Malton 677-3250
RESERVE FORCE
Navy
HMCS York
659 LakeShoreBlW . 369-4803
Ward Room 366-2486
CPO's Mess 368-6825
Men's Mess
659 LakeShoreBlW . 861-1563
Militia
Headquarters Central Militia
Area Downsview . 633-6200
Moss Park Armoury
130 QueenE 368-9267
7th Toronto Regiment RCA
(M) . 369-4992
Officers' Mess 368-6423
Sergeants' Mess 366-9324
48th Highlanders Of
Canada . 369-3296
The Queen's Own Rifles Of
Canada . 369-3281
Avenue Rd Coy
1107 AvenueRd . 484-5655
Denison Armoury
3621 Dufferin 636-5433
Governor-General Horse
Guards . 633-6200
25 Service Bn 633-6200
Fort York Armoury
660 FleetW 369-4813
Duty Medical Officer . . . 369-4811
The Queen's York
Rangers . 369-3265
Sergeants' Mess 366-1404
The Toronto Scottish
Regiment . 369-4537
Sergeants' Mess 368-3178
Officers' Mess 366-0191
709 (Toronto) Communication
Regiment . 369-4500
2nd Field Engineer
Regiment . 369-4588
The Royal Regiment Of
Canada . 369-3677
Officers' Mess 368-3449
Sergeants' Mess 368-9727

GOVERNMENT OF CANADA —Continued
NO CHARGE TO CALLING PARTY FOR
ZENITH OR '800' NUMBERS —Continued
Air
2 Air Reserve Wing
Headquarters Downsview . 633-6200
400 Air Reserve Squadron
Downsview . 633-6200
411 Air Reserve Squadron
Downsview . 633-6200
General Information 633-6200
NATIONAL FILM BOARD OF
CANADA
1 Lombard
Information 369-4094
Chief Librarian 369-4096
Regional Director 369-2235
Film Reservations 369-4092
Distribution
Consultants . 369-4094
NATIONAL RESEARCH COUNCIL OF
CANADA
789 Don Mills Rd
General Inquiries 966-5845
Grants (IRAP) 966-5845
Technical Information
Services . 966-5845
3781 Victoria Park
Rehabilitation Technology
Unit . 499-3222

O

OFFICE OF THE AUDITOR GENERAL
OF CANADA
4900 Yonge 224-4395

P

POST OFFICE
Postal Information 366-7492
Public Affairs 369-3936
Gateway Postal Facility
. Cooksville 625-1956
Staffing&Employment
. Cooksville 625-7351
South Central Plant 461-7611
Staffing&Employment . . 461-2437
East Plant 291-5446
Staffing&Employment . . 438-3771
POSTAL STATIONS
East Metro Retail Sales
Collection&Delivery
Agincourt
4245 SheppardAvE 293-3411
Letter Carriers 293-3327
Ajax
30 King'sCr 683-1900
Letter Carriers 683-2810
Claremont 649-3113
Don Mills
169 DonwayW 444-6271
169 DonwayW 447-2662
Letter Carriers 444-2794
Gormley 887-5119
Locust Hill
Hwy7E . . . . . Markham 294-5692
Markham
21 MainN 294-1451
Letter Carriers 294-0370
Milliken . . . . . Unionville 297-2547
News Revenue
280 Progress 291-9386
Pickering
1740 KingstonRd 683-3812
Letter Carriers 686-2679
Richmond Hill
21 Arnold 884-3297
Letter Carriers 884-1777
Scarborough A
2439 EglintonE 261-5811
If Busy Call 261-5662
Letter Carriers 261-5411
Scarborough B
2530 KingstonRd 261-7511
Letter Carriers 261-5327
Scarborough C
Letter Carrier Depot
1990 Ellesmere . 438-0041
Scarborough D
2075 LawrenceE 755-7991
Letter Carriers 755-0724
Scarborough F
3020 BridletowneCir . . . 497-2182
Letter Carriers 497-7294
Scarborough Malvern Letter
Carrier Depot No 2
27 EstateDr 439-8522
Scarborough Transportation
710 Progress 439-1430
If Busy Call 439-0557
Scarborough Dispatch Depot
155 Midwest 751-6300
Letter Carriers . . . 759-6185
Stouffville
22 MainE 640-2466
Thornhill
7751 Yonge 889-3230
Letter Carriers 889-4770
Unionville
186 Main 297-2122
West Hill
4551 KingstonRd 284-1941
Letter Carriers 284-5610
Willowdale A
5170 Yonge 223-8738
Letter Carriers 221-7081

GOVERNMENT OF CANADA —Continued
NO CHARGE TO CALLING PARTY FOR
ZENITH OR '800' NUMBERS —Continued
Willowdale B
699 SheppardAvE 223-4725
Letter Carriers 223-4742
Willowdale C
1800 SheppardAvE . . . 491-3891
If Busy Call 491-3196
Willowdale D
6035 Bathurst 226-1325
Letter Carriers 226-1717
Willowdale Letter Carrier
Depot No 2
101 PlacerCrt 493-7911
West Metro Retail Sales
Collection&Delivery
Bramalea
150 CentralPark
. Brampton 793-2218
Letter Carriers
. Brampton 793-2219
Brampton
54 QueenE 451-6116
Letter Carriers 451-9334
Clarkson
1156 ClarksonN 822-9962
Letter Carriers 822-9973
Concord
7777 Keele . Thornhill 669-2091
Downsview A
2800 Keele 633-4144
Letter Carriers 635-1560
Downsview B
1011 SheppardAvW . . . 636-6500
Letter Carriers 635-5125
Downsview C
2950 Jane 743-1672
Letter Carriers 743-2068
Erin Mills 4 C Depot No 3
2525 DunwinDr
. Streetsville 828-6412
Etobicoke
577 Burnhamthorpe . . . 621-0761
Letter Carriers 621-7827
Islington A
4975 DundasW 231-3320
Letter Carriers 233-8141
Islington B
25 TheWestMall 622-7259
Kleinburg
10483 Islington 893-1044
Malton
2855 DerryE 677-1907
Letter Carriers 677-1924
Maple
9926 Keele 832-1435
Mississauga A
3025 Hurontario
. Cooksville 279-4941
Letter Carriers
. Cooksville 277-8792
Mississauga B
3100 Dixie . . Cooksville 279-5892
Port Credit
31 LakeshoreRdE 278-7912
Letter Carriers 278-6615
Rexdale A
2110 Kipling 743-8755
Letter Carriers 743-8611
Rexdale B
1686 Albion 749-5469
Letter Carriers 749-4733
Streetsville
145 QueenS 826-3521
Letter Carriers 826-1307
Weston A
2050 Weston 248-9737
Letter Carriers 244-9831
Weston B
19 Toryork 749-3877
Letter Carriers 749-2587
Woodbridge
141 Woodbridge 851-2525
South Metro Retail Sales
Collection&Delivery
Adelaide
Letter Carriers 369-4673
Commerce Court 369-3611
First Canadian Place . . . 369-2120
Royal Bank Plaza 369-2122
Toronto Dominion
Centre . 369-3120
Toronto A
17 FrontW 369-4644
Letter Carriers 369-4023
Toronto B
170 SpadinaAv 369-4676
Letter Carriers 369-4677
Toronto C
1117 QueenW 532-1234
Letter Carriers 534-3983
Toronto D
338 Keele 769-8665
Letter Carriers 769-4476
Toronto E
772 Dovercourt 531-3910
Letter Carriers 534-2909
Toronto F
50 CharlesE 966-6547
Letter Carriers 966-6548
Toronto G
1075 QueenE 465-2360
Letter Carriers 463-3971
Toronto H
2315 DanforthAv 694-5467
Letter Carriers 694-5511

GOVERNMENT OF CANADA —Continued
NO CHARGE TO CALLING PARTY FOR
ZENITH OR '800' NUMBERS —Continued

Toronto J
685 DanforthAv 466-4214
Letter Carriers 463-0342
Toronto K
2384 Yonge 483-1334
Letter Carriers 485-0173
Toronto L
473 Oakwood 652-0170
Letter Carriers 652-0174
Toronto M
2383 BloorW 762-4441
Letter Carriers 762-5211
Toronto N
2930 LakeShoreBlW ... 251-4351
Letter Carriers 251-4773
Toronto O
812 O'ConnorDr 755-0581
Letter Carriers 759-9667
Toronto P
704 SpadinaAv 966-6111
Letter Carriers 966-6112
Toronto Q
27 StClairE 966-6549
Letter Carriers 966-6550
Toronto R
2 LairdDr 421-8777
Letter Carriers 421-7992
Toronto RX
16 ThorncliffeParkDr .. 422-1662
Toronto S
1780 AvenueRd 781-6412
Letter Carriers 781-6510
Toronto T
3019 Dufferin 782-6798
Letter Carriers 782-6583
Toronto U
935 The Queensway ... 251-8802
Letter Carriers 251-8654
Toronto V
25 Ritchie 532-9826
Letter Carriers 532-9885
Toronto W
35 Densley 244-2611
Letter Carriers 244-2610
Toronto Z
473 EglintonW 487-0897
Letter Carriers 487-2293
PUBLIC ARCHIVES
190 Carrier Dr
Federal Records Centre . 675-2546
If Busy Call 667-4534
Central Microfilm 675-2548
If Busy Call 667-4533
National Film Television&
Sound Archives . 675-2086

GOVERNMENT OF CANADA —Continued
NO CHARGE TO CALLING PARTY FOR
ZENITH OR '800' NUMBERS —Continued

PUBLIC SERVICE COMMISSION OF CANADA
180 Dundas W
Employment
Information . 369-3122
Appeals 369-3683
Anti-Discrimination 369-3715
PUBLIC WORKS CANADA
Ontario Region
4900 Yonge
Accounts 224-4204
Design&Construction ... 224-4186
New Toronto International
Airport Project
4900 Yonge 224-4373
Brougham Office
Markham 294-2631
Program Planning&Co-
Ordination . 224-4244
Property Administration . 224-4311
Real Estate Services ... 224-4346
Tendering 224-4240
Director General 224-4100
Inquiries 224-4246

R

REGIONAL ECONOMIC EXPANSION
Ontario Region
55 St Clair E
Analysis 966-6004
Development 966-6004
Incentives 966-6004
General Inquiries 966-6004
REVENUE CANADA
CUSTOMS
Regional Office
55 Bloor W
Bonded Warehouse . 966-8053
Drawbacks 966-8151
Exports 966-8137
Foreign Exchange
Rates . 966-8134
Investigation Service . 966-8032
Refunds 966-8166
Registrar Of
Shipping . 966-8135
Remissions 966-8201
Settlers Effects 966-8005
Tariff Classification&Values
Commodity
Specialists . 966-8184
Rulings&Appeals-D C
A's . 966-6413

GOVERNMENT OF CANADA —Continued
NO CHARGE TO CALLING PARTY FOR
ZENITH OR '800' NUMBERS —Continued

Clearances-Baggage&
Travellers
Airport Terminal 1
. Malton 676-3640
Airport Terminal 2
. Malton 676-3537
Island Airport 364-7967
Clearances-Imported Goods
Exhibitions&
Conventions . 966-8007
Highway Interport
. Cooksville 625-1085
Highway Midcontinent . 255-3475
Highway Toronto
Sufferance . 293-8253
Postal Packages-
Toronto . 369-4581
Postal Packages-West
Toronto . 769-1121
Rail&Marine 966-8036
Toronto International
Airport . Malton 676-3630
Customs Information
9 00 AM To 4 30 PM Mon-
Fri . 966-8022
All Other Times&Holidays
. Malton 676-3643
Excise
Information 966-6561
Audit 966-6585
Audit Offices
Centre 966-6303
East 494-9714
West 621-8341
Belleville ... 613 962-0581
Duty 966-6307
Collections 966-6085
Licensing 966-6083
TAXATION
Refund Inquiries 368-7431
Supplies Of Forms 369-4261
Tax Information
36 AdelaideE . 869-1500
French Language Service . 369-3704

S

SECRETARY OF STATE
Canadian Citizenship
Inquiries
55 StClairE 966-6424
1191 CawthraRd
. PortCredit 271-1793
Court
55 StClairE 966-6424

GOVERNMENT OF CANADA —Continued
NO CHARGE TO CALLING PARTY FOR
ZENITH OR '800' NUMBERS —Continued

Toronto Field Office
25 StClairE 966-6555
STATISTICS CANADA
Information
25 StClairE 966-6586
SUPPLY&SERVICES CANADA
Services
Inquiries 24 FerrandDr . 429-5009
Supply
Regional Supply Centre
295 TheWestMall 622-8111
Contracts-Tenders
295 TheWestMall 622-8111
Disposal Services
(CADC) . 966-6296
Printing
295 TheWestMall 622-8111

T

TASK FORCE ON SERVICE TO THE
PUBLIC
50 BloorW 966-5681
TRANSPORT CANADA
AIR TRANSPORTATION
ADMINISTRATION
Aircraft Accident
Investigation . 224-3445
Aircraft Noise Complaints
. Malton 676-4531
Aviation Safety 224-3193
Air Regulations
General Information . 224-3536
Instrument Rating Flight
Testing Appointments
. Malton 676-3061
Regional Aviation Medical
Officer . 224-3144
LICENCES
Aircraft 224-3237
Aeronautical
Engineering . 224-3124
Pilots 224-3124
Air Traffic Services
Branch . 224-3410
Construction Branch ... 224-3125
Project Tendering 224-3178
Telecommunications
Branch . 224-3449
TORONTO INTERNATIONAL AIRPORT
Airline Flight Information-See
Individual Airline In The
White Pages
Airport Administration
. Malton 676-3473

GOVERNMENT OF CANADA —Continued
NO CHARGE TO CALLING PARTY FOR
ZENITH OR '800' NUMBERS —Continued

Airport Information Counter
. Malton 676-3506
Area Control Centre
. Malton 676-3074
After Hours&Flight Planning
. Malton 676-3011
Aviation Weather Information
. Malton 676-3026
Flight Service Station
. Malton 676-3082
Implementation Team
. Malton 676-3006
Telecommunications Area
Manager . Malton 676-3080
Toronto Island Airport
Control Tower 369-4240
Buttonville Airport
Control Tower
. Unionville 477-6576
Unit Chief . Unionville 477-6747
Inquiries&General
Information . 224-3590
TRANSPORT CANADA
Public Affairs Office . 224-3426
Public Affairs . Malton 676-3580

V

VETERANS' AFFAIRS CANADA
Government Of Canada Pension
Commission
Sunnybrook Medical Centre
Non-Receipt Of War
Disability Pension
Cheques . 486-4748
Reporting Death Of War
Disability
Pensioners . 486-4747
War Disability Pension
Inquiries . 486-4742
Vet Craft Industries
60 Atlantic 531-7045
VETERANS' SERVICES
Toronto North Office
General Information
Office . 486-4724
Out Patients Office 486-3697
Transportation 486-4735
Supply Office 486-4515
Dental Clinic 486-4760
Toronto South Office
11 Front W
General Inquiries 369-4975
Field Services 369-4975

FOR SERVICES NOT LISTED ABOVE CALL . 362-6211

AFTER 5 PM& WEEKENDS&HOLIDAYS CALL . 923-1224

THINKING IT THROUGH

22. Which of the problems on the list might not be solved to your satisfaction, no matter how much help you had? Explain why.

THE INVESTIGATIVE REPORTER

23. Obtain a copy of your local telephone directory. Identify the number to call for the problems on the list which fall under the provincial or local government.

How are laws made?

As you have learned in an earlier part of this chapter, the part of the government which makes laws is known as the legislature. If the federal government wishes to raise taxes or increase prison sentences for violent criminals, it must first pass a law through Parliament. If the provincial government wishes to raise the legal drinking

A reading refers to the consideration of a bill at the various stages in the legislative process. In a parliamentary system, each bill receives three readings in each legislative chamber.

age, it must pass a law through the Legislative Assembly. In either case, the procedure for passing such a law is similar.

Most bills, as proposed laws are called, are thought up and written by the Cabinet. This group consists of the prime minister and a number of leading members of the government party. Having written up such a bill, the Cabinet then passes it on—or introduces it—to Parliament. If both houses of Parliament, the House of Commons and the Senate, approve of the bill, it goes to the Governor-General. This person, the representative of the Queen or King, signs the bill, and it becomes a law. Figure 9 shows in more detail the path from bill to law.

Fig. 9 How a bill becomes an act

1. Idea is discussed and approved by Cabinet. Made into a bill.

2. Bill is introduced to House of Commons. Members have chance to read its terms (first reading).

3. Bill is discussed and voted on in House of Commons (second reading).

4. House of Commons sends bill to a committee where it is examined in detail and necessary changes in wording are made.

5. Voted on, after which the Commons accepts or rejects the entire bill at the third reading.

6. Bill discussed and approved in Senate (usually automatically follows House of Commons).

7. Bill signed by Governor-General, on behalf of Crown.

8. When signed by the Governor-General, the bill becomes a law, unless otherwise indicated.

In a provincial Legislative Assembly, the procedure for making laws is almost identical. The only differences are that there is no Senate, so step 6 is omitted, and the Lieutenant-Governor is the representative of the Crown who signs the bill into law.

The most crucial stage in the House of Commons is the second reading. There are usually a large number of Members in attendance for this stage. They sit in their assigned places as in the diagram on the next page.

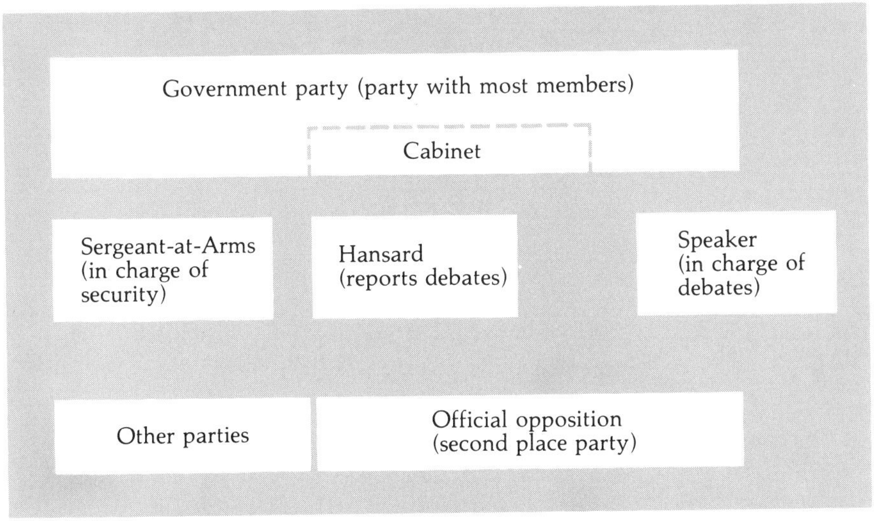

Fig. 10 **Floor plan of the House of Commons**

Government party (party with most members)
Cabinet

Sergeant-at-Arms (in charge of security)	Hansard (reports debates)	Speaker (in charge of debates)

Other parties	Official opposition (second place party)

Members of the government party generally support a bill, explaining why it is needed. Opposition party members sometimes support a bill, but more frequently speak against it. They hope that the bill will be defeated, in which case the government, by tradition, resigns. If the government party has more than half the seats in the Commons, this is unlikely to happen. Members are occasionally caught in a dilemma—their party expects them to vote one way, but their conscience might tell them to vote the other way.

The system generally works smoothly, however, and the passage of a bill into law can be achieved in a relatively short time if necessary.

GETTING THE FACTS

24. Add definitions of the following words to your dictionary of government terms: bill, Governor-General, Lieutenant-Governor. (You may want to look back at an earlier section of the chapter for information on the last two terms.)

USING YOUR KNOWLEDGE

25. In 1978, the Ontario government raised the legal drinking age from 18 to 19 years of age. On the next page, are a series of key dates in passing this new law. Also, in mixed-up order, are the key stages in passing the bill. Your task is to put the stages in their correct order. (Use the diagram "How a bill becomes an act" as your guide.) The stages will then match up with their correct dates.

413

Dates	Stages
April 25, 1978	Bill signed by Lieutenant-Governor on behalf of Crown.
May 25, 1978	
June 12, 1978	Cabinet gives approval to idea to raise legal drinking age to 19 years old. Writes up bill on subject.
June 15, 1978	
June 19, 1978	Changes made by committee approved by Legislative Assembly.
June 22, 1978	
June 24, 1978	Bill introduced to Legislative Assembly. Members have opportunity to learn its major terms.
	Committee asked to look at minor changes in wording of bill. Committee recommends some changes and returns bill to Legislative Assembly.
	Cabinet decides that bill will take effect from December 31, 1978.
	Legislative Assembly discusses and votes on bill, giving approval for it.

THINKING IT THROUGH

26. Imagine that you are an opposition party member. You are preparing to vote on a government party bill to increase prison sentences for violent criminals. There is a good chance that the bill will be defeated and that the government will be forced to resign. If an election were held, your party would become the government, you think. Your party expects you to vote against the bill in the hope of defeating the government. However, you personally support the idea behind the bill, believing it to be a sensible measure to control dangerous crime.

a) Make a list of the advantages of voting with the party. Then make a list of the problems that would occur.

b) How would you vote in this situation? Be sure to give reasons for your choice.

THE INVESTIGATIVE REPORTER

27. Write to the Clerk of the House of your provincial Legislative Assembly, requesting a copy of a recently passed law. Examine the law, especially any summary which may be attached to it.

a) What are the law's main terms?

b) Do you think this law is worthwhile? Why or why not?

Elections—High point in political life

Canada is a democracy. This means that its citizens have a choice about their government. Elections are held regularly, and if the voters do not approve of the actions and policies of the government, they can choose another group of people to be a new government. Normally, no federal government in this country may hold power for more than five years without calling an election. In practice, however, elections are held more frequently than this. In the 60 years between 1920 and 1980, 19 federal elections were held, or one every 3.25 years on average.

This refers to general elections, when there is an election in every riding. If an individual seat in Parliament becomes vacant through a member's death or retirement, what is known as a by-election takes place in that riding. In this way a replacement is found for the outgoing member.

Fig. 11 The national convention of the Liberal party in Ottawa, November, 1982. Why do political parties hold conventions?

Fig. 12 Ed Broadbent, leader of the New Democratic party, greets supporters and news reporters after his re-election to Parliament.

A dissolution [dihs-oh-LOO-shun] or ending of Parliament, which results in an election, may be granted by the Governor-General for one of three reasons. The five year period may have been reached, the prime minister may recommend holding a new election, or the government may have been outvoted in the House of Commons on an important bill. In any of these cases, the Governor-General will issue a document, called a Writ of Election, which authorizes the holding of an election all across Canada.

Canada is divided into 282 districts or ridings each with approximately 100 000 population. In each riding one representative is chosen to represent the voters in Parliament. You must be at least 18 years old and a Canadian citizen to vote in a federal election. In each riding, people (called enumerators) go around from door to door drawing up a list of those eligible to vote. At the same time, any person wishing to be a candidate in the election must notify the official (called the Returning Officer) responsible for running the election in the riding. Candidates must provide a form signed by ten eligible voters in the riding and a deposit of $200.

This deposit is returned to the winning candidate and all losers who obtain at least half as many votes as the winner. Its purpose is to discourage nuisance or joke candidates.

Any eligible voter may stand for election. There are three major parties—the Liberal party, the Progressive Conservative party and the New Democratic party. In each of the 282 ridings across the country, each party normally chooses one person to represent it, and the voters choose from among them. Candidates not representing one of these parties do not have much chance of being elected. In the 1980 federal election, for example, only one of the 282 people chosen by the voters did not represent a major party.

In the weeks before the election, the candidates make speeches and public appearances, while the parties advertise in newspapers and on radio and television. This period is known as the campaign, and most candidates and parties make promises about what they will do if they are elected.

On election day, the voter who goes to a voting station is given a form known as a ballot. This form contains the names of all registered candidates in that riding. The voter chooses one candidate from the list by marking an X in the circle beside the candidates' name. A ballot looks like this.

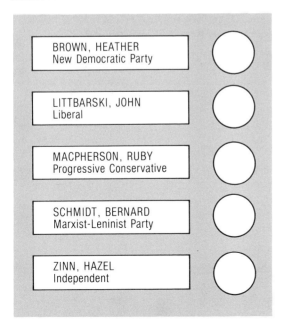

Each voter may choose only one candidate and vote only once. When voting is finished, the ballots are counted and the candidate receiving most votes wins. That person then becomes a member of the House of Commons for the riding.

Similar elections take place in all 282 ridings. These are divided up as shown in the chart in Figure 14.

Fig. 14 Distribution of ridings in Canada, 1981 election

PROVINCE/TERRITORY	NUMBER OF RIDINGS
Newfoundland and Labrador	7
Nova Scotia	11
New Brunswick	10
Prince Edward Island	4
Quebec	75
Ontario	95
Manitoba	14
Saskatchewan	14
Alberta	21
British Columbia	28
Yukon	1
Northwest Territories	2
Total	282

The division of ridings is based on population. Ontario has about 35 percent of Canada's population, and roughly the same percentage of ridings for the House of Commons.

The result of all 282 elections is determined, and the party winning the most elections, and therefore having the most members in the Commons, becomes the government. The second-place party becomes the official opposition.

Fig. 15 Results of federal elections 1962-1980

YEAR	LIBERALS	PROGRESSIVE CONSERVATIVES	NEW DEMOCRATIC PARTY	OTHERS*	TOTALS
1962	100	116	19	30	265
1963	129	95	17	24	265
1965	131	97	21	16	265
1968	155	72	22	15	264
1972	109	107	31	17	264
1974	141	95	16	12	264
1979	114	136	26	6	282
1980	146	103	32	1	282

*Others consists mainly of Social Credit party.

You will see from this chart that, as stated earlier, candidates of the three major parties have won a large percentage of all the seats available.

Elections cause enormous excitement across the land. For weeks before election day the candidates campaign relentlessly and the media cover the travels of the party leaders as they campaign from coast to coast. At no time is interest in the nation's political life higher.

GETTING THE FACTS

28. What are the three reasons which cause a general election?

29. a) What are the qualifications for voting in an election?

   b) What additional items must candidates produce to stand in an election?

   c) How is it decided which party has won an election?

USING YOUR KNOWLEDGE

30. Parties winning elections like to win over half the seats in the House of Commons. If they do, they have what is called a majority government. This means that the governing party can always out-vote the opposition parties on any matters in the House of Commons. Look at the "Results of federal election" chart. Which elections resulted in majority governments? Which ones resulted in the government having less than half the seats (minority governments)?

THINKING IT THROUGH

31. Look at Figure 18 "Canada's major political parties." For each of the following imaginary people explain which party you think they would vote for in an election and why they would vote for this party. If you cannot decide between two parties, state that the person might vote for either party, and explain what the deciding factor might be.

   a) a small business owner in Alberta, who feels that small business people are being squeezed out by large foreign-owned companies;

   b) the mayor of a medium-sized town in Ontario, who feels that the federal government should work strongly to prevent Quebec's separation from Canada;

   c) the managing director of a manufacturing company in British Columbia, who thinks that too much government regulation is strangling the business community;

   d) a university professor in Nova Scotia who feels that the richer people have a duty to help their poorer fellows;

   e) a member of the Legislative Assembly in New Brunswick, who feels that the provinces should be allowed greater freedom to deal with their own problems;

f) a newspaper editor in Saskatchewan who feels that Canadian newspapers need to be protected from growing Americanization;

g) a truck driver in Quebec who feels that the government should own all trucking firms and operate them in the interests of all Canadians;

h) a bank manager in Newfoundland, who feels that people with high incomes are not encouraged to invest their money in banks because of high taxes on interest payments;

i) a doctor in Manitoba who feels that the government should leave the business community to run its own affairs.

THE INVESTIGATIVE REPORTER

32. Write to the Elections Officer of your province's Legislative Assembly. Ask for a copy of the voting qualifications and candidates' qualifications for provincial elections. Are they the same as, or different from, federal election qualifications?

33. Ask the Elections Officer for recent provincial election results, perhaps for the last six elections.

What do politicians do?

Larry Grossman, who represents a Toronto riding in the Ontario Legislative Assembly, has been a member of the Ontario Cabinet since 1975. At the time he gave the following interview he was Minister of Industry and Tourism.

Fig. 16 Larry Grossman, member of the Ontario Cabinet, at work

What's a routine day like for you as a Cabinet minister?

Hectic! It begins around 08.30. I just set that as a rule in my house because I don't want to sacrifice my family life to politics. So I won't leave home until the kids have gone to school. Most of my colleagues have been in their office one hour by that time. They can get a good quiet hour's work done between 07.30 and 08.30.

SUNDAY DEC. 3.	MONDAY DEC. 4.
	09.00 Meetings with assistants to plan week
	10.00 Meeting of Ontario Busi- -13.30 ness Advisory Council
14.00 Asian Society open house	14.00 Legislative Assembly (question period)
15.00 St. Paul's Association Christmas party	15.30 Meeting with Toronto Multicultural Festival Committee
16.00 Progressive Conservative party	
17.00 Cocktail party	17.00 Reception for staff
18.00 Chinese community win- -19.30 ter festival	20.00 Legislative Assembly -22.30 (debate)

Fig. 17 **Weekly schedule of appointments for Larry Grossman**

At noon, almost invariably I'll have a speech to give, or I'll be having lunch to discuss business with someone, which means that noon is no time for a break at all.

The Legislative Assembly starts on Monday, Tuesday and Thursday at 14.00. Being a Minister, I have to be there for question period. That means I get there at around 13.45, and by the time I get back to my office, it's 15.45 or so. Then I have to catch up on my correspondence.

TUESDAY DEC. 5.	WEDNESDAY DEC. 6
08.30 Breakfast with premier	08.00 Breakfast with Toronto area caucus
10.00 Meeting of caucus	
11.00 Meeting with press officer on communications	09.30 Cabinet meeting -12.00
12.00 Address to management accountants of Canada	14.00 Cabinet meets with busi- -15.30 ness representatives from northern Ontario
14.00 Legislative Assembly (question period)	
15.30 Briefing on tourism	18.00 Premier's dinner for retir- -21.30 ing Governor-General
16.45 Interview with *Ottawa Citizen* newspaper	
20.00 Legislative Assembly -22.30 (debate)	

I try to get home for dinner almost every night, from 18.15 to 19.30. Then at 19.30 I'll be off out working again, giving a public speech or in the Legislative Assembly. Once a week I do a cable T.V. show, and that's Wednesday night gone if we do it live. I try to get into my riding office once a week, usually on Monday night. We'll go from 20.00 to 22.30 or so helping people with their problems. That sometimes carries through to weekends, though I do try to keep them free if possible, to spend time with my family.

You must ask yourself sometimes, why did I enter politics?

I didn't enjoy practising law. I had the feeling, sitting in my office, whether I'd been to court that day or handled a real estate transaction, there were a couple of thousand lawyers in the city who could have done the same thing. I didn't think I was changing things very much by what I was doing, so I decided to go into politics to try to change things.

THURSDAY DEC. 8.	FRIDAY DEC. 8.
07.30 Breakfast with caucus	08.45 Taping of cable T.V. show
09.00 Cabinet Committee on Resource Development	10.00 Legislative Assembly (question period)
11.00 Meeting to discuss Ontario trade missions to Europe	11.00 Legislative Assembly -13.00 (debate)
12.00 Lunch with assistant	13.00 Lunch with business leaders
13.40 Photo with school group	15.00 Meeting of Canadian Manufacturers' Association
14.00 Legislative Assembly (question period))	
15.30 Meeting with business group	16.30 Meeting with movie producers
16.00 Briefing on business environment	18.30 Muskoka Progressive -23.00 Conservative Association Christmas party
20.00 Committee to prepare -22.30 government spending plan, 1979-80	Overnight in Huntsville (150 km from Toronto)

What makes it all worthwhile is not all the media attention, which becomes quite routine, as does all the criticism you have to take. What makes it all worthwhile is when someone tells you they were helped by some little change you've made. I can remember, on occasion, going home and telling my wife about such an incident.

We're here to change things for better or worse. At the end of the process I can tell you I'll be able to walk out of government

having felt quite fulfilled. There are some frustrations, but I'll be able to look back and point to the ways I've affected people's lives in this province.

We sure aren't in it for the rubber chicken dinners we have to go to, the routine speeches we have to give, the car and driver that we get. At this point, at the end of the legislative session, I'm physically and mentally tapped right out. You're sure not in it just to see your name in the paper, because after the first couple of weeks it's just like anything else. You're really in it to make things a little better for some people out there, and you hope you did.

Responsibilities of the Hon. Larry Grossman

As a Member of the Legislative Assembly

—to speak in debates on bills
—to help people in his riding who have problems with the government or government programmes
—to answer enquiries from people in his riding about government matters
—to attend social gatherings in his riding to support good causes

As a Member of the Cabinet

—to answer questions in the Legislative Assembly on government bills and policies
—to help the Cabinet draw up new bills
—to ensure members of his party will support government bills and policies
—to help the Cabinet draw up plans for raising money (taxes) and spending it (government programmes)
—to communicate with the media to support government policy
—to meet with all groups having an interest in industry and tourism, and to hear their concerns
—to speak to groups about government policy and programmes

As a Member of the government

—to attend social gatherings as a representative of the government
—to represent Ontario at official functions (dinners, ceremonies, *etc.*)

GETTING THE FACTS

34. Examine Larry Grossman's schedule and list of responsibilities. Make a list of qualities which you think would be necessary to perform the job of M.P.P. and provincial Cabinet minister effectively.

35. In 1982, Larry Grossman received the following salary.

Basic salary for M.L.A.	$31 800
Tax-free allowance	10 600
Minister's allowance	23 000
Total	$65 400

Given this information and the details contained in the preceding section, do you think you would like the job of a Cabinet minister? Explain your reasons fully.

Conclusion

Fig. 18 Canada's major political parties

These "beliefs" have been traditionally connected with these parties, but party policies can and do change.

This chapter looked at how our government works and pointed out many ways government affects you now or might affect you in the future. How do you think you will be involved with our government as an adult? As a tax payer and an elector (voter)? As a civil servant or even a politician? You are one of the people who influences how our government works.

Liberal party believes in	Progressive Conservative party believes in	New Democratic party believes in
—a strong federal government which can overrule provincial interests and hold the country together	—greater provincial control of their own interests through federal-provincial agreements	—increasing harmony between federal and provincial governments
—Canadian control of Canadian resource, broadcast and financial interests	—less government regulation of the economy—for example, foreign ownership of Canadian business should be permitted as long as it is in our interest	—less foreign ownership of Canadian businesses
—higher taxes for richer persons and businesses than for less well-off ones	—lower taxes for higher-income persons, as too-high taxes reduce the desire to work hard	—increased taxes for richer persons and companies, lower taxes for poorer persons
—government ownership of some key businesses such as Air Canada or Petro-Canada	—less government-ownership and more private ownership of businesses	—more government ownership of companies

36. Members of Parliament are elected. Imagine they were hired for the job, and that people had to apply for it, and be interviewed for it.

Using the job advertisement below as a guide, and using the information in the interview to help you, make up an imaginary job advertisement for the position of Member of Parliament.

National Marketing Manager Chemical Products

Duties: To develop a sales team to sell our products across Canada. To establish a network to get our products to retail stores quickly and efficiently.

Qualifications: A university degree in chemistry or a similar subject. At least ten years' experience in sales. (Experience in the chemical industry would be helpful, but is not essential.) Some experience in a management position is a must.

The Candidate: To perform this job well, you will need to be able to inspire your sales team to work hard. You will need to be able to solve problems as they arise. You must be able to communicate with your sales team and customers properly.

The Rewards: We offer $40 000/year to start and the possibility of promotion for the future. We offer the opportunity to travel extensively in Canada. We offer a job which is challenging and satisfying.

Are you Interested? If so, write to us and tell us why you can do this job.

Now answer your job advertisement. Write a letter stating why you wish to apply for the job of M.P. Be sure to state what abilities you have to do the job well.

CANADIAN CHARTER OF RIGHTS AND FREEDOMS

Enforcem
24. (1) Anyone
Charter, have been
jurisdiction to obta
just in the circums
court concludes tha
denied any rights
shall be excluded
circumstances, th
administration o

Gener
25. The g
not be construe
other rights or
including (a) ar
Proclamation c

s and
ed by
ty.

eedom of
nd

m of

ion of
y and to be
s and no
om the date
mbers (a)

imprisonment for five years or a more severe punishment; (g) not to be found guilty on account of any act or omission unless, at the time of the act or omission, it constituted an offence under Canadian or international law or was criminal according to the general principles of law recognized b community of nations: (h) if final

legislature of New Brunswick shall be printed and published in English and French and both language versions are equally auth English or Fren

---

CHARTE CANADIENNE DES DROITS ET LIBERTÉS

Reco
24. (1)
ou libertés c
un tribunal
convenable
instance vis
preuve ont
ou libertés
écartés s'il
susceptib

Di
25
ne porte
autres —
libertés
ou libe
que la
une né
interp
prome
Canad

ui reconnaissent

ts et libertés qui
règle de droit,
ation puisse se
que.

) liberté de
nce, d'opinion et
tres moyens de
té d'association.

procès avec jury lorsque la peine maximale prévue pour l'infraction dont il est accusé est un emprisonnement de cinq ans ou une peine plus grave;) de ne pas être déclaré coupable en raison d'une action ou d'une omission

rendus et les procès-verbaux de la Législature du Nouveau-Brunswick sont imprimés et publiés en français et en anglais, les deux versions des lois ayant également force de loi et celles des autres documents ayant même valeur. 19. (1) Chacun a le droit d'employer le français ou l'anglais dans toutes les affaires dont sont saisis les tribunaux établis par le Parlement et dans tous les actes de procédure qui en découlent. (2) Chacun a le français ou l'anglais dans toutes les affaires dont dans tous les actes de

17 Can the Canadian constitution protect everyone's rights?

In December, 1981, Canada's government sent the above request to
Queen Elizabeth II. It went on to ask her to give Canada a new constitution which contained many new clauses to protect the rights of
its citizens. What observations can you make about the language of
the above request? Is it easy to understand? Why, or why not? Can
you think of any reasons why the request to the Queen was written
in this way?

On April 17, 1982, the Queen followed up on the request made
to her in December. She went to Ottawa, and on Parliament Hill
read the documents which gave the new constitution to Canada.
(The official name is the Constitution Act, 1982.)

The Queen's visit to Canada to sign the new constitution was
the final act in a long drama. Prime Minister Trudeau had made constitutional reform a top priority, right from the time he entered
office in 1968. But there were many disputes between the federal
and provincial governments over what changes were necessary.
Could the federal government draw up a new constitution itself? Or
was provincial agreement necessary? How many provinces would
have to agree with the federal government? Or could Quebec, by
refusing to agree to the new constitution, affect the prime minister's plans? These and other questions had to be ironed out.

In the end, only Quebec refused to go along with the new constitution, but the Supreme Court decided that this refusal should
not stop it from coming into effect. Most of the disagreements faded
into the background, however, and the Queen's presence as the new
constitution was signed into law was a happy and joyous affair for
Canadians.

Chapter overview

A nation's constitution, which is written by the government with the people's approval, is an important document. It describes the way in which the government will work, and what rights the people will have.

For 115 years, the British North America Act of 1867 was Canada's constitution. During this period, which you have read about, major changes took place in Canadian life. As a result by the early 1980s, there was a widespread feeling in Canada that a new constitution was needed. In April, 1982, such a constitution—known as the Constitution Act—was brought into effect.

The new constitution differs from the old one in many ways. One of its most important differences is that the Constitution Act contains guarantees of freedom of speech and religion, while the British North America Act did not. This does not mean that before 1982 Canadians did not have these rights—many of them did. But until 1982, these rights were not guaranteed by the constitution. This meant that citizens' rights could be removed by an act of Parliament. Since 1982, such rights can be removed only by amending or altering the constitution. This action requires the approval of the federal Parliament and at least seven provincial legislatures. Removal of citizens' rights is therefore much more difficult now.

Fig. 1 Signing the proclamation of the new constitution, April 17, 1982

The Constitution Act, 1982 guarantees certain rights to all citizens. For example, if an employer refuses to hire a person because that person is female or French-Canadian, it is considered illegal. The Constitution Act guarantees equal rights for all citizens, regardless of sex or ethnic group. Or, if a province passed a law preventing Indians from fishing on their reserves outside the fishing season, the law would have no effect. Indians are guaranteed this right by the Constitution Act. These guarantees remain in effect until the Constitution Act is changed—a difficult and time-consuming process.

In this chapter you will read about the concerns and demands of three groups—Native people, women and residents of the less wealthy provinces. You will look at what they want, and compare their demands with those rights guaranteed to them by the constitution. Finally, you will decide how effectively their rights are likely to be protected and how likely the various groups are to obtain what they want. At the end of the chapter you will be asked to decide which of the three groups you feel is in the best position to protect itself.

Signposts

What do Native people want?

Women, political life and the constitution

FEATURE: Flora MacDonald: Leading politician

Will the constitution help the less wealthy provinces?

FEATURE: Newfoundland's Brian Peckford

Key words

Inuit	affirmative action	transfer payments
Métis	unconstitutional	equalization
aboriginal rights	party convention	disparity

1867 — British North America Act (Canada's first constitution) passed

1972 — Flora MacDonald elected to Parliament

1979 -80 — Conservative government of Joe Clark
New constitution sent to Queen by federal government

1981 — Brian Peckford elected in Newfoundland

1982 — Queen signs new constitution

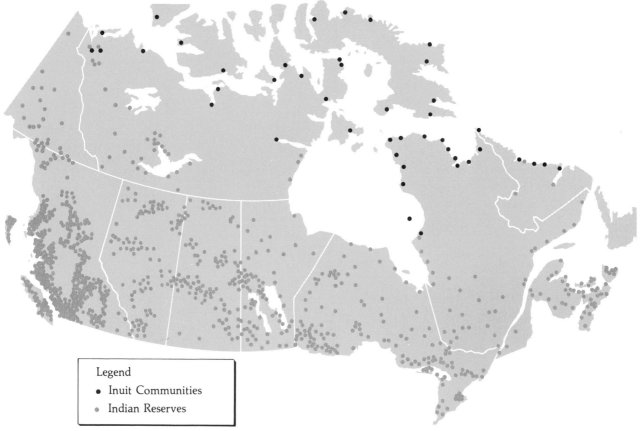

Legend
- Inuit Communities
- Indian Reserves

Fig. 2 Indian reserves and Inuit communities in Canada. Can you suggest areas in which land may be particularly valuable, or rich in resources? In which areas would the land probably be poor, with few natural resources?

Status Indians are those legally recognized as Indians by the federal government. They have the right to live on reserves. Non-status Indians are those who have Indian heritage but are not legally recognized by the federal government and may not live on reserves. These people are frequently only partially Indian.

What do Native people want?

The Native people of Canada may be divided into three groups— *Inuit, Métis* and *Indians*. The Indians are further divided into status and non-status Indians. As you can see, there are major divisions within the Native community. Each group has its own particular interests and problems, but this chapter will deal mainly with the Indians of Canada.

The Indians and the settlers of European descent, who arrived later, had many differences. Unlike European society, for example, many Indian nations did not believe in individual ownership of land. Everyone owned the land, and no one had the right to keep another person off a piece of land. Settlers arrived in Quebec in the 1690s, in Ontario in the 1780s and in the Prairie provinces in the 1850s. When the Europeans, mainly French and British, began to settle Canada, they brought with them their view of individual land ownership. In their view one person could buy and own land and build fences to keep others off it.

Fig. 3 The rights of Native peoples appear to be an important issue today. This picture shows a resources community advisor appointed to discuss the development of oil fields with the residents of Yellowknife. The advisor acts as a link between the oil company and the Indian Band Council.

Indian society rejected this view of land ownership, and agreements had to be worked out to prevent conflict. In their thinking, no one owned land in their society or could keep another person off it. Unfortunately for the Indians, they did not find out what the settlers' view of land ownership meant until it was too late.

In the Prairie provinces, during the 1870s, a series of treaties was drawn up between Canada's government and Indian representatives. Indians were to live on reserves where they retained the right to hunt and fish at will, while the rest of the land passed to Canada's government and eventually to private individuals. In other provinces, especially in the East and in British Columbia as well as in the N.W.T. and the Yukon, many Indians never signed treaties, although they too lived on reserves. Under our constitution, Indian affairs are the responsibility of the federal government. But the Indian groups have recently felt the need to have their rights fully guaranteed by the constitution.

In all provinces, however, Indian reserves tend to be on poor land with few natural resources.

The biggest single concern of Indian groups is that their aboriginal [ab-oh-RIHJ-ih-nul] rights be recognized. They believe that because they were the original people, they have a special claim to the land, which cannot be done away with by treaty or by government law. For example, they believe that hunting and fishing regulations should not apply to them, and that large areas of land, especially in the north, should be returned to them. On the following page, you will see what the Constitution Act says:

The Indian groups are
unhappy with this clause.
They feel that it is too vague,
and that the rights they
enjoy should be specified.

Part II

Rights of the Aboriginal Peoples of Canada.

35(1) The existing aboriginal and treaty rights of the aboriginal peoples of Canada are hereby recognized and affirmed.

(2) In this Act, "aboriginal peoples of Canada" includes the Indian, Inuit and Métis peoples of Canada.

Is this statement sufficient protection for Indians? Let us look at the activities of two Indian groups to see their views on the subject.

The National Indian Brotherhood

Indian bands living on
reserves have some degree of
self-government. Their Band
Councils pass by-laws which
must be obeyed by residents
while on the reserves.

The N.I.B. and its leader Del Riley have launched strong opposition against the Constitution Act. Their opposition was based on two factors. First, they believe it allows the federal government too much power to decide what rights Indians are entitled to. Secondly, they are alarmed that it gives the federal government power to amend or change those rights without consulting Native people.

The N.I.B. organized Native groups in all provinces to oppose the Act, and tried to put pressure on its federal government to change section 35 of the Act. The N.I.B. wanted the Act to spell out exactly what rights Native people have. When this failed, Riley and other N.I.B. leaders went to London. Since the treaties they had signed last century were made with the Crown through the British government and not the Canadian government, they hoped to persuade British courts of law to require that aboriginal rights be spelled out exactly and listed. This move failed and Indian rights remain vague in the Canada Act as section 35 shows.

In addition to the Indians, the
Inuit are trying to have their
special circumstances
recognized. They are
pressing the federal government to grant them a degree
of self-government. The
Dene people of the Yukon
would like to be recognized
as an independent nation.

Are Indian rights fully protected? The N.I.B. feels that they are not and its lawyers are keeping a close eye on future developments to make sure that the federal government does not try to remove or reduce Indians' aboriginal rights.

The Nootka Indians of British Columbia

In the spring of 1982, the Nootka Indians tried to earn their livelihood by catching and selling fish caught off British Columbia's coast. But they had a problem. The Nootkas, residents of Vancouver Island, do not have commercial fishing licences. They believe that, in the words of their leader Tom Sampson, "Our right to the produce of the seas has never been extinguished." In other words, they believe that their aboriginal

rights allow them to fish commercially without a licence.

This is not the view of the federal Fisheries Department. Dennis Duke, fisheries supervisor for the Victoria district, pointed out that the Nootkas risked penalties of up to $5000 under federal fisheries laws. The South Vancouver Island Tribal Council told Ottawa, "We have rights to take fish for food, barter [exchange] and sale, and from now on we are going to do it our way." Fisheries officials believe that the Nootkas' aboriginal rights only allow them to fish for personal, not commercial, purposes without a licence.

The Nootkas fear that the vagueness of section 35 of the Constitution Act does not fully spell out their rights. They are concerned that it guarantees them very little.

GETTING THE FACTS

1. In what way did the Indian view of land and its ownership differ from that of the European settlers who came to Canada?

2. Read section 35 of the Constitution Act, looking up difficult words in the dictionary. Rewrite section 35 in your own words, so that the meaning is clear.

3. What did the National Indian Brotherhood do to try to protect Indian rights? Was it successful? Explain.

4. How does the Nootka view of aboriginal rights to the sea differ from that of federal fisheries officials? Does section 35 of the Constitution Act make it clear which view is correct? Explain.

USING YOUR KNOWLEDGE

5. Why do you think section 35 is so general in its treatment of Native rights? Do you think it will protect those rights fully? Explain.

THE INVESTIGATIVE REPORTER

6. Contact a branch of the federal Department of Indian Affairs and Northern Development. Find out its views on the subject of aboriginal rights. Also, ask the question, "Does the department think that the new constitution is protecting those aboriginal rights?" Write up this information in a report.

7. Obtain the address of a Native peoples' organization in your area of the country. Contact it to find out its view on the subject of aboriginal rights. Try to find out particularly why Native people are unhappy with the phrase "existing aboriginal rights" used in section 35 of the Constitution Act.

Women, political life and the constitution

The British North America Act of 1867 had its name changed in 1982. It is now known as the Constitution Act.

The Governor-General shall, from time to time, in the Queen's name . . . summon qualified persons to the Senate: and . . . every person so summoned shall become and be a member of the Senate, and a Senator.

British North America Act, 1867, Section 24.

(We) have come to the conclusion that the word 'person', in section 24, includes members both of the male sex and the female sex . . . and that women are eligible to be summoned to and become members of the Senate of Canada.

Lord Chancellor, announcing court decision, 1929.

The machine age: Changes in industry and labour

Women received the right to vote in 1922, but at that time it was not expected that they would seek political office themselves.

You read about the fight to have women declared persons, and therefore to be able to take part in political life. For the first 62 years of Canada's existence, women were legally excluded from important aspects of political life, because the word person in the B.N.A. Act was interpreted to mean members of the male sex.

The difficulty was that our first constitution did not guarantee equal rights to men and women. This made it possible to deny the right to vote and run in elections to women, and still be within the law. Since women were limited, by the customs of society, to playing a domestic role, denial of political rights to women seemed logical to many people at that time. As women began to take on other roles, however, these denials became impossible to defend or justify.

After the historic court decision of 1929, women began to play a greater role in the nation's political life. For example, in 1957 Ellen Fairclough became the first female member of the Canadian Cabinet. Thereafter it became important that all prime ministers appoint women to their Cabinet. Despite this, women remained seriously under-represented in politics. It has been estimated that between 1921 and 1968, during which time 15 federal elections were held, only 2.4 percent of candidates were female, and only 0.8 percent of election winners were women.

In recent years, there have been many critics of this situation. Some believe that it was necessary to establish affirmative [a-FIR-ma-tihv] action programmes to increase the number of female representatives.

We recommend that two qualified women from each province be summoned to the Senate as seats become vacant, and that women continue to be summoned until a more equitable membership is achieved.

Recommendation of Royal Commission on the Status of Women, 1970

In other words, all or most Senate vacancies should have been filled by appointing women, until they made up half of its membership. As well, political parties at election time might have been required to

Fig. 4 Why do you think this poster was issued? Try to find similar posters published in your province. Your local library or the Ministry of Labour may be able to help.

Flora MacDonald: A leading politician

Flora MacDonald was born and brought up in Cape Breton, Nova Scotia. After graduating from high school, she went to secretarial college. Always fascinated by political life, she became a member of the Progressive Conservative party. She spent a few years in a variety of jobs but, in 1957, became Executive Secretary to the Progressive Conservative party in Ottawa. In this position she came to enjoy the cut-and-thrust of political life, and planned to become a Member of Parliament.

In 1972, MacDonald ran as Progressive Conservative candidate for Kingston and the Islands in the federal election. She defeated the sitting Liberal Member of Parliament to become Kingston's representative in Ottawa. She was re-elected in the elections of 1974, 1979 and 1980.

As a Member of Parliament she had to make a basic decision. Should she try to become a spokesperson for what are sometimes called women's issues? These include improving pay scales for jobs which are mainly held by women, and providing day care facilities for the children of working women. Or, should she concentrate on issues which are not specifically womens'—such as providing aid to poorer countries or working on Canada's relationship with foreign countries? MacDonald chose the second of these alternatives. She eventually became minister for External Affairs.

In 1976 the Progressive Conservative leader, Robert Stanfield, resigned. MacDonald decided to seek the leadership at a party convention [kuhn-VEHN-shuhn]. Sometime earlier, she was quoted as saying that women are not encouraged to be active in her party and she certainly did not run as a women's candidate. In her campaign speeches, she dealt with broad national and international issues. But in the first round of voting at the leadership convention she finished in sixth position. She withdrew her name from the race, and threw her support behind the eventual winner—Joe Clark of Alberta.

On May 22, 1979 the Progressive Conservative party won a federal election. Prime Minister Clark recognized MacDonald for her previous support by appointing her to his Cabinet. She was given the position of Minister of External Affairs, a senior position, where she was in charge of our relations with other countries. She performed these duties during the short life of Mr. Clark's government. After its defeat, in the election of 1980, she remained and still is a first rank member of the opposition with special interest in international relations.

GETTING THE FACTS

8. Make a chronological list of those events, with their dates, which you consider most significant in Flora MacDonald's life.

9. What issues does she seem to concentrate on?

THINKING IT THROUGH

10. Flora MacDonald decided to concentrate on political issues which concern most Canadians, male and female. Do you think that women politicians should concentrate on women's issues in their political life? Or should they treat such issues as merely another part of their political life—no more or less important than other issues? Discuss this in class.

ensure that half of the candidates were female. Simple as this solution sounds, before 1982, it might have been unconstitutional. It is legally impossible to discriminate against women, by denying them political representation because of gender. Similarly one could not discriminate legally in favour of them by appointing them to office simply because they were female.

The Constitution Act, of 1982, seems to have changed this.

15.(1) Every individual is equal before and under the law . . . without discrimination based on race, national or ethnic origin, colour, religion, sex, age or mental or physical disability.

(2) Subsection (1) does not preclude [prevent] any law, program or activity that has as its object the amelioration [a-mee-lee-oh-RAY-shuhn] of conditions of disadvantaged individuals or groups such as those listed.

Amelioration, in this context, refers to the *improvement* of conditions.

Constitution Act, 1982

Under the terms of this Act, no one may discriminate against individuals because of their sex, but one may give them special treatment (such as increased political representation) to overcome disadvantages they face.

After the 1974 federal election, only nine out of 265 Members of Parliament were women. After the 1981 Ontario provincial election, only six of 125 members of the Legislative Assembly were female. Will the Act, by eliminating discrimination but permitting affirmative action programmes, assist women to play a larger role in Canadian political life? It will take considerable time to know for certain.

GETTING THE FACTS

11. Make a timeline, showing the major events, decisions, reports and figures outlined in this section.

12. What are affirmative action programmes?

USING YOUR KNOWLEDGE

13. Compare section 24 of the British North America Act of 1867 with section 15 of the Constitution Act of 1982.
    a) What important differences do you observe?
    b) Suggest reasons for these differences.

14. Women make up half of the voters in Canada, but have supplied less than one percent of Members of Parliament since they first received the vote in 1922.
    a) What reasons can you think of to account for this?

b) Compare your reasons with those of a classmate of the opposite sex. Are your reasons generally similar or different?

THINKING IT THROUGH

15. Do you think that it would be fair to insist that half of the candidates in an election should be women? Do you think that this should apply even if there were more qualified male candidates than female ones? What are your reasons?

THE INVESTIGATIVE REPORTER

16. Do some research to find out about other women politicians who are active today. These might include Monique Begin, Jeanne Sauvé, Judy Erola or Iona Campagnola. You might also investigate the political life of Judy LaMarsh, who was a prominent member of Lester Pearson's Cabinets.

17. Write to the National Council for the Status of Women in Ottawa. Ask the Council for its views on the subject of affirmative action. Do you agree with its views? Explain your reasons.

18. Write to the Clerk of the House of your provincial legislature. Request a seating plan or membership list. How many members are women? Are they equally divided among all political parties? What conclusions can you draw from this?

19. This section has focussed on women in political life. Do some research on the changing roles of women in another part of society. (For example, what changes have taken place in attitudes towards women in the work force, women in the home, the portrayal of women in advertising?) Present your findings to a group of classmates.

Fig. 5 What do you think are the most important ways in which women's roles have changed since these suffragettes campaigned for their rights?

Will the constitution help the less wealthy provinces?
Newfoundland and Labrador as a test case

These provinces are sometimes called "have" provinces. The others are often called "have-not" provinces.

One of the features of modern Canada is that some provinces are significantly richer than others. In three provinces—British Columbia, Alberta and Ontario—the income of an average person is above that of the average Canadian. People of Quebec have incomes equivalent to that of Canadians as a whole. In the other six provinces, incomes are below the Canadian average. Newfoundland and Labrador is the poorest province of all as seen by the chart on the facing page.

Fig. 6 Comparisons for Canada, Alberta and Newfoundland, 1980

	CANADA	ALBERTA	NEWFOUNDLAND
Income per head of population	$7800	$9300	$5200
Unemployment rate	6.5%	3.2%	15.0%
Average % employment growth (1970-80)	3.1%	5.0%	3.5%
% of provincial government spending provided by federal government	———	18%	53%
Net movement of people, (1970-80)	———	180 000 GAIN	20 000 LOSS
Personal income as a % of Canadian average. (Including government benefits.)	100%	112%	68%

Canada Year Book 1981, 1982

You will see from this chart that Newfoundland and Labrador is behind the Canadian average in almost every category. Moreover, taxes are higher there than in other provinces. Its sales tax of 11 percent is the nation's highest, while Alberta does not have one. An Albertan earning $42 000/year will pay about $12 000/year in income tax. A Newfoundlander with the same income will pay about $14 500/year in income tax.

In general, the less wealthy provinces' problems are caused by small populations, lack of industries and small demand for their resources. (It is notable that our richest province—Ontario—has the largest population and the most industry.)

Through its *Department of Regional and Economic Expansion* (DREE) and other agencies, the federal government gives money or transfer payments, as they are called, to the less wealthy provinces in an attempt to raise their wealth. Total equalization payments to the seven provinces qualified to receive them have risen from $550 000 000 in 1967-8, to $2 300 000 000 in 1974-75 and $3 300 000 000 in 1980-1. While such payments undoubtedly assist these provinces, they cannot bring their income up to the national average, for this would be too costly. The constitution makes no guarantees of equalization, only a commitment to pursue it.

The seven provinces are Quebec, Manitoba, Saskatchewan, Nova Scotia, Prince Edward Island, New Brunswick and Newfoundland and Labrador.

In 1980-1, Quebec with its large population received the most—$1 720 000 000. Saskatchewan with its small population received the least—$40 000 000.

EQUALIZATION AND REGIONAL DISPARITIES

36 (1) The government of Canada and the provincial governments are committed to

(a) promoting equal opportunities for the well-being of Canadians

(b) furthering economic development to reduce disparity in opportunities; and

(c) providing essential public services of reasonable quality to all Canadians.

(2) Parliament and the government of Canada are committed to the principle of making equalization payments to ensure that provincial governments have sufficient revenues to provide reasonably comparable levels of public services at reasonable comparable levels of taxation.

Do you think that these guarantees are sufficient to raise the income of Newfoundland and Labrador to the national average? Its premier, Brian Peckford, does not think they can. He believes the answer to his province's problems is oil.

Fig. 7 Newfoundland and Labrador's potential oil and gas resource areas

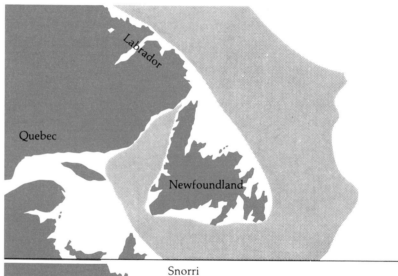

Fig. 8 Actual oil and gas sites offshore Newfoundland and Labrador, 1982

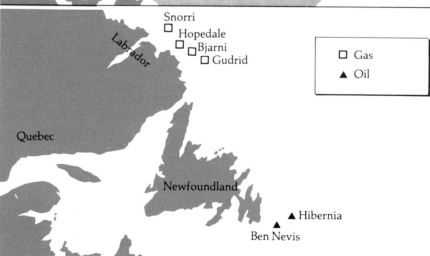

As the accompanying maps show, the areas around the Newfoundland coast are rich in oil deposits. At present many international oil companies are drilling for oil in the coastal waters of the province. But a disagreement has grown up between the provincial and federal governments over the question of oil and gas revenues. Both the federal and provincial government feel that they own the oil and gasfields. Therefore each government considers itself entitled to most of the taxes produced by the fields as they come on stream.

Many other provinces, such as Alberta and Nova Scotia, have been in dispute with the federal government over the question of sharing oil and gas revenues. As of 1982, Newfoundland and Labrador was the only province which had failed to reach an agreement with the federal government over this issue.

Fig. 9 Federal and Newfoundland positions on oil and gas revenues

FEDERAL POSITION	NEWFOUNDLAND POSITION
The Canada Act states that coastal waters are a federal responsibility. Since Newfoundland's oil and gas fields are in coastal waters they are subject to federal control. The Canada Act makes interprovincial trade a federal responsibility. Even if the oil and gas belonged to the province, any of it sold outside Newfoundland comes under federal control. The federal government is prepared to form a joint agency with Newfoundland to administer all aspects of oil and gas production. (A similar agency was set up with Nova Scotia in March 1982.) The federal government would appoint the majority of members to the agency, and it would be directly responsible to the federal minister of energy. Newfoundland would receive the same share of taxes from production as any other energy-producing province (roughly 55%). The deal would last for 42 years.	The oil and gas fields in question were not part of Canada until 1949. In other words, Newfoundland brought them into Confederation and if she left again she could clearly take them out. The fields therefore belong to the province, and must remain under its control. The province is prepared to form a joint agency with the federal government to oversee offshore oil and gas development. The province would appoint a majority of the agency's members, and would receive 75% of all taxes collected from production. When Newfoundland's average income reaches the level of Canada as a whole, its share of taxes would drop to that of any other energy province.

Fig. 10 Brian Peckford

In March 1982 Premier Peckford called a provincial election, using the energy issue as his main campaign item. On April 6, 1982 his Progressive Conservative government won a smashing victory over the Liberal opposition who support the federal position. This seemed to show that most Newfoundlanders feel that their Premier's views are correct. Peckford's second strategy was to take the

Fig. 11 Newfoundland fishermen mending their nets. Are oil and gas likely to be more profitable industries than fishing? Give reasons for your view.

whole issue to the Supreme Court, hoping that it would decide that the oil and gas belong to the province. At the time of his election victory the Court had not announced its decision, but if it adopts the position of Newfoundland and Labrador, the province may finally be on the road to prosperity.

GETTING THE FACTS

20. Write three sentences in your notebook, each of which shows how Newfoundland and Labrador is less well off than Alberta. Be sure that each sentence contains a statistic about both provinces.

21. Identify three major points on which the federal and Newfoundland and Labrador positions about offshore oil and gas differ. Be sure to state the position of each government on the issues. Write the positions in your notebook.

USING YOUR KNOWLEDGE

22. Read the extracts from the Canada Act which deal with equalization and regional disparities. Why do you think Premier Peckford would be dissatisfied with these clauses? Why would he think it necessary to make sure his province controls offshore oil and gas fields, rather than relying on constitutional guarantees?

THINKING IT THROUGH

23. Which position—the federal or Newfoundland and Labrador one—on offshore oil and gas reserves do you support? Explain your reasons fully.

THE INVESTIGATIVE REPORTER

24. a) Use the Canada Year Book or any similar publication to discover whether your province's average income is above or below the Canadian average. (If your province's income has been mentioned in the section you just read, look up the income of another province.)
    b) Suggest reasons for the income level you find.

442

Newfoundland's Brian Peckford

Born on August 27, 1942, Brian Peckford spent his early life in a series of coastal Newfoundland villages. His father was a social worker, and the family quickly became familiar with the problems of poverty and unemployment which plagued the province. Like many young Newfoundlanders, he felt that 20 years of membership in Canada had done little to improve the life of the average person on the island. By 1978, he was leader of the Progressive Conservative party and premier, a position he strengthened by election victories in 1979 and 1982.

Brian Peckford admits that he has little attachment to many parts of Canada, especially the urban sprawl of central Canada. But he is a fiercely proud Newfoundlander. And he is bitter that, despite its considerable natural wealth, Newfoundland and Labrador remains our poorest province. To a large extent, he feels the province has only itself to blame. He believes it has sold off its precious resources at bargain-basement prices and this has done little to raise provincial incomes. For example, an agreement with Quebec signed in the 1960s sells hydroelectric power cheaply to that province. Quebec in turn sells the power to New York State at a huge profit.

Peckford was overjoyed on March 5, 1982 when the Newfoundland Supreme Court made a ruling which may lead to the agreement's being renegotiated to give Newfoundland and Labrador better treatment. He sees the offshore oil and gas fields almost as his province's last chance. He fears that unless it gets a large share of the revenue from the fields, Newfoundland and Labrador will resemble a chronically-ill hospital patient— there will be no hope for an end to its poverty and unemployment.

During the election campaign, Peckford kept the issues simple. JOBS AND A FUTURE was one of the bumper sticker slogans he handed out. A MANDATE TO NEGOTIATE, referring to the need for an oil and gas agreement with the federal government was another. He toured the province by helicopter and car, making speeches about the need to obtain a favourable agreement. The federal government's Energy Minister, Marc Lalonde, accused Peckford of telling "outright lies" about the federal position on oil and gas. But it made no difference. An unusually high percentage of the province's voters cast their ballots in the election, and Peckford's party won again 44 seats to 8.

The patience of Newfoundlanders is wearing thin. A generation after their entry into Canada, they still lag behind in economic development. They feel their problems must be solved soon or the issues will simply be forgotten. In this regard, the impatient and aggressive manner of Peckford seems ideally suited to the mood and demands of the people.

GETTING THE FACTS

25. According to Peckford, why is it that the economic development of Newfoundland and Labrador lags behind the rest of Canada?

THE INVESTIGATIVE REPORTER

26. Obtain copies of books, magazines and newspapers dealing with Newfoundland's economic problems. What developments have taken place since this feature was written (April 1982)? Do these developments seem to have strengthened or weakened Premier Peckford's and his province's position?

27. Obtain publications about offshore oil and gas fields, published by the federal government. (The Department of Energy, Mines and Resources is the department of government responsible for this.) How do federal government views of the issue differ from those of Brian Peckford? Whose views do you support? Why?

Fig. 12 An oil rig off the
coast of Newfoundland.
What do you think it would
be like to work on an oil rig?

Conclusion

Make a copy of the following chart in your notebook.

GROUP	DETAILS OF PROBLEMS/ DEMANDS	WHAT CONSTITUTION SAYS ABOUT EACH GROUP AND ITS PROBLEMS/DEMANDS (YOUR OWN WORDS)	RECENT DEVELOPMENTS (See question 29)
INDIANS			
WOMEN			
NEWFOUNDLAND			

GETTING THE FACTS

28. Review this chapter and the notes you have made on it. Fill in the first two columns of the chart.

THINKING IT THROUGH

29. a) Obtain and study recent newspaper and magazine articles about each group. What recent developments have taken place concerning each group? Summarize these in the third column of this chart.

b) Which of the three groups do you feel is guaranteed the most by the constitution? Which group is guaranteed the least? Explain.

30. Having studied the groups, their problems, the constitutional guarantees and recent developments, which group do you think will most easily solve its problem? Which group will have the most difficulty? Explain.

18 The limits to growth

446

A typical conversation

Petar: Granola bars just went up again. I only have a dollar left after the weekend.

Sonja: I know. A small orange juice is about 55¢ in most places now. With a dollar I couldn't get us both one. Not that I'm offering you one, understand?

Petar: Do you remember when they were less than 50¢ each?

Sonja: Sure. It was just last summer. You could buy a granola bar and an orange juice, and get a nickel's change from a dollar.

Petar: Prices are getting ridiculous, but what can you do about it?

Sonja: Well, we could ask to get our wages from our part-time jobs tied to the cost of living.

Petar: Huh?

Sonja: Well, instead of getting a certain amount an hour, say a dollar, we'd get enough to buy a granola bar, an orange juice and have 15¢ left over.

Petar: So if they went up in price, so would our wages?

Sonja: Right. If they went to a dollar each, we'd get $2.15. If they only went to 75¢, we'd get $1.65.

Petar: Great idea. How do you think the boss will go for it?

Sonja: I'm not sure. But it's the only way you and I can stay ahead of rising prices.

- Does it sound as though Petar and Sonja expect prices to rise or fall? Why do they feel this way? What is their plan to protect themselves from rising prices?

- Do you think their plan is a good one? What are your reasons? Do you think their employers will agree to the plan? What are your reasons?

- As prices go up, fewer people can afford to pay them. Sales of granola bars and orange juice may go down. Manufacturers may be unwilling to raise prices if sales will be badly hurt. If Petar and Sonja and everyone else have more money to spend, will manufacturers be more or less willing to raise prices? What is likely to be the effect on prices of giving everyone more money to spend. Is Petar's and Sonja's plan a good one for everyone? Why or why not?

Chapter overview

In 1967, Canada celebrated its one hundredth birthday as an independent nation. All kinds of festivities were held to mark this historic occasion, the most famous of which was Expo '67 in Montreal.

Generally Canadians were optimistic about the future. High wages and stable living costs had increased the wealth of most people. Energy was cheap and plentiful—gasoline cost around 11¢/L and the price was steady. Unemployment was low, and the economy was growing as the value of production increased steadily. The future looked bright.

Fifteen years later all this had changed. Shortages of fuel and continual price increases were accepted as normal. Prices were rising faster than wages so that people were becoming worse off—the standard of living was falling. Unemployment was high, and the economy was growing very slowly. Forecasts suggested things would get worse. The optimism of the 1960s was replaced by uncertainty and even fear. The following chart illustrates some of these changes:

Fig. 1 Canada's economic performance, 1967, 1973, 1980, 1982

	1967	1973	1980	1982
Rate of inflation	4.0%	9.1%	11.5%	10.9%
Unemployment rate	3.8%	5.5%	7.6%	11.0%
Real growth rate for economy	5.8%	3.5%	2.1%	−4.8%

As you can see, inflation and unemployment climbed steadily, and the growth of the economy became slower.

In this chapter you will read about some of the problems which emerged in Canada during this period. You will learn how people came to recognize that we could not continue to become richer every year, burn more fuel, drive bigger cars, have more jobs and more economic growth than ever before. In short, you will learn about the limits to growth from which Canada could not escape.

Signposts

Energy supplies: A confusing picture >

The problem of unemployment >

Strikes: What do they achieve? >

Timeline:

- 1935
- General Motors workers strike
- 1940
- 1945 — United Auto Workers win union guarantees after 99 day strike
- 1946 — Striking workers win major gains at Asbestos, Quebec
- 1956 — United Auto Workers' strike wins unemployment benefits for laid-off workers at General Motors plants in Ontario
- 1967 — Centennial Year Canadian optimism about future
- 1973 — Middle East countries raise oil prices from $2.10 to $7.75 per barrel
- 1981 — Federal election results show major regional splits (February) Fourth postal strike in 10 years shuts down postal system (July)

FEATURE: Declining productivity: Canada's disease >

Regionalism in Canada: Division in the land >

Key words

economy	Consumer Price Index
standard of living	Unemployment Insurance Programme
OPEC	productivity
inflation	incentive
interest	subsidies

Rate of inflation means the percentage which prices rose that year. If a car costs $10 000 this year and $11 000 next year, its inflation rate is 10 percent. (The $1000 increase is 10 percent of $10 000.)

Unemployment rate means the percentage of the working population unable to find work.

Real growth rate for economy means the percentage increase in goods and services (such as doctors' consultations or babysitting appointments) produced that year. The negative figure for real growth rate in 1982 (–4.8%) means that the economy actually got smaller in that year.

Energy supplies: A confusing future

It seems hard to believe now, but in the summer of 1973, you could buy a litre of regular gasoline in most parts of Canada for 12¢. Later in 1973 the OPEC oil-producing nations increased the price of crude oil from which gasoline is refined. These nations had to pay higher prices for the manufactured goods which they imported, so they

Fig. 2 Where your money goes when you buy a dollar's worth of gasoline.

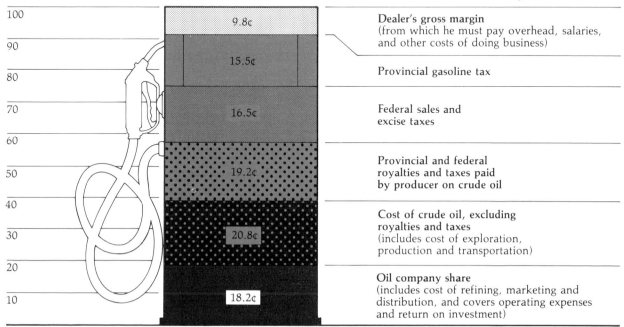

9.8¢	Dealer's gross margin (from which he must pay overhead, salaries, and other costs of doing business)
15.5¢	Provincial gasoline tax
16.5¢	Federal sales and excise taxes
19.2¢	Provincial and federal royalties and taxes paid by producer on crude oil
20.8¢	Cost of crude oil, excluding royalties and taxes (includes cost of exploration, production and transportation)
18.2¢	Oil company share (includes cost of refining, marketing and distribution, and covers operating expenses and return on investment)

These figures are based on retail pump price of 29.7¢/litre of regular gasoline in December 1980

449

Fig. 3 Demand for fuels in Canada

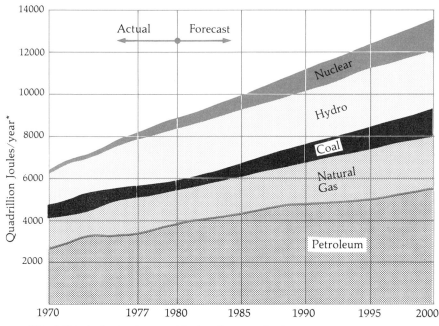

* Quadrillion Joules is a term used to describe amounts of energy

Oil is usually measured in barrels. A barrel contains approximately 159 L.

Oil equivalent means the amount of oil we would consume if all our energy requirements came from oil. In fact much of our energy consumption is in the form of gas, coal, hydro, and nuclear power.

raised crude oil prices. Increase followed increase. A barrel of oil which sold in 1973 for about $2.10 U.S. was worth over $35 U.S. eight years later.

As a result of these increases by OPEC nations, other nations raised the price of their crude oil. Everywhere there were enormous increases in price for items made from oil, particularly fuels and plastic products. In some ways, Canadians were better off than consumers in other countries. While we complained that gasoline cost around 38¢/L in the summer of 1981, people in Britain were paying 82¢. Because our climate is harsher than Britain's, and because the distances we travel between cities are larger, we naturally consume more oil than the British do. Yet oil products like gasoline and home heating fuel have been relatively cheap in Canada, and we also have tended to waste them. In 1978 each resident of Britain consumed the equivalent of 3.8 tonnes of oil. Each Canadian consumed 8.7 tonnes of oil.

Although we pay more than we used to, we still buy oil products relatively cheaply, and we still consume oil at a great rate. Is there an energy crisis? Let us see what two people might say on this subject.

| AN OIL-INDUSTRY REPRESENTATIVE | A GROUP REPRESENTING CONSUMERS |

Q. Is there an energy crisis?

A. Yes. The world is running out of cheaper oil and gas. New sources of oil and gas will be more expensive than present ones. Companies will not seek them without higher prices. Unless we accept the need to secure expensive oil and gas, we are in danger of running out, because new sources will not be brought into production.

There is an oil and gas crisis. We are too dependent on them for energy. Yet we have vast sources of hydro power and can develop other sources of energy as well. An oil and gas crisis—yes. An energy crisis—no.

Q. Why have energy prices risen so much recently?

A. As we run out of our normal supplies, mainly in the south of Alberta and Saskatchewan, we have to open up new oil and gas fields. Although there are huge supplies in the Arctic and northern Alberta tar sands, they are expensive to develop. Unless prices rise, companies will not be able to afford to develop and sell these new supplies and we will run out.

We have relied too much on oil and gas. We are at the mercy of companies who wish to raise prices to increase profits because we have not developed other energy sources enough.

Fig. 4 What would happen to oil refineries like this if the supply of oil runs out?

Q. What should we do in the future?

A. Two things. First we should do as much as possible to conserve. By car pooling, taking the bus and lowering thermostats, we can reduce our consumption. Secondly, we must accept higher prices. These are necessary to make sure new sources are brought into production, and make us secure in our energy supply.

Conserve like crazy! Any way we reduce oil and gas consumption will help. And we must rely far more on wind, solar, hydrogen and tidal power. Instead of wasting money on new oil and gas fields, we should use that money to develop other sources.

Q. Can sources other than oil and gas help?

A. Unfortunately, at present levels of technology, it is doubtful whether they can supply much of our huge energy requirements. It will take at least a generation to develop our technology to this point.

Yes. if we spend money on these sources, we can be free of our reliance on our declining supplies of oil and gas. Let's start now and not wait a generation to solve this problem.

Fig. 5 To what extent can windmills or solar panels provide alternative sources of energy?

The future is confusing. Answers to questions vary enormously. Prices will probably continue to rise over the years. Canadians are unlikely ever again to enjoy the old 'gas-guzzling' habits.

GETTING THE FACTS

1. Why did gas prices rise in 1973?

2. What does OPEC stand for? What is it?

3. Name one way Canada was better off than some other countries after the price hike on oil and gas. Name one way Canada was worse off.

4. Examine the answers of the two representatives to the questions. Make a list of things on which they agree, and a list of things on which they disagree.

USING YOUR KNOWLEDGE

5. Compare the lists you drew up in question 4. Which one is longer? Why?

6. Study the graph in Figure 3 which forecasts demand for energy in Canada and the sources it will come from.

  a) What conclusions can you reach about energy consumption from this graph?

  b) Read the answers to the last question in the interview

above. Which representative—oil industry or consumers' group—would be most likely to agree with the chart's forecast of the future? Explain.

THE INVESTIGATIVE REPORTER

7. Study the chart in Figure 2. Some people charge that the "energy crisis" has been deliberately thought up by oil companies to raise prices and increase profits.

a) Looking at the chart, do you think that the oil companies make a fair or an unfair profit?

b) Find out and record in a chart how much or how little other businesses (such as banks or department stores) make in profits. Compare these with oil company profits. Does this make you want to change your answer to part (a)? Explain.

8. Having read this material, do you think we are facing an energy crisis? Explain.

a) Examine the graph in Figure 3. How much will our demand increase in the rest of this century?

b) Using books, newspapers or magazine articles, find some recent figures about energy supply in Canada. Does it look as though we will be able to increase supplies to keep up with demand? Write a one-page answer and use the statistics found in your text and in your research to back up your statements.

The problem of unemployment

NEW GOVERNMENT PROGRAMME WILL SPEND $113 000 000 FOR UNEMPLOYED

—Newspaper headline

This headline suggests that the federal government in Ottawa is concerned about unemployment. The Canadian government tries to create jobs by employing more people in government jobs or by giving money to companies to help them employ more workers. In this way, as more people find work, the federal government will have to pay less money to unemployed people through its Unemployment Insurance Programme.

If you look at the history of Canada's trade and business over the past 50 years, you will notice two important facts. First, there has been much growth in our economy—we produce more cars, wheat and just about everything else than 50 or 20 years ago. Second, this growth has been uneven. The chart in Figure 6 shows this.

Fig. 6 The value of all goods and services produced in Canada, 1960-80

YEAR	$ DOLLARS
1960	53 000 000
1962	58 500 000
1964	65 600 000
1966	74 800 000
1968	81 900 000
1970	88 400 000
1972	100 200 000
1974	111 700 000
1976	119 100 000
1978	126 100 000
1980	130 400 000

As prices go up, it looks as though production is going up too, when in fact the number of goods produced remains the same. This chart therefore removes inflation from the figures.

Fig. 7 A massive demonstration held in Ottawa in October, 1981. The demonstrators were protesting against government policies which they felt led to unemployment. Do you think such demonstrations do any good?

Canada's economy is greatly affected by developments in other countries, especially the United States. If demand for Canadian goods declines there, for example, through no fault of our own, this will tend to create unemployment in Canada.

Many things cause the economy to speed up and to slow down. Consider the following events and ask yourself whether they would reduce or increase the number of jobs. Whom would they affect the most?

a) Because of increased travel costs, fewer Canadians can afford mid-winter holidays in the sunny south.

b) A Canadian company in Ottawa is chosen to supply navigation equipment for a new American airplane.

c) An Ontario nickel company can produce nickel more cheaply in Guatemala, Central America, and shifts 30 percent of its Canadian production there.

d) An unusually severe winter stops all outside building activity for three months.

e) Canadians decide to trade in their "gas guzzlers" and go on a spree for efficient cars.

f) A bumper crop of peaches, the highest on record, is produced in British Columbia's peach orchards.

g) New word-processing machines can type letters and other material at half the cost of usual methods.

h) Canadians from eastern Canada quit their jobs and move to western Canada in search of more opportunity.

i) Demand for North American cars falls as consumers buy Japanese models in greater numbers.

j) A strike by major league baseball players in the summer of 1981 resulted in the cancellation of many games.

k) The development of cheaper plastic containers has resulted in reduced demand for old-fashioned glass bottles and jars.

Unemployment can be divided into a number of types. There is seasonal unemployment—some jobs are only available at certain times of year. There is technological unemployment—sometimes new methods of producing goods with machines replace humans in the work force. There is cyclical [SIH-klih-kahl] unemployment—demand for certain items decreases owing to changes in the public's taste, or its ability to pay for goods. There is frictional unemployment—some people are between jobs and therefore unemployed for a brief period.

With so many types of unemployment, it is difficult to get rid of the problem entirely. New technology may be providing jobs in factories producing goods, while the same technology is replacing someone in another factory with a machine.

Unemployment is a large problem in Canada at present, and although all political parties wish to end it, our progress in this area is slow.

GETTING THE FACTS

9. Make a line graph to show the information contained in Figure 6. When did the value of all our goods and services rise slowly? When did it rise the most? Is the overall pattern up or down?

10. Name four types of unemployment and explain what each is in your own words.

11. How does the existence of four types of unemployment make the problem more difficult to solve?

USING YOUR KNOWLEDGE

12. Read the events (a) to (k) listed earlier on. Make a copy of the following chart.

REDUCE EMPLOYMENT	INCREASE EMPLOYMENT
a) Fewer holidays in sunny south (travel industry)	

Place each event on the chart in its proper place and in brackets those most affected. To start you off, point (a) has already been put on the chart for you.

13. Copy each event which you put on the left side of the previous chart on the left side of this chart. Opposite each event, write in which of the four types of unemployment it is. Point (a) has already been put on the chart for you.

EVENT	AN EXAMPLE OF
a) Fewer holidays in sunny south (travel industry)	cyclical unemployment

THINKING IT THROUGH

14. There are no simple solutions to the complex problem of unemployment. However, the problem could be reduced. Suggest three ways you think unemployment can best be reduced. Explain your reasons for each choice. Compare and discuss your choices with your classmates.

Strikes: What do they achieve?

When we compare our strike record with that of major industrial countries, the result is surprising.

Fig. 8 Work days lost through strikes, 1978

COUNTRY	POPULATION	WORK DAYS LOST THROUGH STRIKES
Canada	23 000 000	7 400 000
West Germany	64 000 000	4 300 000
France	54 000 000	2 200 000
Japan	110 000 000	1 300 000
Sweden	9 000 000	37 135
United States	217 000 000	36 900 000

If 1000 workers strike for 10 days, this would result in 10 000 (1000 X 10 = 10 000) work days lost.

Canada is a leader in work days lost. In the late 1970s only Italy lost more work days for each worker through strikes than Canada did.

Unfortunately, merely removing the legal right to strike is no solution. It removes the power which employees have to back up their requests for improved wages, working conditions, medical benefits, etc., and replaces it with nothing else. Other methods are sometimes tried. In arbitration, a neutral third party decides on all issues in dispute between an employer and the employees. In mediation, a neutral third party meets with both sides and tries to get them to agree. Both employers and employees are often uneasy

456

about such systems, feeling that they reduce individual powers. As a result, both sides often agree to mediation or arbitration only after a strike, when negotiation between employers and workers has failed.

The Canadian public, frequently trapped in the middle of labour disputes, becomes increasingly frustrated. The question is asked more often. What do strikes achieve? It is true that most strikes cause hardship to employers, workers and customers alike. Yet many important rights, perhaps taken for granted by most workers today, have been won by Canadian workers only after bitter strikes.

The major goal of many early strikes was union recognition. This meant that union supporters wanted managers to recognize a labour union as the representative of all workers employed by a company. At first, managers were unwilling to give this recognition. By the late 1940s, however, union recognition had been won in many industries. From then on, unions were able to bargain with managers to gain higher wages and protection from unsafe or unhealthy working conditions.

The following chart summarizes some of the important strikes in Canadian labour history and what they achieved. (Many of these strikes took place in Ontario and Quebec, since much of our nation's industry is centred there. Please remember that these cases have been simplified in order to fit the chart format.)

Fig. 10 Major achievements won through strikes

STRIKE LOCATION AND DETAILS	CONDITIONS BEFORE STRIKE	CONDITIONS AFTER STRIKE
Workers strike at General Motors plants in Oshawa, Ontario, 1937. Strike lasts 18 days.	All workers suspected by employers of belonging to union are fired. Union activities on GM property impossible.	Workers win right to belong to union without being fired. Union activities outside work hours on GM property allowed.
Union members (United Automobile Workers) at Ford plants in Windsor, Ontario strike, 1945. Strike lasts 99 days.	Although majority of workers belong to union, payment of fees ("dues") to union voluntary. This encourages "freeloaders" who enjoy benefits won by union, but do not pay for them or support union.	All employees must have union membership fees deducted from wages and given to union by employer. Union membership not compulsory, but non-members must have deduction made from wages. (This system is known as the "Rand formula.")
Steelworkers strike at Stelco plants, Hamilton, Ontario, 1946.	"Open shop" (workers may belong to union but not compulsory, even though majority of workers favour union).	"Closed shop" (all workers must belong to union unless majority opposed to union membership).
Asbestos workers strike at Canadian Johns-Manville mines, Asbestos, Quebec, 1946. Strike involves much violence, by police and strikers. It is finally settled, after 5 months, because of involvement of Roman Catholic Church in bringing workers and employers together.	Union membership not compulsory. No overtime pay for weekend work.	Union recognized by employers. Increased wages for shift work and overtime.
United Automobile Workers strike, General Motors plants in Ontario, 1956.	Workers laid off by company when business is bad suffer complete loss of pay. They have no security against sudden losses of pay because of unemployment.	Workers win right to receive "Supplementary Unemployment Benefits" during lay-offs. This gave laid-off workers up to 65 percent of normal take-home pay for up to six months.

After these important victories, labour unions were able to improve pay and working conditions of their members by bargaining with managers. Gradually, the standard of living of workers belonging to a union rose. By the early 1970s, Canada's industrial workers were the second-highest paid in the world. Only U.S. workers were better off.

Some people, mainly those outside labour unions, felt that future strikes were unnecessary. They argued that strikes did too much harm to business and industry, and the benefits won for workers were too small to justify striking. Let us examine a recent Canadian strike to see whether or not this is true. The chart on the next page refers to the postal workers strike of 1981.

Fig. 11 Do you think striking workers value the support of other unions? Why?

Fig. 12 Benefits won by Canadian postal workers, 1981

ITEM	BEFORE STRIKE	AFTER STRIKE
Pay	Most clerks earned $9.33/hour.	Most clerks earned $10.03/hour.
Annual holidays	Four weeks after 10 years employment. Three weeks for less than 10 years.	Four weeks after 8 years. Three weeks for less than 8 years.
Statutory holidays	Eleven days per year, such as Christmas Day, Boxing Day, etc.	No change. (Union had wanted one additional day on January 2.)
Maternity leave	17 weeks leave without pay. After 2 weeks, unemployment fund paid 2/3 regular wages.	17 weeks leave at 93 percent pay paid by Post Office.

To decide whether or not the strike was justified, we must look at the cost to Canada, and compare this with the benefits won by the postal workers. The chart on the next page examines the cost of the strike.

Fig. 13 The known cost of the strike

Postal workers	An average of $2239 in lost wages.
Postal system	Loss of revenue, perhaps $1 000 000/day. Some customers were lost permanently, as businesses switched to more expensive private couriers.
Business losses	A business organization—the Canadian Manufacturers' Association—estimated lost business sales at $7 000 000/day for the 42 day strike, for a total of $294 000 000.
The public	Impossible to estimate in dollars. Massive inconvenience during 42-day shutdown of service.

The whole question is a difficult one. Should a worker put up with what he or she considers unjust conditions simply because a strike might hurt other businesses and other people? Should innocent customers of a business suffer because workers and managers cannot reach agreements through discussion? These are important questions which most of us must eventually answer as business customers, managers or unionized workers.

GETTING THE FACTS

15. Explain the following processes: mediation, arbitration. Why are employers and employees often uneasy with these processes?

THINKING IT THROUGH

16. Strikes are considered to be a way of protecting employees. Select two strikes listed in Figure 10, "Major achievements won through strikes."
   a) What did employees gain?
   b) What were some probable hardships suffered by the employees, customers or other people connected with the industries you selected?
   c) In your opinion, were the strikes worthwhile? Explain.

17. Make a list of arguments in support of strikes. Then list as many arguments as you can against strikes. Select those three arguments from each side which you think are most important. Write a short essay entitled "Are Strikes Justified?" Be sure to examine both sides of the issue. Then, in a concluding paragraph, state your opinion and back it up with reasons.

18. If you had the power to make strikes illegal and to replace them with a system which was fair to employees, employers and the public, what would you replace them with? Describe the things you would do to try to ensure fairness to all.

Declining productivity: Canada's disease

In a Canadian automobile plant, almost three times as many hours of labour are required to build a car as compared to a Japanese factory. Japanese factories are therefore said to be almost three times as productive as Canadian factories. Similarly, many of the most popular clothes in Canada are made in Hong Kong, Taiwan or elsewhere in the Far East where labour costs are lower and each worker produces more articles than a Canadian worker.

Low productivity makes our goods expensive and hurts our exports. In 1978,

Fig. 14 Do we need to increase productivity, or are our markets flooded?

Canada's industries were producing about 88 percent of the goods they could make when run at top capacity. At this rate, each item is more expensive to produce than if the factory were running at capacity.

Why is our productivity so low? There are a variety of reasons including the following.

Absenteeism from work is high, and adds over $7 000 000 000 to our industrial costs (1980 figure).

Our factories are older, have fewer robots than our competitors, and rely on old-fashioned techniques.

Most Canadian workers receive a fixed hourly wage, and have no incentive to work harder.

Energy costs in Canada are low, and do not provide an incentive to find more efficient methods. Japan, for instance, pays high energy prices and its factories burn fuel far more efficiently.

Most Canadian workers work a 40-hour week and must be paid at higher rates for overtime. In Japan, a 50-hour week is not uncommon.

In Canada, managers often regard suggestions from workers as interference. In Japan, suggestions are encouraged, and often increase productivity.

Is higher productivity the answer to our economic problems?

YES. Unless we can improve our productivity, we will lose important markets abroad, and buy more imports at home. If we cannot make our factories more efficient, it will cost us more to produce clothing or automobiles, for example. Other countries will step in and

sell their goods more cheaply than we can, in Europe, South America and elsewhere. As we export fewer goods than before, companies will be forced to lay people off, creating even more unemployment than at present. Make no mistake—this is an economic war. All of us may have to work harder and accept lower wages than we would like. Unless we become more productive, we will suffer economic defeat at the hands of our competitors.

NO. Increased productivity will not solve Canada's problems. Even if we do become more productive, who will buy our goods? There is a surplus of oil, automobiles and other manufactured goods in the industrial world already. The problem of the modern world is that we are convinced we have to grow, to be more productive, although markets are flooded now. As things stand, producers have to keep their goods in storage for too long before they sell them. This is expensive and adds to the final cost. To produce more goods with the same amount of workers makes no sense. Nor is it wise to produce the same number of goods with fewer workers. This is another way of increasing productivity, but only adds to unemployment, which is already too high.

Any way you look at it, increased productivity is not, on its own, a solution to Canada's economic problems.

GETTING THE FACTS

19. Japanese cars tend to be cheaper than domestic ones. What various reasons contained in this feature could possibly account for this?

USING YOUR KNOWLEDGE

20. Which of the two views about productivity as an answer to Canada's economic problems do you support? What are the main arguments to support this view? Why do you support it?

THE INVESTIGATIVE REPORTER

21. a) Consult magazine or newspaper articles and find out how factory managers treat their employees in order to keep them happy and working hard. Write a short report on your findings.

b) Discuss: could some of the methods used in Japan be useful in Canadian factories?

Regionalism in Canada: Division in the land

0800 *The sun to the prime minister*
"Good morning Mr. Trudeau. You are the best prime minister Canada has ever had. Have a nice day."

1800 *The sun to the prime minister*
"Well you've had another rotten day. You are the worst prime minister Canada has ever had. Why don't you resign?"

The prime minister to the sun
"But this morning you said I was the best prime minister Canada ever had."

The sun to the prime minister
"Yes, but I was in the East then."

—Western Canadian joke

During the 1970s, relations between the federal government in Ottawa and the various regions of Canada grew steadily worse. Each region of the country had its own view of how the nation should develop, and the federal government was unable to keep all regions happy. During the February, 1981 federal election the popularity of the Liberal party was so low that the Liberals won only two of western Canada's 77 seats. Yet in Quebec the party was extremely popular. It won all but one of the 75 seats in that province. This difference in popularity of the Liberal party (which formed the federal government) illustrates the impact of regionalism on Canadian thought. When you look at how a typical voter in each of the regions views the nation, enormous differences can be seen.

Fig. 15 The regions of Canada

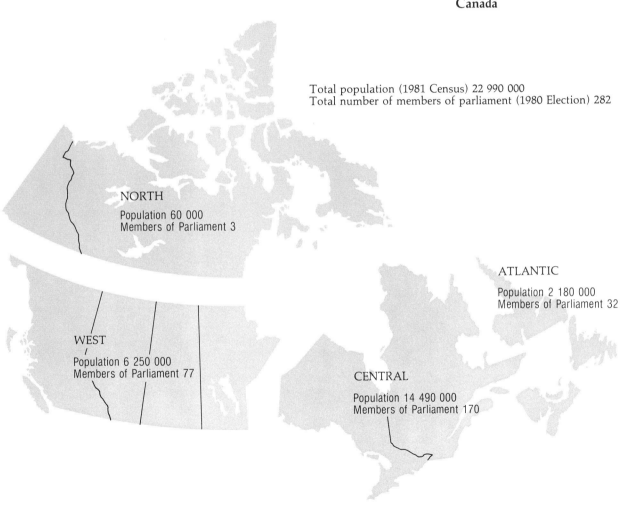

Total population (1981 Census) 22 990 000
Total number of members of parliament (1980 Election) 282

NORTH
Population 60 000
Members of Parliament 3

ATLANTIC
Population 2 180 000
Members of Parliament 32

WEST
Population 6 250 000
Members of Parliament 77

CENTRAL
Population 14 490 000
Members of Parliament 170

In these items, "typical" means that a majority of people in the region might support this view. It does not mean that all, or even nearly all, residents of the region believe this.

A typical central view of Canada

Ours is a particularly fortunate region. The nation's industrial belt is located along a 1000 km strip from Montreal to Windsor, Ontario. About 77 percent of Canada's manufactured goods were produced here in 1977, providing jobs for millions of residents of Ontario and Quebec. Steel, automobile, chemical and textile industries dominate the landscape around our cities producing goods for sale across country and overseas. As a result, our region enjoys a higher standard of living than any other.

Some regions would like to take away from our standard of living. What they do not see is that our industrial system must not be harmed in any way for, if it is, all regions will suffer. The role of the other regions is to support this manufacturing base in central Canada. The nation should strive to produce its resources as cheaply as possible, and to transport them to the manufacturing centres quickly and efficiently. If Canadian oil is cheaper than oil sold elsewhere, our industries will be able to produce goods more cheaply than other countries can. We will then be able to out-sell them in international markets. Cheap resources and cheap transportation to the manufacturing base are the keys to everyone's prosperity.

It makes sense to have manufacturing centred in the region with the largest population and in the region with access to water, rail, road and air transportation. Therefore we should leave things as they are. Central Canada should manufacture the products we need, and the other regions should supply it with raw materials to do so.

A typical western view of Canada

The West produces well over half of the oil and gas at present consumed in Canada, and over 75 percent of the grain products. It does so efficiently and at relatively low cost. For some reason, however, residents of other regions feel that we should continue to provide these items at prices well below those paid in other countries. We are happy to continue providing these much-needed items, but we must have higher prices for them.

In addition to resource production, however, we would like to establish manufacturing industries here. It makes no sense for tractors and other farm machinery to be transported out here all the way from Ontario. We should make it here ourselves. Unfortunately, the railway system prevents this from happening. Because of an agreement between the rail companies and the federal government, it is very cheap to ship raw materials to central and Atlantic Canada. Similarly, manufactured goods coming from the East can be shipped here at very cheap rates. So it makes sense, under this arrangement, for a company to establish a manufacturing plant in

464

Inuvik, Northwest Territories

Edmonton, rapidly-growing capital of Alberta

Montreal harbour

Mining in Ontario

C.N. Tower, Toronto

Fig. 16 Views of Canada. Do you think any of these images present a false impression? Explain your answer.

central Canada and to supply it with raw materials from the West. The transportation charges make this attractive. As a result, industry continues to be concentrated in central Canada, and all the jobs which go with it are denied to the West.

We have about 27.5 percent of Canada's population, but only 18.2 percent of manufactured goods are produced here. Eventually our oil and gas will run out, so we must have industries of our own to provide work when this happens. In the meantime, we must have more for our energy products. It makes no sense to sell oil and gas at prices well below world levels, as we are doing now. Unless these changes are made, the West will not live up to its potential.

A typical Atlantic view of Canada

The region which suffers most from the present economic structure of Canada is neither the West nor the central region. It is the Atlantic region which receives the most unfair treatment.

We have, according to the 1981 census, about 9.5 percent of the nation's population. In addition we have only 32 out of a total 282 Members of Parliament in Ottawa. Because there are so few of us, our views are easily ignored, and because of that, our economy lags behind the rest of the country.

For example, the energy issue hits Atlantic Canadians particularly hard. Two provinces, Nova Scotia and Newfoundland and Labrador, have oil and gas reserves offshore. The federal government claims that it should have over half the tax money which comes from the sale of these resources. This is because it is responsible for the seas around our coast. We feel that the resources belong to the provinces and that they should get the taxes. In fact, Alberta receives roughly twice as much in taxes from the sale of a barrel of oil as we would if we accepted the federal government's view.

The problem is made even worse, however, because our consumers are especially hard hit. Our lower wages and higher unemployment make it difficult to afford rising energy prices.

Our industries are hurt by the railway system. It is expensive to transport manufactured goods from the Atlantic region to the large Ontario-Quebec market, so companies prefer to build their factories in Ontario and Quebec. Thus we lose jobs, and then have to pay high prices for goods manufactured in central Canada. We get hit with high unemployment and high prices all at once.

We must have more grants from the federal government to overcome the problems we face. Also, we must gain complete control of our offshore resources. Unless we do, we are likely to remain a have-not region forever.

See the chapter on the Canadian constitution for a more detailed examination of the dispute between Newfoundland and Labrador and the federal government over offshore oil.

In January, 1983, the energy ministers of Newfoundland and Labrador and the federal government announced that a settlement of the offshore oil dispute was likely in the near future. Many people hope that a growing spirit of cooperation may be developing.

A typical northern view of Canada

The Yukon and Northwest Territories suffer from very large problems in Canada. First, our population is only about 0.25 percent of the nation's total, and our three Members of Parliament do not have enough power to influence the federal government. Secondly, the North does not even have its own government. We are not a province, but are governed by the federal government in Ottawa. All taxes from oil and gas production go to Ottawa, and in return we receive small allowances, but nothing like those which the provinces like Alberta and British Columbia get.

A third problem we face is high living costs—the highest in the land. This is because of the high cost of transporting goods to the North and also our harsh climate. It costs roughly 25 percent more to live in the Yukon than in northern Alberta.

Our distance from the rest of the country is another problem. It is obviously not sensible for a company to build a large factory here where the population is so small. We do not expect this. However, we feel that two things must be done to help us with our problems. First, we must be given a share of taxes from our oil and gas production as if we were a province. That way we could build more roads, hospitals, schools, etc. Second, we must be given subsidies by the federal government to reduce the cost of transporting goods here from the South, and the cost of the large amounts of energy we burn in our harsh climate.

We could be one of the wealthiest regions of Canada, but we are hurt by a very high cost of living, and control of our energy resources by the federal government, thousands of kilometres away. Unless changes are made, the North will be unable to hold on to its present population. People will drift away in search of better opportunities elsewhere, and the North will not develop as it should.

GETTING THE FACTS

22. In your own words, define regionalism.

USING YOUR KNOWLEDGE

23. Turn back to the map at the beginning of this section entitled "The regions of Canada." Look at the information it contains about population and Members of Parliament. Which region do you think has the better chance of making its views well-known in Ottawa? Which region would have the worst chance? Explain.

24. Make a copy of the chart on the next page:

ISSUE	CENTRAL VIEW	WESTERN VIEW	NORTHERN VIEW	ATLANTIC VIEW
Political voice				
Energy prices and taxes				
Manufacturing industry				
Transportation costs				

Read the views of each region and fill in your copy of the chart.

THINKING IT THROUGH

25. Which view of Canada is most justified in your opinion? Imagine that you are writing to the prime minister on the subject. Which view would you support? What evidence would you use?

Conclusion

Figure 17 Canada's economic performance, 1970 to 1982

ITEM	1970	1972	1974	1976 %	1978	1980	1982
Rate of inflation	2.9	7.5	10.8	8.0	9.2	11.5	10.9
Rate of unemployment	5.7	6.2	5.3	7.1	7.4	7.6	11.0
Rate of growth for economy	6.8	7.5	2.2	2.3	2.9	2.1	−4.8

Make a copy of the following graph.

Canada's economic performance, 1970-1990

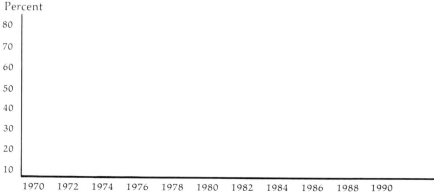

468

Fig. 18 This huge machine is coating a gas pipeline with an anti-rust layer of metal. It is far more productive than human labour. Do you think we should use such machines, even if it means some people might lose their jobs to them?

GETTING THE FACTS

26. a) Take the information in Figure 17 and place it on the graph. Draw a separate line for each item, and make each line a different colour. Beside each line, write what item it represents.

   b) Does the pattern on the graph represent an economy which is getting better or worse? Explain.

THINKING IT THROUGH

27. Extend the lines on the graph past 1982. Assume that they continue in the same direction and at the same slope as between 1978 and 1982. Using these assumptions, what does it appear is likely to happen to the Canadian economy in the 1980s?

28. Do you think that there is any possibility that the situation can be turned around and that the economy can be improved? Which of the problems mentioned in this chapter do you think might be solved? Do you think that there are any new discoveries which might improve the situation? Explain all your answers.

19 What should Canada's role in world affairs be?

Some views of Canada's world role

When I think of Canada, I remember the Canadian troops who freed us from Nazi control in 1945. The German troops who had occupied our country for four years treated us like slaves. The Canadian soldiers who freed us treated us like friends. Many of our young women, including myself, married Canadian soldiers.

Dutch woman

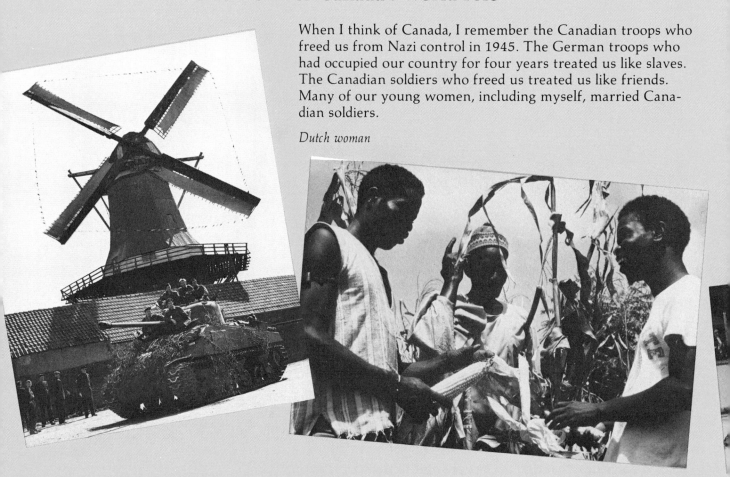

I think of Canada as a nation very concerned with the poorer parts of the world. I think of the farm schemes you have set up in Kenya, and the training which you have given to our people to run them. To me, Canada is a leader in assisting the developing nations of the world.

Kenyan woman

I think of Canadians as a people who lead the world in a few high-technology areas. I think of your Telidon home-computer system and the Short Take-Off and Landing (STOL) aircraft in which you lead the world. You are a people who have chosen to concentrate on a few areas and do them to the best of your ability. As a result, you are world leaders.

German industrialist

To me, Canadians play the role of world go-between. The world is divided into communist and non-communist blocs, each led by its own "superpower." This division threatens the peace of the world, but you have managed to bridge the gap between the two groups. By remaining friendly with both, you have ensured that there is discussion between them, often through you as a third party. Your role as an international peacekeeper is the one that I think is the most valuable.

Swedish teacher

When I think of Canada, I think of Paul Henderson scoring that winning goal against the U.S.S.R. in Moscow in 1972. It proved that we played the best hockey in the world, and united us all for a moment.

Canadian sportscaster

- Pick the two views which best represent your view of Canada's world role. Why did you choose these two?

- Compare your choices with those of your classmates. Have you made similar choices or different ones? Why or why not?

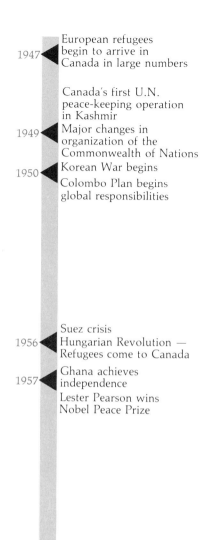

1947 — European refugees begin to arrive in Canada in large numbers

Canada's first U.N. peace-keeping operation in Kashmir

1949 — Major changes in organization of the Commonwealth of Nations

1950 — Korean War begins

Colombo Plan begins global responsibilities

1956 — Suez crisis
Hungarian Revolution — Refugees come to Canada

1957 — Ghana achieves independence
Lester Pearson wins Nobel Peace Prize

1964 — Canada begins participation in peace-keeping in Cypress

Chapter overview

The role which Canada should play in world affairs is unclear. In the past we have enjoyed a close relationship first with Great Britain and then with the U.S. Because they are larger and more powerful than we are, it has been difficult for Canada to play a separate world role of its own. This has been especially true in political and military matters. In some areas we are world leaders. For example, we are the world's leading supplier of potash, nickel, and newsprint. We also lead the world in hydro and nuclear electricity generation. The "space arm" for NASA's space shuttle is a Canadian development. Generally, however, in the field of technology, our relatively small population and available resources have limited the role we can play.

We have to be realistic about our role in world affairs. For instance, Canada cannot be a military superpower like the U.S.A. or U.S.S.R. Our population is too small. We must decide how far we wish to cooperate with other countries and how far we want to "go it alone." In this chapter you will learn about the alternative roles which Canada can realistically play. You also will be asked to solve the problem "what should be our role in world affairs?"

Signposts

International peacekeeper >

Canadian foreign policy: Between the superpowers >

Foreign aid: How we help developing nations >

Canada: A trading giant? >

FEATURE: International hockey: International goodwill? >

What should Canada's role in world affairs be? >

Key words

North Atlantic Treaty Organization (NATO)
North American Air Defense Command (NORAD)
developing nations
foreign aid
Gross National Product (GNP)
Canadian International Development Agency (CIDA)

International peacekeeper

Europeans old enough to remember World War II know that Canada played an important role in defeating Hitler's forces. They remember the 900 Canadians who died in the attempt to capture Dieppe, France in 1942. They remember the Canadian force that took one of the beaches in Normandy in the operation known as D-Day in 1944. Over 700 000 Canadians served in the military between 1939 and 1945. Almost 45 000 Canadians died in the war effort.

After the war, international peacekeeping became a central feature of Canada's foreign and defense policy. You have read about Lester Pearson's efforts to establish the United Nations Emergency Force in 1956. Canada contributed to the United Nations peacekeeping forces in many parts of the world. The following statements from government sources confirm our commitment to this peacekeeping role.

Fig. 1 Canadian troops with the U.N. Force in the Middle East. What sort of jobs would these troops perform?

Defence White Paper (i.e. Statement of policy), 1959.

Minister of National Defence, 1975.

It is the defence policy of Canada to provide forces for the United Nations to assist that organization in attaining its peaceful aims.

The permanent structure of the Canadian Armed Forces will provide for up to 2 000 personnel to be available for United Nations peacekeeping at any one time.

Our role as peacekeeper is taken seriously by our government. As a supporter of international organizations to preserve freedom and to maintain peace, we have gained an international reputation as an important peacekeeping nation.

GETTING THE FACTS

1. Use an atlas to locate each of the countries listed below. On a blank map of the world, colour in these countries and put in their names, and the years in which Canadians served there in United Nations forces. The countries and years are Kashmir (India), 1949; Korea, 1950-4; Vietnam, Laos, Cambodia (Kampuchea), 1954; Israel, 1954; Egypt, 1956-67; Lebanon, 1959; Congo (Zaire), 1960-4; New Guinea, 1962-3; Yemen, 1963-4; Cyprus, 1964-7; India, Pakistan, 1965-6; Aden, 1967; India, Pakistan, 1971; Israel, Egypt, 1973-4.

THINKING IT THROUGH

2. Read the following:

ARGUMENTS IN FAVOUR OF CANADA'S PARTICIPATION IN UNITED NATIONS PEACEKEEPING

1) It is a good way to learn about problems in other parts of the world and to establish a reputation there. This can open doors to future cooperation and trade opportunities.

2) By giving Canada a clear role in international affairs, it gives our people a sense of purpose. In this way it promotes nationalism.

3) It provides Canada's armed forces with a chance to train and practise for operations in action.

ARGUMENTS OPPOSED TO CANADA'S PARTICIPATION IN UNITED NATIONS PEACEKEEPING

1) It costs Canada millions of dollars which could be used to build hospitals, schools and other important items at home.

2) It leads to the deaths of many Canadians involved in keeping peace in parts of the world which do not directly concern us.

474

3) As a peacekeeper, we have often been unable to take sides in a dispute. Sometimes we would have been better off to support the side which we considered to be right.

  a) Add two arguments of your own to each part of the chart.

  b) Which set of arguments (IN FAVOUR or OPPOSED) do you find most convincing? Give reasons for your opinion.

3. Canada sent troops in World War II to join in the fighting. Since then, Canadian troops have generally been used only as peacekeepers—keeping hostile armies apart from each other.

  a) What reasons can you think of why this should be?

  b) Which do you think is the more effective role for Canada to play? Explain your reasons.

Canadian foreign policy: Between the superpowers

A nation's foreign policy is the relationship it has with other countries. Foreign policy deals with such things as who a nation's allies are, who its enemies are, and how it will conduct itself in world affairs. Until the 1920s, Canada did not have its own foreign policy. We automatically followed that of Britain. For example, Canada did not declare war on Germany in 1914. It was assumed that since Britain had declared war, Canada was automatically at war too. Canadian troops were sent at once to join the war.

Fig. 2 Canadian troops supervise the evacuation of refugees, Vietnam, 1968.

In 1927 the Department of External Affairs was founded. This is the part of the federal government responsible for forming Canada's foreign policy. At first, the department acted in a cautious manner. Since Britain and the United States were our most important allies, our foreign policy usually followed theirs. When Britain declared war on Germany in 1939, Canadian troops fought again. The main difference between 1939 and 1914 was that this time Canada declared war separately.

After the war, Canadian foreign policy slowly moved away from automatic support of our oldest allies. In the Suez crisis, for example, Canada supported the removal of British troops from Egypt. Canada no longer followed Britain's foreign policy blindly.

During the 1960s Canada showed that it was prepared to move away from American foreign policy as well. In 1959, a communist revolution in Cuba brought Fidel Castro to power. The U.S. was opposed to the revolution, so it broke off diplomatic relations with Cuba. Trade virtually ended between Cuba and the U.S., but Canada continued both trade and diplomatic relations with Cuba. In 1976, the Canadian prime minister visited Cuba, indicating friendship for the people and government of that country.

Canada also played an important role in welcoming the People's Republic of China back into the world of international affairs. After a communist revolution in 1949, China broke its ties with the western world. It refused to trade with western nations and its politicians had little contact with leaders outside China. By 1970 it was anxious to restore links with the rest of the world. Canada was among the first nations to establish diplomatic relations with China, and did so before the United States.

Another theme in Canadian foreign policy developed during the 1960s. We increased our aid to the world's poorer countries. Some of these countries are not democratic. In Tanzania in Africa, for example, only one political party is allowed to function. Other countries which we assist are anti-American.

Clearly we now establish our own foreign policy. We are a close ally of the United States, and belong to many international organizations with them. For example, both Canada and the U.S. belong to the North Atlantic Treaty Organization (NATO) for European defense, and the North American Air Defense Agreement (NORAD) for our own protection. We also have good relations with countries which do not regard the U.S. as an ally. We are now regarded as an "honest broker" or an impartial judge between the superpowers—the U.S.S.R. and U.S.A. This means that we are respected by both sides, and frequently use our influence to maintain good relations between them. We stand in the middle, trying successfully to be friends with many nations with all forms of government. In this way, Canada makes its contribution to peace and international understanding.

Our friendship with Cuba proved helpful in 1970. That country agreed to accept the kidnappers of British Trade Commissioner James Cross, who had been taken by F.L.Q. members in Montreal. In return for admission to Cuba, the kidnappers released Cross unharmed.

Fig. 3 Distribution of donated supplies to returning refugees in Kampuchea, 1980. Goods given out included corn, soya milk, vegetable oil, dried peas, mosquito netting, sewing kit and cloth.

4. In your own words, define foreign policy.

5. Make a timeline of the following major events in Canada's foreign policy.

Canada recognizes the People's Republic of China before the U.S. does, 1970.

Canada becomes one of the United Nations' original members, 1945.

Canada steps up foreign aid to poor countries, 1975.

Canada declares war on Germany, 1939.

Prime Minister Trudeau makes a speech calling for more international aid to poorer countries, 1981.

Canada supplies troops for the United Nations peacekeeping force in Korea, 1950.

Prime Minister Trudeau visits Cuba, 1976.

All nations are invited to participate in Expo '67 at Montreal in 1967.

Canada opposes Britain's invasion of Egypt, 1956.

USING YOUR KNOWLEDGE

6. Make a copy of the following chart for your notebook.

Events in Canada's foreign policy, 1939-1981

EVENTS INDICATING GROWING INDEPENDENCE FROM BRITAIN	EVENTS INDICATING GROWING INDEPENDENCE FROM THE U.S.	EVENTS INDICATING MAINTENANCE OF CLOSE TIES WITH ALL NATIONS

Place each of the events which were mentioned in question 5 in order in the proper column of the chart. Some events may belong in more than one column.

7. a) Are there any columns in the chart for which there are no entries for the past 25 years? What does this tell you about our foreign policy?

b) Which column has the largest number of entries after 1970? What does this tell you about our foreign policy?

8. If possible, refer back to the chapter in *Discovering Canada*, which deals with Laurier's "juggling act."

a) What are the differences and similarities between that act and Canada's "middle role" today?

b) Do you think that such a middle role is a traditionally Canadian position? Explain.

9. Do you feel that it is a sensible policy to try to maintain a relationship with all nations, rich or poor, democratic or communist? Write a paragraph in which you give your answer, and explain your reasons for your decision.

Foreign aid: How we help developing nations

A study, published in Washington in the summer of 1980, predicted that the world's population would rise from around 4 000 000 000 people to about 6 350 000 000 by the year 2000. Ninety percent of this growth, the study said, would take place in the developing nations, where more than 1 000 000 000 people were already living on the edge of starvation. Unless the rich nations provided aid to these countries, massive world-wide starvation would result.

Like other rich nations, Canada provides foreign aid to developing nations. The United Nations has stated that all rich countries should spend an amount equal to 0.7 percent of their Gross National Product (GNP) on foreign aid. Canada fell below this figure every year during the 1970s. In 1980, Canada's GNP was about $280 000 000 000 and our foreign aid totaled $1 200 000 000. This was 0.43 percent of our GNP. To meet the United Nations' figure, we would have had to increase our spending by about $760 000 000 to $1 960 000 000.

The organization in charge of foreign aid in this country is known as the Canadian International Development Agency (CIDA).

Foreign aid includes such things as food, equipment, money, advice.

In 1977, Canada's Gross National Product (GNP) for each member of the population was $U.S. 8350. We are considered a rich nation. The 1977 figures for Kenya was $U.S. 290, which makes it a poor nation.

Fig. 4 A project in Nigeria to analyse conditions of plant growth. Foreign-funded projects often help increase the yield of vital crops.

It is supported by the federal government. Since the needs of the developing nations are so great and the money available for aid is so limited, CIDA's task is a difficult one. It tries to support projects throughout the world. Because other rich nations provide aid too, CIDA must see that aid does not go to projects already well-supported by other countries but to those who need it most.

Why should rich nations help poorer ones? In response to this question, many people would ask how we could watch our fellow humans suffer when we have so much. There are also very practical reasons why poor nations must be helped. If we raise the wealth of poor nations, they will be able to buy more products from us which they cannot now afford. Thus, in the long run, our own wealth will be increased. In addition, if we help poorer nations we help to prevent division and possible war between North-South countries. (We have already seen the extent of East-West division.)

To meet the United Nations figure, Canada probably will have to spend about $2 870 000 000 in foreign aid by 1985. This represents around $125 per year for each Canadian. In 1980, the total income for each member of the population was only $520 in Ghana and $160 in Bangladesh. In Canada, the figure was just over $12 000. It is likely that what is a relatively small amount in Canada significantly helps the receiving countries. In addition, such spending raises our international reputation considerably.

A project that worked

One of Canada's most successful foreign aid projects involves bees and honey. Between 1971 and 1981, CIDA spent about $1 000 000 establishing beekeeping stations in various parts of the world, which steadily supply much-needed food for very little cost.

The beekeeping project in Ruai, a small village in Kenya, is a good example of this. With the advice of Professor Gordon Townsend of the University of Guelph in Ontario, 12 bee hives and a stock of bees were sent to Ruai. The cost of this equipment was only $150. Professor Townsend spent some time in Ruai advising villagers about beekeeping. A group of people, known as a cooperative, were organized to manage the operation. By 1981 each member was receiving about $700 per year from honey sales. Since the average income in Kenya is less than $350 per year, the Ruai project is very successful indeed.

This project works because it is simple. It produces an item which is of use to the villagers, but does not need expensive equipment or skills which the villagers do not have. The honey and beekeeping fit in with the traditional lifestyle of the villagers who can maintain the beekeeping operation entirely on their own.

A project that failed

One of Canada's least successful foreign aid projects involved fork-lift trucks. In 1972, CIDA spent $4 500 000 supplying 160 trucks to the city of Dar es Salaam in the African country of Tanzania. They were to be used to speed the loading and unloading of ships in the docks.

The trucks were built by a firm in Guelph, Ontario, and shipped directly to Tanzania. By 1975 only 50 of the original 160 were still working. In the hot African climate, machines frequently broke

Fig. 5 What do you think Canadians have to gain from involvement in foreign aid projects?

Fig. 6 One of the many boats of Vietnamese refugees lost in the China Sea. Is foreign aid the only way rich countries can help other people in need? Explain your answer.

down after fewer than 100 hours. No training had been provided by CIDA to make sure that Tanzanian mechanics were able to repair and service them and the repair manuals sent with the machines were in the wrong language. All this was made worse by the failure to send the correctly-sized spare parts from Canada.

The programme failed because it did not really fit the needs of Tanzania. Complex machines designed for use in Canada's cold climate could not be effectively operated in Africa without proper maintenance. By the summer of 1979, fewer than ten of the machines were still working.

The trucks did not fit in with the traditional lifestyle of the dock workers, who were unable to maintain them without proper training. As a result, $4 500 000 of Canadian foreign aid was not spent effectively.

GETTING THE FACTS

10. a) What does each of the following stand for: GNP? CIDA?
    b) In a paragraph for each, describe what the above terms are.

USING YOUR KNOWLEDGE

11. Examine the two case studies, "A project that worked" and "A project that failed." Make a list of those features which you think are important to make a project successful.

12. a) List the reasons why the Tanzania project failed.
    b) Why do you think Canada decided to undertake the project?

THINKING IT THROUGH

13. Examine the three reasons given for providing foreign aid to developing nations. Place them in what you consider to be their order of importance. Why have you put them in the order you did? Can you add any other reasons of your own?

14. a) Make a bar graph showing the amount of money Canada spent on foreign aid in 1980, and the amount we would have to spend in 1985 to meet the United Nations' figure.
    b) Do you think we should try to meet this figure, or should we be spending more money on the needy people in our own country? Give reasons to support your viewpoint.

THE INVESTIGATIVE REPORTER

15. a) Find information about a current Canadian foreign aid project and write a short report on it.
    b) Do you think that the project will succeed? Give reasons for your answer.

In 1977, U.S. exports were $U.S. 184 700 000 000 while its population was 216 700 000. It therefore exported about $841 U.S. (or $890 Cdn.) for every member of the population. Because its manufactured exports make up much more of the total figure in the U.S. than in Canada, this tends to create more jobs for Americans.

Fig. 7 This oil rig, built on an artificial island in the Beaufort Sea, illustrates how it is possible for Canada to be a leader in developing new technology. Do you think we can compete with our international rivals, like the U.S. and Japan, in this sort of technology?

Canada: A trading giant?

In 1977, Canada exported $44 300 000 000 worth of products. In that year, the population was estimated to be 23 200 000. This means that in 1977 we exported approximately $1909.48 worth of products for every member of the population. These figures make us an international trading nation of considerable importance.

Canada sends a wide variety of products overseas. Figure 9 shows that in 1977 motor vehicles and parts were our largest single export item. For every member of the population, we exported $445.64 worth of these products. However, if you add up the first 7 items in the list (all of which are natural products) you will see these products were worth close to half of the total ($828.95 out of $1909.48). More employees are required to produce $1000 worth of manufactured goods than $1000 worth of natural products. Thus, the argument goes, if we concentrated more on manufactured exports, we would reduce unemployment and make the nation wealthier as a result. Can Canada become a trading giant of manufactured products to rival the United States, Japan, or West Germany?

High technology products are one of the fastest-growing areas of international trade. We suffer from considerable handicaps in becoming a world leader in this area. Not the least of these handicaps is our relatively small population. Although our spending on technology for every member of the population compares with a number of our rivals, our small population means that Canada has relatively little money to spend.

Fig. 8 Population, technological spending, spending/population in Canada and selected countries (1972)

COUNTRY	POPULATION	AMOUNT SPENT ON TECHNOLOGICAL DEVELOPMENT (IN U.S. DOLLARS)	AMOUNT SPENT/ POPULATION (IN U.S. DOLLARS)
U.S.A.	210 000 000	22 285 000 000	$106.12
France	52 000 000	2 507 000 000	48.21
Great Britain	56 000 000	2 533 000 000	45.23
Japan	110 000 000	1 684 000 000	15.30
West Germany	62 000 000	2 084 000 000	33.61
Canada	23 000 000	828 000 000	36.00

Fig. 9 Canada's exports, 1977

ITEM	VALUE	VALUE/POPULATION ($)
Wheat	1 827 000 000	78.75
Animals	2 719 000 000	117.19
Metal ores	2 730 000 000	117.67
Oil and gas	4 369 000 000	118.31
Other natural products	2 341 000 000	100.91
Lumber, pulp, paper	4 489 000 000	193.49
Newsprint	2 381 000 000	102.63
Metal goods	3 831 000 000	165.13
Motor vehicles, parts	10 339 000 000	445.64
Other machinery	3 946 000 000	170.09
Other manufactured goods	4 218 000 000	181.81
Other products	1 770 000 000	76.29
Total	44 375 000 000	$1 909.48

In "The new technology: Changes and choices," you learned of Canadian attempts to break into high-technology exports. To the list of items described in that chapter, we should add the CANDU nuclear reactor system.

CANDU is a nuclear power system designed to power electrical generation stations. It was developed in Canada. Other nuclear reactors use enriched uranium. Plutonium, a byproduct, is difficult to store safely. CANDU uses natural uranium fuel with a heavy water moderator which reduce the byproducts and make storage easier.

Fig. 10 CANDU nuclear reactor under construction

Before making a foreign sale, our federal government has required a guarantee from the receiving nation that the uranium which powers CANDU will not be used for making atomic bombs. Sales to Argentina, India, Rumania, Pakistan, South Korea, and Taiwan have encouraged our exporters. In the spring of 1982, however, Mexico backed out of a proposed deal to buy CANDU because of its rapidly increasing cost.

CANDU's supporters believe that we should push its sale vigorously. They feel that Canada can become a giant in world trade by being in the forefront of new technology. CANDU's opponents doubt all this. Some people feel that in selling uranium abroad to fuel CANDU, regardless of the guarantees given, Canada runs the risk of increasing the spread of nuclear weapons. Others think that since our population and our amount of available research dollars are small, we cannot hope to be a world leader in this area forever and that the costs of developing systems such as CANDU are not justified by sales.

In 1974, India experimented with a nuclear explosion using technology supplied by Canada for nuclear research. Clearly, the system of guarantees was not foolproof. More recently, research reactors and electricity stations have been visited by inspectors from the International Atomic Energy Agency, a branch of the U.N., to check on the use of nuclear power.

Between 1978 and 1982 only one foreign sale of CANDU was made.

USING YOUR KNOWLEDGE

16. Look at the chart, "Canada's exports, 1977." Rewrite it in your notebook with our largest single export item or at the top, ranking each one down to the smallest single export item at the bottom.

17. Look at the chart "Population, technological spending, spending/population in Canada and selected countries (1972)." What conclusions can you draw from this chart about our ability to compete with our rivals? Write three observations in your notebook.

THINKING IT THROUGH

18. A number of disadvantages we face in competing in high technology areas are mentioned in this section. If you had the power, what would you do to overcome some of these disadvantages? Are there any you cannot overcome? Explain.

19. a) What arguments do supporters of high technology exports (such as CANDU) use? What arguments do opponents use?
   b) What is your view on the subject? Explain.

International hockey: International goodwill?

In October, 1972, Canada beat the U.S.S.R. in an eight game hockey series. After a slow start, the team came back strongly. When Paul Henderson of the Toronto Maple Leafs scored the winning goal with 34 seconds left to play in the eighth game, the Moscow crowd sat silent and stunned. Team Canada had won the series by four games to three, with one tied. It was clear for all to see that Canadians played the best hockey in the world.

Until the 1950s, Canadian teams had won many international tournaments. Then, for a number of reasons, many of our best players were prevented from playing in such tournaments. As a result, our teams regularly lost to Europeans. For a number of years Canada withdrew from international competition. In 1972, when our best met their best, it looked as though the old days had returned again.

Canada re-entered the World Hockey Championships, but because they were held during the Stanley Cup play-offs, many Canadian players were unable to participate. As a result, the U.S.S.R. and Czechoslovakia dominated the competition. Although Team Canada did win the first Canada Cup competition in 1976, two further tournaments showed the supremacy of Russian hockey.

In the Challenge Cup, played in New York in January, 1979, a National Hockey League All-Star team was beaten 6-0 in the final game by a Russian All-Star team. The worst defeat came in September, 1981. Team Canada lost 8-1 to the U.S.S.R. in the final of the second Canada Cup competition in Montreal.

Many questions were asked about these losses, and many explanations were offered. Scotty Bowman, Team Canada coach in 1981, felt that Canadian youngsters begin to play organized hockey too early. In Russia, he noted, most youngsters concentrate on skating skills until the age of twelve. Only then do they join organized teams. Canadian players join organized teams at a very early age, and learn checking and other skills before they have learned to skate properly. As a result, Bowman stated, Canadian players never learn to be such good skaters as their Russian opponents. Other people felt that accurate passing plays are not emphasized in North America as they are in the U.S.S.R. Whatever the causes, the conclusion is clear. Canada no longer produces the best hockey teams.

Does this matter? Some feel that if international hockey increases international goodwill, it does not matter who wins. The Chinese saying "Friendship first, competition second" states this idea simply. Not all agree with this view, however.

THINKING IT THROUGH

21. Do you think that winning is more important than increasing international understanding? Does it matter that Canada no longer dominates international hockey?

USING YOUR KNOWLEDGE

22. a) Hockey is just one way of promoting international goodwill. What other methods are there? (Consider other sports or the arts, for instance.)

b) Are some methods better than others? Why or why not?

Two Canadians important in the artistic world

Karen Kain was born in Hamilton, Ontario in 1951. She showed great promise as a dancer while very young. In 1962, at the age of eleven, she joined the National Ballet School. After seven years of hard work and constant practice, she was invited to join the National Ballet of Canada.

Fig. 11 Karen Kain

In 1973, Karen competed in the Moscow International Competition for ballet. She won the silver medal (second place) for solo women dancers, greatly impressing the Russian press and critics. She demonstrated that Canadians can successfully compete internationally, not only in hockey or figure skating, but in other areas.

Since this success, Karen has concentrated on playing a variety of roles for the National Ballet. She has toured the world in such ballets as *The Dream*, *Romeo and Juliet*, and has even made her debut as a television actress in *The Littlest Hobo*. In addition she has made guest appearances for Moscow's Bolshoi Ballet and the London Festival Ballet. This talented Canadian has shown the world that we can produce top quality artistic performers.

Gordon Korman was born in 1963. As a child he showed promise as a writer. In grade 7 he wrote a major composition assignment which eventually became his first novel. *This Can't Be Happening at Macdonald Hall!* was published in 1976, when Gordon was only thirteen. In the next six years, he wrote six more books about the heroes he created in *Macdonald Hall*. Bruno, Boots and Bugs Potter have been eagerly received by young Canadian readers.

Gordon enrolled at New York University in 1981, where he began studying film and screenwriting. He is currently negotiating to have some of his novels produced as films. In 1982, *The War with Mr. Wizzle*, another of his stories, was released in the U.S.

This rapid climb to the top has shown that Canada can produce young writers, too. Indeed, Gordon has devoted much time to visiting schools to encourage students to write as a hobby. While still in his teens, Gordon Korman has shown yet another side of the creativity of Canadian youth.

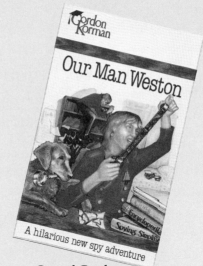

Fig. 12 One of Gordon Korman's many successful novels

THINKING IT THROUGH

23. These two stories suggest that Canada could be successful as a world leader in the performing and creative arts (ballet and fiction writing). Do you think we should concentrate less on competitive sports, like hockey, and more on the arts? Explain your reasons fully.

Fig. 13 CANDU nuclear power plant, Korea. What would Korea gain from a plant like this? What would Canada gain by building the plant?

Conclusion

What should Canada's role in world affairs be?

In this chapter you read about five roles which Canada can play in world affairs. These are listed below.

Possible roles for Canada in world affairs

a) International peacekeeper
b) "Honest broker" between the superpowers
c) Helper of developing nations
d) Trading giant
e) Best hockey-playing nation

It may not be possible for a country with a small population, such as Canada, to effectively play all these roles at once. Some people feel we must pick the roles which we can play most effectively and concentrate on them. Let us assume that this view is accurate in order to do the following exercise.

THINKING IT THROUGH

24. To solve the problem "What should Canada's role in world affairs be?", make a rough copy of the worksheet, and write up your good copy after you have completed your rough copy.

Step 1 has already been done. The problem has been identified.

Step 2 has been done for you. The five possible roles for Canada represent alternative solutions to the problem. This chapter contains

information about each one.

Steps 3 to 6 are your responsibility. With the aid of the information in this chapter, you should follow the steps, in order, to reach your own conclusion. Which of the five roles should Canada try to play? Which of the five roles should Canada not try to play?

Student Worksheet
(Make a copy of this worksheet in your notebook, and use it to do your rough work.)

1. Identifying the problem	What should Canada's role in world affairs be?
2. Identifying the alternative solutions	
International peacekeeping Honest broker Helping developing nations Trading giant Best hockey-playing nation	
3. Collecting information on each alternative	
4. Forming a conclusion	My conclusion is that Canada should try to play these roles: a) b) c)
5. Preparing and presenting your conclusion	Write up your findings and conclusion in good essay form.
6. Evaluating your conclusion	Compare your conclusion with those of your classmates, OR hand your good copy in to your teacher. (Your teacher will tell you what to do.)

Pronunciation key for English words

SYMBOL	EXAMPLE	[PRONUNCIATION. Parts of the word to be emphasized are in capital letters.] RESPELLING
a	bat	bat
ay	say, date, air	[say], [dayt], [ayr]
ah	all, car, lot	[ahl], [cahr], [laht]
eh	let, meant	[leht], [mehnt]
ee	see, hear	[see], [heer]
er	her, learn, fur	[her], [lern], [fer]
ih	sit	[siht]
ī	mīle	[mīl]
ir	sir	[sir]
oh	no, flow	[noh], [floh]
oi	oil, joy	[oil], [joi]
oo	boot, rule, through	[boot], [rool], [throo]
or	corn, door, store	[corn], [dor], [stor]
ow	cow, out, bough	[cow], [owt], [bow]
u	put, look	[put], [luk]
uh	fun, but	[fuhn], [buht]
yoo	few, cue	[fyoo], [cyoo]
ch	chin, beach	[chihn], [beech]
g	go, big	[goh], [bihg]
j	jet, giant, bridge	[jeht], [JĪ-ant], [brihj]
k	kite, cup, back	[kīt], [kuhp], [bak]
ks	tax	[taks]
kw	queen	[kween]
ng	song	[sawng]
s	say, cent	[say], [sehnt]
sh	she, conscious	[shee], [KAHN-shuhs]
th	that, death	[that], [dehth]
th̲	breathe	[bree̲th]
y	yet, union	[yeht], [YOO-nyuhn]
z	zeal, use	[zeel], [yooz]
zh	pleasure	[PLEH-zher]

Pronunciation key for French words

Vowels

(Sounds for which there are no English equivalents)

SOUND	SYMBOL	EXAMPLE	[PRONUNCIATION] RESPELLING
eu	œ (this is a little like the sound in "her")	seul	[sœl]
e, eu	eu (this is a little like the sound in "put")	le, je	[leu], [zheu]
u	u^e (to make this sound, purse your lips as if to whistle and try to say "ee")	rue	[ru^e]
oi	wah (this is a little like the sound in "water," but the lips must be a little more pursed)	voiture	[vwah-TU^{E}R]
ui	wee (this is a little like the sound in "week," but your lips must be a little more pursed)	oui	[wee]

Nasals

(These sounds should be made through your nose, but without actually pronouncing the "n" or "m")

SOUND	SYMBOL	EXAMPLE	[PRONUNCIATION] RESPELLING
an (m), en (m)	ah^n	dans,* vent	[dah^n], [vah^n]
on (m)	oh^n	bon	[boh^n]
ain (m), in (m)	a^n	pain, vin	[pa^n], [va^n]
un (m)	u^n	brun	[bru^n]

*The final consonant of a French word is not usually pronounced.

Glossary

aboriginal Existing from the beginning; first; native. It is used to describe the earliest known inhabitants of a country.

aboriginal rights Special rights to the land and its bounty which Indians and Native peoples claim as original inhabitants of the land—these include the right to fish and hunt game without being subject to government laws.

activist A person who believes strongly in a cause and who is prepared to organize people and to put pressure on opponents to secure goals.

affirmative action A programme by employers to give women and minorities the same opportunities as others in the labour market, to encourage them to go into non-traditional jobs, and to increase their numbers in management.

Americanization The taking on of ways, styles and so on of the people of the United States; American influence in various ways.

amnesty A general pardon especially for political offenses against a government.

arms race The attempt by a nation or group of nations to have not only superior weapons but also a larger number and variety of weapons than another competing nation or group of nations. When the other nation or group of nations responds by trying to do the same, a "race" develops to see which will have the greater military strength.

assimilation To make a minority group as much like the majority as possible; for example, to change people from a traditional Native way of life to the way of life of the Canadian majority.

attrition A gradual wearing or weakening.

backlash A sudden and negative reaction to something.

bias A certain preference or dislike which prevents somebody from judging a situation fairly.

biculturalism Having two cultures; a government policy that encourages a country or a province to have two cultures.

bill of rights A list of the rights and freedoms that a group of people believe in. In nations where a bill of rights has been made law, the government must act to protect the rights and freedoms that are listed.

Blitzkrieg A sudden and lightning attack intended to overwhelm an opponent in hope of a rapid victory.

bloc A group of nations joined together to support each other or to take some action together. The Cold War of the post World War II era has seen the communist (or Eastern) bloc of countries in conflict with the Western (or capitalist) bloc of countries.

branch plant The local office of a company or business which has its main office located elsewhere. Many American firms have Canadian branch plants.

census An official count of the people in one area or one country. The census is used to record the number of people in one place, their jobs, their ages and their marital status.

Civil law The division of law that protects the rights of individuals and deals with disputes between people.

Cold War A conflict between nations or groups of nations carried out by political, economic and psychological (e.g. use of propaganda) means, but without direct military fighting between the hostile nations.

Commonwealth of nations An international association including Great Britain and many of its former colonies.

constitution A system of rules and principles by which a nation or group is governed. These rules may be laws or they may be customs which have been shared by everyone. "Constitution" can also refer to a document stating such rules and principles.

corporation Large business owned by many individuals, run by managers appointed by the owners (shareholders), and usually employing large numbers of workers.

credit A bank's or another financial institution's trust in a person's ability to pay back money. Good credit means a person has a good reputation in money matters. Credit can also mean the amount of money in a person's bank account. Similarly, a country's credit is determined by how rich it is in natural resources.

cultural domination The controlling influence of one culture on another culture.

culture All the social developments that define a certain people or nation at a certain time. These developments include the type of science, art and customs in a particular society.

customs Traditional manners, or ways of behaving.

defendant(s) The person against whom legal action is taken. The defendant is the person who is sued in a civil court. The defendant in a criminal court is called the accused.

defense A protective military system used to guard against attack or harm; the side in a criminal case which represents the accused person. The defense is also the argument the accused and the lawyers of the accused use to support their side of the case.

depression A time when businesses are not doing well, money is scarce and people are out of work.

developed countries Countries that have advanced social services, technology and industry and, generally, a stable economy.

developing countries Countries that are in the process of growing. For the most part, developing countries are neither technologically nor industrially advanced. Therefore, the economies of these countries do not tend to be stable because their trading positions are weak.

discriminate The action of making a distinction between things or kinds of people, often in an unfavourable way.

disparity An inequality or a difference between two things.

displaced person A person forced out of his or her own country by war, famine, political disturbance or another crisis.

distinctive Something which is distinguished from other things by a special or characteristic quality.

domestic market A place or region in one's own country where goods are bought and sold or might be bought and sold.

economic growth Increased production in a country; important to a rise in living standards.

editorial A statement of personal opinion made public through the news media.

energy Power, strength or force. In Canada petroleum is an important form of energy now.

ethnic, ethnic group The racial and cultural group from which a person comes. An example of an ethnic group in Canada would be Italian or Polish Canadians.

exploitation Using, or taking advantage of something. An employer exploits raw materials and machinery by using them. Exploitation of labour is regulated by the government but there are still some places that require their employees to work long hours for little pay. (This is only one example of exploitation.)

fad An item or activity that attracts widespread attention but usually does not stay popular for very long.

federal union A political union in which the members retain some powers over their own affairs and turn some powers over to a central government.

foreign investment The laying out of money in a particular country by a person or a company that is not native to that country in order to make an income or a profit or both.

free enterprise The system under which private business operates for the profit of the owners with little government control.

generation gap A term used during the 1960s to describe the lack of understanding between teenagers and their parents.

glut This is created when the supply of a product is greater than the demand for it.

guerilla war Fighting carried out by armed groups which are usually not part of a country's regular armed forces. Often using hit-and-run tactics, they emerge from hiding places to attack such targets as communication lines and routes, supply storage areas and key buildings as part of a campaign to overthrow the government.

heritage The culture and links with the past which people inherit from their families.

identity A sense of self; can apply to individuals, groups, regions, even nations.

immigrant A person who moves from one country to another.

imperialists In early twentieth century Canada, those who supported a strong connection between Canada and the British Empire, of which Canada was a part, were called imperialists.

imports Goods brought into a country with the purpose of selling them.

income tax A government tax on a person's income above a certain amount.

indictable offence An offence which makes a person liable to be indicted or accused of a crime or any major illegal activity.

industrial base A simple economic system which depends on industrial methods of production, such as factories and corporations. Unless there is such a base already in existence, it is impossible to develop an efficient and productive economy.

inflation A sharp or sudden rise in prices.

international Between or among nations; having to do with relations between nations.

internment camps Places where people could be moved and confined because they were considered to be enemies of the state.

Inuit Native people of the Arctic and Labrador.

investments Money which is used to earn a profit, such as buying stocks and shares, putting money in a bank or buying Canada Savings Bonds.

Je me souviens The motto of the Québécois, which means "I remember."

joint commission Joint commissions have frequently been established to settle disputes between Canada and the United States. A joint commission is made up of representatives of both governments who meet and try to find a solution to a problem or dispute that both sides can accept.

labour force Those people of working age, usually 15-65, who either have work or are seeking it. Students, homemakers, prison inmates and retired people are not considered part of the labour force by government agencies which gather figures and statistics. (It does include laid-off or unemployed workers if they are looking for work.)

la révolution tranquille A period of social and political change in Quebec under Jean Lesage's leadership; in translation, the quiet revolution.

legislature The branch of government that has the power to make laws. In the British North American colonies and in Canada today, the legislature is made up of individuals elected to represent the people of a particular district. These districts are called constituencies.

leisure The time free from required work during which time a person may rest, have fun and do the things he or she likes to do.

maîtres chez nous The campaign motto of Jean Lesage in Quebec, which means "masters in our own house."

market A place, region, etc. for selling and buying goods; can also mean a category of people; e.g. the teenage market.

mass production The making of goods in large quantities by machinery.

media Means of communication such as radio, television, newspapers.

Métis The descendants of the European fur traders and Indians.

middle power A country that is not classed as a big power in terms of its military and economic might nor in its international political influence. It falls somewhere between the great powers and those without much military, economic and political strength.

militia Soldiers who have been trained for military service but work at regular non-military jobs. They can quickly be called up for full-time service in a time of national emergency.

mineral A material obtained from below the ground, such as gold, coal, oil, *etc.*

minority government A minority government is one which holds fewer than half the seats in parliament. A minority government is usually quite weak; it can be out-voted by the combination of members forming the opposition.

monopoly The exclusive or sole control of a service by a person or group.

national identity Refers to those characteristics that give a country a "form" or "shape" or "appearance" that people would recognize as distinctive of that country. Often these characteristics become a source of great pride for the people of that country.

nationalists Refers to people who give the interests of their nation or people a very important place in their thinking and in their actions. They are proud of their people or nation and enthusiastically defend its qualities or characteristics.

neutrality A situation in which a country does not take part in any way in a war, controversy, treaties, or alliances between other countries.

official language A language used in government and in courts of law.

optimism A tendency to believe that everything will turn out for the best.

outmigration Leaving one district to go to another.

pacifist A person who believes that differences between countries should be settled only by peaceful means; an anti-war person.

parole The release of prisoners before their complete sentence is served. A paroled prisoner is supervised and must meet regularly with a parole officer for the rest of his or her sentence. Only prisoners who seem to have reformed are released on parole. A paroled prisoner who commits another crime has to serve the remainder of the original sentence as well as any new one.

participation rate The percentage of working age people who are actively working. If a university student graduates and finds work, the participation rate has gone up, since he/she has moved from outside to inside the labour force.

party convention A large meeting of Members of Parliament of a given party and representatives of party members in each riding. Its purpose is usually to select a leader and to decide on party policy.

perspective A specific point of view in understanding or judging things or events, especially a viewpoint that shows things in their true relations to one another.

plebiscite A direct vote by the citizens in which they express their point of view on an important question or issue.

power politics The aggressive use by a nation, particularly of its military strength, but also its economic and political influence, to attempt to get its way in relations with other countries.

probation Probation is a period of time during which an offender is supervised instead of being sent to prison. Restrictions are sometimes placed on the behaviour of such offenders. For example, an offender on probation may be forbidden to enter a bar.

propaganda A system of spreading ideas to convince people to support a particular viewpoint or way of thinking.

public service Usually refers to something that is done by a government, rather than by an individual or group, for the good of people in that nation.

quality of life The overall standard of life a person has. It includes such things as the amount of money, size of house and number of clothes one has. But it also includes things difficult to measure such as the amount of freedom, security and happiness one has.

reciprocity Refers to a trade agreement between, usually, two countries in which they agree to reduce or eliminate tariffs on all or specific goods imported from each other.

Red Power Organized efforts by Canada's Native people to deal with their problems.

referendum A vote by the people affected on a public issue, proposed law, or other change.

refugee A person who leaves his or her country to seek refuge elsewhere during a time of war.

relief Receiving money, food, etc. from public funds.

reparations Payments (in money or materials) made by a defeated nation to the nations it had fought. As well as punish the defeated nation, the payments are to cover damages done during the war and expenses incurred in fighting the war.

resources The actual and potential wealth of a country. This wealth includes the natural resources (minerals, forests, animals) and the industrial resources (manufacturing or processing plants) of a country.

revenues Taxes collected by the federal or provincial governments. In the case of oil and gas, these taxes are collected as the product is extracted from the ground, and again as its refined product is sold to the consumer.

rights Certain things which a person has first claim to through either law, nature or tradition. For example, a Canadian has the right of free speech; a guarantee in law that a citizen can express his or her opinion on a subject.

satellite A country which is technically independent but which has come under the control or strong influence of another country. The countries of eastern Europe that came under the control of the U.S.S.R. after World War II were called satellites.

scenario An outline for any proposed or planned series of events, real or imaginary.

self-government The government of a country by its own citizens.

social history The study of the past of a people, their customs, living conditions, etc. Social history can be contrasted with political history.

social security A system that gives support to persons in need; for example, family allowances, old age pensions.

socialism A political and economic system where all property and business are owned by the community and where all people share equally in the work and prosperity of the society.

Sovereignty association An arrangement proposed by the Parti Québécois where the Parti Québécois would control and manage their own affairs but keep certain economic ties with Canada.

stalemate An unresolved situation in which further action is impossible or useless.

stocks A part of a company as represented by a piece of paper (a certificate which can be sold to another person). Stocks are divided into standardized units of worth. Buying a stock is like becoming part owner of a company.

subsidy A grant of money given by a government either to another government or to a private group to do something for the public good.

suffragette A woman who militantly demands the right of women to vote.

surplus An amount over and above what is needed, or can be used.

la survivance An unofficial motto of the people of Quebec that means "survival" and refers to the continuation of the Quebecois culture and language.

tariffs Taxes on goods imported into a country. The effect of tariffs is to raise the price of an imported product, so that consumers are more likely to buy things produced in their own country.

technocrat Someone who understands and favours advances in technology.

technology The design and building of complicated and usually expensive products. The higher the technology of a given product, the more research, money and time required to produce it.

technophobe Someone who is afraid and suspicious of advances in technology.

trade (or labour) union An organization of workers, who by acting together, seek to improve their wages, work environment, *etc.*

transfer or equalization payments Taxes collected by the federal government from wealthy provinces to be given to the less wealthy ones. The purpose of this is to bring the incomes of the provincial governments up to the national average.

unconstitutional A law or an action which violates a clause of the constitution and is therefore invalid.

uniculturalism A single culture in one nation.

values The principles, goals and standards held by an individual, group, or society.

veteran A person who had been a member of the armed forces.

veto The power to forbid or prevent one individual, group or branch or an organization or government from taking a particular action.

Index

Credits

Every reasonable effort has been made to find copyright holders of the following material. The publishers would be pleased to have any errors or omissions brought to their attention.

Sources

p.17 © NSL Natural Science of Canada, from *Into the Twentieth Century* (Canada's Illustrated Heritage); p.18 Doubleday Canada Ltd.; p.49 Thomas Allen & Son; p.60 Canadian Imperial Bank of Commerce; p.66 Talon Books; p.69 The Canadian Publishers, McLelland & Stewart; p.71 New Hogtown Press; p.91 University of Toronto Press; p.109 Doubleday Canada; p.117 University of New Brunswick; p.121 Copp Clark Pitman; p.124 McLelland & Stewart; p.125 Macmillan of Canada; p.132 Macmillan of Canada; p.149 Hurtig Publishers; p.167 General Publishing; p.173 Reprinted with permission of the publishers, Peter Martin Associates, distributed by the Book Society of Canada Ltd.; p.176 McLelland & Stewart; p.206 University of Toronto Press; p.225 © NSL Natural Science of Canada, from *A Time of Heroes* (Canada's Illustrated Heritage); p.226 University of Toronto Press; p.230 The Canadian Press; p.265 University of Toronto Press; p.280 McLelland & Stewart; p.356 from *Gutenberg Two*, edited by David Godfrey and Douglas Parkhill, reprinted by permission of Press Porcépic.

Pictures

p.2 Greenaway family; p.8 (bottom) Public Archives of Canada (PAC) C27521; p.9 (top) PAC PA2909, (bottom) PAC PA21609; p.10 PAC PA38567; p.11 PAC C1462; p.12 PAC C22982; p.13 PAC PA 6478; p.14 Western Canada Pictorial Index; p.15 Western Canada Pictorial Index; p.16 Ontario Ministry of Industry and Tourism; p.18 PAC C30953; p.22 PAC C1867; p.24 PAC C5617; p.31 United Nations Reliefs and Works Agency for Palestinian Refugees (UNRWA)/Refugee Documentation Project; p.34 United Nations High Commission for Refugees (UNHCR); p.36 UNHCR; p.39 UNHCR; p.43 UNRWA; p.44 Scott Mission; p.56 PAC PA648; p.57 (top) PAC PA2614, (bottom) Guelph Civic Museum (GCM); p.59 PAC PA2468; p.60 GCM; p.61 PAC PA813; p.65 GCM; p.67 PAC C55113; p.69 PAC C57358; p.70 Saskatchewan Archives Board (SAB); p.71 PAC C95746; p.72 PAC C117471; p.73 (top) PAC C29484, (bottom) City of Toronto Archives (CTA); p.74 C95728; p.75 (top) PAC PA8158; p.77 PAC C5470; p.79 Manitoba Archives (MA) Foote Collection (FC); p.80 Courtesy of Mrs. J.H. Knox/Lawren P. Harris/Art Gallery of Ontario; p.84 MAFC; p.87 Courtesy of Mrs. J.H. Knox/Lawren P. Harris/Art Gallery of Ontario; p.89 SAB; p.91 National Museums of Canada (NMC); p.93 SAB; p.94 MAFC; p.96 Glenbow Archives (GA) NA3181-72; p.97 (top left) Metro Toronto Library (MTL), (top right) CTA; (bottom) Canadian Pacific (CP); p.98 (centre) PAC C5799, (right) PAC C43102; p.101 CP; p.102 CTA; p.103 PAC C89581; p.104 Ontario Archives (OA); p.106 MAFC; p.108 SAB; p.112 SAB; p.113 GA NC6-12955C; p.116 MA; p.119 PAC C623; p.120 PAC 30811; p.121 Private Collection; p.122 PAC C29397; p.123 GA NA3170-1; p.124 MTL; p.125 SAB/Department of Regional Economic Expansion; p.127 PAC/Montreal Gazette; p.130 GA NA2377-1; p.131 PAC C53642; p.132 OA; p.133 M. Filey; p.134 MA; p.136 PAC C38723/Claude Dettloff; p.147 PAC C14160; p.148 National Museums of Canada (NMC)/National Museum of Man (NMM)/Canadian War Museum (CWM); p.151 National Gallery of Canada; p.152 CWM; p.156 PAC; p.158 (top left) PAC PA10830, (top right) PAC C75211, (bottom left) PAC, (bottom right) PAC PA117586; p.159 (top) PAC C26110, (bottom) PAC; p.162 (top) NMC/NMM/CWM, (bottom) PAC PA110919; p.163 (top) PAC, (bottom) PAC C40355; p.165 PAC C46355; p.169 PAC C42726; p.170 PAC PA111369; p.175 Public Archives of Newfoundland (PAN); p.176 PAN; p.177 (top) PAN; p.178 PAC PA111393; p.180 PAC PA 111447; p.181 (top) PAC C49401, (bottom) Provincial Archives of Alberta; p.182 PAC PA111252; p.186 PAC PA96287; p.190 PAC C35680; p.191 PAC C8354; p.202 PAC C90378; p.203 Friends of the United Nations; p.206 PAC PA129625/Montreal Star; p.219 U.S. Air Force; p.220 London Free Press/Tingley; p.227 Refugee Documentation Project; p.229 PAC C7108; p.232 Canadian Forces photo (CF); p.237 CF; p.238 CF; p.239 PAC C94168; p.243 PAC PR111541; p.246 UNHCR/Refugee Documentation Project; p.254 Private Collection; p.257 PAC C68509; p.260 United Church of Canada; p.261 GA; p.263 (top) PAC C17646; p.264 (bottom) PAC C15160; p.266 Ontario Hydro; p.270 PAC PA117465; p.272 PAC PA111214; p.273 J. Zehethofer; p.274 Michel Verreault; p.277 PAC C3702; p.281 PAC C53641; p.282 (top) PAC C5306; p.284 PAC C22859; p.295 PAC C25003; p.300 Multicultural History Society of Ontario (MHSO); p.305 MHSO, p.307 R. Hemingway; p.308 PAC C18743; p.309 MHSO; p.311 Ontario Ministry of Citizenship and Culture/copyright owned by H.M. the Queen in right of Ontario; p.313 Tourism B.C.; p.315 PAC PA40745; p.316 MHSO; p.318 PAC PA111383; p.320 Bruce Clark; p.321 MHSO; p.322 Philip Mallette, Maclean's June 7, 1982; p.325 Andrew Oxenham/National Ballet of Canada; p.327 Phase One Recording Studio Ltd.; p.330 J. Harris; p.336 Private Collection; p.338 Petro-Canada; p.340 Ontario Ministry of Environment (MOE); p.341 MOE; p.342 MOE; p.344 Helena Wehrstein; p.347 Helena Wehrstein; p.348 NASA; p.350 NASA; p.352 Telesat Canada; p.355 TV Ontario; p.357 IBM Canada Ltd.; p.358 MITEL; p.360 IBM Canada Ltd.; p.362 Chrysler Corporation; p.366 Eduvision; p.370 Law Society of Upper Canada/Kenneth Jarvis, Q.C.; p.373 Ontario Ministry of The Attorney General; p.377 Eduvision; p.382 Eduvision; p.385 Eduvision; p.387 Law Society of Upper Canada/Tom Schell; p.388 Eduvision; p.397 Toronto Fire Department; p.399 PAC 2497; p.402 Manitoba Legislature; p.403 Eduvision; p.415 Carl Bigras/Liberal Party; p.416 Photo Features Ltd./NDP; p.417 Photo Features Ltd./NDP; p.417 David Crombie; p.420 Larry Grossman; p.428 Government of Canada; p.431 Imperial Oil Ltd.; p.435 Women's Bureau, Ontario Ministry of Labour; p.436 Flora MacDonald; p.441 Tempofoto; p.444 Photon; p.451 Imperial Oil Ltd.; p.452 Development Education Centre, (DEC) Toronto; p.454 United Press Canada; p.457 Confederation of Canadian Unions/Laurell Ritchie; p.459 Confederation of Canadian Unions/Laurell Ritchie; p.465 (top left) Travel Arctic, (top right) Travel Alberta, (centre) City of Montreal, (bottom left) Ontario Ministry of Industry and Tourism, (bottom right) Ontario Ministry of Industry and Tourism; p.469 Nova Corporation; p.470 (left) PAC 50600, (right) International Development Research Centre (IDRC); p.471 (top) Canadair, (bottom left) CBC; (right) CF; p.473 CF; p.475 CF; p.477 UNHCR/P. Jambor/Refugee Documentation Project; p.479 IDRC; p.481 CUSO; p.481 UNHCR/Refugee Documentation Project; p.484 Imperial Oil; p.486 Atomic Energy of Canada Ltd.; p.489 (top) National Ballet of Canada, (bottom) Scholastic—TAB Publications; p.490 Atomic Energy of Canada Ltd.